Advanced Sciences and Technologies for Security Applications

Indexed by SCOPUS

The series Advanced Sciences and Technologies for Security Applications comprises interdisciplinary research covering the theory, foundations and domain-specific topics pertaining to security. Publications within the series are peer-reviewed monographs and edited works in the areas of:

- biological and chemical threat recognition and detection (e.g., biosensors, aerosols, forensics)
- crisis and disaster management
- terrorism
- cyber security and secure information systems (e.g., encryption, optical and photonic systems)
- traditional and non-traditional security
- energy, food and resource security
- economic security and securitization (including associated infrastructures)
- transnational crime
- human security and health security
- social, political and psychological aspects of security
- recognition and identification (e.g., optical imaging, biometrics, authentication and verification)
- smart surveillance systems
- applications of theoretical frameworks and methodologies (e.g., grounded theory, complexity, network sciences, modelling and simulation)

Together, the high-quality contributions to this series provide a cross-disciplinary overview of forefront research endeavours aiming to make the world a safer place.

The editors encourage prospective authors to correspond with them in advance of submitting a manuscript. Submission of manuscripts should be made to the Editor-in-Chief or one of the Editors.

Juan Cayón Peña · J. Martín Ramírez
Editors

Threats to Peace and International Security: Asia versus West

Current Challenges in a New Geopolitical Situation

Springer

Editors
Juan Cayón Peña
Rector
Universidad Diseño, Innovación y Tecnología (UDIT)
Madrid, Spain

J. Martín Ramírez
Campus de la Berzosa
Nebrija University
Madrid, Spain

ISSN 1613-5113 ISSN 2363-9466 (electronic)
Advanced Sciences and Technologies for Security Applications
ISBN 978-3-031-28335-2 ISBN 978-3-031-28336-9 (eBook)
https://doi.org/10.1007/978-3-031-28336-9

This Springer imprint is published by the registered company Springer Nature Switzerland AG
The registered company address is: Gewerbestrasse 11, 6330 Cham, Switzerland

Preface

This book on THREATS TO PEACE AND INTERNATIONAL SECURITY: ASIA VERSUS WEST-CURRENT CHALLENGES IN A NEW GEOPOLITICAL SITUATION, included in the Springer Series on Advanced Sciences and Technologies for Security Applications, is a result of selected articles on the topic analyzed during the past LXII CICA (7–8 April 2022), co-organized by the Spanish Pugwash, CICA International Foundation & the Nebrija-Santander Chair on Risks and Conflict Management. Let's say a few informative words about each of them.

Over the past few generations, nuclear weapons have turned war between superpowers into a mad act of collective suicide, forcing the most powerful nations on Earth to find less violent ways to resolve conflict. This was the reason for the beginning of the Pugwash Movement, followed by Bertrand Russell and Albert Einstein's Manifesto (1955).

Inspired by their call, in 1957, the Pugwash Movement started its first Conference on Science and World Affairs, which gathered several Nobel Prize winners in the village of Pugwash in Nova Scotia. The strength and reputation of Pugwash derive from the uncompromising dedication of prestigious intellectuals and scientists to work toward averting the existential danger posed by nuclear weapons. It has been following the tradition of "dialogue across divides," through which it has developed the use of scientific, evidence-based policymaking, particularly in areas where nuclear risks are present. Pugwash members can act in several different forums and through their own mechanisms, individually and in association with others, in search of peace and understanding among nations in a world free of nuclear weapons and all other weapons of mass destruction.

Since then, our Pugwash Movement, seeing war as both evil and avoidable, has been present in quite a few international conflicts, such as the mediation in the missile crisis in Cuba, with Robert Mac Namara, Defense Secretary in the Kennedy administration and member of Pugwash. As many of you may remember, the Soviet missiles were removed from Cuba in 1962 in return for an American promise not to invade the island. Many academics consider America's placement of missiles in Turkey as the trigger for the Soviet deployment in Cuba. Soon after the crisis, America quietly removed its Turkish weapons. America didn't have to advertise its concession, and the Soviets got something they seriously wanted.

Anyone interested in the poker game's strategic side will know two things: nuclear deterrence is based on the practical ability to destroy everything, and no rational player would be willing to press the button first. Many years late, according to the unequivocal confession of Robert McNamara, it was learned that total destruction was by no means as close as believed when Kennedy announced the naval encirclement of Cuba, and Khrushchev replied that he would not divert his ships.

Over the past few generations, nuclear weapons have turned war between superpowers into a mad act of collective suicide, forcing the most powerful nations on Earth to find less violent ways to resolve conflict. Some recent examples of the continuous mediating effort of Pugwash could be the incessant and, until now, the unfruitful attempt to help in the unification of Korea, with my modest presence as a mediator in some of our periodical meetings with delegations of both Koreas, and, just in the last years, our participation in the Doha agreement of Afghanistan, led by my since quite a few decades good friend Paolo Cotta, present Secretary-General of Pugwash, who has been kind enough of offering himself as the keynote speaker for explaining us about how it.

Pugwash has reacted by strongly repudiating the violation of the basic principles inscribed in the Charter of the United Nations, highlighting the obligation to settle disputes by peaceful means and to refrain from the use or threat of use of force against the territorial integrity or the political independence of any state. Some have stressed the objective responsibilities of States and the dangers of escalation. In contrast, others have concentrated on suggesting ways to restore peace, including an immediate ceasefire and establishment of dialogue and negotiation. Still, others reflected on different standards applied to similar situations in other parts of the world. Despite the range and diversity of how all of us have expressed our outrage and distress, it is clear to all that some urgent steps must be taken by the leaders of the states concerned to stop armed hostilities and start a process that will lead to lasting peace and understanding.

As the President of Pugwash, ambassador Sergio Duarte, stresses, summarizing the Pugwash statement on the war in Ukraine, issued on 26 February 2022, highlighting the damage made, by the treacherous aggression of Putin's Russia to Ukraine, to the very notion of nuclear weapon non-proliferation: an ominous development, his threat of the possible use of nuclear weapons about which we Pugwashites should with be particularly worried. What is happening is an enormous leap backward! Let's hope that the demise of Putin will be the outcome of this crisis, bringing back Russia to the democratic kind of government that such a civilized and scientifically advanced country deserves.

As stated in the Russell and Einstein Manifesto, we appeal as human beings to human beings: Remember your humanity, and forget the rest!

One of the human concerns is about violence and conflict. Civil society organizations and public opinion are essential instruments to help achieve lasting peace and understanding, and this is one of the main aims of the CICA International Foundation: we believe that the achievement of peace, understood as "the implausibility of war," is possible and may strike deep roots.

Preparing responsible citizens demands attention to the causes and consequences of violent action. Reducing and preventing violence requires understanding the phenomenon's complexity and recognizing the multiple causes of such harmful behavior. Such a basic understanding is necessary if we are to propose positive remedies and point out ways toward peaceful solutions and non-violent alternatives. The present social circumstances add a timely politically charged consideration of possible friendly options. Knowledge of aggression is not only a window to understanding humanity better but also shows that violence involves an intensely emotional individual experience for perpetrators, victims, and witnesses as well.

During the last quarter of the previous century and the beginning of the present one, CICA has addressed different aspects of this topic by scholars from multiple disciplines focusing on this critical individual and societal issue from a multidisciplinary attention. Recently, we have been focusing more carefully on one of its most extreme expressions, terrorism, by organizing joint conferences on the topic with the Society for Terrorism Research, as well as on the analysis and resolution of conflicts.

The international, interdisciplinary, comprehensive approach characteristic of these meetings provides a proper biosocial focus by bringing together multiple disciplines to study the complex relationship between the brain, aggression, and human consciousness more effectively. The main goal is to bridge the persistent gulf between biologically based approaches and those built on the social sciences, in the understanding that real solutions will only be found through integrating insights from the interaction of many different fields and levels. There is no human function that does not involve the brain and social context!

In a nutshell, the primary purpose of our Foundation is to deepen our knowledge about consciousness, the achievement of peace, the resolution of conflicts, and the analysis of aggression and violence at all levels.

The Nebrija-Santander Chair on Risk and Conflict Management serves as a framework for a wide range of teaching and research activities based on the interdisciplinary study of Risks and Conflicts of various kinds, as well as their consequences in the field of Social Sciences, especially Law, International Relations, and Security. With this objective, one must delve into its different facets: knowledge, management, prevention, and resolution of Risk and Conflict.

The nature of both Risks and Conflicts requires an interdisciplinary study since their causes are present at all levels: intrapersonal, interpersonal, intergroup, and international. This necessary breadth of perspectives is reflected in the academic orientation of the Chair members, including political scientists, jurists, historians, members of the armed forces, psychologists, neuroscientists, educators, etc. In this way, the analysis and management of risks and conflicts are fostered at an interdisciplinary level that involves the use of arbitration, reconciliation, mediation, transaction, and negotiation techniques; intervention strategies; conflict mapping; conflict escalation; peacebuilding and maintenance; transitional justice, etc., as well as its repercussion on security and defense, with the consequent civic–military collaboration in the matter.

The scientific response to the main topic of our conference, East vs. West, which is not geographical concepts but geopolitical ones, has been quite encouraging: more than 40 active participants from about 20 countries of four continents: Europe (Czech Republic, Italy, Hungary, the Netherlands, Poland, Slovakia, Serbia, Spain), Asia (Armenia, Iran, Israel); Africa (Nigeria, South Africa); and America (Colombia, Dominican Republic USA, Venezuela). As keynote speakers, we had two prestigious experts:

First Dr. Paolo Cotta-Ramusino, Professor of Mathematical Physics at the University of Milan and Secretary-General of Pugwash since 2002, talked about his participation, leading several Pugwash expert mediators during the elaboration of the Doha Agreement for Bringing Peace, signed in Doha, February 29, 2020, by US Ambassador Zalmay Khalizad, a trusted man of Secretary of State Mike Pompeo, and Taliban leader Abdul Salam Zaeef representing Ashraf Ghan. It was already determined that in 135 days, the troops in Afghanistan present from the Global War on Terrorism (GWOT).

After 9/11 and the withdrawal of sanctions on Taliban leaders, the number of men in the coalition would be reduced to 8,600. Five military bases would be evacuated, and "within 14 months" the abandonment of the country (the deadline was due to close in May 2020). In return, the Taliban's commitment is not to allow the establishment of any organizations or individuals that threaten the security of the USA and its allies, including Al Qaeda or Daesh. The negotiations included negotiations between Afghans to achieve a ceasefire for the country's political future, as well as the release of up to 5,000 prisoners in the hands of the government and 1,000 Afghan government officials imprisoned by the Taliban, and the Emirate promise of not hosting Al Qaeda or ISIS fighters on its territory.

Second the former Spanish ambassador to Afghanistan, Gabriel Ferrán, related the last days of his mission to the unexpected and urgent abandonment of the NATO forces from Afghanistan. Even though he expected to be relieved by the new ambassador, he decided to stay in the country where he had served three years to coordinate the evacuation of hundreds of nationals and Afghans who had collaborated with the Spanish Agency for International Development Cooperation (AECID) before the Taliban took power. Ambassador Ferrán remained at his post with the deputy head of the diplomatic mission in Kabul and the seventeen GEO and other agents who coordinated the mission from the outset, joined by 110 soldiers sent from Spain. Ambassador Ferrán was the last to leave the country, following what the vessel commanders learned to do: They should be the last ones to abandon ship. We admire how he and the soldiers of many countries, Spain included, got the Afghan population out of the Kabul airport.

If I'm allowed a digression, I remember reading in *A study of History* of Arnold JH. Toynbee that "the spirit of sacrifice in defense of a religious, political or economic conception maintains the imperial civilization." In this context, I cannot but be sad hearing what President Biden said after their abandonment of Afghanistan said that the USA would not sacrifice one more soldier except when there was a direct interest from Washington. This means that, at least for Americans, our Western civilization is gone.

Let me finalize with our heartfelt thanks to all of you who have been responsible for the scientific contributions to our new Springer book.

J. Martin Ramirez

Acknowledgments and Introduction

I must begin by thanking Dr. Martín Ramírez for the opportunity to edit this volume and for a life dedicated to the scientific study of violence and conflict, always in search of peace. Dr. Martín Ramirez, through the CICA International Foundation, has been and is probably one of the most critical professors linked to the analysis, management, and resolution of conflicts, with admirable international recognition and experience. Thank you, therefore, in the first place to him and his teaching that we humbly try to follow.

Inextricably linked to the above, it is de rigueur also to thank the CICA International Foundation for organizing the international events this work brings about. CICA meetings are an enormous opportunity for personal and intellectual growth for teachers and students, and for more than forty years, they have become an international scientific reference. In them, we have met and treated most of the book's authors that we now present.

A loving memory to all the authors who have collaborated in developing this work, both to those who have seen their work published and to all those who unfortunately submitted texts that were not finally approved. Without their generous commitment and patience, it would not have been possible for this book to see the light of day.

And finally, once again, thanks also to the prestigious Springer publishing house for trusting us and generously accepting our contributions to better understand a complex world.

By introduction, allow me to begin with a reflection on the current risk that Europe and the world are facing in the face of the conflict between Russia and Ukraine, which is unfortunately present. This was the origin of the preparation of the CICA meeting from which this volume derives, being fundamental to understanding that the use of force and unilateral actions are, in most cases, contrary to international law. And consequently, they endanger global peace and security. In our opinion, it is undeniable that the West has been arrogant and has not respected some red lines set by our eastern neighbors. Still, these errors in no way justify an invasion and a war with irreversible consequences on too many occasions. From these pages, we call the nations to dialogue and negotiate a just and lasting peace, which contemplates the different perspectives and historical and current realities with respect for people and minorities, so often forgotten. On very few occasions, we have been so close to a specific risk of terrible outcomes from the use of nuclear weapons. This reality alone should be enough to make us reflect.

But this book will not only deal in depth with some aspects of the war in Ukraine, but quite the contrary, and always from a multidisciplinary perspective, it will also address other issues that significantly affect the polarization between East and West: from the phenomena terrorists to the problem of nuclear development for peaceful purposes, going through territorial expansionism and the challenges of the ability to create artificial islands in disputed seas, ending with the necessary pedagogy of peace.

Therefore, in our opinion, it seems to be a diverse, multifocal work, which authors rigorously address with very different training and experience. This is our contribution, and we want you to like it.

Contents

Global Perspective

European Challenges

Sovereignty and Defense in the European Union. A Historical and Current Essay

Rogelio Perez Bustamante(✉)

Juan Carlos I University, Madrid, Spain
rogelioperezbustamante@gmail.com

1 Introduction

The European Union has been conceived as a singular and original creation. Currently made up of twenty-seven States, the Union appears less than a State but more than a classic International Organization. The path followed by the European construction is based on functional integration and that integration has been carried out to a great extent through the cession by the States of contents inherent to their own national sovereignty, even when the disintegration of the Sovereignty of the States it has not yet been switched to a desire to establish the elements of authentic European sovereignty.

In his speech, "The Six Books of the Republic", Jean Bodin had evoked the marks of Sovereignty, that is, the signs by which a sovereign power is recognized, among them, the right to mint money appears; right, that has already passed from the States to the European Union, with the construction of the Economic and Monetary Union and putting into circulation in the euro zone the single currency. Another mark of Sovereignty are borders. The European Union has been sustained by the four freedoms of the Common Market, converted into a market without internal borders and consequently has suppressed physical borders, consecrating free movement.

Another of the marks of Sovereignty and absolute power lies in the legislative power, "giving laws to subjects, in general without their consent". The European Union has developed an intense regulatory activity that is transposed to the Member States. Currently there are thousands of normative acts of the Union with its two main characteristics defined by the court of justice: direct effect and primacy.

It has been possible to state that there is no nucleus of Sovereignty that the Member States can invoke as such against the European Union, even though national constitutions contain certain powers that can only be exercised by the powers of the State. This does not prevent them from being attributed to the Union, provided that the Basic Law or Constitution is reformed beforehand, according to the internal procedures of each State (Mrac Ferry 2000).

The European Communities qualified as a supranational organization do not have the characteristics of a State, but, as Robert Schuman would recognize, they exercise certain sovereign powers (Schuman 1953). Consequently, from the outset, the European Communities and the Union would effectively exercise sovereign powers, without becoming sovereign, it holds the exercise, but not the ownership of sovereign state powers.

J. Cayón Peña and J. M. Ramírez (Eds.): *Threats to Peace and International Security: Asia versus West*, ASTSA, pp. 3–36, 2023.
https://doi.org/10.1007/978-3-031-28336-9_1

The Treaties of the Communities and of the Union have continuously used the expression of an "ever closer Union". But this expression would be rejected by Great Britain because it assumed that dilutes the nature of the state. In a shameful cession to prevent the inevitable Brexit, the European Council of February 2016 would address the issue of "Sovereignty", recognizing that the United Kingdom "has not committed itself to greater political integration within the European Union" and consequently, which was not affected by the Preambles of the Treaties referring to the creative process of "an ever closer Union among the peoples of Europe" which does not constitute, according to its interpretation, "a legal basis to extend the scope of application of any provision of the Treaties or secondary EU law" and should not serve to support an extensive interpretation of the competences of the Union or of the powers of its institutions in accordance with the provisions of the Treaties (European Council Feb-2016).

This fear, to recognize as a reality the cessions of Sovereignty, has probably favored the awakening of nationalism and populism. Given this, it is maintained that the refusal to raise the issue of constituent Sovereignty makes it easier to leave this Sovereignty in the hands of actors who are neither legitimate nor responsible and who ultimately decide on the destiny of the peoples of Europe (Constantinesco 2013). On the other hand, globalization has become a factor of erosion of Sovereignty by undermining the exclusivity of the territorial jurisdiction of the State that characterizes its Sovereignty (Arenal 2008, 209–210).

Finally, and this is the object of our interest, another of the marks, the right to form armed forces has been the object of resistance since the origin of European projects, it can be said that maintained up to the present. In the constitutional articulation of the States, the army is entrusted with guaranteeing Sovereignty and independence, defending their territorial integrity and the constitutional order, and this fact is what raises misgivings about the possible attribution to the European Union of a supranational defense policy.

This is how things were until the latest crises suffered by the European Union, the Covid pandemic and the war in Ukraine have made the European States react and rethink their traditional positions, to assume European Sovereignty. Among the marks of Sovereignty is also the right to collect taxes and consequently the States have not wanted to assume a true fiscal integration, they have been forced by circumstances[1], but the Next Generation EU agreement, something unprecedented in the history of the EU, assumes that the Union will issue European sovereign debt or bonds to allocate subsidies and loans to its Member States, paying them by generating its own resources, through direct taxes, which is considered the first step towards fiscal integration in Europe.

Secondly, the crisis caused by the war in Ukraine has updated the application of the concept of Sovereignty to the European Union. In the speech to present the priorities of the French Presidency delivered on December 9, 2021, the President of France, Emmanuel Macron, stated that his activities will focus on three main areas: 1. Carry out a program in favor of European Sovereignty, that is to say, the capacity of Europe to exist in the world as it is and to defend its values and interests; 2. Build a new European growth model; and 3. Create a more "humane" Europe.

[1] Progress has been made in economic integration, as a consequence of the 2008 financial crisis, with the creation of the MEDE or the ESM.

President Macron stated: If I had to summarize in a single sentence the objective of this Presidency that will run from January 1 to June 30, 2022, I would say that we have to move from a Europe of cooperation within our borders to a Europe strong in the world, fully sovereign, free in her choices and mistress of her destiny.

The War in Ukraine recognized as such since February 24, 2022, would precipitate that recognition. On March 10 and 11, 2022, an extraordinary European Council was held in Versailles, which would issue a document called to open a new page of history by consecrating in it, for the first time in an official document, the term "Sovereignty of the European Union". Union" and by expressing in point 7 of said Declaration the following words: "we have decided to assume greater responsibility regarding our Security and adopt new decisive measures to build our European Sovereignty".

The President of the European Council, Charles Mitchel, would confirm the significance of what happened at the informal summit in Versailles, stating: "this Summit will go down in the annals of the European project. I realize that we may not see it right away, but this Versailles Declaration gives impetus to a more sovereign, more independent, more strategic Europe. Because, at Versailles, we decided that fundamentally national issues -energy, defense, certain economic questions- would be dealt strategically with a spirit of European sovereignty".

Reaching Versailles as a new starting point for the Sovereignty of the European Union has required centuries of continuous discussions, debates, philosophical, political, and legal approaches on the need to articulate a political entity, endowed with Sovereignty, that would assume the contents of classical Sovereignty of the European States and consequently would enable the endowment of an army that would protect this new federated reality of nation States. Let's see that long journey from its first manifestations to create a united Europe.

2 The Defense in the First Prefigurations of the Idea of Europe

Constituted during the Middle Ages, the Empire and the Papacy as forms of supranationality, in the first medieval articulation of the political units that were formed in the European space, and that would later take the form of hereditary monarchies, elective monarchies and federative republics, appeared the first attempts to reunify Christianity, as reflected by Dante in his treatise "On Monarchy" and the Norman lawyer Pierre Dubois, who proposes to establish a universal Council whose main mission would be to end wars and recover the Holy Land, by advancing, at the same time, in interesting projects of political and social reforms. Arbitration appeared to ensure peace.

Even more advanced would be the project of the King of Bohemia, George of Poděbrady, who prefigures the idea of building an Assembly of representatives of the Princes that would vote by a simple majority, a Court of Justice, a confederal budget and a common army, exhorting the sovereigns Christians to mobilize and take common military action to expel the Turks from Europe.

Pope Pius II would manifest himself committed not only to the defense of Christianity, but also to the defense of Europe. The third article of that project prohibited the violation of the peace by a sovereign over the territory of another. The fourth article dealt with the solution of armed conflicts between various sovereigns belonging to the Union and the sovereigns who did not belong to it, and in the fifth article, the solution of armed conflicts between sovereigns who did not belong to the Union (Draus 2009, 63–67). This project made it possible to understand that under the pretext of a war against the Turks it was a question of creating a European federation, among the Christian sovereigns, endowed with a common army.

At the beginning of the Modern Age, the formation of the modern State would take place, within the framework of profound transformations in the mechanisms of government and in the exercise of power. The consequence of which would be the emergence of nation states and the ambition of European political hegemony. The concept of Sovereignty appeared with Jean Bodin, in his great work from 1576, "*The Six Books of the Republic*" emanating from a rational representation of the power of the State that is embodied in a unitary power: the will of the monarch (Bodin 1986).

For Bodin, in a proposal that corresponds to a rationalization process on the nature of States, Sovereignty is the pillar of the State structure: "Sovereignty is the absolute and perpetual power of a Republic… That is, the greatest power of command". The Sovereignty is absolute and perpetual because neither the power nor the position is limited to a certain time (Read 2021).

Thomas Hobbes will base his thought of sovereign power on the destructive character of the State of nature, which is the war of all against all. Faced with this, individuals will adopt a social contract that establishes a higher authority (Hobbes 2022). Reinterpreting the conceptual legacy, Rousseau will maintain that Sovereignty is only real when it resides in the people. The town that for Hegel is the concrete, dissolves in the State that is the abstract.

Ensuring the European balance against the ambitions of the States would be the objective of the European Union projects that emerged throughout the Modern Era in the historical scenario of the theoretical articulation of Sovereignty. These projects proposed the construction of a Confederation of States without integrating the nascent concept of Sovereignty into it. The Security and Defense of a sovereign State that is constituted as one of the main elements of Sovereignty, is shared in the Confederation of States, as it was originally conceived as the protection against military attacks by third parties (Gerbet 1999, 14–15).

Emeric Cruzé in his work *Le Nouveau Cynée* considers peace as the requirement of good sense in its project for the European Union, understanding that universal peace is what should inspire Christian princes and from it comes its project to create an Assembly of Ambassadors who must make decisions by majority (Fenet & Guillaume 2004). Cruzé suggests the creation of a permanent Assembly or Senate of States, based in Venice, free movement of goods or people and unification of weights or measures.

In a more advanced idea, the Duke of Sully (1560–1641), carried out a Union project against the hegemony of the Habsburgs, on the basis of a Treaty of peace and mutual assistance. The Union and Confederation that he proposes will have the purpose of uniting the sovereigns in a single body of republic in which there is a loyal and perpetual association in a "fraternal community of arms and designs". This Confederation of States, called "Very Christian Republic" would be under the tutelage of a Council of Europe, made up of six provincial councils and a General Council. Sully demands free trade and the removal of customs barriers.

In this project by Sully (Buisseret & Barbiche 1970–1988), the very Christian Republic must have armed forces, made up of contingents from each of the fifteen political entities whose Union he proposes, made up of six elective monarchies, six hereditary monarchies and three republics. In short, the "Grand Dessein", a title assumed by the president, Kennedy, reader of Sully 's work at Harvard University, from which he would take the title for the design of his foreign policy; It arises with a proposal for a concert between the Christian States that pursued the establishment of an era of collective security and prosperity.

According to the calculations of the Duke of Sully, the armed forces should include one hundred and seventeen ships, two hundred and twenty thousand infantrymen, fifty-three thousand eight hundred cavalrymen and two hundred and seventeen artillery pieces. This army will carry out a continuous war against the Turks, then considered as the enemy of Europe. The Peace of Westphalia of October 24, 1648, that would consecrate non-interference in international relations and the internal order of each sovereign State.

Between 1600 and 1715 Europe only knew seven years of peace. That period would end in 1713, with the set of Treaties signed in the Dutch city of Utrecht and in the German city of Rastatt, which allowed the end of a dynastic conflict, the succession of the Spanish Crown, which caused numerous battles and caused hundreds of thousands of victims. France managed to accentuate its leading role in international relations and Great Britain obtained important concessions that meant the breaking of the commercial monopoly that Spain had maintained during the s. XVI and XVII, on the other side of the Atlantic. Both Treaties would give rise to a new drawing between the borders of Europe.

In 1713, the same year as the Treaty of Utrecht, Charles - Irénée Castel de Saint-Pierre published his work *Memory to make peace in Europe perpetual* (St. Pierre 1986). In order to establish a lasting peace in Europe, the Abbot of Sant Pierre suggests the constitution of a "perpetual arbitration", to make a Treaty of Union, to form a perpetual Congress and to create a "European Union" or "European Society". Against the system of balance between the powers, he proposes the system of the "Permanent Society in Europe" that should ensure perpetual peace among the sovereigns of Europe, where trade should constitute an important aspect of the European Union.

In the third article of his project, he deals with the military contingents that each sovereign state must provide in the event of a war that threatens the Union, and the fourth article establishes the behaviour to be followed in the event of a war declared by the Union against a European sovereign.

Rousseau will summarize that project by proposing a federation of princes that could mediate in wars by adopting the same solution, one establishing a permanent diet made up of nineteen members, including Russia and the Pope, using military sanctions as an element of pressure. Its difference with the above remains in the conception of the Abbé de Saint Pierre, universal peace applies both to internal order and to external events, while Rousseau does not accept that internal peace presupposes or demands the unconditional obedience of the people to the sovereign, because for him internal peace must, first of all, presuppose the elimination of the causes of the revolts and the elimination of the tyrannical government. In his reflection he questions whether Sovereignty is susceptible to division and distribution (Vayssiere 2007).

Based on a reflection of the approaches of the Abbot of Sant Pierre and Rousseau, Immanuel Kant assumes in his work "For Perpetual Peace" (1795) the progress of the political consciousness of constitutional and liberal ideas and the appearance of first revolutionary movements, proposing that the law of nations should be based on a Federation of free States subject to a single law (Kant 2019).

Considering the project of perpetual peace as another form of Treaty that establishes Peace as an imperative of reason, and understanding that, in every State, the civil Constitution must be republican, the law of nations must be founded on a federalism of free States and cosmopolitan law must be restricted to the conditions of universal hospitality. Kant proposes the federative Union as an idea of reason. Perpetual peace will be nothing more than a hypothesis inviting us to think about the political history of humanity in terms of a movement towards peace.

Montesquieu, who would be in favour of a system of political parties and intermediate bodies, would accept the idea of a "Society of Societies", anticipating the prospect of a federation of republics. The novelty would consist in the acceptance of shared power, guaranteed by a constitution. Madison and Hamilton will give birth to a political formula unprecedented in the world such as the American Federal Constitution of 1787.

Europe will develop the transforming ferment of the American Revolution, while the French Revolution would bring to civilization the right of peoples to determine their destiny. The Congress of Vienna would bring together the great European powers, victorious over Napoleon, as well as the other States, to draw up and sign the conditions of peace, determine the borders and try to establish a new political order. The search for European balance would be accompanied by the consecration of the principles of legitimacy and monarchical restoration and Christian brotherhood in direct opposition to the revolutionary brotherhood of the peoples. Almost all European states would join the Holy Alliance.

Congress of Vienna would symbolize the political reconstruction of Europe, under the tutelage of the four great powers: England, Austria, Prussia and Russia. The most brilliant exposition of the idea of a unified Europe would be offered at that time by Claude-Henry de Rouvroy, Count of Saint- Simon, who, in 1814, would write together with the historian Agustin Tierry, a work entitled *On the Reorganization of European Society. On the necessity and on the means of uniting the peoples of Europe in one body politician* (De Saint-Simon 2014).

Saint - Simon would advocate a European Community, established on the parliamentary system, based on a political system like the English system. One king, two chambers and the administrative, scientific and economic elites: "*Europe will have the best possible constitution if all nations are each governed by a Parliament, recognizing the supremacy of a general Parliament made up of all national governments and vested with a power to judge their differences*" (Carbonell 2001, 87). The European Parliament should also play a political role abroad. This project would not get the support of the diplomats gathered at the Congress of Vienna.

Along the XIX century the different ideas about a united Europe would have as a common thread a Europe constituted as a Community of interests, but also as a system of socialist and revolutionary federations. But, above all, of a Europe as a system of arbitration and cooperation. In that framework, the Congresses for Peace would occupy a preponderant place, an idea that came from the United States, and that would propose the celebration of a first International Congress in London in July 1841, to study the possibility of establishing universal peace.

This Congress effectively held in 1843 with the exclusive participation of Americans and English, would decide for arbitration as a solution to resolve their differences. A second Congress, held in Brussels in 1848, also with the presence of Americans and English, plus Belgians, French, Dutch and Spanish, would postulate the creation of a disarmament system and the creation of international arbitration. Under the same ideology, the third Peace Congress would be held in Paris in the summer of 1849, presided over by Victor Hugo (1802–1885), who would deliver a famous opening and closing speech[2].

But peace was not possible and after the war of 1870 and the Lugano Peace Congress of 1872, Victor Hugo sent a letter to his European compatriots urging them to build the United States of Europe, under the model of the United States of America, with democratic institutions. In his thinking, the key to his European project lay in the alliance between France and Germany. France would contain England, Germany would contain Russia and the European continent would march towards peace, towards a Universal Republic founded on peace and freedom and where borders would be abolished.

The United States that had suffered the Civil War would overcome the so-called reconstruction era (1865–1877), with a process that would lead to the restoration of national unity and the strengthening of the national government. After the American Civil War, where some 620,000 casualties were recorded on both sides, the United States emerged as a great power, whose army would confront the Native American tribes and take part in the Spanish-American War, subjecting its actions to the Monroe Doctrine, under the principle of non-intervention of the United States in European conflicts.

3 The Idea of Europe and of an Integrated Defence in the Scenario of the Two World Wars (1919–1949)

European nationalisms, moved by their colonizing ambitions, their demographic growth and the development of capitalism, would collide with each other from the end of the s. XIX. Germany would become the centre of gravity of European politics, while the rivalry between the great powers over the division of the colonial world would be the

[2] There will come a day when weapons fall from your arms, you too! A day will come when France, you Russia, you Italy, you England, you Germany, you all, nations of the continent, without losing your distinct qualities and your glorious individuality, you will merge into a superior unity and you will constitute European fraternity just as Normandy, Brittany, Burgundy, Lorraine, Alsace, all our provinces merged into France'. He called what corresponds to the vision of Enlightenment Perspectives 3 contemporary federalists the 'United States of Europe'. He imagined technical progress going hand-in-hand with this fraternal advance: 'Thanks to the railways, Europe will soon be no larger than France was in the Middle Ages! Thanks to steamboats, it is now possible to cross the Ocean more easily than one used to cross the Mediterranean! Soon man will travel round the earth like the Gods of Homer crossing the heavens in three strides. In but a few years, the electric wire of concord will surround the globe and embrace the world.

cause of the greatest conflicts. The two European blocs, the Triple Entente, made up of France, Russia and Great Britain, and the Triple Alliance, made up of Germany, Austria-Hungary and Italy, would confront each other in a general catastrophe caused by the assassination of Archduke Franz Ferdinand in Sarajevo, leading to a conflict on a European scale first and then on a world scale.

The intervention of the United States in World War I supposed the overcoming of the Monroe doctrine becoming the main figure of the final events of the war, President Thomas Woodrow Wilson, who would present to Congress on January 8, 1918 the Fourteen points, among which was the elimination of economic barriers and guarantees of reduction of arms to the maximum degree.

The Treaties of Paris and Versailles falsely closed a time in history that was followed by the February 1917 revolution, the Russian civil war of 1918 and the constitution of the Soviet Union, in a devastated Russia with an economy in ruins. Stalin would seize the administrative apparatus of the State and proclaim socialism in a single country, producing the international and internal consolidation of the USSR.

The League of Nations that emerged in 1919 from the Treaty of Versailles was, according to its creators, the first effective movement towards the organization of a world political and social order, whose main objective would be to guarantee peace through collective security and the construction of peace through cooperation.

The collective security system, which embodied the political dimension of the Company, would be regulated by articles 8 to 17 of its founding agreement, where the guidelines for a political and legal system of war prevention were established in which different notions interacted: the guarantee of the territorial integrity and independence of the States, collective assistance, arbitration, the limitation of the right to use war and a punitive system of sanctions.

The task of peace required in turn the adoption of a constructive principle of solidarity and international cooperation to which articles 23 to 25 of the Covenant of the League of Nations were devoted. But, the American isolation policy and the ineffectiveness of the League of Nations, were projected in a difficult scenario in which the Treaty of Versailles had created deep prejudices. The Locarno Treaties, signed in October 1925, would consecrate a climate of understanding and relaxation between Germans, British and French.

European defence was hardly going to be a central issue in a conflict-generating world in which new pro-European projects appeared that aspired to unite nations. At this time, from 1922, the ideas of the diplomat Richard de Coudenhove-Kalergi, who expressed the need to build the United States of Europe, would be disseminated in the main newspapers of European countries. His thought would be exposed in a book of 1923 founding, a year later, the Pan-European Union, with headquarters in Vienna and national sections in various European countries. In his Paneuropa project, he does not include Russia as he considers it a Eurasian country and Great Britain, which he conceptualizes as an intercontinental Empire (Saint-Gille 2003).

Kalergi would meet in Vienna from October 3 to 6, 1926, the first Congress of the Pan-European Union, which would be attended by 2,000 delegates from 24 countries and where they would consider freedom, peace as the foundation of the association of sovereign states, prosperity and culture. The Pan- European Union proposed a military alliance as a third point, within the framework of a balance between France and Germany, suggesting the European negotiation with the USSR (Coudenhove-Kalergi 1965).

In 1923 he foresaw the appearance of Eurosceptics, "*who then divided into four main groups; the chauvinists, the communists, the militarists and the protectionist industrialists. For Kalergi, of the four, the first would be the most impulsive but not the most dangerous, the second would seek to enter the European federation in order to denaturalize it from within, the third would see Paneuropa as the main obstacle to his reason for being; war, and the fourth would be the most dangerous because it would be configured by those industrialists who survive thanks to the intervention of their states in the natural international commercial traffic and who, therefore, could not compete within a pan-European bloc*" (Faramiñán Fernández-Figares 2014, 198).

Years later, at the end of his life, Coudenhove-Kalergi in his work *Europe, World Power* will assess the status of his project to establish an integrated Federation of States and will reflect on the fact that the withdrawal of American forces from Europe is nothing more than a question of time and that Europe must be united and assume the consequences of stopping the blows of destiny (Coudenhove-Kalergi, & Auclères 1972, 206). This precision raised generically does no more than warn that constituted Europe as a fourth world power must have a military force.

In his final considerations, he will allude to the modern weapons that threaten Europe with destruction in the event of a new war: "*The technique of weapons has progressed after the last war, so that any hope of reaching a future war is absurd. The last war was the last duel between the European peoples and groups of peoples, the next war will be a double suicide, the ineluctable ruin of the victor and the vanquished*" (Coudenhove-Kalergi, & Auclères 1972, 222).

The first statesman to present a political project for the European Union in the interwar period was Aristide Briand, whose most notable action had been the signing of the Locarno Treaty. Precisely in Locarno, Briand affirmed in his brilliant opening speech: "Away with the rifles, the machine guns, the cannons, I move on to conciliation, arbitration and peace". The spirit of Locarno would lead to the Briand- Kellogg Pact or Pact of Paris, agreed on August 27, 1928, which supposed the assumption by those States of a moral commitment and a principle of renunciation of war, committing themselves to submit in their litigations to international arbitration. With that Treaty, the United States, Great Britain, Germany, France, Italy and Japan, renounced war as a means of resolving conflicts and to which a total of 62 States would join.

Briand, who had accepted the honorary presidency of the European Movement in 1927, would deliver a speech before the Assembly of the League of Nations in which he declared himself in favour of creating "a kind of federal bond" in Europe, an association that would act above all in the economic domain, which is the most pressing issue, but I am sure that also on the political point of view, or the social point of view "*the federal bond, without touching the common sovereignty of nations, could configure that association that It would be well done*" (Pérez-Bustamante 2008, 59–60).

Briand evokes the idea of a federal bond, respect for Sovereignty and the notion of association and within it, a consultation between the Heads of Government, to prevent conflicts in Europe. The twenty-six European Member States of the League of Nations would entrust Aristide Briand with the preparation of a Memorandum that would be published on May 1, 1930 and presented to the Assembly of the League of Nations on September 8, 1930, in which he placed the accent more in the economy than in politics, understanding that "*any possibility of progress on the path of Economic Union is rigorously determined by the issue of Security and this issue is closely linked to that of making progress on the path of Political Union. It is on the political plan that the constructive effort must be carried out, tending to give Europe its organic structure*" (Lang 1998, 32).

But those visionary proposals would fail, in a context marked by the crisis of 1929, which affected the European economy and particularly Germany, where, in the 1930 elections, the nationalists obtained more than six million votes and in the 1932 elections, reached thirteen and a half million votes, opening the way to the appointment of Hitler as Chancellor, ready from his first days to breach the Versailles agreements and promote the militarization of Germany.

The "Lebensraum" would become an ideological principle of Nazism that provided a justification for German territorial expansion in Central and Eastern Europe. Nazi Germany supported other Axis nations with their own versions like Fascist Italy's living space and the Hakko Ichiu of the Empire of Japan, who proposed the Greater East Asia Co-Prosperity Sphere of 1940, a year before the Pearl Harbor attack.

After the invasion of Poland, the French and British governments mutually undertook not to negotiate the armistice separately and to carry out a common action of reconstruction after peace in the framework of future solidarity. Churchill and de Gaulle meet in London, at the Carlton Club, to consider the creation of a Franco-British Union, a project in which the resources of the two countries would be pooled. The two governments declare that France and Great Britain will henceforth not be two nations but one, a Franco-British Union will be created, every citizen of France will immediately enjoy British citizenship and every British subject will be a citizen of France (Gates 1981).

During the war there would be only one cabinet, made up of halves, under which would be all the sea, land and air armies. Marshal Petain judged the British proposal dishonourable, condemned in absentia De Gaulle would appear before the microphones of the BBC on June 18, 1940 to deliver his historic appeal to resistance.

Jean Monnet, who was present, will receive from Churchill the task of being part of the British purchasing mission - the British Supply Council in Washington, and from there he will personally participate in the Prêt-bail agreements, as the main weapon program launched by the United States during World War II, in order to provide war material to friendly countries without directly intervening in the conflict entered the war, effectively putting an end to the Neutrality Laws of the 1930s.

Monnet will be one of the editors of the Victory Program, as documented in the Balance Sheet, for 1941 and 1942, aimed at a great objective, the multiplication of American war production, managing to accelerate the production and delivery of aircrafts that allowed the Roya Air Force to win the Battle of Britain against the Luftwaffe. Keynes states that Monnet's intervention was capital and "it could be that he reduced the duration of the war by a year".

The British leadership was willing to create some kind of European federation, under British constitutional principles and consequently without a formal constitution. The British would never be willing to dilute their Sovereignty in a European federation.

At the end of World War II, the defense of Europe would be based on the Franco-British cordial entente, embodied in the Dunkirk Treaty of 1947, whose preamble establishes mutual assistance, to frustrate any resumption of a German policy of aggression.

The next advance within the framework of a veritable fever of activity related to the defense of Europe would come about with the Brussels Treaty of March 7, 1948, through which the organization of military, economic, social, and cultural cooperation between its Member States, as well as a mutual defense clause, through the creation of an international organization called the Western Union. As a secret objective it is established that when circumstances allow it, Germany, Austria and Spain should form part of the Brussels Treaty.

These treaties would arise within the framework of intergovernmental collaboration without any transfer to supranationality. The North Atlantic Treaty of 1949 would establish a political-military organization among the signatory countries, in order to comply with their security and collective defense and whose article V states the solidarity of its members in case of an armed attack, before which, the rest of the member countries will come to its defense.

With the failure of British leadership, the United States understood that France had to take on a sufficiently ambitious project to integrate Europe economically, with a high degree of supranationality, including the Federal Republic of Germany, which in September 1949 elected Konrad Adenauer as Chancellor. The Franco-German question would be the axis of the European construction.

At the end of 1949, everyone agreed that the defense of Europe was insufficient, while Truman announced that the Soviet Union had exploded its first atomic bomb with the consequent loss of the atomic monopoly by the United States. The German rearmament was a military necessity, but before the rearmament the integration of the German Federal Republic had to be resolved.

4 Security and Defense in the Scenario of the European Communities (1950–1990)

In that context, the functionalist pragmatism of Jean Monnet would emerge, enshrined in the Schuman Declaration of May 9, 1950 and the first Community Treaty, developed by Jean Monnet and his collaborators, which gave birth to the European Coal and Steel Community, in the founding idea of the Declaration of May 9, 1950: "The pooling of coal and steel production will immediately ensure the establishment of common bases, of economic development, the first stage of the European federation and will change the destiny of these regions (nations) long focused on the production of weapons of war of which they were victims" (Gerbet 1962).

This first Community Treaty assumed the creation of a common authority, the High Authority, made up of independent personalities assigned on a parity basis by the governments and a president elected by common agreement, whose decisions would be executive.

But the Korean War, which began on June 25, 1950, would lead to a new scenario in the process of European unification. By then, it was clear that the European defense situation was unacceptable. The allies had 10 divisions in the Federal Republic of Germany and according to the experts, eighteen were required to carry out dissuasive actions and fifty-four to defend the Rhine, the USSR had 22 divisions in the satellite countries and more than one hundred in reserve.

Precisely then, the idea of transposing the technique of uniting coal and steel to the military field would take shape, proposed with the Pleven Plan, the creation of the European Defense Community, through the constitution of a "European army" in which the German troops, thereby avoiding the creation of a German army, while increasing troops from the European continent, facing the direct Soviet threat (Clesse 1989, 200–201). With a European army, as the prestigious professor and politician André Philippe would say to the Assembly, "there would no longer be any problem of a national nature".

Jean Monnet was in favor of German rearmament in a supranational European framework and got down to work, to forge a military project on a European scale, with the same men with whom he had made the European Coal and Steel Community Treaty. General Eisenhower, who met with Jean Monnet on June 27, 1951, would join the project to create a European Defense Community.

The solution would be an expanded Schuman Plan based on the CECA Institutions and creating a European army, whose main characteristics would be the unity of equipment, organization and command and where the national, basic unit would be the battalion and the superior unit, the division, formed by the union of battalions of different nationalities. Financing would be done through a common budget.

The British would again refuse to enter a Defense Community, Anthony Eden would state: "It is only when the plans for the unification of Europe take on a federal character that we cannot take part, since we cannot subordinate ourselves or leave control of our politics to a federal authority" (Eden 1960, 50–52). In an attempt to hinder the march towards the signing of the Treaty, Moscow will launch the offer to reunify Germany in exchange for its neutralization (VanDijk 1999).

This would lead to the CED Treaty, signed in Paris on May 27, 1952, in which the main institutions would be: a European Defense Authority that would act as a European Defense Minister; a Council of Ministers whose assent will be required when the Authority must make important decisions; a Parliamentary Assembly (made up of the same delegates provided for in the Schuman Plan for the Coal and Steel Community) that will examine the management of the Authority and, to a certain extent, the funds allocated to it, and a Court of Justice to rule on legal disputes that may arise between the Authority and the States, there would be a joint European Defense Fund to cover all the expenses of these integrated forces and receive financial contributions from the member States and foreign aid from other States, equating the validity of the Treaty with the CECA, in fifty years.

However, the supranational institutions desired by Jean Monnet were not contained. The null will of the politicians to build a federal Europe left the future of the CED buried. The failure of the ratification of the Treaty, in France dominated by the nationalism of General de Gaulle and by the French Communist Party, liberated by the death of Stalin, ended the dream of European defense. Jean Monnet recounts in his Memoirs how he had been attacked by De Gaulle, in November 1953, when he accused him of being "the inspirer of a stateless European army". Disappointed, he would resign the presidency of the High Authority, of the first Community.

Robert Marjolin, involved in the Marshall plan, first Secretary of the OECD and one of Jean Monnet's main men, will say in his Memoirs that "Europe's inability to unite resulted from a decision implicitly made by Europeans after World War II. World Cup, that of trusting the Americans for their defense". For Eisenhower, the States of Western Europe should provide the necessary forces, for its territorial defense, Churchill understood that the survival of the West did not depend on the conventional rearmament of Europe, but on the atomic supremacy of the United States.

The Brussels Treaty of Cooperation and Collective Security, signed on October 23, 1954 in Paris, by which the Western European Union would be created, reactivated the 1948 Treaty and would try to build a more integrated Europe in Defense by strengthening the anchorage German in the Euro-Atlantic and Western space, achieving its reconciliation with France and the resolution of the Saar problem, but also restoring confidence in the countries of Western Europe, in particular, in terms of arms control, although in reality, it would not do but to recognize the weight of the Atlantic dimension of Western European defense, placed under the command of NATO.

At the same time, the entry of the Federal Republic of Germany into NATO took place, with the consequent integration of the West German armed forces in the integrated military structure of the Atlantic Alliance. It is not new to affirm that the Western European Union would later relinquish many of its powers, de jure or de facto, while the Atlantic Alliance would remain as the reference framework for the collective security of European countries.

The European defense scenario would be altered again by the positions of General de Gaulle, elected President of France in 1958, forced to coexist with the European Communities, an integrating and supranational project with which he never agreed and against which he would try to articulate an intergovernmental political Europe "the Europe of the Homelands", based on the political cooperation that it would present through the Fouchet plans.

De Gaulle would maintain an attitude of mistrust towards the United States, which had already existed since World War II, on November 2, 1959, he would deliver a resounding speech in which he stated: "NATO has ceased to be an Alliance, it means subordination, we cannot accept the Guardianship of the United States, the Defensive Integration System has ceased to exist, France's defense must be French. It is absolutely necessary that France defends itself by itself and with its own means".

Fouchet Plan I would be the first step on the road to a common foreign policy and the Fouchet Plan II proposed on January 18, 1962, would highlight in its preamble the commitment of the States to increase their defence capacity, but would omit any reference to NATO. In any case, I would accept foreign trade and the economy remaining within the community structure, but foreign policy and defence would be managed intergovernmentally. His idea of creating a European defence, separate from the Atlantic alliance, supported by France's nuclear arsenal, would be contested by President Kennedy who would state: "I believe that it will be many years before the European nations are capable of defending themselves without the presence of the United States" (Guinea 2021, 134).

With the aim of constituting a European block independent of the United States, on January 22, 1963, de Gaulle would sign the Elysée Treaty with Adenauer, establishing greater cooperation between France and Germany in international relations, defense, and education, with a specific program for the organization of military summits. The Treaty did not mention NATO, but the ratification by Germany would include a preamble referring to the "close association between Europe and the United States of America" and the "common defense within the framework of the North Atlantic Alliance with the United States of America", which led to an angry reaction from De Gaulle, who would have to accept the preamble imposed by the Bundestag.

Confronted with its community partners, it would cause a paralysis of the European Economic Community with the "Empty Chair Crisis", demanding the principle of unanimity when the governments understood that vital interests were at stake, as well as the limitation of the powers of the Commission, ensuring its control by the Council. Thus, the Luxembourg Compromise, January 28–30, 1966, would be reached, which by imposing unanimity would reject the federal evolution of the Community, betraying the spirit of the Treaties of Rome.

Determined to maintain the development of nuclear weapons, in March 1966, General de Gaulle would announce his departure from the integrated command of the Atlantic Alliance. The French armed forces would be withdrawn from NATO's integrated command and Supreme Headquarters Allied Powers Europe (SHAPE) by moving from Roquencourt, near Paris, to northern Belgium. France would continue in the Alliance and with its troops stationed in West Germany.

In that divided Europe, on August 21, 1968, the USSR invaded Czechoslovakia, to repress the country's internal reforms. The Soviet performance caught Europeans and Americans by surprise. The New York Times reported the intervention of 650,000 men equipped with the most modern and sophisticated weapons in the Soviet military catalogue. The United Nations condemned the invasion, but neither the WEU nor NATO, absorbed by the conflict in Asia, considered intervening and a curtain of silence was imposed on the occupation. A NATO communiqué would state that the North Atlantic Alliance would remain the indispensable guarantor of European security and that its existence was more necessary than ever.

The arrival to the presidency of George Pompidou, on June 20, 1969, would bring with it the relaunch of the European community project, agreed at the Hague Summit, on December 1 and 2, 1969. In it, the States in agreement, to allow Europe to play its part in international detente, the balance of the world and the protection of peace (Gallung 2021).

Cooperation in Foreign Policy would then constitute the preliminary piece of European Political Unification (Rapport Davignon) of July 20, 1970, but in that consultation and agreement mechanism, for Political Cooperation, Defense was left out, due to the divergences of the States on the role of NATO. The entry of Great Britain into the Communities, carried out in 1973, would reinforce the defensive capacity of the Communities by having an additional Member State with a seat on the United Nations Security Council, but it would stop the supranational projection of the Communities and the Union European.

The last Summit of Heads of State and Government, held in Paris, in December 1974, would commission Leo Tindemans to explore the path to reach the creation of the European Union. Tindemans, Prime Minister of Belgium, was convinced that his country should be a loyal member of the Atlantic Alliance. NATO would continue to be the continental defensive umbrella and recognized that, thanks to NATO, Europe had a security climate that had allowed it to undertake community construction, but it also assumed that Europe should carry out an analysis of defense problems and increase a greater autonomy in the question of armament.

With the birth of the European Council in 1975, a forum was made possible for the leaders of the States of the European Community that would acquire a prominent role over the years, guiding the future actions of the Communities in matters of Security and Defense. The Dublin European Council of March 11, 1975 highlights in its Conclusions a Declaration on the Conference on Security and Cooperation in Europe, in which the Heads of State and Government would reaffirm the will of the Nine to continue and identify their Policies of Detente and Cooperation with Europe.

The Commission itself would act through its President Françoise Xavier Ortolli, presenting, on June 26, 1975, the Report entitled "The European Union", where, detailing the scope and legal nature of a possible Union, it was stated that "the Security of each Member State affects the Security of other Member States and of the Community as a whole". Security was then presented as a fundamental element in the future construction of a united Europe and it was recognized that, although the Atlantic Alliance played and would continue to play a decisive role in the security of Western Europe, it was specified that there would not be a true Union "if the issues of defense are simply set aside when the Union begins to establish itself.

Likewise, there was concern about the different situation of the Member States with respect to NATO and the WEU and it was understood that the construction of the European Union was the way to make Defense a field of potential competence for the Union, specifying that it would be desirable the alignment of the defense policies of the Member States and the development of a common arms and equipment policy, possibly through the creation of the European Armaments Agency.

If the European Council took leadership away from the European Commission and then assumed the need to attribute to itself an eminently political nature that would lead to accentuating its leading role, in Foreign Policy and Defense Policy, the European Parliament would go even further by presenting a constitutional proposal embodied in a draft European Union Treaty, promoted by most of the Parliamentarians.

Its rapporteur, the federalist Altiero Spinelli, would have as its objective the achievement of a federal union and in that project, he would develop the international relations of the Union, in articles 63 to 69 consecrating the method of Joint Action and instituting the method of cooperation that it could be extended to the matter of armament, defense policy and disarmament.

The Spinelli Treaty project, which would be adopted by Parliament on February 14, 1984, would not be successful, but it would promote or manage to engage the Member States in a reflection on the reform of the Communities that would culminate in 1986 with the Single European Act, whose title III in its article 30 would develop Political Cooperation including "a closer cooperation in European Security issues", representing for the States, the preservation of the technological and industrial conditions necessary to safeguard their Security, without undermining their Sovereignty, nor hindering their Political Cooperation within the framework of the Western European Union or NATO.

In 1985, Mikhail Gorbachev, General Secretary of the CPSU, would come to power, ready to carry out a partial liberation of the socialist system and to maintain a position of dialogue with the United States, ready to take steps towards détente. On December 8, 1987, the Intermediate-Range Nuclear Forces Treaty was signed in Washington, the most detailed and rigorous in the history of nuclear arms control.

Elected President of the Presidium in 1988, he would introduce Perestroika, through which new freedoms would be granted to citizens, and glasnost, which meant clarity and transparency in political processes and in favor of democratic control. The opening of the Berlin Wall on the night of November 9–10, 1989 would symbolize the end of the Cold War and profoundly modified the European political space and, consequently, the horizons of the European Union. The countries of Eastern Europe would become democratic states and begin to make trade agreements with the European Economic Community, while the Soviet Union would transform its political regime, establishing a presidential regime. The Atlantic Alliance would undertake to cooperate with the countries of Central and Eastern Europe, guaranteeing the stability of their borders.

Those years of long negotiations would allow the United States to coincide, together with its European allies and the Soviet Union, in the necessary reform of their relations, for their part, the Communities would gain momentum that would lead to Political Union.

5 Security and Defense in the Treaties of the European Union (1992–2009)

In the midst of the great political transformations that had been taking place on the European scene, fundamentally the end of the Soviet Union, German unification and the political and economic reconstruction of the Eastern European States; The European Council in Rome in 1991 was decisive in emphasizing the attention of the Communities on the Foreign Relations and Security policy, according to a continuous evolutionary process, and at the same time unitary, based on general objectives defined in a new Treaty.

It was then understood that the Common Foreign and Security Policy would be established on an intergovernmental basis and security and defense issues would be included in it; a taboo subject since the failure of the CED in 195 and that would constitute the greatest innovation of the Maastricht Treaty, in this field. The European States were aware that the disintegration of the USSR would produce a reduction in the American presence in Europe, but various proposals would be debated in the joint Security and Common Defense, including the Franco-German proposal and the Anglo-Italian proposal.

The two major debates would focus on the Common Defense and the role of the WEU. The first would lead to the constitution of a Command made up of common armed forces structures, under a single integrated command, compatible with NATO structures, considering the idea of creating a European intervention force, for peacekeeping operations and humanitarian. As for the role of the WEU, in the Franco-German idea, which proposed a properly European defense, it should become one of the instruments of the Political Union of which it would be a part, while in the British-Italian idea that proposed an Atlanticist vision, the WEU, on the one hand, would be the "defense" component of the European Union and, on the other, a means of reinforcing the European pillar of the Atlantic Alliance.

The Compromise between the different security and defense positions would be formulated in article J-4 of the Maastricht Treaty, according to which the Common Foreign and Security Policy will include issues related to the Security of the Union and may conclude in the future in the establishment of a Common Defense Policy. The Union will demand that the Western European Union elaborate and implement the decisions and actions of the Union that have repercussions in the field of Defense (Cloos 1993).

In this way, with the Union Treaty, progress had been made in the construction of a political Europe and in the incipient construction of a Security and Defense Europe, but the divergences of conception and the demand for unanimity in the Council The European Union prevented the European Union from establishing a true Common Foreign and Security Policy. Jacques Delors, who had stated that the fact that the Union did not have a legal personality would cause problems in the long run, was disappointed in relation to the Policy of Defense, since the intergovernmental model -the Greek temple-, adopted by the Maastricht Treaty, would be inoperative, warning, once again, that the community method was the only one that could make the European space work (Delors 2004, 489).

During the Franco-German Summit held in La Rochelle on May 22, 1992, Mitterrand and Kohl decided to create Eurocorps, an army corps open to all WEU nations. The Petersberg agreement, of June 19, would define the missions that could be entrusted: the common defense of the allied countries and peacekeeping missions. The headquarters was established in Strasbourg and in the following years Belgium joined in 1993, Spain in 1994 and Luxembourg in 1996.

The disintegration of Yugoslavia would create an instability that would lead to a long period of wars, the end of which in western Yugoslavia would conclude in 1995 with the Dayton Accords, peace talks sponsored by the United States. However, in 1996, the war in Kosovo would begin, which would end with the bombing of Yugoslavia by NATO in 1999. At the end of the war, Kosovo would be recognized as an independent state by most countries.

Between 1992 and 1996 the European Union had adopted twelve "Common Actions" essentially in the former Yugoslavia, the Middle East and Africa, but the European Union had not acted as such in the Yugoslav crisis. Its most important countries, France, the United Kingdom, Germany, and Italy, had formed the Contact Group with the United States and Russia.

At the Summit, held on January 10 and 11, 1994, NATO would again assume European defense, adapting to the reinforcement of the European Security and Defense Identity, while assuming that the WEU was complementary to NATO. Great Britain would emphasize this issue by recalling that the European Union's defense action should be intergovernmental, based on cooperation between national States and not dictated by supranational bodies, but that intergovernmentalism was precisely the paralyzing element of the Union in Foreign Policy and Defense Policy.

The appointment of Javier Solana Madariaga, as Secretary General of NATO, made on December 5, 1995, would coincide with the reorganization of the political and military structure of the Atlantic Alliance and its basic strategies. On the other hand, on May 27, 1997, the NATO-Russia founding act was signed in Paris, which put an end to hostilities between Russia and NATO, allowing NATO to act in the war in Kosovo, under the authorization of the Council of United Nations Security.

By mid-January 1995, work had already begun on a reform of the Maastricht Treaty, identifying among its objectives the reform of Foreign Policy and, within it, of Defense Policy, evidenced in the conflict of the Former Yugoslavia and in humanitarian catastrophes. The attitude of the States was very different, the United Kingdom, which became intransigent, wanted to have a free hand on a global scale and at the same time refused to distance itself from the United States. France wanted a true Common European Foreign Policy, with the support of Germany, to reaffirm the international role of the European Union, although Germany remained faithful to its Atlantic commitment.

Italy, close to the United States, aspired to develop its influence in the Mediterranean. Spain appeared among the greats, thanks to its influence in Latin America. The medium and small countries had a limited horizon in foreign policy, some continued to give priority to the Atlantic Alliance, the neutrals - Ireland, Sweden, Austria and Finland - were not interested in a military alliance.

This is how the Saint Malo Summit was reached, which would be held on December 3 and 4, 1998, and in which the President of France, Jacques Chirac, met with the British Prime Minister, Tony Blair, in a bilateral meeting that is usually considered the starting point of the European Security and Defense policy. The Saint Malo Declaration would be considered as a response to the war in Kosovo in which it was appreciated that the International Community and, in particular, the European Union and its Member States had not intervened to stop the conflict. The Summit would give rise to a Joint Declaration that called for the establishment of "independent" and "credible" military means for the European Union. It would specify the relationship with NATO, committing the European Union to act "when the Alliance as such is not compromised" and "without necessary duplications".

After the European Councils of Cologne, June 3 and 4, 1999, and Helsinki, December 10 and 11, 1999, a Rapid Reaction Force of 60,000 men was created that could be deployed within 60 days and during one year, what would be called the so-called Helsinki Headline Global. In any case, the events of that decade made possible, under the leadership of France and Germany, a general consensus in the development of the Defense Policy, something in which Great Britain would always refuse to assume greater integration. The fundamental purpose would be the progressive integration of the WEU into the EU.

The Treaty of Amsterdam, which would enter into force on October 2, 1999, established the figure of the High Representative for Foreign Policy in the figure of the Secretary General of the Council, assisted by a Planning Unit for the Early Warning Policy. Although this Treaty would improve the decision-making process, introducing the notion of common strategies, and transferring the Petersberg missions from the WEU to the EU, anticipating the eventual integration of the WEU into the European Union, the CFSP proved insufficient to allow the European Union to play an international role that corresponds to its demographic and economic importance, articulating the European Security and Defense Policy (ESDP).

For its part, Eurocorps, which had intervened in 1998 and 1999, would be offered by France and Germany to the service of the European Union and, following a decision of November 22, 1999, would be transformed in 2002 into a European rapid reaction corps. The dramatic end of the Kosovo War and its terrible consequences, including the so-called Balkan syndrome, nearly 100,000 soldiers undergoing check-ups to verify their health status, would once again leave us open to reflection on the defense policy of the European Union.

The Franco-German Summit in Toulouse, on May 28 and 29, 1999, advocated the creation of a European rapid reaction corps, based on Eurocorps. The European objective set by the European Council in Helsinki, on December 10 and 11, 1999, would be to constitute a European rapid reaction force of 60,000 to 80,000 men, which meant a reserve of 150,000 men.

Beginning in November 2000, two Conferences would be held to agree on military capabilities and obtain the necessary national commitments to achieve the Helsinki objectives. The Member States decided to establish a "European Action Plan for Capabilities", to fill the gaps that had been observed in order to rationalize the defense efforts of the Member States. Within this framework, 19 working groups would be created to study the most important gaps in the Helsinki global objective.

Meanwhile, the concept of Sovereignty was already present in the academic debate (Cazzaniga and Zarka 2001). On February 26, 2001, a new Treaty of the European Union was signed: the Treaty of Nice, whose main objective, if not the only one, would be to establish the principles and methods of the institutional system that would allow the great enlargement, of the European Union, to the countries of central and eastern Europe, the Baltic countries, and the islands of Cyprus and Malta. That Treaty would hardly deal with Defense policy, although it would develop enhanced cooperation more widely and would cede control and strategic direction of crisis management operations to the Political Committee, now also called Security.

By then, the Fifteen had found a compromise formula between their divergent positions on their relations with NATO, agreeing that the progressive definition of a Common Defense Policy, which could lead to a common defense if the European Council so decides… Does not affect to the specific nature of the Security and Defense Policy of certain Member States… Which consider that their common defense is carried out within the framework of NATO.

On December 16, 2002, the EU-NATO Declaration on Common Foreign and Security Policy was made in which both reaffirmed their determination to strengthen their capabilities for the Atlantic organization, reserving a greater role for Europe. This Declaration would pursue three objectives: the European Union will ensure that the European members of NATO that are not part of the ESDP are associated as far as possible with the ESDP, NATO will lend its support to the ESDP and give the EU a guaranteed access to NATO planning capabilities and the two organizations will agree on advantageous arrangements for their common capability needs.

Barely a month later, on March 27, 2003, the Berlin+ Agreements were signed, laying the foundations for NATO-EU cooperation in the field of crisis management. The EU would accede to NATO's operational planning, with a view to effective use in the framework of EU-led military planning of crisis management operations.

At a time when the European Union was facing the great challenge of its institutional and organizational reconstruction, the terrorist attacks of September 11, 2001, against the United States, were taking place, which meant the appearance of terrorism on a global scale, and with a global impact, as a key factor to take into account when building security. The European Union, which assumed that challenge, would celebrate, on December 14 and 15, the Laeken European Council in which a Convention would be articulated with the mandate to draft a Constitutional reform project[3]. Its President, Valéry Giscard d'Estaing, would focus one of the debates on strengthening the European identity on Foreign Policy.

One of the eleven Working Groups would have as its objective the Security and Defense Policy, and would be chaired by Michel Barnier, considering as main points of examination: the need or not to include a collective defense clause in the Treaty, indicate the appropriate mechanisms, to guarantee the respect of the Member States, of their commitments, in terms of military capabilities, to guarantee that decision-making during the execution of an operation is made quickly and efficiently, to ensure that the military and civilian elements of the EU coordinate and plan properly and, lastly, consider the possibility of including in the Treaty forms of cooperation in the field of armaments, as well as the creation of an Armaments Agency.

Those issues would be dealt with from September to December 2002 and the approaches would take shape in various documents. The main protagonist in the debates would be the proposal of the Foreign Ministers of France and Germany, Dominique de Villepin and Joschka Fischer, who proposed transforming the CFSP into a "European Security and Defense Union", greater flexibility in the decision-making process, annex to the Treaty a protocol on the improvement of military capabilities and develop, or include in the Treaty, a European Arms Policy with a view to a European Arms market, along with the creation of a European Arms Agency.

In the conclusions of the "Defense" group it was recognized that the European Defense Policy cannot be defined without referring to NATO. Eleven EU Member States were then members of NATO and under Article 5 of the Washington Treaty they were bound by a collective defense clause. Likewise, the closest Cooperations that existed between the Member States in the field of armament and the military field (Eurcopos, Euroford, Euromaford, European Air Group, Multinational Division and General Staff of the first German-Dutch Corps) would be remembered. Several members of the group would propose a collective defense clause and the creation of a European Armament Agency.

The final contributions to that Defense Working Group would include crisis management, with the expansion of the Petersberg Missions, they would assume a common Solidarity and Security clause or a collective defense clause in the Treaty, they would defend the improvement of capabilities and armament, creating a European Agency and would strengthen the institutional framework, maintaining the existing structures and creating a political personality in the Council to coordinate efforts in the field of Defence.

Those proposals would largely go to the draft European constitution: Art. I-11 and I-15 on the competence of the Union in Common Foreign and Security Policy; art. 1–27.2 on the Minister of Foreign Affairs and his contribution to the formulation of the Common

[3] The constitutional idea had already been raised since the election of the European Parliament by universal suffrage and would take shape in the draft Spinelli Treaty of 1984 and in the Herman project of 1993.

Security and Defense policy; art. III-205 on the expanded version of the Petersberg Missions; art. III-205-paragraph 7, on the action of a European Agency for Armaments, research and military capabilities; art-. III-205, Sect. 6, instituting permanent structured cooperation and article I-42, instituting the solidarity clause.

The attacks in New York had a harsh response and finally provoked, on March 20, 2003, the invasion of Iraq by a coalition led by the United States. The American decision would divide the European continent: France and Germany had proposed that the UN inspectors continue to investigate bombs of mass destruction, an American argument, while Great Britain, Spain, Poland, and various Eastern countries aligned themselves with the The United States, who proposed to the United Nations a Resolution that would allow them to start the bombers, but that proposal was rejected by France and Germany, along with China and Russia. The division between the countries of the European Union would highlight the scant integration in Foreign Policy and Defense Policy.

The European Council of 12 and 13 September 2003 would adopt the document on the "European security strategy". A text written under the authority of the High Representative of the European Union, for the CFSP, Javier Solana Madariaga, with the aim of better identifying the threats, defining the strategic objectives of the Union and identifying the political implications for Europe. This document would endure, being replaced on June 28, 2016 by the "Global Strategy of the European Union". On the military plane, the Ministers of Defense would adopt, in April 2004, the Franco-German-British proposals for the creation of tactical groups of 1,500 elite soldiers who could be deployed to crisis points outside European territory, at the request of the UN..

A few months later, on July 12, 2004, the European Defense Agency was created, with the aim of supporting the Defense efforts of the European Union, whose Statute, headquarters and operating procedures would finally be defined in the CFSP 2015 Council Decision /1835, of October 12, 2015. The Agency was born with the idea of allowing the development of European weapons programs, but it would be limited by the lack of resources and the need to operate unanimously. Its meager budget in 2015 was 30,000 million euros. In September 2004, a European gendarmerie force would be created, made up of 800 gendarmes, from five countries (Spain, France, Italy, the Netherlands and Portugal), to intervene in operations to maintain order and security in the outgoing regions of conflicts.

The failure to ratify the Constitutional Treaty would give way to a long period of reflection in which there was no lack of voices in favor of establishing a true Security and Defense Union. On December 13, 2007, a new Union Treaty was signed in Lisbon in which the Common Foreign and Security Policy would be renamed the Common Security and Defense Policy, being developed in the second section, articles 42 to 46 of the Treaty of the European Union, integrated into the Common Foreign and Security Policy and established with the aim of establishing for the Union the capacity to operate on the basis of civil and military means, in external projection and in the Security of the Union.

The provisions relating to the Defense Policy would be identical to those contained in the Treaty that establishes a Constitution for Europe, prepared by the Defense group, under the presidency of Michel Barnier, coming largely from the aforementioned Franco-German contribution, of November 2002. The main innovations of the Lisbon Treaty would be the updating of the Union's missions, the creation of the European Defense Union and the "permanent structured cooperation", as well as the introduction of the mutual defense clause. The set of decisions, with the notable exception of the decisions related to the implementation of permanent structured cooperation, the participation of this cooperation and the Statute of the European Defense Agency, would continue with Unanimity.

After the entry into force of the Lisbon Treaty, produced on December 1, 2009, all the functions of the WEU would be incorporated into the European Union. The UEO had maintained during the first decade of the s. XXI a small number of powers and activities, included in the modified Brussels Treaty of 1954 that was still in force, among them, the contracting of mutual assistance in case of armed aggression against one of the countries of the Treaty, in accordance with the Article V of the Treaty, although the Treaty of the European Union had established, under the Lisbon reform, that article 42 maintain a clause of mutual assistance in case of armed aggression, the presentation of an annual parliamentary report on its activities and particular on arms control in accordance with article IX of the Treaty and the holding of sessions of the Parliamentary Assembly of the WEU.

On March 31, 2010, the ten member states of the WEU would announce the dissolution of the organization and the transfer of its capabilities to the European Union, in collaboration with NATO. On July 30, 2011, the WEU would cease to exist and the Luxembourg National Archives would become the repository of its documentation.

By then, a worrying scenario hung over Eastern Europe. The aspirations of Georgia and Ukraine to become members of NATO and the NATO Summit held in Bucharest in April 2008, in which President George W. Bush had offered a Membership Action Plan to both countries, had awakened the misgivings of Russia, for whom the Russian military deployment in the Black Sea was vital.

Vladimir Putin would state that NATO enlargement would be seen as a direct threat to Russia's security. Russia would start, four months later, on August 7, 2008, a war in South Ossetia and Abkhazia, being the first time since the dissolution of the USSR that the Russian army intervened in an independent State, to achieve political objectives. The European States would not react and the violation of the territorial integrity of Georgia opened the way for Russian action, similarly in a possible future with other neighboring States.

6 The Defence of the European Union in a New Scenario of Tensions (2014–2022)

After the entry into force of the Lisbon Treaty, on December 1, 2009, two opposing views were maintained within the Union: one that advocated the creation of a European army and a strong Security and Defense policy, a position maintained by Germany and France, with the strong support of the European Parliament; and of the position of the United Kingdom and Poland, more Atlanticist, which prioritized the preferential framework of NATO.

On November 2, 2010, the two nuclear powers of the European Union, France and the United Kingdom, concluded the Lancaster House Cooperation and Defense

Treaties in London, including, in an operational section, Arms Cooperation and the rapprochement of their nuclear industries. Defending. The path chosen by the States was not the community route, but the strengthening of their national bases for defense and blocking the advance of the Union. We would see this attitude endorsed by the veto of the United Kingdom to a possible increase in the budget of the European Defense Agency, which in 2012 would again freeze its economic development for the third time and for the third year.

A new moment of tension would arise in Eastern Europe as a result of the events that occurred in Ukraine at the end of 2013, once an attempt to sign the Association Agreement with the European Union took place, leading to the fall of a government favorable to a Customs Union with Russia. Those events facilitated Vladimir Putin's decision to annex Crimea, where, after a military intervention, a Declaration of Independence was produced on March 16, 2014, and the illegal annexation to Russia on March 18.

The European Union would respond by imposing economic and commercial sanctions, described by Moscow as unacceptable, condemning the conflict and expressing its hope that the Russian Federation would respect Ukraine's national sovereignty and territorial integrity. The sanctions did not alter Russia's road map in the East Caucasus scenario.

Consequently, a new period of European Defense policy began in September 2014, under the presidency of Jean Claude Juncker at the head of the Commission. Juncker would revive the debate on the European army in a scenario in which the European Union was surrounded by an increasing number of international crises. The crises in Ukraine, Syria and Libya and what some would call an "arc of instability" on the European fronts. Juncker would not miss any occasion to emphasize that a European army would help design a common foreign and security policy: "You do not have a European army to mobilize it, but a common army would serve to show Russia that we are serious about defending the values of the European Union. The then German Defense Minister, Ursula von right Leyen, would rule in favor of such a proposal (DW 2015).

The construction of a common army had been made possible by article 42.7 of the Union Treaty, but there was no political will to achieve it. The resistance to this rapprochement in recent decades had become evident on the part of some governments of the Member States. Germany was not willing to risk the advantages of the energy supply provided by Russia, who had captured former German Chancellor Gerhard Schröder himself, who, since January 2009, had been a member of the board of directors of the Russian-British oil group TNK-BP, position for which he received a salary of 200,000 euros per year.

Another of the most reluctant to the military development of the Union was the United Kingdom, which, at the European Council in February 2016, requested new conditions of permanence in the Union, and so they were offered with the intention of keeping it in the Union. In one part of annex 1, a decision on "a new regime for the United Kingdom in the EU", a section would be dedicated to "Sovereignty" in which it was recognized that the United Kingdom "has not committed itself to greater integration policy within the EU and that the references made in the Treaty and the preambles to the process creating "an ever closer Union among the peoples of Europe" does not constitute a legal basis, to extend the scope of application of any provision of the Treaties or of the derived law of the EU" and "neither should they serve to support an extensive interpretation of the competences of the Union or of the powers of its institutions".

It was also recognized that the references to an ever closer Union between peoples "are compatible with the different paths of integration available to the Member States and do not oblige all Member States to seek a common goal". Finally, it is said that "article 4, paragraph 2, of the Treaty of the European Union confirms that national security will continue to be the exclusive responsibility of each Member State" (European Council, feb-2016). Undoubtedly, these cessions, which would not be able to stop the sovereigntist drift of the United Kingdom and its exit from the European Union, represented a brake on the process of European construction, a distortion of the Treaties themselves and, above all, of the founding spirit of European construction.

On June 23, 2016, they would hold a referendum in which 51.8% of the British would vote in favor of withdrawal and thereby definitively distance themselves from a greater rapprochement with the rest of the Union nations. On March 27, 2017, the United Kingdom launched that complex withdrawal process, inexorably initiating the procedure described in article 50 of the Treaty of the European Union. Brexit was a serious setback for the European Union's Defense Policy, despite the relative involvement of Great Britain in the CSDP, but also an opportunity because Great Britain had always been a critical actor, or even an obstructor, in the initiatives of the European Union in matters of defense and in the possible communitisation of said policy.

The departure of Great Britain would finally take place on January 31, 2020. Let us remember that Great Britain had signed the Lancaster House Treaties with France that had launched the Battle Groups, tactical units, made up of 1,500 troops, an initiative that Germany had joined, just then, in March 2018, the United Kingdom withdrew from this project, which was considered vital in the construction of defense Europe.

In sum, the implications of the United Kingdom's exit from the EU's Common Security and Defense Policy were important because it meant, first and foremost, the loss of one of the two nuclear powers and of a permanent member of the United Nations Security Council (with the right to veto). In second place, the United Kingdom was the country that invested the most in defense, representing 24% of the total of the EU Member States in 2016 and, in addition, it had already committed to increasing its budget by 0.5% per year in the period 2020, 2021 and an investment of 178 billion pounds in the following ten years in military equipment. Its military spending was already 4.7%, well above Germany, France and Italy.

Consequently, his departure meant the loss of one of the countries with the highest investment in defense R&D&i, representing, together with France and Germany, 92% of the two billion EU funding. Consequently, this withdrawal caused the European Union to lose defense spending, a global footprint and military capabilities, which reduced its capacity as a security actor on the international scene.

At a Conference on Defense and Security in Prague, held on June 9, 2017, Jean Claude Juncker would once again insist on the need for the European Union to make more common efforts in Defense because, in his own words, it could not be "outsourced" your protection. In that speech, he would insist that the European Security and Defense policy did not undermine the role of NATO, nor did it seek to compete with the Alliance, stating that "NATO has been and will continue to be the cornerstone of European security for decades."

This intervention was not accidental, it was a response to the new situation that arose with the United States. Relations between the European Union and the United States, during the presidential term of Barack Obama, had been extremely cordial, starting in 2014. Precisely, because of the crisis in Ukraine and the Russian annexation of Crimea, Obama would then announce an initiative of 3,400 million dollars, to reinforce the presence of the United States in NATO. Obama had even given his support to the TTIP, the Transatlantic Trade and Investment Association, which had opened its round of negotiations on July 8, 2013, and which would continue without difficulties until 2016.

The Republican candidate Donald Trump was going to accede, on January 20, 2017, to the presidency of the United States and by then he had already declared himself against maintaining the expense that security entailed in Europe, being the country that maintained most of the NATO budget.

Trump would demand that NATO allies substantially increase their military spending and dedicate 2% of their GDP to Defense, a commitment that had already been made at the Prague Summit in 2002 and Newport in 2014, but only five members of all 28, including the UK, Poland, Greece, and Estonia, had met them. On July 11, 2018, at the Summit of the North Atlantic Organization in Brussels, Trump would describe as delinquent the countries that did not allocate the committed 2% of GDP, now demanding that the States double their defense spending up to 4%, alleging that the United States allocated 4.2% in real figures and directing his greatest criticism at Germany, whom he described as a hostage of Russia due to its energy dependence.

At the G7 Summit in Quebec, held in August 2018, during a trade war with European countries, Trump would question Article 5 of the Washington Treaty, referring to the commitment to mutual defense. That hostile position would be constantly maintained and at the NATO 70th anniversary summit, held in London on December 4, 2019, the President of France Emanuel Macron would declare that the Atlantic Alliance was in a state of "brain death", stating that the issue was not just talking about money, but about having a clear strategy about what the Alliance should be.

The European Union was aware of the need to address defense policy, and on the occasion of the 60th anniversary of the founding of the European Communities, it would hold a meeting with European leaders in Rome on March 25, 2017, where would issue a declaration in which it would be clear that the Union was ready to assume its responsibilities and help create a more competitive and integrated defense policy in a vision committed to strengthening its common security and defense, albeit in cooperation and complementarity with NATO, taking into account the circumstances and legal commitments.

That conviction would have materialized in the European Council of June 22, 2017, where the Heads of State and Government agreed on the need to launch an inclusive and ambitious Permanent Structured Cooperation, to reinforce the security and defense of Europe, assuming to agree on a common list of criteria and commitments, together with concrete capacity projects, in order to initiate this cooperation. At the same time, the Commission would issue a Communication on the creation of a European Defense Fund, constituted as the main instrument of the Union, to support cooperation in defense matters. The remaining institutions, the Council and the European Parliament would adopt the final decision on its creation, with the Fund starting to operate on January 1, 2021, with a total budget of 7,953 million euros, for the period 2021–2027.

Before the American elections, on November 3, 2019, it had been suggested that if Trump was re-elected, he could even end the United States' membership in NATO. The American President had decided to withdraw about 12,000 soldiers from Germany, stating that this was "a delinquent country that has not paid its contributions to NATO". The question raised by the European countries was that Europe was no longer the axis of potential NATO conflicts, the debate on NATO operations not contemplated in article 5 of the North Atlantic Treaty generated controversy.

It seemed clear that a change had to be faced in the NATO financial system, reducing its excessive dependence on the initiatives of each country, betting on a more efficient distribution of the economic burden to balance the costs that were recorded on the countries that worked the most in the common defense of Europe. Each national budget must then anticipate how far national defense is covered and what remains to complete it with common defense.

The question of whether the European Union should decide whether to continue depending mainly on the United States, for the Defense of Europe, was already on the horizon when throughout 2019 the change of personalities at the head of the institutions of the European Union took place.

The European Council would be chaired, from July 2, by the Belgian Charles Michel who would state that the European Union was a fervent defender of multilateralism and an international order based on rules, announcing that the Union would reinforce its capacity in the domain of security and defense and that the High Representative for Foreign and Security Policy would present in November 2021, a first draft of a strategic compass, which would be approved at the European Council in March 2022, dedicated to defence.

In addition, a new political declaration on relations with NATO would be made before the NATO Summit in June 2022. Ursula von right Leyen, President of the Commission, from December 1, 2019, would announce in her speech on the State of the Union, delivered on September 15, 2021, the project to create a European rapid reaction force of 5,000 soldiers, anticipating that there would be strategic autonomy "there will be missions in which NATO or the UN will not be present, but in which the European Union should be".

The withdrawal from Afghanistan, decreed by President Biden, on August 18, 2021, closed Western liberal interventionism in Iraq, Syria, Libya, Yemen and finally, Afghanistan with many failures. American neglect forces the European Union to definitively consider its solvency in Security and Defense policy and this possibility only seems to exist if the European Union equips itself with a military force capable of mobilizing and if that force has strategic autonomy.

Josep Borrell, would assume, from December 1, 2019, the position of Vice President of the European Commission, High Representative of the European Union for Foreign and Security Policy and would affirm that the international order that the West has led during the last centuries it has entered a singular crisis, from which new global leadership may be born. China is playing a thriving role on the international stage, defending multilateralism, in the face of an absent G7 and G20, a United Nations Security Council paralyzed by the intransigence of the permanent powers and with international organizations also witnessing struggles of power between states. In short, an openly unequal scenario in the distribution of power and divergent when assuming global leadership to respond to the challenges of globalization.

In this increasingly competitive and multipolar scenario, and in which the appearance of a global pandemic such as Covid-19 was to constitute a phenomenon of enormous political, economic and human disturbance, Borrell means that the European Union should play a role in outlining greater security and defense of European ideals and values, as well as of its own vital scenario in the face of the great challenges of the 21st century that may take the form of health, energy, migratory, cybernetic, or even military crises. For Borrell, reinforcing the EU Security and Defense Policy is not a luxury; it is a necessity, a necessity that essentially lies in three major areas on which the defense policy of the European Union should focus.

In the first place, the "Permanent Structured Cooperation" under way with 46 projects, and the collaboration of third countries. Second, under the adoption of the "Strategic Compass", which will be formalized at the end of 2021 and will be launched in 2022. Third, the adoption of a "Coordinated Annual Review on Defense" that will provide the first comprehensive overview of the European defense landscape, including the defense industry. Defense, in which it can be seen that European defense is still too fragmented.

Josep Borrell would point out that while the United States has one large war tank, Europe currently operates 16 different types. In the maritime realm, 30 different types of corvettes, frigates, and destroyers, compared to four surface combatant ships in the US. On the operational side, the CSDP's commitment in terms of personnel and expenses barely accounts for 7% of total operational commitments from Member States…

Finally, he would state that "in this scenario, the European Union must assume new commitments: a new advance in integration and the assumption of maturity in an area that par excellence has occupied the leading role of the Member States. Today it is time to change that role to Europe, but the speed of this development will be propitiated by the events that occur in the theater of International Relations".

In this way, the battle to strengthen the security and defense of the European Union continued, which the European Councils had already been dealing with since June 2018, in which the Permanent Structured Cooperation and the negotiations on a European Fund for Defending.

7 The Invasion of Ukraine and the Commitment to Give the European Union Sovereignty in the Field of Defence

If during 2019 the main concern of the European Union was to close a Withdrawal Treaty and a trade agreement with the United Kingdom, during 2020 it would deal with dealing with the COVID-19 pandemic, which constituted an unprecedented challenge, to Europe and the whole world. At the same time, the European Union would try to stop or mitigate the economic damage by assuming an economic recovery plan through an ambitious multi-year financial framework 2021–2027, reinforced by a "Next Generation EU" net debt instrument endowed with 750,000 million euros to 2018 prices. That decision was a historic milestone in the framework of European sovereignty, as the Union assumed a common and solidarity debt, backed by community structures, to help Member States emerge from the crisis.

On the foreign stage, the presidential elections in Belarus, held in August 2020, were the subject of major protests, demonstrations and repression. The re-election of Lukashenko, linked to Putin's Russia, would be discussed. The European Union would not recognize the results and would mobilize 3 million euros to support the victims of the repression and finance the independent media.

The European Council, on October 1 and 2, 2020, would express its solidarity with Lithuania and Poland, in the face of the retaliatory measures taken against them by Belarus. In that scenario, the President of Ukraine Volodymyr Zelensky would approve on September 14, 2020, a new National Security Strategy for Ukraine that provided for "the development of the distinctive association with NATO, with the aim of joining NATO".

In response, on February 21, 2021, the Russian Ministry of Defense announced the deployment of 3,000 paratroopers to the Ukrainian border for "large-scale exercises " in the months of March and April 2021. Russian troops to the Ukrainian border, although the Russian and Belarusian authorities would deny any invasion plans, although by the end of April more than 100,000 soldiers had already gathered on the Ukrainian border and on the Crimean peninsula.

From March 16, NATO would carry out the largest military exercises in its history. The military exercises organized by the United States Army "defender Europe " which were joined by 25 other countries with the aim of maintaining and improving interoperability between US troops and those of other NATO countries, was joined in parallel by the NATO, which would carry out its". Stadfast Defender 2021" exercises in the Black Sea region at the end of May, where 20 countries of the alliance participated.

On March 24, 2021, President Zelensky would sign decree number 117/2021 approving the "strategy of vacating and reintegrating the temporarily occupied territory of the Autonomous Republic of Crimea and the city of Sevastopol", using military means to achieve it.. The European Union that announced holding a strategic debate with Russia would then limit itself to describing the presence of Russian troops on Ukraine's borders as "illegal, disruptive and provocative, carried out against the European Union, its member states and outside the union" (Extraordinary European Council 2021).

On the Kremlin page, Vladimir Putin would publish, on July 12, 2021, an extensive essay, entitled "*On the historical unity of Russians and Ukrainians* ". The thesis he defended is that "in recent years a wall had been built between Russia and Ukraine, to great misfortune and common tragedy." For Putin, "Russians, Ukrainians and Belarusians are all descendants of ancient Russia, which was the largest state in Europe"... But, he continued, "the United States and the EU countries have systematically and constantly pressured Ukraine to reduce and limit economic cooperation with Russia" ... "I am sure that the true sovereignty of Ukraine is possible only in partnership with Russia" (Putin 2021). Putin would declare that "Ukraine never had a genuine state tradition" (Düben 2020).

Dmitry Medvedev. Vice President of the Russian Security Council would express the same arguments, publishing, on October 11, 2021 (Medvedev 2021), an article in which he argued that Ukraine was a "vassal" of the West and that, therefore, it did not make sense for Russia to try to dialogue with the Ukrainian authorities, whom he described as "weak", "ignorant" and "unreliable".

Volodymyr Zelensky had assumed a pro-European and Atlantic position. On October 12, 2021, during the XXIII European Union - Ukraine Summit, the Agreement on the Greater European Air Space would be signed. On December 17, 2021, Russia formally requested NATO to abandon any military activity in Eastern Europe and Ukraine and to sign an agreement preventing possible acceptance of Ukraine's NATO membership.

It was therefore proposed that Russia and NATO does not deploy additional troops and weapons beyond their May 1997 limits - prior to the NATO accession of any of the former communist Eastern European states. De facto it meant that NATO would have to abandon any military activity in the Ukraine, Eastern Europe, the Caucasus and Central Asia.

The approach proposed by Moscow entailed an unaffordable cost both for the Member States of the European Union and for the US administration itself, which was not going to give up its plans to maintain and revive the structure of NATO, with the specific weight both military and economic organization, to increase its power on the global stage.

While the European Council of December 16, 2021 highlighted the urgent need for Russia to lower the tensions generated by the increase in the military presence along its border with Ukraine and its aggressive rhetoric (European Council Dec-2021), Russia would culminate its struggle with a proposal for an Agreement made on December 17 to the NATO states and, in parallel, he would hold a meeting with Xi Jinping weeks before the aggression on Ukraine where, possibly, on February 4, 2022, he detailed his plans for Ukraine to the Chinese leader.

A new informal European Council, meeting on February 17, 2022, would highlight the scant strength offered by the European Union, verified by the observations made by Charles Michell, who would limit himself to highlighting: "the unbreakable unity of the European Union, both internally and with its NATO partners, the commitment to diplomacy, support, assistance and solidarity with Ukraine and the defense of European values, urging Russia to reduce tension" (European Council, Feb-2022).

However, the President of the European Commission, Ursula von right Leyen, would speak in a personal capacity, in favor of Ukraine's accession to the European Union, stating, when asked by a Euronews journalist about the country's membership in the Union, that "in time, in fact, they will belong to us. They are one of us and we want them among us" (Euronews 2022).

On February 21, 2022, Russia recognized the Donetsk and Luhansk People's Republics, and the following day, the Russian Federation Council authorized the use of military force. The invasion of Ukraine began on the morning of February 24, 2022. Without a declaration of war, Russia placed its troops on the territory of Ukraine and began to bomb the main Ukrainian cities bordering both its country and Belarus, developing a strategy destined to quickly bring down the capital Kyiv and neutralize the figure of the president, Zelensky.

The extraordinary European Council, held on February 24, 2022, would limit itself to condemning, with the utmost firmness, the military aggression, demanding that Russia unconditionally withdraw all military forces and equipment from all Ukraine and fully respect the integrity territory, sovereignty and independence of Ukraine.

In this new framework of events, the European Union would assume the need to use the concept of "sovereignty", for the European Union, and after once again condemning Russia's military aggression against Ukraine and applauding the courage of its people, it would re-launch its responsibility to maintain its own security and increase its strategic action in defense matters, as well as reduce its energy dependence (European Council March-2022).

The European Union seemed determined to build a "European sovereignty", in the face of the rise of authoritarianism. French President Emmanuel Macron was determined to raise the question of European sovereignty in the semester in which France held the presidency of the Council. For several years he had been proposing this idea, described in some way in a speech in the European Parliament on April 17, 2018, claiming to build "authentic European sovereignty" in the face of the rise of authoritarianism in countries such as Russia and China, the unilateral temptation of The United States of Donald Trump or the triumph of "illiberal" democracy in Member States such as Hungary or Poland. Macron would maintain that the refoundation of the European Union is the only way to protect citizens in globalization "in the face of the great transformations of the world, we need a sovereignty stronger than ours that is complementary and not substitutive" (Macron 2018).

The European Council of March 24 and 25 would reaffirm the "Versailles Declaration", recognizing the European aspirations and the European option of Ukraine, as established in the Association Agreement. By then, several million Ukrainians had fled their homes, finding refuge and safety in the European Union, thanks to the temporary protection mechanism.

The Versailles declaration and its content would be recalled again by the President of the European Council, Charles Michel, on October 21, 2022, who, regarding the strategic autonomy of the European Union, would emphasize that "this is a key moment to reinforce European defense in very close ties with NATO", stating that they were actively working on a new declaration between NATO and the European Union.

In that context, an important novelty would take place. A few days earlier, at an extraordinary European Council, held on October 6, 2022, the first meeting of the European Political Community (EPC) was convened, with the aim of promoting political dialogue and cooperation and reinforcing security, stability and the prosperity of the European continent. This initiative would bring together, together with the 27 Member States of the European Union, another 17 European States, including Georgia, Ukraine and Turkey and, in particular, the United Kingdom, which having left the Union in 2020 joined a common defensive strategy.

The EPC appeared with the historical name of the failed European Political Community born in 1952, giving a political body to the treaty of the failed European Defense Community and in 1953 to the failed treaty of the European Political Community. It had taken 70 years for the European Union to seem determined to create a common defence in a new scenario of assumption of sovereignty, recalling the old Treaties of the 1950s and now making it possible for a future Treaty to be held in this decade is proof of this will to build a powerful federal Europe recognized as such on the global stage.

The will to act in a European Space superior to that formed by the states of the Union would be symbolically reflected on October 17, 2022, with the presence of the European Union Force (EUROFOR Althea), initiating military manoeuvres in Bosnia, through of the "rapid response 2022" exercises, to show the European Union's commitment to a European future for all and to dissuade any destabilization of the country, in this case Bosnia, which is intended to be given the Statute of a candidate country in an immediate time. Accession to the European Union.

The fate of a European army seems to be cast. The demand for a European army had been continuous. Guy Verhofstadt, author of a work entitled *Le mal européen* to which he would dedicate chapter 18 "An army for Europe" (Verhofstadt 2016), would intervene on September 14, 2022, in the presentation of the Commission Report, criticizing the intervention of the President of the Commission: "I thought there was a black hole in his speech, not as big as those that have been discovered at the moment, but that is the absence of defence, because I think that we are really going to live in a totally new world order, with enormous problems for our security. And you never know what happens if tweeting Trump comes back to the US, then we'll be on our own for our own safety. Therefore, a defence community is an absolute necessity.

Today we are spending €240 billion on defence in Europe, the same amount as China, four times more than Russia. We have 130 weapon systems in Europe. We have a world record for soldiers in the world: 2.4 million. And we are powerless. That is at least the sentiment of most people.

So, my request is when we have a convention, and thank you for supporting it so clearly, we must also talk about that and we must present, I should not say a copy, but a draft like the Treaty of Paris of 1952, negotiated by Adenauer, de Gasperi and Robert Schumann. That is the way to go. Do not forget. And fill the black hole, please".

The war with Ukraine leaves opens the need for a complete transformation of the European Union, which completely reforms its Common Foreign and Security Policy and its Common Security and Defense Policy, so that they are unique at European level, as exclusive competence, with which is endowed with a unified leadership, and a European army, capable of dissuading third States from attacking the Member States of the Union. In the same way, a single energy policy is required, based on a European search for energy resources, so that no State has scarcity or insecurity, and the trans-European energy networks are built from a European strategic vision and not from the Member States.

The mistake of the European Union has been to ignore Putin's threat when he stated that he would allow the accession to the European Union, but not to NATO, of the countries bordering its territory. If the European Union had made them members, the war would have been avoided, but not only was Ukraine not made a member or a candidate, until the war had started, (June 2022 European Council, but even as late as 2017 discussed putting into force the Association Agreement signed in 2014, and he had to assume that Putin would carry out his threats. The European Council has really been knocking on Russia's doors looking for an understanding, and it would do so until its failure, with the invasion of Ukraine Since then, it has not had much chance of stopping the conflict. On the global stage, the United States, which resolutely supports Ukraine with military weapons, and China, which supports Russia's military action from afar, in a geopolitical tug-of-war, They seem to be the two great political actors capable of stopping this war.

The General Assembly of the United Nations has condemned the aggression, but the Security Council has not been able to adopt any Resolution of condemnation, under the Russian veto. Millions of Europeans try to rest in the summer of 2022, while millions of Ukrainians have left their country that is in open war. Autumn and winter present a bleak outlook, which will spread over cold Europe. One more highly sensitive element is the nuclear threat wielded by Russia: "If a war breaks out against Russia, there will be no winners. They won't even have time to blink."

In the month of November of this year 2022, when we are finishing these pages, two lines of action seem evident: that of the European Union with NATO, which will probably be the subject of a document presented at the end of this year, and that of the United States with Russia that apparently are holding talks to avoid nuclear escalation and openly request that Ukraine agree to negotiate the end of hostilities.

References

Arenal, C.: Globalization, growing interdependence and globalization in international relations. *Vitoria-Gasteiz International Law and International Relations Courses* 1 (2008): 181–268, p. 209–210 (2008)

Bodin, J.: Los Seis Libros de la República, lib. 1, cap. 8, Paris: Fayard (1986)

Buisseret, D., Barbiche, B.: *Les Œconomies royales de Sully* volume I (1572–1594) and volume II (1595–1599), Paris : Librairie C. Klincksieck (1970–1988)

Carbonell, C.O.: *Saint-Simon's L'Europe*. Private, p. 87 (2001)

Cazzaniga, G.M., Zarka Y.C.: *Penser la souveraineté à l'époque moderne et contemporaine*. Vol. 1. Librairie Philosophique J Vrin (2001)

Clesse, A.: *Le Project de CED Du Plan Pleven au «crime» du 30 aout. History d'un misunderstanding European*. Baden -Banden: Nomos, pp. 200–201 (1989)

Cloos, J.: *Le Traité de Maastricht: genèse, analyse, commentaires*. Vol. 28. Emile Bruylant, pp. 481–489 (1993)

Constantinesco, V.: Is the souveraineté est-elle soluble dans l'Union européenne ? L'Europe in Formation **368**(2), 119–135 (2013)

Coudenhove-Kalergi, R.N., Auclères D.: *Europe, puissance mondiale*. Stock, p. 206 (1972)

Coudenhove-Kalergi, R.N.: *Una vita per l'Europa*, Ferro Edizioni: Milano (1965)

De Saint-Simon, H.: *Of the reorganization of the European society*. Editions Rivages (2014)

Delors, J.: *Mémoires*, Paris: Editions Plon p. 489 (2004)

Draus, F.: *Critique historique de l'idee européenne*. Vol. 1. François-Xavier de Guibert, p. 63–67 (2009)

Düben, B.A.: 'There is no Ukraine': Fact-Checking the Kremlin's Version of Ukrainian History". *LSE International History*. London School of Economics, 1 July 2020. https://blogs.lse.ac.uk/lseih/2020/07/01/there-is-no-ukraine-fact-checking-the-kremlins-version-of-ukrainian-history/

DW: Verbatim words of Jean Claude Juncker and Ursula von right Leyen (2015). Collected by at https://www.dw.com/en/juncker-calls-for-collective-eu-army/a-18302459

Eden, A.: Memories. Vol. III (1945–1957), pp. 50–52. Noguer Publishing House, Barcelona (1960)

European Council: Conclusions 18 and 19 February (2016). http://data.consilium.europa.eu/doc/document/ST-1-2016-INIT/en/pdf

Extraordinary European Council, Brussels (May 2021), chaired by Charles Michel. https://www.consilium.europa.eu/media/49817/2425-05-21-euco-conclusions-en.pdf; https://data.consilium.europa.eu/doc/document/ST-5-2021-INIT/es/pdf and https://www.consilium.europa.eu/media/49007/250321-vtc-euco-statement-en.pdf. European Council, Brussels (December 2021), chaired by Charles Michel https://www.consilium.europa.eu/media/53622/20211216-euco-conclusions-es.pdf

European Council, Brussels, chaired by Charles Michel (informal meeting of Heads of State or Government), February 2022. https://www.consilium.europa.eu/en/press/press-releases/2022/02/17/remarks-by-president-charles-michel-following-the-informal-meeting-of-the-members-of-the-european-council/

European Council, Versailles, chaired by Charles Michel (extraordinary meeting of Heads of State or Government) – Versailles Declaration, March 2022

Faramiñán Fernández-Figares, J.M.: Paneuropa, the attempt at a united Europe at the crossroads of the interwar period. In: *War and Conflict as Dynamic Elements of Society: Institutions, Law and Security*, pp. 181–202, 198 (2014)

Fenet, A., Guillaume, A.: *Le Nouveau Cynée ...*, Presses Universitaires de Rennes (2004)

Gallung, J.: "Pax Bruxellana" The European Superpower, *Perspectives*, pp. 51–63 (2021)

Gates, E.M.: *End of the Affair: The Collapse of the Anglo-French Alliance, 1939–40*. George Allen & Unwin, London (1981)

Gerbet, P.: *La Genèse du plan Schuman, des origines à la declaration du 9 mai 1950*, Lausanne, Center de recherches européennes (1962)

Gerbet. P.: *La construction de l'Europe*. Imprimerie National: Paris p. 14 and next (1999)

Guinea Bonillo, J.: *Historia de la Política de Seguridad y Defensa de la Unión Europea*. Aranzadi, p. 134 (2021)

Hobbes, T.: Leviathan: Or the Matter, Form, and Power of an Ecclesiastical and Civil State. Lebooks Publisher (2022). https://www.consilium.europa.eu/media/54800/20220311-versailles-declaration-en.pdf

Interview with Ursula von right Leyen, for Euronews on May 19, 2022. Available at https://www.euronews.com/2022/02/27/ukraine-is-one-of-us-and-we-want-them-in-eu-ursula-von-der-leyen-tells-euronews

Kant, I.: *About perpetual peace. A Philosophical Sketch*. Editorial Verbum (2019)

Lang, P.: *Le Plan Briand d'Union Fédérale Européenne*. Vienna (1998)

Macron's speech in the European Parliament on April 17, 2018. https://www.elysee.fr/en/emmanuel-macron/2018/04/17/speech-by-emmanuel-macron-president-of-the-republic-at-european-parliament

Medvedev, D.: Почему бессмысленны contacts с нынешним ukrainian руководством [Why the contacts with current leadership_ukrainian do not have sense]. Published in Russian in *Kommersant* (2021). https://www.kommersant.ru/doc/5028300

Mrac Ferry, J.: La cuestión del Estado Europeo. Gallimard (2000)

Pérez-Bustamante, R.: Political and legal history of the European Union. Edisofer, pp. 59–60 (2008)

Progress has been made in economic integration, as a consequence of the 2008 financial crisis, with the creation of the MEDE or the ESM

Putin, V.: Article on the historical unity of Russians and Ukrainians, 25 January 2021. Available on the Kremlin website: http://en.kremlin.ru/events/president/news/66181

Read, D.: The Right of Sovereignty: Jean Bodin on the Sovereign State and the Law of Nations. University of Oxford Press (2021)

Saint-Gille, A.M.: La "Paneurope": un débat d'idées dans l'entre-deux-guerres. Presses Paris Sorbonne (2003)

Schuman, R.: *La Communauté européenne du charbon et de l'acier*, Ed. LGDJ, p. 7 (1953)
St. Pierre, A.: *Projet pour rendre la paix perpétuelle en Europe*. Paris, Fayard, Corpus des oevres de Philosophie en langue française (1986)
The constitutional idea had already been raised since the election of the European Parliament by universal suffrage and would take shape in the draft Spinelli Treaty of 1984 and in the Herman project of 1993
VanDijk, R.: *East and West and the Division of Germany, 1945–1953: A Reassessment of the "Missed Opportunities" for Unification*. Ohio University (1999)
Vayssiere, B.: *Europa y soberanía: La noción de Estado, de los pensadores clásicos a las realidades actuales. S. XX*. Revue de Histoire, presses des Sciences Po, 3 (95), pp. 151–166 (2007)
Verhofstadt, G.: *Le mal européen*. Plon (2016)

The Hegemonic Rivalry Between the United States and the People's Republic of China: European Union's Place

Gracia Abad-Quintanal(✉)

Nebrija University, Madrid, Spain
gabad@nebrija.es

Abstract. If anything characterises the current state of the international system, it is the re-emergence of great power rivalry. This rivalry has two main consequences: the re-emergence of traditional security problems and the challenge to the international order established since the Second World War. The powers at the centre of this rivalry for the dominance and design of the world order include the People's Republic of China, which has risen dramatically, now wields considerable comprehensive power and seeks to use it to project its influence. Against it, the United States takes a posture of resistance, containment and defence of the existing liberal international order and seeks relentlessly to enlist Europe's support in this effort. However, Europe, while increasingly aware of the challenge posed by the People's Republic of China, has not yet opted for a decisive alignment with Washington, probably because, at least in the short term, the relationship with Beijing also brings it benefits, but above all because it prioritises problems that are geographically closer and that may seem more pressing.

Keywords: China · US · Europe · China · EU · International order · Great power

1 Introduction

One of the defining features of the current international context is undoubtedly the re-emergence of rivalry and competition between great powers. This circumstance has two main consequences that are, moreover, easily visible:

- The evolution and transformation of security, marked by a strong return to traditional threats.

Indeed, from now on, alongside non-traditional challenges such as Islamist terrorism, cyber-threats or the spread of infectious diseases, migratory and refugee flows, energy price hikes or commodity price hikes - to name but a few - and often intermingled with these non-traditional challenges, as evidenced by the emergence of hybrid warfare or conflicts in the grey zone, the role of traditional threats -like the Russian invasion of Ukraine- must also be taken into account.

- The challenge to the established international order since World War II by a number of states, most notably the People's Republic of China (PRC) and the Russian Federation (Sánchez 2022).

J. Cayón Peña and J. M. Ramírez (Eds.): *Threats to Peace and International Security: Asia versus West*, ASTSA, pp. 37–46, 2023.
https://doi.org/10.1007/978-3-031-28336-9_2

2 The Rise of the People's Republic of China: The Rebirth of Power Rivalry

In this context of competition between powers, the People's Republic of China undoubtedly deserves a place. It is not in vain that the PRC is one of the main advocates of an alternative international order, and has experienced a rise that should be considered the most significant event in decades. In this respect, it should be stressed that this rise, far from being accidental, is the result of a careful strategy in the framework of which, as we shall see, it has skilfully played with the rules of the game of an international system in whose design it did not participate. Thus it is currently in a position to foster the emergence of another what turns it into an openly revisionist power when it has had the power to do so (Campbell and Rapp-Hooper 2020).

Thus, China's conviction, expressed even by Yang Jiechi, member of the Political Bureau of the Chinese Communist Party Central Committee and head of the Office of the Foreign Affairs Commission of the Chinese Communist Party Central Committee, that China's great power status entitles it to a new global role incompatible with unchallenged US dominance, is clear (Xuetong 2021, 2).

However, as Shi Ze, a former Chinese diplomat based in Russia, points out, it is important to realise that while "Russia wants to break the current international order [...] China wants to improve and modify it, not break it". While it is clear that it wants to change it to its liking and according to its interests, the differences in approach are also obvious (Christensen 2021, 7).

Consequently, it is in the rise of the People's Republic of China (Anere 2022) where lies the key, or at least one of them, to the reborn rivalry between powers that we mentioned. A rivalry Chinese President Xi Jinping himself is well aware of, as evidenced by his statement that "the game of the great powers is becoming increasingly difficult, and the world has entered a new period of turbulence and change" (Blanchette, 2022).

However, as we pointed out, the People's Republic of China can now adopt this revisionist attitude (Sendagorta 2020, 23) and become a leading actor (Weissmann 2015, 153) in the competition between great powers because it has real comprehensive power (Abad-Quintanal 2008), or "structural power", if we want to use Susan Strange's conceptualisation (Strange, 1988) as a starting point. If, according to this author, structural power is made up of four elements (knowledge structure, financial structure, security structure and production structure) it is remarkably interesting to see how China has progressed in relation to all of them.

2.1 The Rise of the People's Republic of China: Its Structural Power

2.1.1 Security Structure

Over the course of the past few decades, China has witnessed a veritable revolution in military affairs, not only acquiring more modern weaponry and equipment - advanced air defences, silent submarines, anti-ship missiles, and air transport and amphibious forces, to name but a few - but modernising the entire functioning of its armed forces and defence. This has led to significant institutional reforms, for example, reducing the People's Liberation Army - from 5 million troops in the 1980s to approximately 2 million today (Sommer 2018) - by improving training and capacity building, adopting new doctrines and conducting joint military exercises with other states. It has also prioritised cyber capabilities and artificial intelligence-based weaponry.

All these changes have turned the PRC into a military power ready for combat if necessary (Xuetong 2021, 6). It is also a maritime military power, even though it was once a land-based military power at most (Marshall 2017, 52), precisely because it now prioritises the sea over land, unlike in the past. Indeed, the PRC's naval expansion has led it to have one of the largest navies in the world today. However, we cannot overlook the air force, which is now considered to be the third largest in the world and the second largest in Asia-Pacific.

Nor can we ignore the changes in the nuclear doctrine since, although the People's Republic of China seems to remain faithful to the "no first use" doctrine -as it appears in its 2019 White Paper-, it nevertheless gives the impression that it is abandoning its approach of maintaining only a minimum deterrence capability (Mohan 2022, 3). Thus, the PRC is building new silos on its territory, expanding its missile and submarine arsenal and increasing the number of nuclear warheads it has, while modernising its nuclear programme as a whole (Mohan 2022, 10).

All these developments have unsurprisingly translated into steady and sustained increases in China's defence budget in recent years that have been viewed with considerable concern by other states:

This evolution is even more striking if we compare the progression of Chinese military spending with that of other powers and states. However, it is also interesting to see the results of this spending. A comparison between China's capabilities and those of the United States shows that despite the enormous transformation undergone by the Chinese armed forces, there are elements in which the weight of the past is still felt and which could put the United States at an advantage, such as the preponderance in China's case of the land army or China's inferiority in terms of attack helicopters and long-range missiles.

2.1.2 Financial and Production Structure

Perhaps the best known but no less important aspect of the spectacular rise of the People's Republic of China is economic growth. Economic growth is no longer based solely, as in the past, on the manufacture of low-priced products and exports, but rather on aspects such as the purchase of real estate, debt and critical infrastructures, with all that this entails in terms of penetration into the economies of third countries; investment in strategic sectors, the promotion of the use of renminbi and cryptocurrencies, and what is known as the "Chinese dual economy", made public in May 2020. The so called "Chinese dual economy" means the generation of a double circuit, domestic and international, with which the Beijing government seeks to protect the Chinese economy, reducing dependence on foreign markets and, with it, vulnerability to the pressure they may exert (Xuetong 2021, 5). A dual-circulation strategy that President Xi Jinping himself explained by stating that "only by being self-sufficient and developing the domestic market can vibrant growth and development be achieved, regardless of the hostility of the outside world" (Haas 2021, 5).

Although China's growth strategy had so far proved to be effective, as can be seen in the graph below, and at first, after the pandemic it seemed that it would continue to be so, today the data provided by China's own national statistics bureau cast doubt on the sustainability of this growth. On the contrary, we see that this growth has fallen to an approximate figure of 3% and that the PRC does not expect to go, at least in the next five years, beyond 4% growth, a far cry from what the Chinese economy needs to create employment.

On the other hand, and this is an issue that is not likely to improve in view of what we have just discussed, this economic growth has also had its dark areas, some of which may have a tremendous destabilising potential for the Asian giant: this is the case of the notable inequality of this economic growth, a growing problem for the People's Republic of China.

In any case, this growth strategy seems far from being exhausted, as evidenced by the commitment to cutting-edge technology sectors: digitalisation, biotechnology, artificial intelligence and robotics, in particular. The commitment to these sectors is beyond doubt if we take into account the very significant public investment dedicated to them. In this respect, it is worth noting the importance of the "Made in China 2025" strategy, with which Beijing is trying to ensure its leadership in the sectors we are dealing with and to consolidate its increasingly pre-eminent position in networks and cybersecurity, artificial intelligence and robotics.

As is also the case with the Russian Federation, the PRC does not hesitate to use unorthodox means to try to condition the positioning of public opinion on a global scale, even resorting to the use of cyber-attacks that weaken the political systems of other states and citizens' confidence in democracy (Christensen 2021, 7).

2.1.3 Knowledge Structure

However, we would not have a full understanding of China's progression in terms of its structural power if we do not refer to its knowledge structure and the extent to which it is able to influence the definition of the prevailing ideational framework, as well as the definition of the rules of the game.

At this point it is necessary to highlight the importance of Beijing's diplomacy - notably more assertive than in the past. Indeed, perhaps one of the most visible manifestations of the PRC's shift since the arrival of Xi Jinping has to do with the so-called "diplomacy offensive" which, paradoxical as it may seem, has translated into the development since 2012 of a notably offensive diplomacy, the so-called "Wolf Warrior Diplomacy". China, which in the past had always opted for a low-profile policy, trying to hide its true interests or ambitions, is now opting for a much tougher and nationalistic foreign policy (Blanchette 2022), resolutely oriented towards "China taking its place in the world" (Brands and Sullivan 2020), as Xi Jinping himself pointed out in 2017, and is also much more willing to take risks (Weissmann 2015, 159), including the generation of conflicts. At this point we cannot overlook the Civil-Military Fusion Plan either.

At the same time, China has not hesitated to favour regime change when and where convenient and to influence the trajectory of political systems to suit its preferences.

More subtle, if possible, has been the influence derived from the so-called 'Beijing Consensus', possibly because this largely stems from an earlier point in time, although it was subsequently endorsed by President Xi Jinping himself in November 2017, after the 19th Chinese Communist Party Congress. Thus, he indicated that 'China's path could be an alternative to the so-called Washington Consensus', particularly, for states that wanted to 'accelerate their development while preserving their independence' (Christensen 2021, 6). What is undeniable is that the demonstration that the combination of economic freedom and political freedom - market economy and democracy - encapsulated in the "Washington Consensus" may not be the only possible formula if sustainable growth is to be achieved has proved tremendously attractive to many states, particularly those led by non-democratic elites who feared being dislodged from power.

In this sense, China will not miss the opportunity to foster an ideological context that is favourable to it by trying to counter the idea that Western political values can have universal validity or appeal to everyone (Xuetong 2021, 4) and by being aware of the potential conflict between its values and those of the West (Zhao 2019, 378). At the same time, it will strive to gain respect for its political and economic model and increasingly influence existing norms, rules and institutions to be more in line with its preferences (Haas 2021, 7).

In this respect, the growing weight of the PRC in defining the rules that govern global governance and, closely related to this, in international organisations (Brands and Sullivan 2020) cannot go unmentioned. A weight that is not unrelated to Beijing's ability to have Chinese nationals or nationals of other states, but with national or personal affinity with China in key positions in processes and organisations. A recent example is that of the WHO and its approach to the Covid 19 pandemic (Abad-Quintanal 2022a, 78), clearly influenced by the preferences of the People's Republic of China, despite the fact that it has been demonstrated that the management of the pandemic by this state has not exactly been the most efficient, but neither has it been the most respectful either of citizens' rights and freedoms or of states' own internal legislation. Part of the explanation for this influence should probably be sought in the figures of the organisation's last two directors general, both the current one, the Ethiopian Tedros Adhanom Ghebreyesus, an admirer of the PRC, with which he has an ideological affinity, and his predecessor, the Chinese Margaret Chan Fung Fu-chun.

3 The PRC'S Projection of Influence and Its Transformation into a Revisionist Power

This capacity, this structural power of the People's Republic of China which allows us to speak of its rise as a power translates into its will to project influence over different regions (Leandro 2015), starting with its own, to condition the rules on which global governance is based and, ultimately, to redefine the world order in a way that is more in tune with Chinese interests and preferences. These efforts are clearly depicted in the so-called "Three Wars Strategy" (García 2022).

3.1 Projecting Influence in Asia

China's military and purely economic projects in the Pacific and Indian Oceans over the past few decades must necessarily be interpreted in the context of a broader strategy to consolidate its influence and seek to become the undisputed hegemonic power in the area encompassing both oceans, and thus in Asia as a whole.

This is the perspective from which we have to view China's creation of the so-called "String of Pearls" connecting the Arabian Sea with the South China Sea across the entire area around the Indian subcontinent and through the Straits of Malacca. This "string of pearls" would be made up of a series of ports, bases and sites where the PRC is present, thus maintaining control over the whole area. Specifically, we are referring to sites such as the port of Gwadar in Pakistan, the container port of Hambatota, the port of Chittagong, the port of Sittwe in Burma and the presence in Djibouti and the Maldives.

In a similar vein, it is necessary to analyse the One Belt, One Road project, the so-called "New Silk Road", launched in 2013, which connects Africa and Europe by sea and land, respectively, with the Chinese coast in an effort to prevent, as far as possible, these states from taking positions that run counter to the interests of the PRC in different forums and on different issues (Christensen 2021, 13).

A project which, in geographical terms, has not stopped expanding (Sommer 2018) and which, in its maritime dimension, is nothing more than China's attempt to control Rimland, according to the term coined by Nicholas Spykman, who, as Christian Blasco reminds us, pointed out that control of this area was key to projecting global hegemony (Blasco López, 2022, 3).

At the same time, the perhaps best known, at least in recent years, dispute over the islands in the South China Sea, namely the two archipelagos of the Paracelsus Islands and, above all, the Spratly Islands, would be but one more element of this overall strategy. This is a crucial one, since this area is key for Beijing in order to consolidate its control over its Pacific front (Brands and Sullivan 2020, 1) and to try to prevent another power, probably the United States, from projecting force and calling into question its hegemony in the region.

Control of the South China Sea is key for China to be able to implement its A2AD strategy vis-à-vis the US, a strategy that seeks to block the passage of the United States beyond the first island chain and which explains the PRC's efforts in recent years to improve its maritime capabilities by investing in a deep-sea navy. Needless to say, that the repeated references to piracy made by Beijing are in no way convincing.

However, these efforts would be insufficient to achieve their objectives for the time being, since the United States, through a combination of air and naval forces (Abad Quintanal 2017, 9), articulated in terms of the Air Sea Battle and Joint Operational Access concepts (Friedberg 2014, 75; Le Miere 2014, 14), would have achieved, at least so far, its access capacity and thus its maritime advantage over the PRC. Thus, if the United States decides to penetrate the area with its nuclear attack submarines or nuclear ballistic missile submarines, it can do so, as China does not have the submarine capabilities to prevent it from doing so.

3.2 China as a Revisionist Power: The Challenge to the International Order

However, the idea that a state should increase its structural power and consolidate or reinforce its status as a power or that, precisely as such a power, it should seek to project influence does not per se call into question the international order. In fact, the PRC itself has long been in this situation without questioning it. However, the situation changes when the PRC ceases to be a power that preserves the status quo and becomes a revisionist power. This is exactly what has happened in the course of the last decade with the People's Republic of China: a power that had consolidated itself as such in the context of the international order born of the Second World War. In addition, very skilfully, had been able to reach a preponderant position by playing with the rules of a system in whose design it had not participated, has reached a point where it does wish to change the international order for one more in line with its preferences and interests, and in the ordering of which it does take part. A redesign in which, as we have already seen, it would not be alone, but would have well-disposed support, starting with the Russian Federation with which, if we are to believe the words of Xi Jinping last March, it would be united in a "partnership without limits" (Blanchette 2022, 1). Needless to say that while there is no reason to deny the partnership, its unlimited character seems rather exaggerated.

In any case, and as we have argued, the People's Republic of China may be the first systemic challenger since the demise of the Soviet Union, because, like the Soviet Union, it advocates a political, economic and social system that is different from the one sponsored by the West. Consequently, today as then, it will be necessary for the West to counter the winds of change from Beijing if it is to defend the existing international order.

Now, while the systemic nature of the challenge is the same, there are some elements that make the current situation different from that of the Cold War years. Among these elements, probably the most important is what has to do with the main stage where this confrontation between models is taking place: whereas during the Cold War the main theatre of the confrontation between the Western allies and the USSR was Europe, today the main stage in the confrontation between the Western and Chinese models is the Indo-Pacific.

This circumstance is not without relevance for a Europe that, at least in principle, would have reason to feel less involved in what is happening on non-European soil and, consequently, less impelled to contribute to the defence of the liberal international order born of the Second World War.

4 The Response to the Chinese Challenge

4.1 The US Response

The United States has long been aware of the revival of great power competition. In fact, as early as the end of 2017, the US National Security Strategy released by the Trump Administration echoed the new framework generated by great power competition while identifying the People's Republic of China as a "revisionist power" and "strategic competitor" that sought to "shape a world opposed to US values and interests" (Zhao 2019, 371), a line that has been maintained in the documents produced in the following years. Thus, the 2018 National Defence Strategy stated that the central challenge for the following years would be to "manage the strategic competition posed by China and other states" (Zhao 2019, 372).

In this situation, Washington's priority becomes the containment of China, which it sees as a systemic competitor as the US recalls in its recent National Security Strategy

(NSS 2022, 23). An aspect in which, on the other hand, a clear continuity can be seen since the end of the Cold War. This containment and competition are thus at the root of a trade and investment policy (Arezina 2019, 289) that seeks a lesser economic relationship with China, increased tension over Taiwan and the South China Sea, and ultimately the US Indo-Pacific strategy (Zhao 2019, 372).

Indeed, rivalry with China and the growing (maritime) projection of the PRC explain the US efforts to try to assert its role and presence in the Indo-Pacific, the adoption of this concept as a central aspect of its foreign, security and defence policy, and ultimately the implementation of an Indo-Pacific strategy.

On the other hand, it should be noted that within the framework of these efforts to contain China, Washington sees Europe as an indispensable partner, seeking the involvement of both NATO - the new strategic concept that emerged from the Madrid Summit in June 2022 describes China as a "strategic challenge" - and the EU in this scenario, which is undoubtedly considered a strategic priority. In this sense, as Thomas Christensen points out, President Biden's team does not hesitate to recognise that "alliances and partnerships are the main strength of the United States in its competition with China" (Christensen 2021; Rodríguez-Rata, 2022), as it is through cooperation in these frameworks that it hopes to preserve the current international order based on rules, norms and values and not solely on force.

Washington insists on recalling China's character as an authoritarian state, opposed to American values and political ideals in particular and Western values and ideals in general (Zhao 2019, 378). Hence the importance the US attaches to curbing China's further rise as a way of 'safeguarding the liberal international order' (Arezina 2019, 313).

4.2 The Position of the European Union

In contrast to this perspective, we see how the greater distance and lesser relationship that Europeans have traditionally had with the "theatre" in which the current systemic contest is taking place means that Europeans, while in no way questioning the existence of common values on both sides of the Atlantic, do differ markedly in the degree of priority that should be assigned to the different challenges, the aims and objectives to be achieved and the means to do so.

In this sense, from the European perspective, the priorities are, on the other hand, conflicts at the continent's borders and neighbourhood and their consequences; the threat posed by terrorism; political and social polarisation; and the emergence of strong nationalist and populist movements, some with a clear authoritarian imprint.

In fact, as late as December 2020, the EU concluded an investment agreement with China, strengthening relations with the Asian giant in this area (Christensen 2021, 12).

However, the EU, which has been increasingly uncomfortable with the assertiveness of Beijing's diplomacy since 2008 (Christensen 2021, 12; Campbell and Rapp Hooper 2020, 1), is gradually becoming aware of the challenge represented by the People's Republic of China. Thus, as early as March 2019, the European Commission defined China as 'a partner, a competitor and a systemic rival' 'seeking to promote alternative forms of governance' and, in 2021, it decided to prepare a strategy for the Indo-Pacific (Abad-Quintanal 2022b, 14) which was finally published on September 16th 2021 (European Commission (2021)).

At the same time, the European Union is working to develop ways to protect intellectual property and limit the possibilities of information theft and espionage by China (Christensen 2021, 12).

For its part, the People's Republic of China seems interested in pursuing an approach aimed at dividing Europe and the United States, clearly positioning itself in favour of the development of capabilities and the enhancement of strategic autonomy on the part of the former as a way of "counterbalancing US hegemony" (Blasco López 2022, 9). At the same time, it would do everything possible to prevent Washington from building a united front with the EU in the face of growing Chinese power. In this sense, Foreign Minister Wang Yi himself called on the EU to "transcend systemic differences and not draw lines along ideological lines" (Haas 2021, 9).

5 Conclusion

Consequently, and although this position has until recently been questioned by many, it is undeniable that for the first time since the end of the Cold War there is a global competition between two political, economic and social models. A competition in which the features that will characterise the new world order are being decided.

In the context of this contest, the People's Republic of China, which has established itself as a major power over the last few decades, is naturally trying to ensure that this order reflects its preferences and is doing so by all the means at its disposal, means that have only increased with the passage of time. However, the PRC is not alone in its bid. Alignment with Russia, resulting largely from antagonism with the West in general and the United States in particular, is increasingly visible, particularly in the area of security, where there has been no shortage of joint military exercises, arms sales and cooperation in the framework of the United Nations (Christensen 2021, 13).

The challenge is therefore not only growing, but also increasingly complex. Consequently, defending the status quo and the existing international order will require unified and determined action by the United States, the European Union - and to a large extent Europe - and third states on all continents.

However, in the face of the US's firm commitment to the defence of the international order, the Europeans, with their different geographical position and approaches, are still undecided given the existence of political and security issues that they consider more urgent and geographically closer and the advantages that, at least in the short term, they believe can be derived from an understanding with the People's Republic of China.

References

Abad-Quintanal, G.: The Indo-Pacific and Southeast Asia: the impact of external strategies on Southeast Asia and ASEAN's response. UNISCI J. (59) (2022a)

Abad-Quintanal, G.: Managing a Pandemic: the securitisation of health and the challenge for fundamental freedoms. In Stanford, B., Foster, S., Espaliú Berdud, C. (eds.) Global Pandemic, Security and Human Rights. Routledge (2022b)

Abad-Quintanal, G.: De la Revolución en Asuntos Militares a la carrera de armamentos en Asia-Pacífico. Documento de Opinión. IEEE (2017)

Abad-Quintanal, G.: La Política Exterior y de Seguridad China o la Búsqueda del Poder Integral. Atenea, Año V, No **37**, 12–18 (2008)
Anere, J.M.: A new era of chinese foreign policy. Diplomacy (2022). https://www.diplomacy.edu/blog/a-new-era-of-chinese-foreign-policy
Arezina, S.: U.S. – China relations under the Trump administration: changes and challenges. China Q. Int. Strat. Studies **5**(3), 289–315 (2019)
Blanchette, J.: Xi Jinping's Faltering Foreign Policy. Foreign Affairs (2022). http://www.foreignaffairs.com/print/node/1128637
Blasco López, C.: Perspectivas geoestratégicas de la Unión Europea con relación a los Estados Unidos, China y Rusia. Documento de Opinión. IEEE (2022)
Brands, H., Sullivan, J.: China has two pathas to global domination. The Big Think (2020). https://foreignpolicy.com/2020/05/22/china-superpower-two-paths-global-dominarion-cold-war/
Campbell, K., Rapp-Hooper, M.: China is Done Biding Time: The End of Beijing's Foreign Policy Restraint? Foreign Affairs (2020). http://www.foreignaffairs.com/print/node/1126187
Christensen, T.J.: There will not be a new Cold War. Foreign Affairs (2021). http://www.foreignaffairs.com/print/node/1127274
European Commission. The EU strategy for cooperation in the Indo-Pacific (2021). https://ec.europa.eu/info/sites/default/files/jointcommunication_indo_pacific_en.pdf
Friedberg, A.L.: Beyond Air-Sea Battle. IISS. Routledge (2014)
García Cantalapiedra, D.: La Estrategia de las Tres Guerras: La guerra política con características chinas dentro de la Gran Estrategia de la República Popular China. Documento Opinion, 29/22. IEEE (2022). https://www.ieee.es/Galerias/fichero/docs_opinion/2022/DIEEO29_2022_DAVGAR_China.pdf
Haas, R.: How China is responding to escalating strategic competition with the US. China's Leadership Monitor (2021). www.brookings.edu/articles/how-china-is-responding-to-escalating-strategic-competition-with-the-US/
Leandro, F.J.: Four circles of Foreign Policy. Asean Weekly (2015). https://www.chinadailyasia.com/asean-weekly/article-5696.html
Le Miere, C.: The spectre of an asian arms race. Survival **56**(1), 139–156 (2014)
Marshall, T.: Prisioneros de la geografía. Península (2017)
Mohan, P.: China's Nuclear Ambitions, the implications for India, and the future of Global Disarmament. Observer Research Foundation Issue Brief, Issue No 560 (2022)
Rodríguez-Rata, A.: Cómo la OTAN continúa rodeando a China pese a la amenaza rusa. La Vanguardia (2022). www.lavanguardia.com/internacional/20220416/8194840/como-otan-continua-rodeando-a-rusia-pese-a-la-amenaza-rusa.amp.html
Sánchez, R.: Borrell, en la Conferencia de Seguridad de Munich. Rusia y China quieren redefinir el orden mundial. ABC (2022). www.abc.es/internacional/abc1-borrell-conferencia-seguridad-munich-rusia-y-china-quieren-redefinir-oden-mundial-202202201352_noticia..
Sendagorta, F.: Estrategias de Poder, Deusto (2020)
Sommer, T.: China's relations with its neighbours and the West will define the next world order. The Security Times (2018). www.the-security-times.com/chinas-relations-wit-its-neigbours-and-the-west-will-define-the-next-world-order/
Strange, S.: States and Markets. Blackwell (1988)
The White House. National Security Strategy (2022). https://www.whitehouse.gov/wp-content/uploads/2022/10/Biden-Harris-Administrations-National-Security-Strategy-10.2022.pdf
Weissmann, M.: Chinese foreign policy in a global perspective: a responsible reformer "striving for achievement." JCIR **3**(1), 151–165 (2015)
Xuetong, Y.: Becoming Strong. Foreign Affairs (2021). www.foreignaffairs.com/print/node/1127541
Zhao, M.: Is a new cold war inevitable? chinese perspectives on us-china strategic competition. Chin. J. Int. Polit. **12**(3), 371–394 (2019)

The Case of David vs. Goliath?
Reflections on the International Regulation of the Use of Force in Relation to the Russia–Ukraine Conflict

Noémi Nagy(✉)

Department of International Law, University of Public Service (Ludovika), Budapest, Hungary
nagynoemi@uni-nke.hu

1 Introduction

On 24 February 2022, Russian President Vladimir Putin declared a "special military operation" against Ukraine, provoking the general resentment of the international community, and possibly marking the beginning of a new era in international relations and the international legal order. This paper explores aspects of the conflict that are relevant from an international legal perspective, more specifically, legal norms on the use of force (*ius ad bellum*). Whereas rules of *ius in bello* (applicable during an armed conflict, i.e. international humanitarian law) and international criminal law are just as important in the protracted war, these will be mentioned only to the extent necessary for understanding the ongoing legal proceedings.

The paper aims to scrutinize the most important legal grounds that have been invoked in pursuit of justifying the Russian invasion of Ukraine, involving the international regulation of the use of force, the right to (collective) self-defence, and the right of peoples to self-determination in connection with the two breakaway regions of eastern Ukraine (Luhansk and Donetsk). In this context, the role of the most relevant international organizations – the UN, the NATO, the European Union (EU), the Council of Europe, and the International Criminal Court (ICC) – will also be presented, along with the possible legal consequences of the conflict.

2 Events Leading to the Current Conflict and the Response of the International Community

On February 22, 2014, the pro-Russian President of Ukraine Viktor Yanukovych fled the country, after months of protests had destabilised his power. On the very same day Russian military forces invaded the Crimean Peninsula, and on March 16, 2014, via a controversial referendum the population of the territory declared its secession from Ukraine and the establishment of the Republic of Crimea, which Russia immediately recognized as an independent State. On March 18, Crimea requested its accession to the Russian Federation, which was accepted on March 21. At the same time, an armed

The manuscript was closed on 22 October 2022. The author is grateful to Tamás Hoffmann and Norbert Tóth for their valuable comments to the manuscript.

J. Cayón Peña and J. M. Ramírez (Eds.): *Threats to Peace and International Security: Asia versus West*, ASTSA, pp. 47–61, 2023.
https://doi.org/10.1007/978-3-031-28336-9_3

uprising with Russian military support broke out against the Ukrainian authorities in the eastern Ukrainian counties of Donetsk and Luhansk, populated mainly by ethnic Russians, and on May 11, 2014, following a referendum, the People's Republics of Donetsk and Luhansk were proclaimed. Since then, there has been an ongoing armed conflict between the territories of eastern Ukraine and Ukraine, in which Russian military forces have actively participated (Hoffmann 2022, pp. 2–3).

Tensions between Ukraine and Russia culminated on February 21, 2022, when President Vladimir Putin announced that the Russian Federation recognizes the independence of separatist entities in eastern Ukraine, and would send Russian "peacekeeping" troops there. On February 24, the Russian army indeed launched an invasion against Ukraine which triggered a broad-reaching, swift, and surprisingly unified condemnation by the international community. Intergovernmental organizations around the world have unanimously rejected the Russian aggression and demanded that Russia immediately withdraw its forces and abide by international law. After the UN Security Council was prevented to act by a Russian veto on 25 February, the UN General Assembly (UNGA) adopted – by an overwhelming majority of 141 against 5 (Russia, Belarus, North Korea, Eritrea and Syria) – a resolution on 2 March. The document deplored "in the strongest terms" the aggression by Russia and affirmed the international community's commitment to the sovereignty, independence, unity and territorial integrity of Ukraine, whereas calling for unimpeded access for humanitarian assistance (UNGA 2022). A month later the UNGA suspended Russia from its membership at the UN Human Rights Council, after disturbing photos had emerged from the city of Bucha, a suburb of the capital, Kyiv, with hundreds of civilian bodies found in the streets and in mass graves following Russia's withdrawal from the area (UN News 2022).

Several organs of the Council of Europe also condemned the aggression of Russia as a "blatant breach of international law", including the Parliamentary Assembly, the Congress of Local and Regional Authorities and the Committee of Ministers. As a result, the Russian Federation was expelled from the organization on 16 March 2022 (Committee of Ministers of the Council of Europe 2022). The EU member states all firmly underlined that "the use of force and coercion to change borders has no place in the 21st century. Tensions and conflict should be resolved exclusively through dialogue and diplomacy" (European Council 2022a). This was not just a hollow declaration, but a promise followed by various (ongoing) sanctions on Russia from economic and diplomatic measures through sanctions against individuals and entities to restrictions on media and economic cooperation (European Council 2022b).[1] NATO (2022) has also condemned "in the strongest possible terms Russia's brutal and unprovoked war of aggression against Ukraine".

In the following section we are going to see why international response could be so prompt and uniform. Notwithstanding alleged political, security-related and historical

[1] The prohibition of the use of force is an obligation *erga omnes*, i.e. an obligation under general international law which a State owes to the "international community as a whole". Where a breach of such an obligation occurs, the States shall endeavour to bring the breach to an end, and are entitled to take non-forcible countermeasures under conditions analogous to those applying to a State specially affected by the breach (Yiallourides et al. 2018, p. 29).

justifications (Putin 2022a),[2] the evaluation of the Russian actions in terms of international law are clear cut: we are dealing with a textbook case of aggression. The purpose of this paper is not to decide who is right in the conflict – evidently, there are no black and white events in the history of mankind. It merely aims to present the relevant international legal regime on the use of force – this obviously can be challenged, a new world order may be created, but that does not change the legal nature of the conflict under the current status quo. All the more so, because Putin (2022a) himself referred to the provisions of the UN Charter in pursuit of legitimizing his actions, which makes it only logical that his arguments should be scrutinized in the context of international law as it stands today.

3 The Modern Regulation of the Use of Force in International Law

Although the topic of use of force by States has in the recent decades produced vigorous debate in the United Nations and other international organizations, national parliaments, academia and the media, the rules on it can be expressed very simply.[3] According to Article 2(3) of the UN Charter international disputes shall be settled by peaceful means, and Article 2(4) requires all Members to "refrain in their international relations from the threat or use of force against the territorial integrity or political independence of any State, or in any other manner inconsistent with the Purposes of the United Nations". Unlike the 1928 Kellogg–Briand pact[4] (see Wright 1933), the Charter prohibits not only war, but the use of force of any kind. The rule received universal acknowledgment and quickly became part of customary international law, as affirmed by the International Court of Justice in the *Nicaragua v. United States* case (ICJ 1986, paras. 34, 174).

Yet, the prohibition on the use (and threat) of force is not absolute. As the wording of Article 2(4) of the UN Charter and the UN General Assembly resolution on the principles of international law (UNGA 1970) suggest, force is permissible in circumstances consistent with the purposes of the United Nations. Chapter VII of the UN Charter ("Action with Respect to Threats to the Peace, Breaches of the Peace, and Acts of Aggression") outlines that States can resort to the use of military force against other States in two[5] instances: when such act is authorised by the UN Security Council (UNSC) as part of the collective security system, or in the case of – individual or collective – self-defence. Chapter VII provides the framework within which the Security Council may take enforcement

[2] Putin's non-legal justifications include that historically, Ukraine has been part of Russia and is not a legitimate state; references to past allegedly unlawful uses of force by Western nations in Iraq, Syria, Libya and Yugoslavia; the "threatening expansion" of NATO towards Russia's borders, etc. For the detailed refutation of these (and other) arguments, see Green et al. 2022.

[3] As Aust (2010, p. 205) explains, the difficulty lies in how these rules apply in particular circumstances.

[4] Treaty between the United States and other Powers providing for the Renunciation of War as an instrument of national policy.

[5] The third option (the use of force against "enemy States") has never been invoked in practice and by all means has become obsolete by now, when all entities universally recognized as States are members of the United Nations. UN Charter, Article 107 (cf. Articles 53 and 77). See, Wood 2006.

action, sometimes acting under the auspices of a regional intergovernmental organization or arrangement. It allows the UNSC to "determine the existence of any threat to the peace, breach of the peace, or act of aggression" and to make recommendations or to resort to non-military and military action to maintain or restore international peace and security. As known, the Security Council did not authorize the Russian actions against Ukraine. Due to the Russian veto, it was not able to pronounce itself on the evaluation of the crisis, either (UNSC 2022a). This leaves us with the second possibility, the right to self-defence, which is the most frequently invoked norm in cases of interstate violence in the post-World War II international legal order (Hoffmann 2022, p. 5). Was Russia in fact acting in self-defence as claimed by President Putin (Nebenzia 2022a)?

4 Regarding the Self-defence Argument

Article 51 of the UN Charter contains the following provision:

> "Nothing in the present Charter shall impair the inherent right of individual or collective self-defence if an armed attack occurs against a Member of the United Nations, until the Security Council has taken measures necessary to maintain international peace and security. Measures taken by Members in the exercise of this right of self-defence shall be immediately reported to the Security Council and shall not in any way affect the authority and responsibility of the Security Council under the present Charter to take at any time such action as it deems necessary in order to maintain or restore international peace and security."

Hence, States may legitimately resort to the use of armed force as a reaction to an "armed attack" against their territorial integrity. The meaning of "armed attack" causes significant controversy in international law (Ruys 2010). The ICJ rejected the idea that an armed attack may include "not only acts by armed bands where such acts occur on a significant scale but also assistance to rebels in the form of the provision of weapons or logistical or other support". Such assistance may be regarded as a threat or use of force, or amount to intervention in the internal or external affairs of other States, but for the purposes of self-defence, it is necessary to show that an armed attack is attributable to a foreign State (ICJ 1986, para. 195; cf. ICJ 2004, para. 139).[6]

However, Ukraine did not attack Russia, so the only way the Russian actions could be considered lawful is if we accept the concept of anticipatory (often referred to as preemptive) self-defence. This means that the inherent right of States to defend themselves is also accorded as a preventive measure, taken in anticipation of an armed attack, and not merely in response to an attack that has actually occurred. The narrower interpretation of this concept is supported by several States and legal scholars (Van den hole 2003,

[6] In the *Nicaragua* case (ICJ 1986), Judge Higgins strongly opposed this view and argued that the act involving the use of force from actors other than a State, such as groups of insurgents or terrorists, may also give rise to the exercise of the right of self-defence by the attacked state. The use of force in self-defence against non-State actors remains a highly contentious issue in modern international relations, especially in the aftermath of the 9/11 terrorist attacks on the World Trade Centre.

pp. 80–90; Värk 2003, p. 36), and was also expressed in the report of the High-Level Panel commissioned by Secretary-General Kofi Annan (2005, para. 124), stating that a State can take military action as long as the threatened attack is imminent. However, the notion of imminent attack was finally not included in the declaration adopted by UN member states (Hoffmann 2022, p. 7). The broader version of the concept of anticipatory self-defence, that would authorize the use of force against distant threats, is even more controversial and almost unanimously rejected by the international community (Corten 2021, pp. 403–435; Gray 2018, pp. 248–256).[7] Furthermore, it would most certainly go against the traditional definition of self-defence, which was formulated in the 1837 *Caroline* case[8] and became accepted as part of customary international law.[9] According to this definition, self-defence is an instant, overwhelming necessity that leaves no choice of means and no time for deliberation. Also, for the self-defence to be lawful in international law, the counter-attack must be necessary (no viable alternative exists) and proportional (limited to the necessity) (Aust 2010, pp. 209–210). Even if Russia could prove the existence of a self-defence situation, its actions would definitely not meet the requirements of necessity and proportionality (Hoffmann 2022, pp. 14–15). That anticipatory self-defence is excluded from the ambit of Article 51 is also supported by the ICJ (2005, para. 148): "Article 51 of the Charter may justify a use of force in self-defence only within the strict confines there laid down. It does not allow the use of force by a State to protect perceived security interests beyond these parameters."

Russian official statements made several vague references to distant security threats stemming from Ukrainian territory, including terrorist activities, neo-Nazism, the access to or development of nuclear, biological and chemical weapons, and most importantly, the eastward expansion of NATO (Putin 2022a, 2022b; Nebenzia 2022b; UNSC 2022b). Putin himself declared that "Russia launched a pre-emptive strike" (Putin 2022b), and although it was put as "a matter of life and death", a real threat to the very existence of Russia and to its sovereignty (Putin 2022a),in fact no persuasive arguments, let alone

[7] One of the biggest supporters of the concept is the United States of America. As the former President George W. Bush set out in the 2002 National Security Strategy: "For centuries, international law recognized that nations need not suffer an attack before they can lawfully take action to defend themselves against forces that present an imminent danger of attack. [...] We must adapt the concept of imminent threat to the capabilities and objectives of today's adversaries. [...] The greater the threat, the greater is the risk of inaction – and the more compelling the case for taking anticipatory action to defend ourselves, even if uncertainty remains as to the time and place of the enemy's attack." *The National Security Strategy of the United States of America*, 2002, p. 15. Cited by Hoffmann 2022, p. 8.

[8] The case originated from a dispute between the British Government and the US Secretary of State, Daniel Webster, regarding the destruction of an American vessel in an American port by British subjects. The reason was the use of the vessel to transport munitions and groups of Americans, supporting the Canadian rebels against British rule. The US Government declared that the attack on the vessel constituted an attack against American territory, whereas the British Government responded by claiming the right to self-defence. The subsequent diplomatic correspondence between the parties laid down the key elements of legitimate self-defence. See, Shiryaev 2007–2008, p. 82.

[9] Although there is a strong debate about the post-1945 applicability of the Webster formula, see Kajtár 2016.

evidence existed which could have substantiated the threat of an imminent armed attack by Ukraine (Hoffmann 2022, pp. 8–10). This excludes the legal possibility of Russia to recourse to individual self-defence.

However, Article 51 of the UN Charter also recognizes *collective* self-defence, which means assistance to a State in a situation of individual self-defence. This norm is also of customary nature, the requirements of which are clarified in the *Nicaragua* judgment: for a third-party State to lawfully intervene on behalf of another State a State must first publicly announce that it has been attacked (declare itself a victim) and then specifically request assistance (ICJ 1986, paras. 199, 232; Walker 1998, p. 354). Importantly, the request has to be made by an established (recognized) State.[10] This leaves us with the question: did the people of the two territories of the Donbas region have the right to self-determination, secede from Ukraine, and establish their independent States?

5 Regarding the Self-determination Argument

The argument that Russia lawfully intervened in defence of other States by sending "peacekeeping forces" is, again, a very problematic element in the Russian line of justification, since the Donetsk People's Republic and the Luhansk People's Republic at the time were recognized by no other States but the Russian Federation.[11] In fact, both the UN General Assembly (2022, point 5) and UN Secretary General António Guterres (2022) expressly pointed out that the decision of Russia to recognize the statehood of Donetsk and Luhansk is a violation of the territorial integrity and sovereignty of Ukraine.

Self-determination – the right of all peoples to decide their own destiny in the international order – is a core principle of international law, arising from customary international law, but also enshrined in a number of international treaties. The concept was born in the eighteenth century as related to popular sovereignty (rule by the people), and came to the fore as a political doctrine after the First World War, championed by US president Wilson's famous 14 points. The idea was that people should have a right to decide their own future and live within their own territorial units, and in theory this became basis for the Peace Treaties of Paris (Tóth 2018, [4–9]). To develop friendly relations among nations based on respect for the principle of equal rights and self-determination of peoples features in Article 1(2) of the UN Charter as one of the purposes of the United Nations. The meaning of the principle is explained briefly in the common provision (Article 1[1]) of the two major human rights treaties of the UN, the International Covenant of Civil and Political Rights, as well as the International Covenant of Economic, Social and Cultural Rights: "All peoples have the right of self-determination. By virtue of that right they freely determine their political status and freely pursue their economic, social and cultural development." Self-determination was further enunciated in several General Assembly resolutions (including UNGA 1960 and 1970), yet, notwithstanding universal

[10] On the issue of collective self-defence of contested States, see Fisher (2020).

[11] The two "republics" were later also recognized by Syria, North-Korea, South Ossetia and Abkhazia – the latter two being unrecognized States themselves. The DPR and LPR, along with the Zaporozhye and the Kherson regions, were officially annexed by Russia on 30 September 2022 (Kremlin.ru 2022). For a thorough explanation of the legal status of the two republics before the current war, see Korotkyi and Hendel 2018.

acknowledgment,[12] both the content of the right as well as who can assert it has been the subject of extensive debate and controversy.

Contrary to widespread public belief, self-determination is not an automatic right to independence. Contemporary legal thinking usually distinguishes between internal and external aspects of the concept, where internal self-determination refers to the right of peoples to freely determine, without external interference, their political status and to pursue their economic, social and cultural development (self-government or autonomy within the existing boundaries of a country). In turn, external self-determination may include the establishment of a sovereign and independent state (independence/secession from the larger politico-legal entity), free association or integration with an independent state, or emergence into any other political status. However, the modern (post World War II) state practice of recognition shows that external self-determination leading to independence has been interpreted in very narrow terms (Ker-Lindsay 2012, pp. 24–38). Primarily, it has come to be regarded as a right applicable to the decolonisation process or to other limited cases where the territory is under military occupation (Ker-Lindsay 2013, p. 841), as clearly confirmed by the ICJ's advisory opinion on the unilateral secession of Kosovo:

> "During the second half of the twentieth century, the international law of self-determination developed in such a way as to create a right to independence for the peoples of non-self-governing territories and peoples subject to alien subjugation, domination and exploitation." (ICJ 2010, para. 79.)

In any other context, self-determination is seen as being wholly subordinate to the principle of territorial integrity (Ker-Lindsay 2013, p. 841). As emphasized in Resolution 1514 (XV) of the UNGA, the right to self-determination cannot be construed as

> "authorizing or encouraging any action which would dismember or impair, totally or in part, the territorial integrity or political unity of sovereign and independent States conducting themselves in compliance with the principle of equal rights and self-determination of peoples as described above and thus possessed of a government representing the whole people belonging to the territory without distinction as to race, creed or colour" (UNGA 1970).

However, the second part of this provision may allow a broader interpretation of external self-determination, expanding it to scenarios when the government in fact does not represent the whole population. The advocates of this interpretation (including myself) accept the concept of remedial secession as a last resort for minority groups suffering from systematic or structural discrimination, or serious human rights violations (Cassese

[12] Some even claim that it has *jus cogens* status, but this idea is not endorsed by the majority of the international community: "even if it is accepted that the Declaration [on Principles of International Law], which includes desiderata as to the content of future international law, is heterogeneous, and thus not of the nature of jus cogens in every one of its propositions, the fundamental principles of the Charter embodied in it – and hence the principle of self-determination of peoples – as enunciated in General Assembly resolution 2625 (XXV), are nevertheless of the nature of jus cogens" (Gros Espiell 1978, para. 72).

1995, p. 119; Murswiek 1993, pp. 26–27; Tomuschat 2006, pp. 38–42). Whereas there exists some support to this theory in jurisprudence (Vidmar 2010, pp. 39–40),[13] it is generally accepted that minorities within an established State do not have the right to self-determination under international law. As Judge Koroma argued in his dissenting opinion (para. 4) in the Kosovo case:

> "International law does not confer a right on ethnic, linguistic or religious groups to break away from the territory of a State of which they form part, without that State's consent, merely by expressing their wish to do so. To accept otherwise, to allow any ethnic, linguistic or religious group to declare independence and break away from the territory of the State of which it forms part, outside the context of decolonization, creates a very dangerous precedent." (Cited by Ker-Lindsay 2013, p. 841.)

To put it another way, the consensual answer to the question of "Who constitutes a people?" for the purposes of self-determination, is the whole population of a fixed territorial entity, specifically peoples oppressed by a colonial or foreign military power (Tóth 2018, [17]).

Even if remedial secession were legal under the existing norms of international law, there are two problems with its exercise in the current case. Firstly, the very circumstances under which the people of the two breakaway regions declared their independence via referendums held on 11 May 2014 are very obscure (Cavandoli 2016, p. 883). Secondly – although the UN Human Rights Monitoring Mission repeatedly disclosed serious human rights concerns (OHCHR 2023)[14] –, there has been no convincing evidence provided that the people of the Donbas region were victims of such extreme abuses that could not be remedied through any other ways but secession.[15] There is certainly no ground

[13] The most prominent judicial pronouncement underpinning the theory of remedial secession is that of the Supreme Court of Canada in the *Quebec* case: "There is no necessary incompatibility between the maintenance of the territorial integrity of existing states, including Canada, and the right of a 'people' to achieve a full measure of self-determination. A state whose government represents the whole of the people or peoples resident within its territory, on a basis of equality and without discrimination, and respects the principles of self-determination in its own internal arrangements, is entitled to the protection under international law of its territorial integrity." (Supreme Court of Canada 1998, para. 130, also calling for the surpass of a certain threshold, para. 135.).

[14] Most importantly, persisting grave violations of human rights, including arbitrary detention, torture and ill-treatment in the territories controlled by the self-proclaimed republics were not only attributable to the government of Ukraine, but also to the occupying armed groups. The latest (thirty-fourth) report was published on 27 September 2022 (OHCHR 2022).

[15] As Russia itself explained in its intervention in the Kosovo case: "conditions [authorizing secession] should be limited to truly extreme circumstances, such as an outright armed attack by the parent State, threatening the very existence of the people in question. Otherwise, all efforts should be taken in order to settle the tension between the parent State and the ethnic community concerned within the framework of the existing State" (ICJ 2009, para. 88).

for claiming that the Kyiv regime had perpetrated genocide[16] against the ethnic Russian population of East Ukraine (Gill 2022a, p. 123; Sayapin 2018) which could lead to a possible humanitarian intervention – another highly controversial issue in international law.[17]

6 What is Next? – Possible Legal Consequences of the Conflict

From the very beginning of the Russia-Ukraine war, there have been widespread claims in the international community (including by U.S. President Joe Biden) that President Putin should be held responsible for being a "war criminal" (Thebault et al. 2022). Formal investigation by Prosecutor Karim Khan was launched on 2 March after the situation was referred to the International Criminal Court by 43 State Parties (ICC 2022). Ukraine is not party to the Rome Statute (the founding treaty of the ICC), but it has twice exercised its prerogatives to accept the Court's jurisdiction over alleged crimes under the Rome Statute occurring on its territory, pursuant to Article 12(3) of the Statute. The first declaration accepted ICC jurisdiction with respect to crimes committed on Ukrainian territory from 21 November 2013 to 22 February 2014, whereas the second declaration extended this period on an open-ended basis to encompass ongoing crimes committed from 20 February 2014 onwards. The scope of the situation encompasses any past and present instances of war crimes, crimes against humanity or genocide committed on any part of the territory of Ukraine by any person from 21 November 2013 onwards. In turn, the ICC does not have jurisdiction over the crime of aggression, because it was not committed by the nationals or on the territory of a State Party, nor has the UN Security Council referred this situation to the ICC Prosecutor (Rome Statute of the International Criminal Court 1998, Article 15 *bis* (5) and Article 15 *ter*). In any case, there is mounting evidence that Russia has been committed several war crimes, crimes against humanity, and potentially genocide,[18] which will most certainly lead to criminal trials (unless Russia wins the war and a new international legal order will be created).

Bringing individuals in front of the ICC is but one available legal avenue. The responsibility of Russia as a State can be established by the International Court of Justice

[16] For genocide, an intent to destroy, in whole or in part, a national, ethnical, racial or religious group, as such must be proved (Convention on the Prevention and Punishment of the Crime of Genocide 1948, Article II). Whereas there is no doubt that Ukrainian authorities did commit human rights violations against members of the Russian minority, it is very questionable whether these atrocities were committed with the actual intent of destroying Russians as an ethnic group.

[17] Due to space constraints, I cannot elaborate on the inapplicability of the implicit claims of humanitarian intervention, protection of nationals and intervention by invitation to the invasion of Ukraine. On these issues, see Gill 2022b; Green et al. 2022, pp. 14–16, 21–27.; Hoffmann 2022, pp. 15–23.

[18] See the most recent report of the Independent International Commission of Inquiry on Ukraine (2022). The OSCE Moscow Mechanism's mission of experts also issued two reports (2022a, 2022b) on violations of international humanitarian and human rights law in Ukraine, and under its extended mandate (Council of the European Union 2022), the European Union Advisory Mission for Civilian Security Sector Reform in Ukraine also provides support to Ukrainian authorities to facilitate the investigation and prosecution of any international crimes committed in the context of Russia's military aggression (EUAM Ukraine 2022).

(for violating any provisions of international law) and the European Court of Human Rights (for violating the European Convention on Human Rights). As early as February 26 Ukraine in fact initiated proceedings against Russia in front of the ICJ, basing the jurisdiction of the Court on the compromissory clause of the Genocide Convention,[19] to which treaty both States are parties. In its application, Ukraine "emphatically" denied the Russian allegations of genocide, and requested the Court to indicate provisional measures to protect the people of Ukraine by ordering Russia to suspend its military actions (ICJ 2022a). Whereas the Court did provide for the requested provisional measures (ICJ 2022b, para. 86.),[20] it was cautious not to pre-empt any finding of the merits stage (Green et al. 2022, pp. 25–26):

> "At the present stage of the proceedings, it suffices to observe that the Court is not in possession of evidence substantiating the allegation of the Russian Federation that genocide has been committed on Ukrainian territory. Moreover, it is doubtful that the Convention, in light of its object and purpose, authorizes a Contracting Party's unilateral use of force in the territory of another State for the purpose of preventing or punishing an alleged genocide" (ICJ 2022b, para. 59).

The future outcome of this and another ongoing proceedings before the ICJ, initiated by Ukraine in January 2017 (ICJ 2017), will shed further light on the events preceding the current conflict.

The first judicial institution to rule against Russia following its invasion of Ukraine was the European Court of Human Rights (ECtHR) on March 1, ordering interim measures including a halt to attacks on civilians and civilian objects: "The Court has regard to the current military action which commenced on 24 February 2022 in various parts of Ukraine and considers that it gives rise to a real and continuing risk of serious violations of the Convention rights of the civilian population, in particular under Articles 2 (right to life), 3 (prohibition of torture and inhuman or degrading treatment or punishment) and 8 (right to respect for private and family life) of the European Convention on Human Rights" (ECtHR 2022).[21] This is the tenth interstate case brought by Ukraine against Russia – in addition to a case brought by Russia against Ukraine – that deals with prior episodes of the conflict (Milanovic 2022; ECtHR 2023). Although Russia is not party to the European Convention of Human Rights any more, the Court's jurisdiction applies to

---

[19] "Disputes between the Contracting Parties relating to the interpretation, application or fulfilment of the present Convention, including those relating to the responsibility of a State for genocide or for any of the other acts enumerated in article III, shall be submitted to the International Court of Justice at the request of any of the parties to the dispute." (Convention on the Prevention and Punishment of the Crime of Genocide 1948, Article IX.).

[20] "The Russian Federation shall immediately suspend the military operations that it commenced on 24 February 2022 in the territory of Ukraine; [and] shall ensure that any military or irregular armed units which may be directed or supported by it, as well as any organizations and persons which may be subject to its control or direction, take no steps in furtherance of the military operations…".

[21] The interim measures were extended on April 1, 2022.

events that took place before the entry into effect of its denunciation, that is, 16 September 2022 (Council of Europe Newsroom 2022), even if the chances for the enforcement of its judgments under the present circumstances are low.

7 Concluding Remarks

Despite being euphemistically called a "special military operation" by President Putin and other Russian officials, the Russian Federation's actions against Ukraine qualify as a textbook case of war of aggression under international law. Acts of aggression include, *inter alia*, the invasion or attack by the armed forces of a State of the territory of another State, whether on the land, sea or air (UNGA 1974, Articles 1 and 3).[22] Aggression falls within the broader scope of "force", which is prohibited by international law since 1945, the establishment of the UN, with the only exceptions of self-defence and UN Security Council authorization.

Wars, nevertheless, are not rare occurrences in international relations, although after the Second World War the vast majority of them have been waged within States. What makes the present conflict exceptional is, however,

> "not merely the scale of the military intervention, but also the thinly veiled intention to annex a significant part of Ukraine's territory, despite Russia's previous explicit acceptance of Ukraine's sovereign statehood and territorial integrity in several international treaties" (Hoffmann 2022, p. 32).

As proven in this paper, under the existing regime of international law, the Russian invasion lacks any sound justification. On the contrary, it is "without doubt one of the most serious and flagrant violations of the core international legal rule prohibiting the use of armed force" since 1945 (Gill 2022a, p. 125). It may even be interpreted as an attempt to return to the pre-twentieth century legal order when war was a sovereign prerogative, waged for a "just" cause (Douzinas 2022), when States could undertake military interventions simply to support their broader geopolitical interests. However, as things stand today, the vast majority of the international community do not support Russia in this endeavour, on the contrary, they seek the restitution of the modern international order, and call for the accountability of the perpetrators.

Whereas the ICC has no jurisdiction to prosecute the crime of aggression committed against Ukraine, many – including the President of Ukraine (Zelenskyy 2022) – ponder the possibility of creating a special international tribunal to that effect (Just Security 2023), and individual criminal responsibility will most likely be invoked for those committing war crimes and crimes against humanity – on behalf of both Russia and Ukraine. Furthermore, awaited judgments of the International Court of Justice and the European Court of Human Rights may also contribute to serving justice to the parties concerned under the current framework of international law.

[22] These provisions are repeated verbatim in Article 8*bis*(2) of the Rome Statute as modified in 2010, Kampala.

References

Annan, K.: In Larger Freedom: Towards Development, Security and Human Rights for All. Report of the Secretary-General. UN Doc. A/59/2005, 21 March 2005. https://digitallibrary.un.org/record/543857

Aust, A.: Handbook of International Law, 2nd edn. Cambridge University Press, Cambridge (2010)

Cassese, A.: Self-determination of Peoples: A Legal Reappraisal. Cambridge University Press, Cambridge (1995)

Cavandoli, S.: The unresolved dilemma of self-determination: crimea, donetsk and luhansk. Int. J. Human Rights **20**(7), 875–892 (2016)

Charter of the United Nations. San Francisco, 26 June 1945. https://treaties.un.org/pages/ViewDetails.aspx?src=IND&mtdsg_no=I-1&chapter=1&clang=_en

Committee of Ministers of the Council of Europe. Resolution CM/Res(2022)2 on the cessation of the membership of the Russian Federation to the Council of Europe, 16 March 2022. https://search.coe.int/cm/Pages/result_details.aspx?ObjectId=0900001680a5da51

Convention on the Prevention and Punishment of the Crime of Genocide (1948). https://treaties.un.org/pages/ViewDetails.aspx?src=IND&mtdsg_no=IV-1&chapter=4&clang=_en

Corten, O.: The Law Against War: The Prohibition on the Use of Force in Contemporary International Law. Hart Publishing (2021)

Council of Europe Newsroom. Russia ceases to be party to the European Convention on Human Rights (2022). https://www.coe.int/en/web/portal/-/russia-ceases-to-be-party-to-the-european-convention-on-human-rights. Accessed 19 Jan 2023

Council of the European Union. Council Decision (CFSP) 2022/638 of 13 April 2022 amending Decision 2014/486/CFSP on the European Union Advisory Mission for Civilian Security Sector Reform Ukraine (EUAM Ukraine) (2022). https://eur-lex.europa.eu/legal-content/EN/TXT/?uri=CELEX:32022D0638

Douzinas, C.: A Short History of Just War. Critical Legal Thinking (2022). https://criticallegalthinking.com/2022/03/15/a-short-history-of-just-war/. Accessed 19 Jan 2023

ECtHR. Inter-state applications. https://www.echr.coe.int/Pages/home.aspx?p=caselaw/interstate. Accessed 19 Jan 2023

ECtHR. The European Court grants urgent interim measures in application concerning Russian military operations on Ukrainian territory. Press Release (2022). https://hudoc.echr.coe.int/eng-press?i=003-7272764-9905947. Accessed 19 Jan 2023

EUAM Ukraine. How EUAM supports Ukraine in fighting impunity for war crimes (2022). https://www.euam-ukraine.eu/news/infographics/how-euam-supports-ukraine-in-fighting-impunity-for-war-crimes/. Accessed 19 Jan 2023

European Council. Conclusions, 24 February 2022a. https://www.consilium.europa.eu/en/press/press-releases/2022/02/24/european-council-conclusions-24-february-2022/

European Council. Infographic – EU sanctions against Russia over Ukraine (since 2014) (2022b). https://www.consilium.europa.eu/en/infographics/eu-sanctions-against-russia-over-ukraine/. Accessed 19 Jan 2023

Fisher, R.M.: Defending Taiwan: collective self-defense of a contested state. Florida J. Int. Law **32**(1), 101–146 (2020)

Gill, T.D.: The Jus ad Bellum and Russia's "Special Military Operation" in Ukraine. J. Int. Peacekeeping **25**, 121–127 (2022a)

Gill, T.D.: Remarks on the Law Relating to the Use of Force in the Ukraine Conflict. Lieber Institute (2022b). https://lieber.westpoint.edu/remarks-use-of-force-ukraine-conflict/. Accessed 19 Jan 2023

Gray, C.: International Law and the Use of Force, 4 edn. Oxford Public International Law (2018)

Green, J.A., Henderson, C., Ruys, T.: Russia's attack on Ukraine and the jus ad bellum. J. Use Force Int. Law **9**(1), 4–30 (2022)
Gros Espiell, H.: Implementation of United Nations Resolutions relating to the Right of Peoples under Colonial and Alien Domination to Self-Determination. 20 June 1978, E/CN.4/Sub.2/405(vol.I) (1978). https://www.un.org/unispal/document/auto-insert-186956
Guterres, A.: UN Secretary-General's press encounter on Ukraine (2022). https://www.un.org/sg/en/content/sg/press-encounter/2022-02-22/secretary-generals-press-encounter-ukraine. Accessed 19 Jan 2023
Hoffmann, T.: War or peace? – international legal issues concerning the use of force in the Russia-Ukraine conflict. Hung. J. Legal Studies **63**(3), 1–44 (2022)
ICC. Situation in Ukraine, ICC-01/22 (2022). https://www.icc-cpi.int/ukraine. Accessed 19 Jan 2023
ICJ. Military and Paramilitary Activities in and against Nicaragua (Nicaragua v. United States of America), Judgment of 27 June 1986 (1986). https://www.icj-cij.org/public/files/case-related/70/070-19841126-JUD-01-00-EN.pdf
ICJ. Legal Consequences of the Construction of a Wall in the Occupied Palestinian Territory, Advisory Opinion of 9 July 2004 (2004). https://www.icj-cij.org/public/files/case-related/131/131-20040709-ADV-01-00-EN.pdf
ICJ. Armed Activities on the Territory of the Congo (Democratic Republic of the Congo v. Uganda), Judgment of 19 December 2005 (Merits) (2005). https://www.icj-cij.org/public/files/case-related/116/116-20051219-JUD-01-00-EN.pdf
ICJ (2009). Written statement of the Russian Federation. April 17, 2009. https://www.icj-cij.org/public/files/case-related/141/15628.pdf
ICJ. Accordance with International Law of the Unilateral Declaration of Independence in respect of Kosovo, Advisory Opinion of 22 July 2010 (2010). https://www.icj-cij.org/public/files/case-related/141/141-20100722-ADV-01-00-EN.pdf
ICJ. Application of the International Convention for the Suppression of the Financing of Terrorism and of the International Convention on the Elimination of All Forms of Racial Discrimination (Ukraine v. Russian Federation) (2017). https://www.icj-cij.org/en/case/166
ICJ. Allegations of Genocide under the Convention on the Prevention and Punishment of the Crime of Genocide (Ukraine v. Russian Federation), Application instituting proceedings submitted by Ukraine, 26 February 2022a. https://www.icj-cij.org/public/files/case-related/182/182-20220227-APP-01-00-EN.pdf
ICJ. Ukraine v. Russian Federation, Order on Provisional Measures, 16 March 2022b. https://www.icj-cij.org/public/files/case-related/182/182-20220316-ORD-01-00-EN.pdf
Independent International Commission of Inquiry on Ukraine (2022). Report, 18 October 2022, A/77/533. https://www.ohchr.org/sites/default/files/2022-10/A-77-3737%20-ADVANCE-UNEDITED-VERSION.pdf
Just Security series. Prosecuting the Crime of Aggression Against Ukraine. Council of Foreign Relations. https://www.cfr.org/article/case-creating-special-tribunal-prosecute-crime-aggression-committed-against-ukraine. Accessed 19 Jan 2023
Kajtár, G.: The Caroline as the 'Joker' of the law of self-defence – a ghost ship's message for the 21st century. Aust. Rev. Int. Eur. Law **21**, 3–25 (2016)
Ker-Lindsay, J.: The Foreign Policy of Counter Secession: Preventing the Recognition of Contested States. Oxford University Press, Oxford (2012)
Ker-Lindsay, J.: Preventing the emergence of self-determination as a norm of secession: an assessment of the Kosovo 'unique case' argument. Eur. Asia Stud. **65**(5), 837–856 (2013)
Korotkyi, T., Hendel, N.: The legal status of the donetsk and luhansk "Peoples' Republics". In: Sayapin, S., Tsybulenko, E. (eds.) The Use of Force against Ukraine and International Law: Jus Ad Bellum, Jus In Bello, Jus Post Bellum, pp. 145–170. T.M.C. Asser Press, The Hague (2018). https://doi.org/10.1007/978-94-6265-222-4_7

Kremlin.ru. Signing of treaties on accession of Donetsk and Lugansk people's republics and Zaporozhye and Kherson regions to Russia (2022). http://en.kremlin.ru/events/president/news/69465. Accessed 19 Jan 2023

Milanovic, M.: The Russia-Ukraine War and the European Convention on Human Rights. Lieber Institute (2022). https://lieber.westpoint.edu/russia-ukraine-war-european-convention-human-rights/. Accessed 19 Jan 2023

Murswiek, D.: The issue of a right of secession – reconsidered. In: Tomuschat, C. (ed.) Modern Law of Self-Determination, pp. 21–40. Martinus Nijhoff Publishers (1993)

NATO. NATO's response to Russia's invasion of Ukraine (2022). https://www.nato.int/cps/en/natohq/topics_192648.htm. Accessed 19 Jan 2023

Nebenzia, V.: Letter dated 24 February 2022 from the Permanent Representative of the Russian Federation to the United Nations addressed to the Secretary-General. UN Doc. S/2022/154 (2022a). https://digitallibrary.un.org/record/3959647

Nebenzia, V.: Letter dated 19 March 2022 from the Permanent Representative of the Russian Federation to the United Nations addressed to the Secretary-General. UN Doc. S/2022/249 (2022b). https://digitallibrary.un.org/record/3906945

OHCHR. Office of the High Commissioner for Human Rights, Ukraine. https://www.ohchr.org/en/countries/ukraine. Accessed 19 Jan 2023

OHCHR. Report on the human rights situation in Ukraine, 1 February to 31 July 2022 (2022). https://ukraine.un.org/sites/default/files/2022-09/ReportUkraine-1Feb-31Jul2022-en.pdf. Accessed 19 Jan 2023

OSCE Moscow Mechanism's mission of experts. Report on Violations of International Humanitarian and Human Rights Law, War Crimes and Crimes Against Humanity Committed in Ukraine since 24 February–13 April 2022 (2022a). https://www.osce.org/odihr/515868. Accessed 19 Jan 2023

OSCE Moscow Mechanism's mission of experts. Report on Violations of International Humanitarian and Human Rights Law, War Crimes and Crimes Against Humanity Committed in Ukraine (1 April – 25 June 2022), 14 July 2022b. https://www.osce.org/odihr/522616. Accessed 19 Jan 2023

Putin, V.: Address by the President of the Russian Federation (2022a). http://en.kremlin.ru/events/president/transcripts/67843. Accessed 19 Jan 2023

Putin, V.: Address by the President of Russia at the military parade (2022b). http://en.kremlin.ru/events/president/news/68366. Accessed 19 Jan 2023

Rome Statute of the International Criminal Court (1998). https://www.icc-cpi.int/sites/default/files/RS-Eng.pdf

Ruys, T.: 'Armed Attack' and Article 51 of the UN Charter: Evolutions in Customary Law and Practice. Cambridge University Press, Cambridge (2010)

Sayapin, S.: An alleged "genocide of Russian-speaking persons" in Eastern Ukraine: some observations on the "Hybrid" application of international criminal law by the Investigative Committee of the Russian Federation. In: Sayapin, S., Tsybulenko, E. (eds.) The Use of Force Against Ukraine and International Law: Jus Ad Bellum, Jus In Bello, Jus Post Bellum, pp. 313–326. T.M.C. Asser Press, The Hague (2018). https://doi.org/10.1007/978-94-6265-222-4_15

Shiryaev, Y.: The right of armed self-defense in international law and self-defense arguments used in the second Lebanon war. Acta Societatis Martensis **3**(1), 80–97 (2007–2008)

Supreme Court of Canada. Reference re Secession of Quebec, 1998 CanLII 793 (SCC), 2 SCR 217 (1998). https://canlii.ca/t/1fqr3

Thebault, R., et al.: Biden calls for Putin 'war-crimes trial' as world leaders issue fresh rebukes. The Washington Post (2022). https://www.washingtonpost.com/world/2022/04/04/russia-ukraine-war-news-putin-live-updates. Accessed 19 Jan 2023

Tomuschat, C.: Secession and self-determination. In: Kohen, M.G. (ed.) Secession: International Law Perspectives, pp. 23–45. Cambridge University Press (2006)

Tóth, N.: A népek önrendelkezési joga [Peoples' right to self-determination]. In: Jakab, A., Fekete, B. (eds.) Internetes Jogtudományi Enciklopédia, Nemzetközi jog rovat [Internet Encyclopedia of Law, International law section] (2018). http://ijoten.hu/szocikk/a-nepek-onrendelkezesi-joga. Accessed 19 Jan 2023

UNGA. Declaration on Granting Independence to Colonial Countries and Peoples, Resolution no. 1514 (XV), 14 December 1960. https://digitallibrary.un.org/record/662085

UNGA. Declaration on Principles of International Law concerning Friendly Relations and Co-operation among States in accordance with the Charter of the United Nations. Resolution no. 2625 (XXV), 24 October 1970. https://digitallibrary.un.org/record/202170

UNGA. Definition of Aggression. UN Doc. GA/RES/3314 (XXIX), 14 December 1974. https://digitallibrary.un.org/record/190983

UNGA. Eleventh Emergency Special Session: Aggression against Ukraine. UN Doc A/RES/ES-11/1, 2 March 2022. https://digitallibrary.un.org/record/3965290

UN News. UN General Assembly votes to suspend Russia from the Human Rights Council (2022). https://news.un.org/en/story/2022/04/1115782. Accessed 19 Jan 2023

UNSC. Security Council Fails to Adopt Draft Resolution on Ending Ukraine Crisis, as Russian Federation Wields Veto. 8979th meeting, SC/14808 (2022a). https://press.un.org/en/2022/sc14808.doc.htm. Accessed 19 Jan 2023

UNSC. UN Security Council 8991st meeting, 11 March 2022, UN Doc. S/PV.8991 (2022b). https://documents-dds-ny.un.org/doc/UNDOC/PRO/N22/284/83/PDF/N2228483.pdf?OpenElement

Van den hole, L.: Anticipatory self-defence under international law. Am. Univ. Int. Law Rev. **19**(1), 69–106 (2003)

Värk, R.: The use of force in the modem world: recent developments and legal regulation of the use of force. Balt. Def. Rev. **2**(10), 27–43 (2003)

Vidmar, J.: Remedial secession in international law: theory and (lack of) practice. St Antony's Int. Rev. **6**(1), 37–56 (2010)

Walker, G.K.: Anticipatory collective self-defense in the charter era: what the treaties have said. Cornell Int. Law J. **31**, 321–376 (1998)

Wood, M.: United Nations Charter, Enemy States Clauses. Max Planck Encyclopedia of Public International Law (2006). https://opil.ouplaw.com. Accessed 19 Jan 2023

Wright, Q.: The meaning of the pact of Paris. Am. J. Int. Law **27**(1), 39–61 (1933)

Yiallourides, C., Gehring, M., Gauci, J.-P.: The use of force in relation to sovereignty disputes over land territory. The British Institute of International and Comparative Law (2018)

Zelenskyy, V.: We must create a Special Tribunal on the crime of aggression against Ukraine – address by President Volodymyr Zelenskyy to the participants of the public debate "War and Law" in Paris (2022). https://www.president.gov.ua/en/news/mayemo-stvoriti-specialnij-tribunal-shodo-zlochinu-agresiyi-78285. Accessed 19 Jan 2023

mutually the great powers vie for power for maximizing their quota at the cost of other competitors. Therefore, they attempt to modify the existing reality on their behalf to establish a solid hegemonic position that ensures an acceptable level of security [3].

According to Realism, it would be the exact structure of the international system the cause that induces States to make war, and not their innate Will to Power, as asserted by Hans Morgenthau [4]. From the realist's point of view, the perception of States' security assumes a prominent position; even if they did not have any bellicist intent, the fear for their safety would pressure them to prepare aggressive measures to prevent attacks from abroad [5].

Based on this assumption, the realist interpretative model gave excellent proof in interpreting international events as well as in terms of predictiveness also respect to the current conflict in Ukraine and, in particular, the offensive realist theory by Mearsheimer.

For the realist theory and Mearsheimer's research, one of the essential points is that the international system lacks any overall central authority in which it can intervene to protect one State victim of the attack: the international system is an anarchist system. In a system of this type, each State should defend its safety on its own behalf. Nevertheless, the State's military capacity that generates offensive ability is a quantifiable element. Unfortunately, another element breeds fear about safety, and that is unmeasurable: States cannot know the true intentions of competitors, and it is a critical point. Of course, those intentions can now also be peaceful, but in the future, they might change. Many factors could generate a hypothetical change of intentions, not least the changes introduced by the new national leadership [6].

The combination of these elements contributes to generating fear; consequently, the reaction of the States will be to increase their aggressive capacity to neutralize that of the other. Thus, the State will be able to achieve and perceive a higher degree of security, which means survival.

According to Mearsheimer, for one State, the higher degree of hegemony manifested, the higher chance it has to survive, not only if it remains untouched in its territory but also if it can defend its autonomy in internal decision-making [7].

That means that the survival of the State requires an aggressive attitude, as the internal drives to domain play a less relevant role [8].

Mearsheimer confers an essential role to the hegemony: the great powers, to ensure their survival, act to move the center of power towards them and enhance their regional hegemony by preventing other States from assuming power [9].

In this regard, Mearsheimer has shown how the United States, throughout its history, applied the theory of aggressive Realism to establish itself as hegemonic power from the moment when it gained independence from Britain in 1783 until the Cold War period, thus preventing the Soviet Union to rule the Eurasian continent.

When the Soviet system collapsed, the United States became, in fact, the sole global superpower: the international system took the unipolar form, and the aim was to preclude the rise of any opponents to maintain that position of superiority [10].

Another approach in the realist school different from the aggressive one by Mearsheimer, which we have outlined, is that of the defensive Realism advocated by K. Walz and B, Posen [11]: according to these authors, the States to protect their survival would be more inclined to defend their position, in the international system, and less to attack. The States outcome would be to ensure possible security: the costs resulting from aggression would be enormous, and it would be appropriate to achieve a realistically possible level of security molded on moderate behavior in an overall balance of powers.

Although Realism has predictive power, it is not so popular in the West, as Mearsheimer and Stephen M. Walt recognize [12]. The realist theory holds an essentially pessimistic view, and understandably Western leaders would have trouble reaching an agreement on international targets justified by power politics, although history proves that often happened.

Nevertheless, if Realism does not enjoy a good reputation in the West, which has been the most accredited theory in the international system since the end of the Cold War? The answer is the international liberal system.

The international liberal approach, rooted in the Enlightenment tradition, relies on three key issues. First, for the Liberals, the States are key players in international politics, and certain internal features affect their conduct. A democratic country will produce good results in the international field, while a dictatorial regime will produce the worst results. Second, the willingness to cooperate of a democratic State will be amplified compared with that of an authoritarian State, which will be prone to violence and oppression to achieve its ends.

Finally, the more Liberal democrat States populate the world, the more power politics become an unusable instrument as well as an unessential factor within the international framework.

An essential condition for such a model would be to achieve a liberal economic order in which free trade and solid economic interdependence would be a safety guarantee to neutralize power politics [13].

That is precisely the foreign policy pattern the United States and the West have shaped since the end of the Cold War until now.

According to Mearsheimer, that model – unlike Realism - fits well with the idea that Americans have about themselves and the outside world: the liberal geopolitical approach, optimistic and moralistic at the same time, accords with the deep feeling of American society connecting it with the needs of the USA foreign policy [14]. Thus, the war can be viewed - obviously - as a horrible phenomenon yet acceptable, mainly when it was used for liberal purposes like to export democracy or to topple tyranny. In this perspective, the defense and expansion of liberal values and the market economy would act as positive points for pacifying the international framework [15].

According to Mearsheimer, in reality, scholars who support the international liberal system and the role of the United States in the world have performed as real realists and inspiring policies based on the power logic [16]. Indeed, with the fall of the Soviet system, it seemed that the idea that international liberal order might have been the ultimate pivot for promoting peace and prosperity worldwide; however, the liberal pattern runs exclusively in a unipolar system but not when forming a multipolar one, and it was an overlooked aspect. At that event, the liberal-democratic expansion strategy fails to preserve peace, and on the contrary, it leads to opposite effects and is doomed to fail [17].

The analysis of evolution in the international power distribution clarifies the causes which have led first to the conflict between Ukraine and Russia in 2014 and then to its second bloody phase: this raised the legitimate concern on the inadequacy of the international liberal approach, which it seems to be unable to guarantee stability, safety, and peace.

2 How Did It Get to the Current Situation?

Events occurred, and policies adopted have contributed to causing the current situation. As previously mentioned, we need to go back to the transition from communism to capitalism to understand where the current conflict has its roots. In the wake of the Soviet collapse, the liberal-democratic system represented the inevitable model to guarantee peace and cooperation between the States, thus the end of history [18]. However, expectations for the normalization of the international scenario contained elements that would have frustrated those aspirations.

The significant relevance of the historic moment led Charles Krauthammer, an influential conservative thinker, to theorize that:

> «The unipolar moment means that with the close of the century's three great Norther civil wars (World War I, World War II, and the Cold War) an ideologically pacified North seeks security and order by aligning its foreign policy behind the United States. [...] And for the near future, it is the shape of things to come» [19].

The significant changes, which were taking place in Eastern Europe, yielded a high degree of enthusiasm; however, in Russia, that sentiment was not so great in proportion. The transition from a centrally planned to a market economy entailed within the society a phase of critical issues. According to historian Paul Bushkovitch, the transition to a market economy – often implemented through savage Liberalism - brought forth a cortege of secondary effects such as social Darwinism and the spreading of criminogenic phenomena. Enormous wealth began concentrating in a few hands, often due to bribery and wild speculation, while the condition of large sections of the working classes was even more deteriorating. The capitalist shock therapy did not envisage transparency, more democracy, and mechanisms of social equalization. On the contrary, much opaqueness occurred, allowing the western community to use that country as an enormous effective money laundering method. If for the West, the Eltsin period meant the beginning of a new and normalized world, democratic and liberal, for the Russian collective imaginary, that moment was the symbol of anarchy, misery, and deep uncertainty for the nation's future [20].

In addition, the Asian financial crisis spread at the end of the 1990 s had considerable repercussions in Russia that forced a dramatic devaluation of the ruble to ensure the necessary competitiveness and productivity to the national economy: however, it did not avoid the country's default [21].

The situation was made worse with the outbreak of war in Chechnya – one of the country's major hubs of petroleum activities -, which refused any agreement with Moscow once it proclaimed its independence. From '94 to '96, the first Chechen war was a disaster for Russia and certified its downgrading as never before. During that period, the Russian Federation's international downgrading was enormous: to the social, economic, and cultural disintegration that was suffering that country [22], it joined the leading

Western role implemented by NATO [23] and was encouraged by a vast Russian process of demilitarization [24].

In the second half of '90, the excellent relations between president Eltsin and President Bill Clinton failed to neutralize the heavy tensions that were taking place: the Kosovo war and the NATO bombing of Serbia in 1999 exacerbated them. The bombing without the Un Security Council's authorization humiliated Russia, which could not support its long-standing ally, thereby confirming the evident subjection to NATO's activism. In 1999, NATO initiated a progressive eastern expansion with Poland, Hungary, and the Czech Republic. In the same year, NATO adopted a new policy. With the Alliance's New Strategic Concept [25], NATO could support operations even in areas outside of those established in 1949: the bombing of Serbia was the demonstration.

There is concern that NATO's expansion of that time was motivated by those countries' concern for the resurgent Russian imperialism: however, the weak position of Moscow ruled it out. Undoubtedly, the end of the USSR had encouraged an unusual international scenario characterized by the possibility of genuine cooperation, not only political, between Russia and the West. Nevertheless, preserving that favorable situation required the retention of the Russian weakness. However, for Russia would not be easy to remain subject to the US-led unipolar international approach if the situation had changed.

Despite the USSR's historical failure, different leaning from the Western unipolar settings had not wholly vanished, as evidenced by Yevgeny Primakov [26], first foreign minister and then premier of the Russian Federation and a fervent supporter of multipolarism. Even in the light of a new perception of the global system aroused by the attack on the Twin Towers on September 11, 2011, Primakov, in an article that appeared in Russia in Global Affairs in September 2003, reaffirmed his idea of a multipolar order, which sketched out during the time he held government positions:

> «The events of September 11 have instigated a heated confrontation between the two contrasting methods for ensuring world order. On the one hand, it is argued that the ongoing efforts to preserve the world order should be organized under the auspices of particular collective agencies, such as the United Nations. On the other hand, the U.S. is pushing forward with a singularly minded agenda of "unilateralism" where it wants to unilaterally address mankind's vital problems on the basis of Washington's biased views of the global situation» [27].

At the end of his political parable and given that, he was not enjoying good health; President Eltsin resigned from his position on December 31, 1999, appointing Vladimir V. Putin [28] as his successor. However, Putin's rise to power immediately did not produce a paradigm shift in Russian foreign policy, quite de contrary: at least until 2004, with the start of the Color Revolution, Putin showed himself significantly open to authentic collaboration policies with the West and of appeasement about NATO, especially concerning Ukrainian question [29]. By contrast, to the political openness, Western responses proved to be below expectations and were perceived from the Russian side as inadequate: This triggered the rebirth of the national consciousness, supported by large slices of widespread consensus and even markedly anti-Western [30].

That was also because, since the beginning of 2000, Russia activated an objective process of transformation and reconstruction: the economic recovery revitalized the domestic market; that produced growth as the path towards prosperity based mainly on oil and gas sales to Europe. In addition, the tourism, culture, and publishing sectors showed strong signs of an upturn, allowing the country to reappear on the international stage as an emerging power and regain an essential role after a ten-year absence [31].

The early years of 2000 were crucial for many aspects. In May 2002, in Italy in Pratica di Mare, Putin signed the Declaration of Rome, in other words, an agreement that instituted a council with 20 participants, including Russia. It was a strategic partnership with NATO to build «a harmonious coordination of actions in many areas opens up broad opportunities for creating a common security space from Vancouver to Vladivostok» as Putin stressed [32]; yet, the American invasion of Iraq in 2003 cleared the emerging spirit of cooperation. Iraq was charged with weapons of mass destruction and to protect Al Qaeda; the evidence was false, and - bypassing the ONU - the George W. Bush administration invaded Iraq. The Russian perception of U.S. aggression was proof of unipolarism and indeed not a counter-terrorism action; in addition, Russia interpreted U.S.'s military action as interference in the Middle East for destabilizing many States such as Syria, Iraq, and Iran, which represented for Russia as a protective cordon.

In 2004, the expansion process of NATO continued with the inclusion of Estonia, Latvia, Lithuania, Slovakia, Bulgaria, and Slovenia: for some countries of Central and Eastern Europe, the enlargement process added, as a complement, an increasing ideological challenge towards Russia. In creating a multipolar order, the interest and national sovereignty became a cornerstone of the Russian Federation's policy, which often declined politically and socially in a conservative direction [33].

The renewed willingness for autonomy and redefinition of international order exposed the Russian Federation to a confrontation between two conflicting worldviews, even with the introduction of moral considerations. From the Russian's point of view, the collision became evident with the Western vision and liberal-democratic values: it could not guarantee international security, even more claimed by the new emerging poles. Putin's speech in Munich in 2007 was significant in delineating a new approach: «I want to emphasize this – no one feels safe! Because no one can feel that international law is like a stone wall that will protect them. Of course, such a policy stimulates an arms race. The force's dominance inevitably encourages a number of countries to acquire weapons of mass destruction».

With that speech, the president of the Russian Federation refused to be acquiescent toward the unipolar approach and even depicted the Western order as lacking in moral foundation:

> «However, what is a unipolar world? However, one might embellish this term, at the end of the day it refers to one type of situation, namely one center of authority, one center of force, one center of decision-making. It is world in which there is one master, one sovereign. In addition, at the end of the day this is pernicious not only for all those within this system, but also for the sovereign itself because it destroys itself from within.
>
> Moreover, this certainly has nothing in common with democracy. Because, as you know, democracy is the power of the majority in light of the interests and opinions

of the minority. [...] I consider that the unipolar model is not only unacceptable but also impossible in today's world. In addition, this is not only because if there were individual leadership in todays – and precisely in today's – world, then the military, political and economic resources would not suffice. What is even more important is that the model itself is flawed because at its basis there is and can be no moral foundations for modern civilization» [34].

Signs of explicit impatience coming from Putin, especially on security issues, found little attention from the Western side, and indeed, in response, in August 2008, U.S. Secretary of State Condoleezza Rice and Polish Foreign Minister Sikorsky signed a bilateral agreement to build a U.S. base in Poland for the installation of long-range ballistic missiles. Besides, the official motivation from the Western side was that the installation of the missiles would contain threats from Iran; however, Moscow-again-perceived that project as a direct threat. The following year, President Obama withdrew the project in his first term, but it was re-started in 2011 and is currently nearing completion in Redzikovo in northern Poland [35].

The 2008 was also an important year for the issue involving Georgia. The affair involving the former Soviet country was similar to what would happen a few years later in Ukraine. With the 2008 Bucharest Summit, NATO declared that it would accommodate the Euro-Atlantic aspirations of Ukraine and Georgia to become members of the Alliance [36]. Putin, a guest at that summit, opposed NATO's intentions, however, causing no effect on the Western line, especially considering Russia too weak to stop it [37]. At that point, the Russian Federation intervened militarily in Georgia to defend the self-proclaimed republics of South Ossetia and Abkhazia (which proclaimed independence as early as 1992) and moved toward Tbilisi, the Georgian capital, as a warning and to mark a red line.

The picture of international relations between the West and Russia should be complete with other circumstances to understand the process that led to the Russian-Ukraine conflict. In particular, it relates to the NATO bombing of Libya and the overthrow of Qaddafi, and then to the war in Syria: that war also began in 2011 and saw Russia's direct participation, in 2015, in defense of Syrian President Bashar al Assad, who was in danger of being overthrown by pro-American rebels coalesced with the Islamic State established in Raqqa since 2014. To the lack of space, we will not examine those events, but below is given a part of a powerful speech by Putin delivered at the U.N. General Assembly two days before the military intervention. He warned the United States against continuing with its unipolar approach also to avoid the risk of falling into a generalized conflict that would end the current system of international:

«We all know that after the end of the Cold War the world was left with one center of dominance, and those who found themselves at the top of the pyramid were tempted to think that, since they are so powerful and exceptional, they know best what needs to be done and thus they don't need to reckon with the UN, which, instead of rubber-stamping the decisions they need, often stands in their way. That's why they say that the UN has run its course and is now obsolete and outdated. Of course, the world changes, and the UN should also undergo natural transformation. Russia is ready to work together with its partners to develop the UN further based on a broad consensus, but we consider any attempts to undermine the legitimacy of the United Nations as extremely dangerous. They may result in the collapse of the entire architecture of international relations, and then indeed there will be no rules left except for the rule of force. The world will be dominated by selfishness rather than collective effort, by dictate rather than equality and liberty, and instead of truly independent states we will have protectorates controlled from outside» [38].

The analysis of the last two decades is vital to understanding what happened on February 24, 2022, which was not a bolt unexpectedly. It was indeed the possible conclusion of a process studded with difficulties in relations with the West, or rather between the United States and the Russian Federation. Nevertheless, it was also a period of concrete dialogue that, at certain moments, had new momentum with both the experience of President Obama and the presidency of Donald Trump [39].

3 The International Liberal System: The Ideological Battle

To international tensions mentioned above joined a new source of instability arising from diverse factors, such as when Russia had to compete with the phenomenon of the so-called colored revolutions [40]. The occurrence of those movements involved the countries belonging to the former Soviet space and especially Georgia and Ukraine: with this last, the situation deteriorated so much to provoke, in 2014, the outbreak of the first violent crisis resulting in the annexation of Crimea to Russia and the separatist conflict in the Ukrainian region of Donbass [41]. In 2014, in addition to the countermeasures the West established against Russia regarding economic sanctions, a strong resurgence of the ideological battle increased, unusual since the end of the Cold War. Russian attitude on the Ukrainian issue led Western politicians, also supported by various scholars, to a prognosis that envisaged a kind of regression of Putin's regime toward an authoritarian, repressive, if not openly, fascist system [42]. Not for nothing, as mentioned earlier, the ideological element plays a prominent role in the concept of the international liberal order especially concerning the expansion of democratic values.

According to scholars Alexei Miller and Fyodor Lukyanov, Western criticism about Putin's Russia had turned into outright demonization. However, not much on concrete issues of international politics, as on the diversity of values from the Western system. As a result, the representation of the Russian government, in the eyes of the West, was something of an international headquarters coordinator and financier, at the same time, of all those forces and political expressions that worldwide were declared as non-liberal or even anti-liberal: the aim was to foment an intense political-ideological battle for protecting Western values [43].

The overriding purpose was to demonstrate the radical diversity between the two value systems, emphasizing a supposed non-reconcilability between the Russian and Western worlds.

Vladimir Putin did not shy away from the logic of ideological confrontation, which he sought to use for opposite purposes by making it an essential element of various public occasions [44].

On the one hand, non-Russian or Westernized Russian scholars attempted to interpret the difficulties of interlocution between the Western and Russian worlds by resorting to the chronic and atavistic backwardness of the latter. On the other hand, there were other currents more inclined to appreciate the differences as a natural consequence of Russian ideology characterized by its own identity and historical specificities rooted deep within the Eurasian entity [45].

This cultural approach, whose origins date back to the late 1800s with the figures of N. Danilevsky and M. Leont'ev, forerunners of classical Eurasianism in the 1920 s–30 s, has not exhausted its propulsive momentum and has survived the collapse of the Soviet system to reappear in the present day. Some aspects of that debate, while not simplifiable and which should be placed in proper perspective, had political repercussions on partnership models with some former Soviet countries. Since 2011, Russia has sponsored the construction of the Eurasian Customs Union, on the pattern of the European Union, and which then was finalized in 2015 with the Eurasian Economic Union [46]; the explicit goal in a multipolar perspective, was to build an economic and strategic alliance with countries disengaged from the pattern of cosmopolitan Liberalism.

By the way, the main characteristic, not-only narrative, of Vladimir Putin's period is the centrality of the concept of national sovereignty in union with references to traditional values [47] but in a complex articulation where even the concept of democracy would not be absent, as demonstrated by a speech he gave at July 20, 2022, at the forum Strong Ideas for a New Time of the Agency for Strategic Initiative:

> «Sovereignty is about freedom of national development, and thus, the development of every individual. It is about the technological, cultural, intellectual and educational solvency of a state – that is what it is. No doubt, responsible, active, nationally minded, and nationally oriented civil society is the most important component of sovereignty.
>
> I am convinced that in order to be strong, independent, and competitive, we need to improve the mechanisms for people to participate in the country's life and to make them more open and fairer. That includes mechanisms for direct democracy and people's involvement in addressing the critical problems facing society and the public» [48].

On the sovereignty issue and State survival, Putin's speech on January 15, 2020, before the Russian Federal Assembly was noteworthy:

> «Russia can be and can remain Russia only as a sovereign state. Our nation's sovereignty must be unconditional. We have done a great deal to achieve this. We have restored our State's unity. We have overcome the situation when oligarch clans essentially usurped certain Powers in the government. Russia has returned to international politics as a country whose opinion cannot be ignored. We have created powerful reserves, improving our country's stability and its capability to protect its citizens' social rights and the national economy from any attempts of foreign pressure» [49].

The reasons that guided Western policy, with the support of part of the international academic community, to describe the Putin regime as an alternative to liberal democracy seem clear also by taking into consideration the contents of an article by J.J. Mearsheimer on the ideological forms of a unipolar international order:

> «The key issue is whether the unipole has a universalistic ideology, one that assumes that its political system should be exported to other countries. If the unipole makes this assumption, the world order will be ideological. The sole pole, in other words, will try to spread its ideology everywhere and remake the world in its own image [...] Liberalism, of course, contains within it a powerful universalistic strand, which stems from its emphasis on the importance of individual rights. The liberal story, which is individualistic t its core, maintains that every person has a set of inalienable or natural rights. As such, liberals tend to be deeply concerned about the rights of people worldwide, regardless of which country they live in. Thus, if the unipole is a liberal democracy, it is almost certain to create an international order that aims to reshape the world in its own image» [50].

It is therefore evident that under Putin's leadership, Russia has re-positioned itself as a power in the international arena, and it produced resistance from the West; on that front, the security issue has persisted with its unipolar approach, and to protect that vision they made use of ideological means.

The following section will present certain aspects of how the confrontation between Russia and the West has developed based on ideological categories with the employment of accusations of neo-imperialism, illiberalism, and even fascism and what the actors were.

4 Forms of Historical Revisionism

Zbigniew Brzezinski was the first in 2004 to use an impressive juxtaposition toward the Russian leadership by comparing Putin to the figure of Mussolini. However, without mincing words, Hillary Clinton, Secretary of State in the Obama administration, used the category of fascism to define the nature of the Russian regime during the first Russian-Ukrainian crisis in 2014 that led to the annexation of Crimea to the Russian Federation. Later, part of the Western academia had no scruples in using the category of fascism against Russia, which, from being an object of research for comparative purposes, ended up becoming a political tool of delegitimization [51].

Together with the predictions raised in the international arena about a return of fascism, another phenomenon seemed to corroborate them: the rapid electoral rise in Europe and the United States of populist and sovereignist movements sparked concern, often situated on radical right-wing positions, but not just to the right, mainly because they were bearers of intense criticism of the Western liberal democratic system and institutions [52].

The contestation of the Western value system by those radical political phenomena that the traditional political taxonomy would have placed in the right radicalism activated a general alarm bell about the return of fascism enough to employ this category as a bogeyman to counter better any element that challenged the model based on liberal democratic values [53].

The outlook of the danger of fascism, even rising from inside the Western democracies, combined with Russian international assertiveness, declined according to a vision so different from Western universalist conceptions. Thus, as the idea of the normalization of Russia disappeared, the countermeasures materialized with the resumption of solid ideological conflict.

The countries of East Central Europe, also moved by the need to ensure their security, which they perceived as unstable, were protagonists in a cultural battle oriented toward a new historical narrative and alternative to the dominant Russian one, prevalent since the end of World War II.

The revisionist intent became evident on January 25, 2006, when the Parliamentary Assembly of the Council of Europe adopted Resolution No. 1481/2006 entitled "Need for international condemnation of crimes of totalitarian communist regimes" [54].

In connection with that, various political forces amended this Resolution, ensuring an explicit equation between Nazism and Communism was not explicit - as would have wished the Baltic States, Bulgaria, Ukraine, and the Czech Republic. However, it did hold a call to all member States, particularly the various communist or post-communist parties, for a profound re-examination of the history of past regimes so that they would distance themselves appropriately and unambiguously [55].

The process of historical reinterpretation continued in 2008 with the approval of a Declaration by the European Parliament based on Resolution 1481/2006 of the Parliamentary Assembly of the Council of Europe: with the Declaration, the Parliament affirmed that « the mass deportations, murders and enslavements committed in the context of the acts of aggression by Stalinism and Nazism fall into the category of war crimes and crimes against humanity» therefore, as the day in 1939 when was signed the non-aggression pact between Nazi Germany and the Soviet Union [56] was August 23, that day was proclaimed as «day of Remembrance for Victims of Stalinism and Nazism, in order to preserve the memory of the victims of mass deportations and exterminations, and at the same time rooting democracy more firmly and reinforcing peace and stability in our continent» [57]. Parliament justified the equating of Nazism and Stalinism by the fact that «the influence and significance of the Soviet order and occupation on and for citizens of the post-Communist States [were] little known in Europe» [58].

Parliament justified the equating of Nazism and Stalinism by the fact that.

The Molotov-Ribbentrop Pact became a means to break up the political legitimacy of the Successor State of the Soviet Union and to involve it as a participant and accomplice of the Third Reich's responsibility for the outbreak of World War II. Nonetheless, this argument would have been on a collision course with the traditional Russian interpretation: Nonetheless, this argument would have been on a collision course with the traditional Russian interpretation: Russia continued to recognize itself among the powers that defeated Nazism with the sacrifice of millions of lives. That belief settled in Russian common sense to the point that it became a factor of national foundational, and in addition, according to the Russian position, responsibility or complicity should have been sought in those collaborationist components widely present in Central and Eastern European countries during the period of German occupation [59]. It became clear that the looming conflict would not be easy to resolve.

In 2009, another European institution, the Organization for Security and Cooperation in Europe (OSCE), contributed in support of the European Parliament's positions. With the Vilnius document, the parallels between Hitler's regime and that of Stalin became even more evident because those regimes «brought about genocide, violations of human rights and freedoms, war crimes and crimes against humanity». Vilnius Declaration of the OSCE Parliamentary Assembly and Resolutions Adopted at the Eighteenth Annual Session on 29 June to 3 July 2009, https://www.oscepa.org/en/documents/annual-sessions/2009-vilnius/declaration-6/261-2009-vilnius-declaration-eng/file.

In 2019, ten years after the OSCE pronouncement, the European Parliament - as usual - under the pressure of some Central and Eastern European countries - passed a Resolution on the importance of European remembrance for the future of Europe in which it reaffirmed the condemnation of all totalitarianism combining the historical experience of Nazism with that of Soviet communism [61].

Vladimir Putin commented on that Resolution as groundless and shameless lies. Nevertheless, according to Putin, at the «attempts to distort this historical truth [about the WWII]» to the «heirs of Nazi accomplices joined them, now it has come to some quite respectable international institutions and European structures» [62].

5 Conclusion

This chapter highlighted how the policies of NATO enlargement to the East have combined ideological battles based on historical revisionism. The liberal international order - by its nature - acting on the two planes intended to extend and gradually homogenize the East society to Western Europe society but not to counteract Russian expansionist aspirations of which there is no evidence [63]. Neo-imperialist attempts did not characterize Russia in the era of the 2008 Bucharest summit, and NATO, equally, wanted to proceed with its will to East enlargement. Yet, Western intentions negatively affected Russian perceptions because of that evolution, and Angela Merkel and Nicolas Sarkozy realized what kind of danger might arise from it [64].

Starting from the first Russian-Ukrainian crisis in 2014, the United States provided substantial military support in supplying weapons and training Ukraine to use them, and NATO's commitment was gradual but steady. Besides, in 2021, the Alliance launched a massive campaign of military exercises in which Ukraine always participated. All this placed the relations between the West and the Russian Federation on a dangerous inclined plane that would degenerate into Russian aggression in February 2022.

Hence, it seems clear that in international politics, the security of States is a crucial element strictly related to the policies of other States: security and the extent of its perception by other States become a decisive factor for international stability or it is opposite [65].

From the end of the Cold War to the present, realist theory has revealed a considerable power to predict tensions and conflicts in a more high-performance manner than liberal or neoconservative theory: however, advocates of Realism remain largely absent from mainstream information, and they have little chance of guiding government choices and public opinion sentiment [66].

References

1. Walt, S.M.: What would a Realist world have looked like?, in Foreign Policy (2016). https://foreignpolicy.com/2016/01/08/what-would-a-realist-world-have-looked-like-iraq-syria-iran-obama-bush-clinton/
2. Mearsheimer., J.J.: La tragedia delle grandi potenze (Luiss University Press, Italian Trans.). (p.31). (Original work published 2001). The Tragedy of Great Power Politics, New York: W.W. Norton & Company (2019).
3. Mearsheimer., J.J.: La tragedia delle grandi potenze (Luiss University Press). New York: W.W. Norton & Company. (Original work published 2001). pp. 32 (2019)
4. Morgenthau, H.J. (2017). Politica tra le nazioni. La lotta per il potere e la Pace (Luiss University Press). (pp.81). (Fifth ed., New York: Alfred A. Knopf, 1978)
5. Frenkel, B.: Restating the realist case: An introduction. (1996). https://doi.org/10.1080/09636419608429274
6. Mearsheimer., J.J.: La tragedia delle grandi potenze (Luiss University Press). (p. 380). New York: W.W. Norton & Company. (Original work published 2001) (2019).
7. Mearsheimer., J.J.: La tragedia delle grandi potenze (Luiss University Press). (p. 381). New York: W.W. Norton & Company. (Original work published 2001) (2019).
8. Mearsheimer., J.J.: La tragedia delle grandi potenze (Luiss University Press). (p. 33). New York: W.W. Norton & Company. (Original work published 2001) (2019).
9. Mearsheimer., J.J.: La tragedia delle grandi potenze (Luiss University Press). (pP. 381–382). New York: W.W. Norton & Company. (Original work published 2001) (2019).
10. Mearsheimer., J.J.: La tragedia delle grandi potenze (Luiss University Press). (pp. 384–385). New York: W.W. Norton & Company. (Original work published 2001) (2019).
11. Waltz, K.N.: Theory of International Politics. McGraw-Hill (1979)
12. Walt, S.M.: Why do people hate Realism so much? (2022). https://foreignpolicy.com/2022/06/13/why-do-people-hate-realism-so-much/
13. Mearsheimer, J.J.: Bound to Fail, The Rise and fall of the Liberal International. Order (2019). https://doi.org/10.1162/isec_a_00342
14. Mearsheimer, J.J.: La tragedia delle grandi potenze (Luiss University Press), pp. 53–54 (2019). New York: W.W. Norton & Company. (Original work published 2001).
15. Mearsheimer, J.J. (2019). La tragedia delle grandi potenze (Luiss University Press). (pp. 54-55). New York: W.W. Norton & Company. (Original work published 2001).
16. Mearsheimer, J.J. (2019). La tragedia delle grandi potenze (Luiss University Press). (pp. 55-56). New York: W.W. Norton & Company. (Original work published 2001).
17. Mearsheimer, J.J. (2019). Bound to Fail, The Rise and fall of the Liberal International Order. . https://doi.org/10.1162/isec_a_00342
18. Fukuyama, F.: La fine della storia e l'ultimo uomo (UTET, Italian Trans.). The End Of History and the Last Man New York: Free Press (2020). (Original work published 1992)
19. Krauthammer, C.: The Unipolar Moment. Foreign Affairs, 70 (1). America and the World, 1990/1991, p. 25 (1990)
20. Bushkovitch, P.: Breve storia della Russia, Dalle origini a Putin. Einaudi. (pp. 523–524). See also BARTLETT, R. (2005). A History of Russia. Palgrave Macmillan (pp.288–291); Shekhovtsov, A. (2018). Russia and the Western Far Right, Tango Noir. New York: Routledge. For aspects of the transition to a market economy in Russia in the early 1990s, see also EBRD (European bank for reconstruction and development), 1994–2008. London: Transition report. Shleifer, A. Treisman, D. (2004). A normal country. in Foreign Affairs, March/April 2004 (pp. 20–38) (2013)

21. The default that the Russian government had to declare in the summer of 1998 was a severe blow for Russia; among other things, a year later the Interior Ministry estimated that 40 percent of the Russian economy was in the hands of crime along with about 50 percent of the banks. See., di Nolfo, E. (2000). Storia delle relazioni internazionali 1918–1999. Roma-Bari. Laterza. (p.1397)
22. Bushkkovitch, P.: Breve storia della Russia, p. 524. Einaudi, Dalle origini a Putin (2013)
23. In optics of a policy of containment of the Soviet Union on April 4, 1949, in Washington with the participation of twelve countries, the United States, Canada, Great Britain, France, Belgium, Holland, Luxembourg, Portugal, Italy, Norway, Iceland, and Denmark, signed the North Atlantic Treaty. In August 1949, with the end of the atomic monopoly and the proclamation of the People's Republic of China, the US administration wanted to take measures to update the containment policy. A debate ensued that would lead in April 1950 to the adoption of the National Security Council. With Resolution No. 68, the basis for the subsequent militarization of the American presence in Europe, the Atlantic Pact changed into the North Atlantic Treaty Organization (*North Atlantic Treaty Organization*, NATO). See, DI NOLFO, E. (2000). Storia delle relazioni internazionali 1918–1999. Roma-Bari. Laterza. (pp.774–775)
24. Trenin, D.: The Revival of the Russian Military: How Moscow Reloaded. Foreign Affairs, **95**(3), pp. 23–29 (2016). http://www.jstor.org/stable/43946854
25. It is interesting to observe the attention that NATO gave to the Ukrainian issue back in 1999: «Ukraine occupies a special place in the Euro-Atlantic security environment and is an important and valuable partner in promoting stability and common democratic values. NATO is committed to further strengthening its distinctive partnership with Ukraine based on the NATO-Ukraine Charter, including political consultations on issues of common concern and a broad range of practical cooperation activities. The Alliance continues to support Ukrainian sovereignty and independence, territorial integrity, democratic development, economic prosperity and its status as a non-nuclear weapons state as key factors of stability and security in central and Eastern Europe and in Europe as a whole». https://www.nato.int/cps/en/natohq/official_texts_27433.htm#:~:text=At%20their%20Summit%20meeting%20in,years%20of%20the%20Cold%20War
26. Primakov, Y. was Minister of Foreign Affairs of Russian Federation between 1996 and 1998, when he became Prime Minister
27. Primakov, Y.: A World without Superpowers. Russia in Global Affairs. n.3. (2003) https://eng.globalaffairs.ru/articles/a-world-without-superpowers/
28. Laruelle, M. Radvanyi, J.: Understanding Russia, the Challenges of Transformation. Rowman&Littlefield. (pp.48–52). See also, Ivanter, V.V. Sapir, J. (2012) (2019). L'economia russa nella crisi finanziaria. Eurasia, Rivista di Studi Geopolitici, (1), Parma, 79–93
29. See the following official speeches by Vladimir Putin. http://www.en.kremlin.ru/events/president/news/41841. http://www.en.kremlin.ru/events/president/transcripts/21308. http://www.en.kremlin.ru/events/president/transcripts/21598,. http://www.en.kremlin.ru/events/president/news/43122
30. Ferrari, A.: Russian Foreign Policy between Westphalia and Greater Eurasia. Milano (2018). In: COLOMBO A. MAGRI, P. (Eds), Big Powers are Back. What about Europe? (ISPI Annual Report), p. 47. LediPublishing
31. Bushkovitch, P.: Breve storia della Russia, Dalle origini a Putin. Einaudi, pp. 527–528 (2018)
32. See, http://www.en.kremlin.ru/events/president/news/43121
33. Laruelle, M., Radvanyi, J.: Understanding Russia, the Challenges of Transformation. Rowman & Littlefield. pp. 78 (2019)
34. President Putin's Speech and the Following Discussion at the Munich Conference on Security Policy, February 10, 2007. Vladimir Putin's speech can be found in English and Russian on the Kremlin's official website http://en.kremlin.ru/events/president/transcripts/24034

35. Orsini, A.: Critica della politica internazionale. Roma: Paper First, pp. 46–49 (2022)
36. Issued by the Heads of State and Government participating in the meeting of the North Atlantic Council in Bucharest on 3 April 2008, https://www.nato.int/cps/en/natolive/official_texts_8443.htm
37. Mearshiemer, J.J.: The Causes and Consequences of the Ukraine War. (2022)https://www.russiamatters.org/analysis/causes-and-consequences-ukraine-war, Accessed 21 July 2022
38. Vladimir Putin's speech to the United Nations General Assembly on September 28, 2015. http://en.kremlin.ru/events/president/news/50385
39. According to the analysis of Dmitry Trenin, former director of the Carnegie Moscow Center, Putin bet politically on President Trump as a promoter of essential changes in the global system. President Trump's approach was founded on the politics of force and great power rivalries, thus recognizing Russia as one of the major powers in the world «[…] Trump is replacing liberal universalism with a version of great-power politics that is not focused on promoting U.S.-favored values. To be sure, it is a policy of strength, but it is clearly preferable to the policy of values, since it rests on a transactional approach to international affairs and allows for compromise. […] Thus, Putin, a consummate here-and-now politician, not only cannot afford the luxury of tuning out the Trump presidency and waiting it out: He has no reason to shun Trump. […]. Now, much of the world is following Russia's choice, including the Trump administration. This means that, for all the disparity in power and difference of interests, the Kremlin and the White House now talk the same language. And they talk». See also, D. TRENIN, Why Putin Isn't Sweating the Midterms, November 6, 2018, article originally published in Politico Magazine, currently in Carnegie Endowment for International Peace, https://carnegiemoscow.org/2018/11/06/why-putin-isn-t-sweating-midterms-pub-77663
40. By Color Revolutions, we mean a series of political and social mobilizations that affected a number of countries in the former Soviet space (Georgia, Ukraine, Kyrgyzstan). They were characterized by a marked pro-Western sentiment and in favor of deeper liberal and democratic changes
41. In November 2004, Ukrainian presidential elections are canceled due to widespread protests over suspected fraud in favor of pro-Russian Prime Minister Yanukovych, supported by outgoing President Kucma. With U.S. support, supporters of contending candidate Juscenko start the "orange revolution." The elections were repeated in December of the same year when pro-European Juscenko was elected. See, Ferrari, A. (2014). Oltre la Crimea, Russia contro Europa? Milano: Istituto per gli Studi di Politica Internazionale. See also, Laruelle, M. Radvanyi, J. (2019). Understanding Russia, the Challenges of Transformation. Rowman & Littlefield.; Cardini, F. Mini, F. (2002). La Guerra e la storia. Roma: Paper First, Roma
42. Timofeev, I.: Per una "nuova normalità" tra Russia e NATO. Limes Rivista italiana di geopolitica (9). Roma: Gruppo ed. L'Espresso, pp. 108–109 (2016)
43. Miller, A., Lukyanov, F.: Restraint Instead of Assertiveness: Russia and a New Era in World Politics (2017) https://eng.globalaffairs.ru/articles/restraint-assertiveness/
44. In a speech in September 2013 during a plenary session of the international forum of the Valdai Club and before an audience of Russian and foreign politicians, analysts and researchers, Vladimir Putin argued his thesis by also resorting to moral categories in addressing the issues of Western values: «Another serious challenge to Russia's identity is linked to events taking place in the world. Here there are both foreign policy and moral aspects. We can see how many of the Euro-Atlantic countries are actually rejecting their roots, including the Christian values that constitute the basis of Western civilization. They are denying moral principles and all traditional identities: national, cultural, religious and even sexual. They are implementing policies that equate large families with same-sex partnerships, belief in God with the belief in Satan». See also, http://en.kremlin.ru/events/president/news/19243.

45. Vittorio Strada spoke about the Russian ideological conception in a study published while the Soviet Union was collapsing: according to the author, the Russian ideology was formed by a set of tendencies and different inclinations aimed at discovering for the country an original path based on historical, geographical, social and cultural conditions that could not be reduced to the imitation of Western patterns. See, Ferrari, A. (2019). Russia and the Post-Western World, in COLOMBO, A. Magri, P. The End of a World, The Decline of the Liberal Order, ISPI Annual Report. Milano: Gruppo ed. L'Espresso. (p. 97). Regarding Russian ideology, see Strada, V. (1991). La questione russa. Identità e destino.(pp. 40–41)
46. Ferrari, A.: Russian Foreign Policy between Westphalia and Greater Eurasia. Milano: LediPublishing, pp. 48–53, (2018)
47. Alekseenkova, E.: Russia First? The New Constitution's Impact on Domestic and Foreign Policy, in Ferrari, A., Tafurro Ambrosetti, E..: Forward to the Past? New/Old Theatres of Russia's International Projection, p. 19. ISPI, LediPublishing, Milan (2020)
48. Panel discussion ASI, Strong Ideas for a New Time, July. 20 2022, http://en.kremlin.ru/events/president/news/69039
49. Putin, V.: Presidential Address to the Federal Assembly, http://en.kremlin.ru/events/president/news/62582, January 15, 2020, also mentioned by ALEKSEENKOVA, E. Russia First? The New Constitution's Impact on Domestic and Foreign Policy, in Ferrari, A. Tafurroo Ambrosetti, E. (2020) Forward to the Past? New/Old Theatres of Russia's International Projection. Milan: Ispi, LediPublishing, pp.19 (2020)
50. Mearsheimer, J.J.: Bound to Fail, The Rise and Fall of the Liberal International Order, in International Security, Vol.43, n.4, pp. 7–50, https://doi.org/10.1162/isec_a_00342
51. Laruelle, M.: Is Russia Fascist?, p. 3. Cornell University Press, Unraveling Propaganda East and West (2021)
52. Taggart, P.: I nuovi partiti populisti nell'Europa occidentale, In M. TARCHI (a cargo de), Anatomia del populismo, Antologia della rivista Trasgressioni, Diana Edizioni, pp.338–340 (2019)
53. The theme of the imminent fascist danger was used in connection with different figures, such as those of Donald Trump, Angela Merkel, y Vladimir Putin or between Israel and the Islamic world with reciprocal accusations of racism, due to segregationist policies or similar policies to those of Nazi extermination. See, LARUELLE, M: Is Russia Fascist?, p. 19. Cornell University Press. p, Unraveling Propaganda East and West (2021)
54. http://assembly.coe.int/nw/xml/XRef/Xref-XML2HTML-en.asp?fileid=17403&lang=en consultado 19 mayo 2022

55. Malksoo, M.: Criminalizing Communism: Transnational Mnemopolitics in Europe. In International Political Sociology (2014). https://doi.org/10.1111/ips.12041.pp.82-99
56. Between July and the first two weeks of: because of the strengthening relations between Poland, Britain, and France - Hitler felt his isolation increasing and wanted to complete military plans to invade Poland before Britain and the United States could activate the military apparatus for war purposes. What Stalin was interested in instead was to counter the level of weakening that occurred in 1938. According to the Soviet leader, the new appeasement policies would bring the danger closer to the borders of the Soviet Union; he, therefore, thought cynically of taking advantage of conflicts within the capitalist countries as Lenin did in 1922 with the Treaty of Rapallo. On August 23, the non-Aggression Pacts were signed, which contained a general political scope (refraining from carrying out mutual acts of aggression, not providing aid to those who attacked the other party, and future consultations on problems of common interest), along with additional secret protocols. The Pact represented the reversal of alliances, and the secret protocols indicated the spheres of influence that the two sides established relative to Eastern Europe. The first article dealt with the area of the Baltic States and established Lithuania's northern border, representing the boundary between Soviet and German influence. The second article referred to Poland and placed the border between the two areas between the Narew, Vistula, and San rivers. The problem of maintaining an independent Polish state whose boundaries would be decided later. The third article affirmed Soviet interest in Bessarabia and the Reich's total disinterest regarding that area. The fourth article confirmed the total secrecy of the protocol. See, E. DI NOLFO, Storia delle relazioni internazionali 1918–1999. Laterza, Roma-Bari **2000**, 297–299 (August 1929)
57. Declaration of the European Parliament on the proclamation of 23 August as European Day of Remembrance for Victims of Stalinism and Nazism , https://www.europarl.europa.eu/doceo/document/TA-6-2008-0439_EN.html
58. Frenkel, B.: Restating the realist case: An introduction (1996). https://doi.org/10.1080/09636419608429274
59. Laruelle, M.: Is Russia Fascist?, p. 2. Cornell University Press, Unraveling Propaganda East and West (2021)
60. Frenkel, B.: Restating the realist case: An introduction (1996). https://doi.org/10.1080/09636419608429274
61. European Parliament resolution of 19 September 2019 on the importance of European remembrance for the future of Europe, https://www.europarl.europa.eu/doceo/document/TA-9-2019-0021_EN.html
62. Vladimir Putin's statement, Interfax, December 11, 2019, https://www.interfax.ru/world/687610, accessed June 12, 2022
63. Mearsheimer, J.J.: The Causes and Consequences of the Ukraine War. Horizons: Journal of International Relations and Sustainable Development, 21, 12–27 (2022). https://www.jstor.org/stable/48686693
64. See https://www.reuters.com/article/us-nato/ukraine-and-georgia-face-uphill-battle-on-nato-bid-idUSL0179714620080401, and https://www.dw.com/en/angela-merkel-opens-up-on-ukraine-putin-and-her-legacy/a-62052345
65. Walt, S.M.: An International Relations Theory Guide to the War in Ukraine, in Foreign Policy. (2022)https://foreignpolicy.com/2022/03/08/an-international-relations-theory-guide-to-ukraines-war/
66. Walt, S.M.: What a Realist World Have Looked Like, in Foreign Policy (2016). https://foreignpolicy.com/2016/01/08/what-would-a-realist-world-have-looked-like-iraq-syria-iran-obama-bush-clinton/

Far East Challenges

China's Borderless Expansionism. Could Be a Threat to International Security?

Juan-José Delgado-Morán[1(✉)], Claudio-Augusto Payá-Santos[2], and Roger Sanz-Gonzalez[3]

[1] Universidad Pablo de Olavide, Sevilla, Spain
jjdelmor@upo.es
[2] Cátedra Universitaria de Inteligencia académica, Alicante, Spain
info@catedrainteligenciaacademica.com
[3] Universidad Isabel I de Castilla, Burgos, Spain
roger.sanz@ui1.es

Abstract. In recent decades, China has established itself as a world economic power. While some Western countries question the leadership of their rulers, and weak governments are created, with little capacity for action, China is the only one of the five world powers that maintains an authoritarian regime, and the Government admits that the establishment of control measures helps to the growth of the country. While it is debated to become the first world power, it is worth asking if the absence of freedoms is one more boost to the development of the Asian country outside its borders. China´s strategy is going based on advance quietly, without attracting the attention of other opponents. This advance is aided by controlled public opinion within the borders. While the actions of democratic countries are influenced by the media, in China that does not count. Henry Kissinger in an article published in The Washington Post in the summer of 2009 already announced that "the axis that forms the backbone of the world is no longer the Atlantic", but the Pacific. Two powers dispute hegemony: that of democracy, although "imperfect" and that of the authoritarian system. There is no doubt that the world is at a crossroads towards something new. In this, it is worth asking if greater democracy is synonymous with more risks. The Polish sociologist Zygmunt Bauman (1925–2017) already anticipated it when he said that greater control translates into greater security and balance; while the more freedom a country has, its insecurity increases (Bauman 2006). Are China and the United States within these statements? Will a new world order be possible without a confrontation between them? To what extent do their government structures influence economic expansionism? Asia has long ceased to be the Far East, and its importance is increasingly decisive on the board. The Polish sociologist Zygmunt Bauman (1925–2017) confronts the concepts of security and freedom. The dilemma applied to the Chinese case has its own connotations, clarifying that it is an exceptional case. The China system supports strong contradictions that make the analysis interesting. While security within its borders has gradually increased, its expansionism abroad has positioned it as an emerging power, and has opened the way to new markets.

Keyword: China · Freedoms · Expansionism · Legislation · Authoritarianism

J. Cayón Peña and J. M. Ramírez (Eds.): *Threats to Peace and International Security: Asia versus West*, ASTSA, pp. 81–96, 2023.
https://doi.org/10.1007/978-3-031-28336-9_5

1 National Legislative Framework "Short Life to the Constitution"

The Chinese republic federal constitution approved on 4tf December 1982, by the Fifth Assembly and contains the core system Principles on which the current Chinese system is based. However, the duration of the previous constitutions in the Asian country did not cover a great period of time. In less than 30 years, it had four different constitutions, which correspond to the political stages that the country has gone through. The idea of creating a first constitution arose after the 1949 Revolution. It was at that moment that the Chinese Communist Party took hold and marked the ideological doctrine of the system. A short time later, in 1954, the first Constitution was established, which was in force for almost two decades, until in 1975, in the IV Assembly, a new order was approved. It is the most radical constitution and places imperialism and socio-imperialism as threats. It uses belligerent language against foreign enemies (Russia and the US) and also against its own internal enemies.

After the death of Mao Zedong (1976), the Fifth Assembly approved the 1978 Constitution. Although this text speaks of equal rights between men and women, in its article 53 it grants the State, among other issues, birth planning. The validity of the text was not long, since in 1982 the new Constitution was created, still in force. Not free of modifications, the current text has been amended five times: 1988, 1993, 1999, 2004 and 2018.

1.1 Conceptual Framework Limitations

Chapter III of the Chinese Constitution, in its Sect. 2, includes the foundations by which the President of the Republic must be governed. Both he and the vice president are elected by the National People's Assembly, the supreme body of state power and which exercises the country's legislative power. The renewal of the deputies of the Assembly occurs every five years and has a permanent body, which is the Permanent Council of the National People's Assembly. The reform of the Constitution must be made at the proposal of the Permanent Committee or at the proposal of more than 1/5 of the deputies of the Assembly. In addition to electing the president, it is the function of the Assembly to reform the Constitution and also supervise its fulfillment. Its powers are very clear within the Chinese legal system, and, just as it has the power to appoint the president, also that of the heads of the ministries, that of the president of the Central Military Commission, or that of the Supreme People's Court, among many others.

The last reform carried out by the Assembly, approved in March 2018, eliminates the term limit, since the 1982 Constitution established that no president could be perpetuated in government for more than two periods of five years. Xi Jinping, the current president, who became president of the country in 2013, will be able to stay in power beyond 2023 with the new reform. He thus accumulates the greatest power in decades. The proposal was approved by eliminates the term limit, since the 1982 Constitution established that no president could be perpetuated in government for more than two five-year terms. Xi Jinping, the current president, who became president of the country in 2013, will be able to stay in power beyond 2023 with the new reform.

He thus accumulates the greatest power in decades. The proposal was approved by eliminates the term limit, since the 1982 Constitution established that no president could be perpetuated in government for more than two five-year terms. Xi Jinping, the current president, who became president of the country in 2013, will be able to stay in power beyond 2023 with the new reform. He thus accumulates the greatest power in decades. The proposal was approved by2,958 votes in favor, two against and three abstentions.

1.2 The Political Control Reflected in a 21st Century Regulatory Framework

After the 1949 revolution, the Communist Party exercises control over all institutions. Its policies have been adapted to the different situations and the necessary reforms have been carried out at all times for the survival of the system. Control over the population has been decisive since the mid-twentieth century to the present. Behind the policies undertaken by the Government is always the Party, it should be remembered that the president of China is also the general secretary of the Chinese Communist Party. The system, in short, controls everything. Some laws have been reformed according to new developments or circumstances.

1.2.1 National Security Law (2015)

This legal framework approved in July 2015, manifests, once again, the domination of the Communist Party over the institutions in China. It gives powers to the State over the domain of the digital space and its corresponding development. Likewise, the Law includes government control over scientific development and international cooperation. It also considers that a greater response to nuclear threats is necessary. The National Security is defined in these legislative rules as a "condition in which the government of a country, its sovereignty, unity and territorial integrity, the welfare of its people, the sustainable development of its economy and society and other major interests are relatively secure. And are not subject to internal or external threats" (Xinhua 2015).

The NGO (Non-governmental organization) *Amnesty International* consistently consider that Law would further limit freedoms inside and outside the country. Of the 155 members entitled to vote on this Law in China, an overwhelming majority voted in favor of this Law, with only one abstaining.

1.2.2 Counterterrorism Law (2015)

In December 2015, China passed the first counterterrorism Law in its entire history. Processed by the National Popular Assembly, it once again gives broad powers to the Government. It even imposes restrictions on reporting terrorist acts (EFE 2015). Until now, China relied on regulations such as the Criminal Law or the Emergency Response Law in the absence of an Anti-Terrorism Law as such. One of the main problems of the Law is the obligation for companies to provide the Government with access to all their procedures. In this way, all its internal functioning can be controlled by the Government. Similarly, companies are required with servers and user data in China to provide the authorities with the records of their information, encryption codes and to censor any content linked to terrorism. Institutions or individuals may not generate or disclose information on terrorist incidents. With this law, China also opens up the opportunity to participate abroad, and send soldiers to fight against terrorism.

1.2.3 Cybersecurity Law (2017)

The Cybersecurity Law, which came into force in May 2017, was no less controversial for the Asian country. Foreign complaints did not take long to appear due to possible limitations on their business possibilities. According to the Government and the Chinese authorities, this Law is about safeguarding data protection, as announced at the time by the country's authorities. However, what might seem positive, goes back into the limitations on users and government control. In this way, users are prohibited, by means of this Law, from publishing content on the Internet that threatens the national honor of the country or that affects the socialist system, or the economic and social order.

As for companies, the legislation includes periodic security reviews for those entities that operate in key sectors of the country. This set off all the alarms about the possibility of industrial espionage or an attempt by the country to attack industrial property.

The entities, national or foreign, are obliged, according to this Law, to store the data obtained in China on servers that are within the Chinese national territory. In the case of wanting to transfer data abroad that involves more than a million and a half people, they must submit it to a security review.

1.2.4 National Intelligence Law (2017)

This law constitutes one of the greatest concerns for the countries that dispute hegemony with China (Delgado and Teano 2019; Liz 2021). Any person, institution or company of Chinese nationality is obliged to collaborate and assist public security in the terms that the government determines through legislation. In this way, it is worth reflecting on whether the obligations applied to Chinese interests are not limited to what is under its territorial domain and, therefore, as the Dr Scot, the law allows intelligence agencies to insist on these aspects with the warning of potential non-compliance with the laws and that, under the historical context of the actions of said government agencies, it is a serious risk for Chinese society both because it means that not only Chinese citizens are obligated subjects (Payá and Luque 2021).

In the same vein, it should be understood that the different alerts from counterintelligence agencies about, for example, technological giants such as Huawei may have a high degree of commitment of interests, directly or indirectly, due to the applicability of the law extraterritorially.

2 Bauman's Sociology Applied to the Chinese Case

Two images recently went viral in China. The first of them is framed in 1901, in the signing of the Bóxer or Xinchou protocol, by the Japanese photographer Y Sui Tsu. The image shows the ministers of different countries in front of the Chinese negotiators. In this black and white photograph, China is represented by elderly men, while the rest of the countries have a more youthful appearance. This snapshot has gone viral on social networks compared to another more recent one. In the second, the Chinese show a youthful appearance, while the Westerners are the ones who transmit old age. These two images do not fail to represent the reality of the change that the country has experienced. China has changed the world. Now it is a country that grows and expands.

The strategy he maintains, with its imperfections, it brings the regime closer to its world hegemony. Along this path, it is fighting to be closer to the United States, its main competitor. One is closer to democracy, another to authoritarianism. At this point, it is worth asking if the authoritarian system gives China an advantage in maintaining further expansion (Delgado et al. 2020a).

The Polish sociologist Zygmunt Bauman (1925–2017) confronts the concepts of security and freedom. The greater the freedom, according to what he explains, the less security would be. On the other hand, when security is greater, freedom could be reduced (Bauman 2006). This statement can be applied to the Chinese case, clarifying that it is an exceptional case. His system maintains strong contradictions that make the analysis interesting. While security within its borders has gradually increased, its expansionism abroad has positioned it as an emerging power and has opened the way to new markets.

According to Bauman's theory, China has maintained control, and with it, communal values in domestic perspective of action. If the Polish sociologist warns that the Internet and the new information possibilities have squandered communal barriers, China has taken special care to curb them and impose limits on its territory (Payá and Delgado 2016).

What is really admirable is that the country has managed to establish itself as the second world economy, without relinquishing control of its borders in each and every one of the areas in which the stability of the regime could manifest any danger.

2.1 Increase of Internal Control Capabilities

That China has had an iron control on its borders is not new. As an authoritarian system, which it is, it maintains its own characteristics. The 1978 Constitution in its first article defines it as "a socialist state of popular democratic dictatorship, led by the working class and based on the worker-peasant alliance".

Not much further, at that same point in the Magna Carta, it is stated that the socialist system is the basic pillar of the People's Republic of China and prohibits "all sabotage by any organization or individual against the socialist system." There is no room for interpretation of what the Magna Carta says. The Chinese are bound to accept the socialist system and are explicitly prohibited from challenging it. State control responds to the interests of the Communist Party (PCCh). It is who sets the line to follow through different control agencies (Ministries of Information, Departments, etc.). And in every company, media outlet, or school there is an association or group that represents the CCP and controls everything in each one of them.

The Chinese Communist Party is the one that marks all the decisions and is protected by the Constitution itself. It is the world political party with the most millions of affiliates, a total of 67 million. It is not, however, the only political party in the country. There are eight others, always tolerated by him, and between all of them they do not have half a million members. Despite the fact that this control exercised by the Government in China was already legislated in the approach of its current Constitution, the latest laws have increased control (Colomo 2018).

Experts of the digital age such as Bill Gates have already reflected that the birth of the Internet would mean a change equal to or greater than what was once the printing press of Johannes Gútenberg (Sahagun 2004). What was clear is that the network of networks bridged the gap between states, as Bauman also argues. The barriers of community were dissolved, as the sociologist would surely point out.

China refused from the beginning to get more freedom in exchange for reduced security. The country, in recent years, has only strengthened itself in this area (Delgado and Teano 2020). Among this establishment of control measures, the last thing the current president has opted for has been a reform of the Constitution. With this, among other things, what he has achieved is a perpetuation in power. Xi Jinping, the current president, who became president of the country in 2013, will be able to remain in power beyond 2023, when he would finish his term. He amasses the most power in decades. The United States, as the main power, sees in the laws and rules of the democratic system some limits that all similar societies maintain to guarantee rights and freedoms.

With the arrival of Xi Jinping in 2013, an interest in control was already evident that was greater than that which had existed in previous governments. This can be seen, for example, when he heads the National Security Commission. Until then, predecessor presidents had chosen to delegate this responsibility to third parties. At that time, a greater power is already assumed by the Chinese leader.

Xi Jinping also chairs the commissions of Civil and Military Development, Foreign, Taiwan, Deepening Reform, Internet, Military Reform, and Economic Affairs. In addition to reinforcing its power, China has developed new laws to control and dominate the population and the companies established in the country. The National Security Law of 2015 provides greater powers to the State over the domain of digital space and its corresponding development (Pollpeter et al. 2015).

While certain uncertainties or instabilities in democratic countries put their growth or stability in the markets at risk, China has an element in its favor such as the ability to anticipate, to maintain control of the country. All this added to the political stability granted by perpetuation in power and social control, even more so after the abolition of term limits.

In this context, the Asian country is testing a Social Credit System. It is intended to reward or penalize citizens according to their actions. Based on that, those who do not fulfill their obligations could be penalized with a ban on buying train or plane tickets for one year. After a year, this prohibition would be reviewed, and it could be decided to maintain it or not. With all this, it is reflected that China has reformed its laws in recent years with numerous reforms. Far from advancing towards greater democracy, the laws have been tightened in their quest to maintain internal control of their borders.

2.2 The Chinese Democratic Rate Growth and the Population Approval

Less than 5% of the world population lives in a full democracy, according to the report published by The Economist Intelligence Unit (Democracy Index 2018).

According to this index, the United States would have a score of 7.98 in 2017, which according to The Economist would be an imperfect democracy. The North American country is positioned at its lowest level. In 2006, it was among the perfect democracies, maintaining a rating of 8.22.

As far as China is concerned, it´s still an authoritarian country and registers a score of 3.10 out of 10. It has lost a score level in the last year from 3.14 to 3.10. Since 2004, it would have risen slightly in the ranking from 2.97, although without major variations during these years. It remains below countries like Cuba, with 3.31 (World Bank 2018).

As for the image of the country abroad, almost half of Americans consider seeing China as something positive or negative. 47% say they see their main competitor as something unfavorable, while 44% see it as something positive. Also, inside and outside the country, the opinion is different. A Chinese citizen residing in Spain points out that the limits established by the system affects in different manner the people who reside there and those who go abroad. Those who have been abroad, as she explains, have been able to learn about other networks and other possibilities that when they return to their country, they miss not being able to have free access to them.

On the other hand, society considers the expansionism of the country abroad to be positive. The Chinese population applauds the foreign policy that the country has carried out in recent decades, although especially that of Xi Jinping, it has consisted of the "peaceful rise" of Hu Jintao, adding a search for a greater role and participation of China in the international sphere, understanding by role and participation the acquisition of more power in the IMF, World Bank or United Nations.

With all this, despite the absence of freedoms of the authoritarian regime, it can be deduced that China maintains control of the population, and it considers many of the measures developed to be positive, understanding them to be positive for the country's economic growth.

3 China Foreign Policy: A Silent Expansionism

China's strategy abroad involves silence, it is how economic expansionism and the exploitation of new resources are guaranteed. One of China's weaknesses is its lack of raw materials, which means that it has to source from abroad. In the 19th century, Africa witnessed how the colonialism of countries plundered its territory. Today, the colonization that part of the continent is undergoing is somewhat different.

Africans, far from seeing Chinese interference as a problem, applaud it and see it as beneficial to their economy. In fact, the Forum for Cooperation between Africa and China (FOCAC) is a meeting point between leaders and businessmen.

Success is none other than that of not interfering in internal issues and trying to ensure that countries do not oppose their entry through their complacency, something that perhaps the powers that colonized Africa in the 19th century did not know how to do adequately.

Speaking to Xinhua, Guan Yingmin, representative of the government of Heilongjiang province, in the north of the country, indicated that the region's investment figures were inflated by at least 20%, which would be equivalent to around 15.7 billion euros. Dollars. Although the general perception is that the numbers offered by Beijing at the national level are more transparent than those of local governments, many analysts consider that the growth of the Asian giant is lower than that indicated by official figures (Economist 2015; 2018).

3.1 Relations Between Authoritarian Policies and Expansionism

Most of the five economies that are going to grow the most, 60%, are authoritarian governments, while the rest, 40%, would be imperfect democracies. This would show that the government system of a country does not determine growth forecasts. The countries that will grow the most, according to the forecast, next year are those that are developing. Its growth achieves the best percentage with respect to the GDP of its economy, but its economy is not very influential worldwide, as it is not among the great powers. One would then wonder what the situation is and how these two elements are combined in the largest economies worldwide.

The United States is the first and main world economic power. If the level of democracy of the major powers is related to the percentage of the economy they represent worldwide, it can be seen that China is the only power that maintains a suspense in the level of democracy, with a 3.10. The country, with an authoritarian regime, has managed to consecrate itself as the second world power, and relies on that authoritarianism for its economic expansion.

Chinese expansionism abroad is aided by internal control at home. The reforms carried out by the Government strengthen its policies abroad and give it greater economic security.

The control policy carried out by the Chinese Government translates into greater "tranquility" and security for the institutions, and reduces the uncertainty of political change. In this way, the Chinese economy benefits from the political and social stability of the country. The theory exposed by Bauman is applicable to the Chinese case. The country gets greater security in exchange for giving up its freedom and maintaining an authoritarian system. Authoritarian regimes, on the other hand, are not directly related to greater economic expansionism. The case of China is an "exceptional" case as it is the only one of the five great powers that has an authoritarian system (Liz 2021; Liz 2018). The case of China is explained by the "collective conscience" of society, since they consider that control is justified with greater progress for the country.

3.2 The NATO Vision Statement of China's Expansionist Position

The Madrid meeting held in June 2022 by the North Atlantic Treaty Organization (NATO), allowed the meeting the leaders approved a new strategic concept that will define the roadmap for the alliance for the next decade. The concept defines Russia as "the most significant and direct threat to the security of the allies, to peace and stability in the Euro-Atlantic area."

NATO's strategic concept considers that "China's declared ambitions and coercive policies challenge our interests, security and values" declaring it a systemic challenge. Likewise, NATO also considers that «The strategic association between Russia and China and its attempts to undermine the rules on which the international order is based go against our values and interests».

In reply to the NATO summit conclusions, Chinese Foreign Ministry spokesman Zhao Lijian draw attention that de NATO's new "strategic concept" stubbornly adheres to the wrong positioning of "systemic challenges" to China, stains China's foreign policy, makes irresponsible comments on China's military development, national defense policy, and encourages confrontation. The spokesman warned NATO that it is completely useless to exaggerate about the so-called "China threat". NATO must immediately stop making baseless accusations and provocative comments against China, and abandon the outdated concept of the Cold War mentality and the zero-sum game (Delgado et al. 2019).

From China's perspective, the GSI can be understood as a practical experience of the concept of a community with a shared future for all mankind in security. In addition to becoming the third initiative, after the Belt and Road Initiative (2013) and the Global Development Initiative (2021) for global governance proposed by China during its new era (2012-current) and facing the 20th Congress of the Communist Party of China (CPC) to be held in November this year.

4 China and Its Geopolitical Motivations for the Antisatellite Weapons Test

As Vilanova (1985) points out in his book "From the double decision to Star Wars", the arms race has acquired its own dynamics whose autonomous force moves through centers of interest and various pressure groups, for which you need to analyze your problem. It is worth noting that, in January 2007, the People's Republic of China became the third country to conduct a successful test that destroyed an inactive weather satellite, launching a ballistic missile at an altitude of approximately 530+ miles (hardly the altitude which is used for US and Japanese imaging intelligence satellites). Before achieving it, there were three failed attempts (Zissis 2007).

The foregoing refers to the concept of hybrid threats, since, as Mazurier y Payá (2018) explains, these can be understood as those actions that, in a synchronized and coordinated manner, seek the objective of deliberately attacking the systemic weaknesses of the States, as well as their institutions (Delgado et al. 2020). In addition, the author points out that these hybrid threats are generated through different media and target sectors, be they political, economic, military, social, informational, as well as infrastructure or legal matters. Finally, Payá and Delgado (2017), shows that cyberspace is used as a versatile tool for the fulfillment of its respective purposes.

Chinese space activities and anti-satellite tests come as a response to advances, space technology and the US ectocratic strategy, this is supported by several comments made by PLA officials and Chinese analysts, who also point out that the ASAT test seeks "attack their vulnerability in a certain way as a consequence of the currently existing satellite dependency" (Kan 2007, p. 3). This fact, however, loses force because in 2020 the United States managed to reach space by its own means, a situation that will be explained later.

China's reasons for testing are likely military and diplomatic, say Michael A. Levi and Adam Segal of the Council on Foreign Relations (CFR). In this sense, "by demonstrating its ASAT capacity, China exposes its fear of a US space missile defense system that could neutralize its nuclear arsenal and therefore prohibit space weapons" (Levi and Segal as cited in Zissis 2007, paragraph 3).

In essence, by demonstrating its ability to use ASAT weapons, China exposes its military growth in space to its neighboring countries and to the world at large. But more importantly, from an American perspective, China's ability to destroy satellites demonstrates that it can attack weaknesses in the US military, and in particular break confidence in satellites for intelligence gathering and surveillance operations. High-precision weaponry (Payá et al. 2015). A nation with the ability to destroy satellites also threatens to seriously affect essential daily functions, from financial transactions to telephone communications and electrical networks, as well as controlling time signals and global positioning satellite (GPS) (Zissis 2007).

Likewise, Beijing has met with Moscow in its long-running efforts to convince the US to sign a treaty banning the deployment of weapons in space. As Anguiano (2001) puts it, China's deterrent power against projectile systems or defensive missiles would be totally neutralized if they could be deployed and perfected. For this reason, the author points out the importance for China of international treaties providing this nuclear arms control, in order to be able to allocate the country's economic resources for the well-being of its population instead of the development of nuclear power.

5 China's Arctic Policy: Reactions Provoked

At the beginning of 2018, China published its first White Paper on the Arctic, which is entitled "China's Arctic Policy". The document details China's interests, priorities and policies towards the Arctic. During the official launch of the White Paper, China's Vice Foreign Minister, Kong Xuanyou, stated that "the document may be updated in the future, in order to keep it in line with emerging changes" (cited in SCIO, 2018b, paragraph 19, own translation). Thus, it is clear that China does not hesitate to expand the scope of its goals in the Arctic region. Although this is not new for China to position itself with respect to the Arctic, it is the first time that it has broadly developed its vision of the region's problems, as well as a policy of international cooperation and development of natural resources (Kassow 2015; Sun 2020; Mazurier et al. 2020).

China is emphatic in stating that Arctic problems have a global impact and proclaims itself as a "responsible power" on Arctic issues (SCIO 2018a). In this way, it emphasizes its right based on a moralistic logic and the obligation to participate in the development of the region and contribute to the construction of a "shared future for humanity -in the Arctic-" (SCIO 2018a, para. 1, own translation).

On the other hand, investigations affiliated with institutions such as the People's Liberation Army of China (PLA) indicate that navigation and satellite surveillance technology in the Arctic are a priority, and in other investigations sponsored by the Chinese Ministry of Education (with the PLA involved) describe the Arctic as a budding arena for great powers to fight for influence over trade routes and resources (Havnes and Seland 2019), conceiving the area as a focus of geopolitical competition.

Despite this, the National Strategy for the region, launched by the US government in 2016, does not indicate an explicit concern regarding China's actions (Arctic Executive Steering Committee 2016). However, as of 2019, with the launch of a new National Strategy for the Arctic, there is a marked shift in US policy in the region, which is seen in a context of strategic competition between the US power and Russia and China: (Weidacher 2020).

This document articulates the Department of Defense (DoD) strategy for the Arctic region (…). It is (…) anchored in the priorities of the National Defense Strategy (NDS) 2018 and its focus on the competition with China and Russia as the main challenge for the security and prosperity of the United States (Department of Defense United States of America, 2019, p. 2, own translation).

Thus, the document points out the multidimensionality of China's actions in the Arctic, which include: China's icebreakers, the Xuelong and Xuelong 2 (…), and civil investigation efforts, which could support a future strengthened Chinese military presence in the Arctic Ocean, which could include the deployment of submarines in the region (Department of Defense Arctic Strategy, 2019, p. 4, own translation) (Mark 2017; Zhen 2019).

So Beijing's current actions are seen as possible harbingers of an eventual Chinese military presence in the Arctic. In turn, the document indicates that China is increasing its presence in the Arctic "through the economic plan, investments in strategic sectors of the Arctic states and scientific activities" (Department of Defense United States of America 2019, p. 4), highlighting that Beijing has research stations in Iceland and Norway, and that it has developed large infrastructure projects in the region (Koivurova et al. 2019).

In this sense, although China and Russia maintain close economic cooperation in the Arctic, Moscow has shown concerns regarding Chinese policy in general in the region, essentially because Russia sees itself as an "Arctic power" and has a strong military projection in the region. Due to this, Russia prefers to keep the Arctic "closed" in terms of security, treat the region as part of its domestic policy and maintain its military predominance in it, thus, there is a conflict of interest between the need to open the Arctic to external States in the economic field, which collides with the security ambition of closing the Arctic –security not only in the military sense, but also in the sense of ensuring the income generated in the Arctic (Kassov 2015, para. 4, own translation) (The Arctic Institute 2019).

Therefore, Moscow would view with suspicion any attempt by Beijing to consolidate itself militarily in the region:

"China's growing interest in the Arctic has strengthened the surveillance of the Russian army, which is very sensitive to security issues" (Hong 2018, p. 17, own translation).

Canada, for its part, prefers that governance in the Arctic remains dominated by Arctic states:

"Canada's official position indicates that it prefers a regional governance regime dominated by the Arctic states" (Lackenbauer et al. 2018, p. 132).

In addition, although it is not something that has been explicitly pointed out by the Canadian government, there is a fear among the academic community and security experts in Canada that the sovereignty over the maritime routes of the Canadian northwest is undermined due to the fact that China believes "that the Arctic is open to the international community" (Hong 2018, p. 17).

With regard to Norway, the Nordic country has welcomed China's involvement in research projects in the Arctic, thus, in 2010, the then Minister of Research and Higher Education, Tora Aasland, said: "we are happy to that China is now investing greater efforts in polar research" (Gulliksen (2019); quoted in The Nordic Page, 2010, para. 2, own translation).

The trade relationship between China and Iceland, the first European country to sign a free trade agreement with the Asian giant in 2013, has also sparked interest in the Arctic. The trade agreement exposes the interest of both countries in cooperation on

Arctic issues and on the same day it was signed, Ólafur Ragnar —Icelandic president— created the Arctic Circle governance forum and invited Beijing to be part of it (Cornet 2018; Dams et al. 2020a).

Thus, after several years of intense cooperation, in 2018 the China Polar Research Institute opened the China-Iceland Arctic Scientific Observatory (PRIC) in the north of Iceland, whose initial focus was to serve as an observatory of Northern Lights has expanded into satellite remote sensing research, monitoring activity that could have security implications in the medium or long term and that could generate concern within the Atlantic Alliance, since Iceland is a strategic point in the surveillance of the Euro-Atlantic zone (Dams et al. 2020b). Furthermore, "Iceland, without an army, depends on the United States to guarantee its security, while the latter seems to gradually engage in a polar wrestling match with China" (Cornet 2018, p.13, own translation).

In this sense, in 2018, China invited Iceland to participate in the Silk Road, and given the indecisive position of the European country towards the proposal, the US Secretary of State, Mike Pompeo, stated during a visit to Iceland in 2019 that China's ambition in the area makes the United States-Iceland relationship essential and welcomed the "rejection" by the Icelandic government of the proposal, despite the fact that the authorities did not publish any formal opposition (Ríkey 2019).

6 Conclusions

Reflection on China in the Arctic

It is clear that Beijing develops a multidimensional policy and strategy in the Arctic that seeks to achieve its geopolitical objectives in the region, evidenced both by its interest in participating in the governance of the Arctic, and through its actions at the diplomatic level, economic, scientific, investment, military (on an initial scale) and research, exercised both at the governmental level and through non-state actors. In this sense, the Arctic emerges as a geopolitical region of great importance, not only because of its richness in natural resources, but also because it can become an important commercial navigation route and connection between Asia and Europe, and also because there is the possibility of projecting geopolitically in a region under a complex legal regime.

So, it is concluded that China's actions in the region emerge as a hybrid threat for countries like the United States, because Beijing employs a combination of "conventional and unconventional activities, military and non-military, that can be used in a coordinated manner by actors state and non-state to achieve specific political objectives" (European External Action Service 2018, para. 2, own translation). This reaffirms the concerns expressed by countries such as Russia, which worries about an eventual Chinese military consolidation in the Arctic, and by Canada, which fears that the Chinese vision of the Arctic could undermine its sovereignty in the region (Global 2017).

Reflection on China in Space

The People's Republic of China has increased its advances in the space field, which has allowed it to carry out multiple studies for the execution of tests such as ASAT, which has been identified as a hybrid response threat to US space geopolitics. The existing tensions between China and the United States and the search for space power have driven specialization in both countries, whether to create expert government organizations in launching and creating space weapons, or for the development of space geopolitics through the strengthening of diplomatic ties with others through regional and international cooperation. In this sense, China has promoted increasing its political closeness with South American states due to an ideological and geographical strategy based on its expansion interests in the spatial plane. To this is added that the cooperation managed with countries such as Argentina, Brazil, Chile and Ecuador, can be seen as an element that comes to strengthen its astro-strategy.

The United States has seen outer space as a new means of power and continues to exercise its dominance under realistic visions of International Relations, such as weapons capabilities. Therefore, through programs such as SpaceX, where the country reached space by its own means, it sends a message where it seeks to show the space capabilities it has and, unlike countries like China, it is moving away from space cooperation which; however, it should not be left out completely as it can be a key element. The latest space launches of the main powers already mentioned, such as China, the United States and Russia joining, but also of countries such as Saudi Arabia or Israel, are a reflection of the new space age. Interests in space resources.

Terrestrial geopolitics crossed borders until it reached outer space, which allowed taking classic concepts of said discipline and creating new ones such as astropolitics and Astro-strategy, terms that manage to explain the behavior and decisions of these actors both on planet Earth and in the world. Outer space. Like the definitions mentioned above, the latest discoveries and space activities support the concept of ectocracia and make it a present reality.

Reflection on Chinese Expansionism

Chinese expansionism abroad is aided by internal control at home. The reforms carried out by the Government strengthen its foreign policies and produce greater economic security. The control policy carried out by the Chinese Government translates into greater "tranquility" and security for the institutions and reduces the uncertainty of political change. In this way, the Chinese economy benefits from the political and social stability of the country. The theory exposed by Bauman is applicable to the Chinese case. The country gets greater security in exchange for giving up its freedom and maintaining an authoritarian system. Authoritarian regimes are not directly related to greater economic expansionism. The case of China is an "exceptional" case as it is the only one of the five great powers that has a system lacking freedoms.

The case of China is explained by the "collective conscience" of society, since they consider that control is justified with greater progress for the country and, therefore, for its well-being. China has a flexible legislation to the interests of the Communist Party. It is explained by the numerous reforms undertaken to the Magna Carta, depending on the political moments (1988, 1993, 1999, 2004, and 2018). The flexibility derives from government control and the concentration of powers around the president. The Antiterrorist Law and the National Security Law of 2015, or the Cybersecurity Law of 2017 corroborate an increase in control by the Government, both for the Chinese themselves and for the multinational companies with a presence in the country. China is the country with the greatest social inequalities in the world. China maintains an expansionism abroad. It uses a silent tactic, without attracting the attention of the great powers.

References

Anguiano, E.: The People's Republic of China as a nuclear power. Asian Afr. Stud. **36**(114), 129–153 (2001). www.jstor.org/stable/40313396

Bauman, Z.: Community: Seeking Safety in a Hostile World. Themes for the 21st Century. First published in 2001 by Polity Press. Reprinted 2006 (2006)

Beiser, E.: Encarcelan a una cifra récord de periodistas, en tanto Turquía, China y Egipto pagan poco precio por la represión. En Comité para la Protección de los Periodistas (CPJ), 13 diciembre 2017. https://cpj.org/es/2017/12/encarcelan-a-una-cifra-record-de-periodistas-en-ta.php

Colomo, J.: Constitución de la República Popular China Xavier Colom (2018). http://www.javiercolomo.com/index_archivos/Const/Cons_Ch.htm

Cornet, A.: From the "Polar Silk Road" to the Arctic Rimland: A case study of the Belt and Road challenges for the European Union the Route for the European Union]. Institute of International and Strategic Relations (2018). https://www.irisfrance.org/wp-content/uploads/2018/10/Asia-Focus-90-Anglais-1.pdf

Dams, T., van Schaik, L., Stoetman, A.: Presence Before Power: China's Arctic Strategy in Iceland and Greenland, Amsterdam, Netherlands: Clingendael, p. 34, June 2020

Dams, T., van Schaik, L., Stoetman, A.: Presence before power China's Arctic strategy in Iceland (2020)

Delgado Moran, J.J., Teano, F.: El concepto de hidrohegemonia como marco de análisis de los conflictos transfronterizos por el agua. Pensando en el caso Chino. Agua Y Territorio / Water and Landscape (14), 97–104 (2019). https://doi.org/10.17561/at.14.4437

Delgado Morán, J.J., Jiménez Reina, J., Jiménez Reina, R.: Seguridad cooperativa como medida de prevención y respuesta de la Unión Europea. Revista Científica General José María Córdova **18**(29), 61–85 (2020a). https://doi.org/10.21830/19006586.520

Delgado Moran, J.J., Mazurier, P.A., Paya Santos, C.A.: The race to securitize the arctic in a post-cold War scenario. Revista de Pensamiento Estratégico y Seguridad CISDE **4**(1), 59–64 (2019)

Delgado Morán J.J, Teano, F.: Gendering migration: securitization and integration media narratives in Europe. Vergentis. Revista de Investigación de la Cátedra Internacional Conjunta Inocencio III **11**, 93–126 (2020)

Delgado-Morán, J.-J., Jiménez-Reina, J., Cremades-Guisado, Á.: Analytical approach to emergent hybrid threats phenomena. case study: EU and Colombia. In: Ramírez, J.M., Biziewski, J. (eds.) A Shift in the Security Paradigm. ASTSA, pp. 49–68. Springer, Cham (2020). https://doi.org/10.1007/978-3-030-43253-9_5

Greenland [Presence before the power of the Chinese Arctic strategy in Iceland and Greenland]. The Clingendael Institute. https://www.clingendael.org/pub/2020/presence-before-power/

Gulliksen, S.: Norwegian Foreign Minister Ine Eriksen Søreide: - Not an unexpected outcome. High North News, 8 May 2019. https://www.highnorthnews.com/en/not-unexpected-outcome

El Economista: (2015). http://www.eleconomista.es/economia/noticias/7220298/12/15/Varios-gobiernos-locales-chinos-admiten-la-manipulacion-de-datos-economicos.html

El Economista: (2018). http://www.eleconomista.es/economia/noticias/7573379/05/16/La-desigualdad-economica-en-China-emprendia-a-caer-se-cumple-la-teoria-de-Kuznets.html

EFE: (2015). https://www.efe.com/efe/espana/mundo/china-se-arma-con-su-primera-y-controvertida-ley-para-la-lucha-antiterrorista/10001-2798650

Pew Global: (2017). http://www.pewglobal.org/2017/04/04/americans-views-of-china-improve-as-economic-concerns-ease/

Havnes, H., Selan, J.: The Increasing Security Focus in China's Arctic Policy. The Arctic Institute (2019). https://www.thearcticinstitute.org/increasing-securityfocus-china-arctic-policy/

Hong, N.: China's interests in the Arctic: opportunities and challenges. Institute for China-America Studies (2018). https://chinaus-icas.org/research/chinasinterests-in-the-arctic-opportunities-challenges/

Democracy Index 2018 (2018). https://i2.wp.com/eleclectoral.com/wp-content/uploads/2018/03/Indice-de-democracia-2017.png

Kan, S.: China's Anti-Satellite Weapon Test. [Chinese Anti-Satellite Weapon Test]. CRS Report for Congress (Order Code RS22652) (2007). https://fas.org/sgp/crs/row/RS22652.pdf

Kassow, J.: 'Western' Sanctions will not create a Chinese-Russian Alliance. The Arctic Institute (2015). https://www.thearcticinstitute.org/westernsanctions-china-russia/

Koivurova, T., et al.: China in the Arctic and the Opportunities and Challenges for Chinese-Finnish Arctic Co-operation. Government's analysis, assessment and research (2019). https://julkaisut.valtioneuvosto.fi/bitstream/handle/10024/161371/8-2019-China_Arctic_andFinland.pdf

Mazurier, P.A, Payá Santos, C.A.: Amenazas Híbridas: Teoría de la Hibridez y Nuevo Orden Internacional. Ed. Thomson Reuters (2018)

Mazurier, P.A., Delgado-Morán, J.J., Payá-Santos, C.A.: The meta-tragedy of the commons. climate change and the securitization of the arctic region. In: Ramírez, J.M., Biziewski, J. (eds.) Security and Defence in Europe. ASTSA, pp. 63–74. Springer, Cham (2020). https://doi.org/10.1007/978-3-030-12293-5_5

Lackenbauer, W., Lajeunesse, A., Manicom, J., Lasserre, F.: China's Arctic ambitions and what they mean for Canada. East Asia-Arctic Relations: Boundary, Security and International Politics (8), 1–262 (2018). https://www.econstor.eu/bitstream/10419/200718/1/978-1-55238-903-4.pdf

Mark, A.A.: Tensions in the South China Sea. A conflict of difficult solution. New Magazine of Politics, culture and art. No. 161 (2017)

Liz-Rivas, L.: Algunas bases neurológicas sobre la violencia y la agresión, en. Conflictos y diplomacia, desarrollo y paz, globalización y medio ambiente coord. Por Emilio José García Mercader, Claudio Payá Santos. César Augusto Giner Alegría (dir.), Juan Jose Delgado Morán (dir.). Thomson Reuters, pp. 943–955 (2018)

Liz-Rivas, L.: Geopolítica hidro-hegemónica china en la cuenca del río Mekong. URVIO. Revista Latinoamericana De Estudios De Seguridad (30), 108–120 (2021). https://doi.org/10.17141/urvio.30.2021.4770

World, B.: World Bank (2018). http://www.worldbank.org/es/news/press-release/2018/01/09/global-economy-to-edge-up-to-3-1-percent-in-2018-but-future-potential-growth-a-concern

Payá Santos, C.A., Delgado Morán, J.J.: El uso del ciberespacio para infringir el terror. Estudios en Seguridad y Defensa **11**(22), 91–108 (2016). https://doi.org/10.25062/1900-8325.211

Payá-Santos, C.A., Delgado-Morán, J.J.: Use of cyberspace for terrorist purposes. In: Ramírez, J.M., García-Segura, L.A. (eds.) Cyberspace. ASTSA, pp. 197–209. Springer, Cham (2017). https://doi.org/10.1007/978-3-319-54975-0_12

Payá Santos, C., Luque Juárez, J.M.: El sistema de inteligencia criminal ante las nuevas amenazas y oportunidades del ciberespacio. Revista Científica General José María Córdova **19**(36), 1121–1136 (2021). https://doi.org/10.21830/19006586.855

Payá Santos, C., Delgado Morán, J.J., Fernández Rodríguez, J.C.: Los medios de producción de inteligencia, en el análisis actual de los conflictos. Estudios En Seguridad y Defensa **10**(20), 5–17 (2015). https://doi.org/10.25062/1900-8325.31

Pollpeter, K., Anderson, E., Wilson, J., Yang, F.: China Dream, Space Dream: China's Progress in Space Technologies and Implications for the United States. US-China Economic and Security Review Commission (2015). https://www.uscc.gov/sites/default/files/Research/China%20Dream%20Space%20Dream_Report.pdf

Europapress: (2018). https://www.europapress.es/economia/macroeconomia-00338/noticia-pib-china-crecio-69-2017-acelera-primera-vez-2010-20180118093237.html

Reporter Without Borders: (2018). https://www.rsf-es.org/news/reporteros-sin-fronteras-condena-la-violencia-policial-contra-periodistas/

Rikey, G.: Pressure in the Arctic: China-Iceland Relations in the Era of US-China Rivalry. Institute for Security & Development Policy (2019). https://isdp.eu/pressure-in-the-arctic-china-iceland-relations/

Sahagun, F.: From Gutenberg to the Internet: The International Information Society. Forge, Madrid (2004)

European External Action Service: A Europe that protects countering Hybrid Threats (2018). https://eeas.europa.eu/sites/eeas/files/hybrid_threats_en_final.pdf

Sun, Y.: Defining the Chinese Threat in the Arctic. The Arctic Institute (2020). https://www.thearcticinstitute.org/defining-the-chinese-threat-in-the-arctic/

The Arctic Institute: The Arctic Institute's Reaction to the 2019 Department of Defense (DoD) Arctic Strategy (2019). https://www.thearcticinstitute.org/the-arctic-institute-reaction-2019-department-defense-dodarctic-strategy/

The State Council Information Office of the People's Republic of China [SCIO]. China's Arctic Policy (2018a). http://english.scio.gov.cn/2018-01/26/content_50313403.htm

The State Council Information Office of the People's Republic of China [SCIO]. SCIO briefing on China's policy on the Arctic (2018b). http://www.scio.gov.cn/32618/Document/1618357/1618357.htm

Vilanova, P.: Some notes on the new cold war. From the «double decision» to «Star Wars». Affers Int. (6), 71–79 (1985). www.jstor.org/stable/40550269

Xinhua: (2015). http://spanish.xinhuanet.com/china/2015-07/01/c_134372895.htm

Zissis, C.: China's Anti-Satellite Test. Council on Foreign Relations (2007). https://www.cfr.org/backgrounder/chinas-anti-satellite-test

Zhen, L.: Could China's 'experimental' ship be the world's biggest nuclear-powered icebreaker? [Could Chinese "Experimental" Ship Be World's Largest Powered Icebreaker?]. South China Morning Post (2019). https://www.scmp.com/news/china/military/article/3002455/china-build-30000-tonnenuclear-powered-ship-described

Weidacher, C.: The Emergence of a Sino-Russian Economic Partnership in the Arctic? [The emergence of a Sino-Russian economic alliance in the Arctic?]. The Arctic Institute (2020). https://www.thearcticinstitute.org/emergence-sino-russian-economic-partnership-arctic/

The Philippines, Factor of Stability in Southeast Asia

Federico Yaniz(✉)

Eurodefense-Spain, P.O. Box 50.359, 28.080 Madrid, Spain
federo101@hotmail.com

Abstract. The Republic of the Philippines is an archipelagic country of Southeast Asia, The Philippines (2022). It is situated in the western Pacific Ocean and consists of about 7,600 islands and islets lying about 500 miles (800 km) off the coast Vietnam. Manila is the capital, but nearby Quezon City is the country's most-populous city. Both are part of the National Capital Region (Metro Manila), found on Luzon, the largest island. The Philippines takes its name from Philip II, who was king of Spain during the first years of the colonization of the islands by the Spaniards in the 16th century. The Philippines was under Spanish rule for 333 years and later for 48 years was under U.S. tutelage. For that reason, the Philippines has unique cultural and historical ties with the West. Spain, and the United States. It is, one of only two predominantly Roman Catholic countries in Asia (the other is tiny East Timor) and it is after India the second most-populous Asian country with English as an official language, World Atlas (2018). The Philippines are geographically part of Southeast Asia, but the country is culturally strongly Hispanic-American. Nearly four centuries of Western rule have left an indelible imprint on the Philippines, serving as a conduit for the introduction of Western culture and as the catalyst for the emergence of a sense of Philippine unity. The Christian churches built by the Spaniards provided a spiritual anchor and the educational system established by the United States and expanded by the Filipinos has become a sign of cultural unity and social progress, Nevertheless, increased attention to Asian history and literature and the revival of dormant traditions has strengthen the Asian heritage without abandoning the Philippines Western cultural ties. The Philippines has been and still is a supporter of the development of the concept of archipelagic states in the Law of the Sea, Churchill et al. (2022). Since 1898 the Philippines keeps a special relationship with the U.S. The Japanese occupation and the independence of the Philippines were no obstacles for keeping in force that link. In the context of the volatile situation in the Indo-Pacific region the visit of Mr. Blinken to the Philippines in August 2022 was relevant. The Statement on the on U.S.-The Philippines relationship published 5 August 2022 reflects the importance of U.S.-Philippines relations and specially security cooperation, U.S. Department of State (2022). The statement makes clear that bilateral defense agreements continue to supply the foundation for that relationship.

Keywords: Euro-American · Spanish rule · Asian heritage · Southeast Sea · Socio-economic · Economic zone · Archipelagic states · ASEAN

J. Cayón Peña and J. M. Ramírez (Eds.): *Threats to Peace and International Security: Asia versus West*, ASTSA, pp. 97–110, 2023.
https://doi.org/10.1007/978-3-031-28336-9_6

1 Introduction

The Philippines has been, and still is, an ardent supporter of the development of the concept of archipelagic states in the Law of the Sea. In fact, the Philippines, together with Indonesia, Fiji, and Mauritius, took part actively in the first meeting of the archipelagic states in New York on 13 March 1972. They worked hard to formulate the principles for the archipelagic states, including their rights and obligations. They sent the outcome to the then coming third UN Law of the Sea Conference, which was going to start in 1973. Nevertheless, they still had basic differences on the details, especially on the criteria for their status as archipelagic states, their rights and obligations over the archipelagic waters, and the rights of other states over those waters. At the suggestion of the Philippines, another meeting took place in Manila on 25–26 May 1972 (Mauritius did not take part in that meeting), trying to further formulate the agreed principles, Severino (2011). After lengthy discussions, including on a trip to Corregidor across Manila Bay, three basic principles approved: the definition of an archipelagic state; the sovereignty of an archipelagic state over the waters within its archipelagic baselines, and "innocent passage" of foreign vessels through such sea lanes as appointed by the archipelagic state. One confusing issue was the nature of the lines drawn by the Treaty of Paris of 1898, in which Spain delivered sovereignty over the Philippines to the United States. The Philippines later claimed that the lines defined in the Treaty were territorial in nature and encompassed an extension of sea outside of the Philippines island group, up to the extent of 250 miles from the Philippines' coast lines. This provision is relevant for the disputes on the South China Sea and the West Philippine Sea over the sovereignty on the Spratly islands that are a group of Islands, reefs, islets, and cays claimed by Asian countries namely the Philippines, Vietnam, Brunei, Malaysia, Taiwan, and People's Republic of China. The establishment of Chinese installations on the Spratly islands put the United Nations Convention on the Law of the Sea or the Law of the Sea Convention (LOSC) as an essential international instrument affecting the maritime entitlements of the Philippines.

2 Early Philippines History

30.000 years ago, migrants from Indonesia and other places arrived in the Philippines archipelago, see One World-Nations online (2011). Additional migrations took place over the centuries and social and political organization developed and evolved in the archipelago. Barangay, a Malayan word for boat, came to denote a communal settlement. Familiar groups were under the leadership of a chief o "datu." Within the barangay there were broad social divisions: nobles, freemen, dependent landless agricultural workers, and slaves. Very soon, Indo-Malay migrants were joined by traders and craftsmen from China. A major development was the introduction of Islam to the Philippines by traders from the Indonesian islands. By A.D. 1500, Islam established in the Sulu Archipelago and spread from there to Mindanao; it reached the Manila area by 1565. During the introduction of Islam came the Christianity with the arrival of the Spaniards.

Ferdinand Magellan was an explorer of Portuguese origin subject of the Hispanic Monarchy from 1518. In 1519, he led initially the 1519 Spanish expedition to the East Indies across the Pacific Ocean. The members of the expedition were the first Europeans to land in the Philippines. They arrived in March 1521 during the Spanish expedition to circumnavigate the globe. Magellan claimed land for the king of Spain but he died fighting a local chief. Following more Spanish expeditions, the first permanent settlement was in Cebu in 1565, Marquez Montero (2021). After defeating local rulers, in 1571 the Spaniards established their capital at Manila, and they named their new colony Philippines after King Philip II of Spain. In doing so, the Spanish sought to acquire a share in the lucrative spice trade, develop better contacts with China and Japan, and gain converts to Christianity. Only the third objective was successful. Catholic religious orders oversaw Christianizing the local population. The civil administration was based upon the traditional village organization and used local leaders to rule for Spain. Nevertheless, Muslims and upland tribal peoples remained detached and not integrated.

In the Philippines, commerce centred around the Manila galleons (Cartwright 2021), which sailed from Acapulco on the west coast of Mexico (New Spain), Puig-Samper Mulero (2019). Shipments of silver and coins were exchanged for return cargoes of Chinese goods, mainly silk and porcelain. During the Seven Years' War (1756–63), British East India Company forces captured Manila. Although the Philippines was returned to Spain at the end of the war in 1763, the British occupation marked the beginning of the end of the old colonial order. Rebellions broke out in the north, and Muslims raided from the south. In addition, the Chinese were resentful of Spanish discrimination. After the restoration of Spanish control of commerce there were reforms aimed at promoting a new economic development of the islands and making them economically independent from New Spain. The galleon trade ended in 1815, and from that date onward the Royal Company of the Philippines promoted direct trade between the archipelago and Spain. Crops were cultivated for trade with Europe and South America, but profits diminished after Spain's colonies in South America became independent. In 1834 the Royal Company was abolished, and free trade recognized: Your guide to the world (2021). Manila, with its excellent harbour, became an open port for Asian, European, and North American traders. In 1873 other ports opened to foreign commerce, and by the late nineteenth century the Philippines economic was based on three crops: tobacco, abaca (a type of buff-colored fiber), and sugar.

3 Advancing Towards Democracy

Chinese immigration increased in the late nineteenth century and Chinese mestizos became a feature in social and economic life. Filipino native elite class became increasingly receptive to liberal ideas and called the "ilustrados". However, conservative Catholic continued to dominate the Spanish establishment. Despite prejudices against native priests and nuns, members of the religious orders became prominent to the point of leading insurrections against the establishment. Additionally, upper class Filipinos returning from education abroad brought innovative ideas to incite a resistance.

José Rizal was one of the early nationalist leaders. He was a physician, scientist, scholar, and writer and his writings as a member of the "Propaganda Movement" had an impact on the awakening of the Filipino national awareness. Rizal returned from Spain to launch the "Liga Filipina", a nonviolent political organization, but he was prosecuted, and the league was dissolved, Rizal (1930). Rizal lived also in exile from

1892 to 1896 in far-away Dapitan, a town in Mindanao which was under the missionary authority of the Jesuits, Ordaz Gargallo (1947) The nationalist movement split between the reform-minded medium class members and more revolutionary and independence-minded groups that eventually joined the Katipunan, a secret society founded by Andres Bonifacio in 1892. The Katipunan had 30.000 members when in 1892 it rose in revolt against Spain. Rizal was not a member of the Katipunan but was condemned and executed on December 30, 1896. Rizal's death filled the rebels, led by Emilio Aguinaldo as president, with new determination. However, Spanish troops defeated the insurgents and Aguinaldo, and his government went in December 1897 into exile in Hong-Kong.

The Spanish-American War broke out in April 1898 and the Spanish fleet was defeated at Manila. Aguinaldo returned with his 12,000 troops and was able to keep the Spanish forces bottled up in Manila. When the U.S. troops landed the Americans did not recognize the inclusion of Aguinaldo in the new situation and very soon fighting between American and Filipino troops broke out. On June 12, 1898, Aguinaldo issued a declaration of independence. Nevertheless, a Treaty was signed by the United States and Spain on December 10, 1898, Treaty of Paris (1898). Spain ceded the Philippines, Guam, and Puerto Rico to the United States, recognized Cuban independence, and gave $20 million to Spain. A revolutionary congress promulgated a constitution on January 21, 1899, and two days later inaugurated Aguinaldo as president of the new republic. After hostilities broke out in February 1899, Aguinaldo captured by March 1901 and his forces defeated. Aguinaldo's call his forces to lay down their arms, but their resistance continued until 1903. From 1898 to 1935 was the first phase of the U.S. rule over the Philippines. During that time, Washington considered its colonial mission as one of protection and preparation of the Philippines for future independence. There were two legislative bodies: a popularly elected Philippine Assembly and Philippine Commission. The "ilustrados" formed the Federalist Party and presented a statehood platform that had a limited appeal. In 1905 the party, renamed the National Progressive Party, assumed a platform of independence. The Nationalist Party formed in 1907 and dominated politics until after World War II.

The second phase of the U.S. rule from 1936 to 1946 characterized by the establishment of the Commonwealth of the Philippines and the occupation by Japan during World War II. Legislation passed by the U.S. Congress in 1934 contemplated a 10-year period of transition to real independence. Under the country's first constitution approved by plebiscite in 1935, Manuel Quezon elected president of the Commonwealth died in exile in 1944 and his successor was Vice President Sergio Osmeña. Japan attacked the Philippines on December 8, 1941, and occupied Manila on January 2, 1942. Japan set up an independent republic, opposed by underground and guerrilla activity. A major element of the resistance against the Japanese in the Central Luzon area were the "Huk" (short for Hukbalahap, or People's Anti-Japanese Army), Gojo (1984). U.S. and other allied forces invaded the Philippines in October 1944, and on the second of September 1945 the Japanese surrendered.

4 Independence from the United States

To follow the whereabouts of the Presidents, I have used the information provided by Studocu (2022), enriched with details from specific biographies in different encyclopaedias and documents. With the Philippines having a presidential system, to follow the Philippine politics, it is necessary to know the trajectory of the country's presidents.

World War II had been demoralizing for the Philippines, and the islands suffered from rampant inflation and shortages of food and other goods. The Allied leaders wanted to purge officials who collaborated with the Japanese during the war and to deny them the right to vote in the first post-war elections. Commonwealth President Osmeña, however, countered that each case should considered on its own merits. The successful Liberal Party presidential candidate, Manuel Roxas y Acuña, was among those collaborationists. Independence from the United States came on July 4, 1946, and Roxas was sworn in as the first president.

The United States continued to maintain control of twenty-three military bases and installations and in March 1947, and a bilateral treaty signed by which the U.S. continued to provide military aid, training, and materiel. The aid was at the right time, as the "Huk" guerrillas rose again, this time against the new government. They changed their name to the People's Liberation Army and demanded political participation, disbandment of the military police, and a general amnesty. Negotiations failed, and a rebellion began in 1950 with communist support. Better trained forces and conciliatory moves were able to offset "Huk" effectiveness.

Ramón Magsaysay of the Nationalist Party was elected president in 1953 and embarked on widespread reforms that benefited tenant farmers in the Christian north while exacerbating the Muslims in the south. The remaining "Huk" leaders captured or killed; the movement disappeared by 1954. After Magsaysay's death in an airplane crash in 1957, Vice President Carlos P. Garcia succeeded him. On the next election, Garcia won the elections the same year. He advanced the nationalist theme of "Filipinos First," reaching agreement with the United States to relinquish large areas of land no longer needed for military operations.

In 1961 the Liberal Party candidate, Diosdado Macapagal, became president, "One World - Nations online" (2011). Macapagal sought closer relations with Southeast Asian neighbours. However, negotiations with the U.S. over military bases led to considerable anti-American feelings. Diosdado Macapagal was the ninth president of the Philippines, serving from 1961 to 1965, and the sixth vice president, serving from 1957 to 1961. He was also a member of the House of Representatives and in 1970 he headed the Constitutional Convention.

Nationalist Party leader Ferdinand Marcos dominated the political scene for the next two decades, beginning with his election to the presidency in 1965. Marcos initiated ambitious public works to improve the quality of life of the Filipinos. At the same time, he tried to get as much as possible economic and military aid from the U.S. while resisting Philippines involvement in Indochina. In 1967 the Philippines became an initial member of the Association of nations of Southeast Asia, World Atlas (2021). Marcos became the first president to be re-elected (in 1969), but early in his second term economic growth slowed, the crime rate increased, and a new communist insurgency led by the new Communist Party of the Philippines (Marxist-Leninist) was on the rise.

In 1969 the Moro National Liberation Front founded and conducted an insurgency in the South of the archipelago. President Marcos declared martial law on September 21, 1972, that it did last until January 17, 1981. During that period, he called for self-sacrifice but Marcos's friends and his wife, Imelda Romualdez-Marcos, engaged in corruption. With her husband's support, Imelda Marcos built her own political power, becoming governor of Metropolitan Manila and minister of human settlements. The previously non-political armed forces became highly politicized, with relevant positions given to Marcos's loyalists. In 1979 the U.S. reaffirmed Philippine sovereignty over U.S. military bases but continued to provide military and economic aid to Marcos. The end of the Marcos era occurred when his political rival, Liberal Party leader Benigno "Ninoy" Aquino, jailed for eight years by Marcos, was assassinated at the Manila International Airport on August 21, 1983, when returning from the Unites States. Marcos's friends charged with this crime were acquitted. Aquino, however, became the centre of indignation against the Marcos's regime. The Roman Catholic Church, old political opposition groups, the business elite, the left wing, and factions of the armed forces began to exert pressure on the regime. There also was foreign pressure but Marcos, confident with the support given by President Reagan, called a presidential election for February 7, 1986. When the National Assembly proclaimed Marcos the winner, Cardinal Jaime Sin and key military leaders rallied around the apparent majority vote winner, Aquino's widow, Corazon Cojuango Aquino. The People Power Movement (a popular uprising of priests, nuns, and ordinary citizens, and children, supported by military units), after weeks of political unrest, got that President Regan convinced Marcos to retreat to the United States for exile, Jose Mario Bautista Maximiano (2022).

5 Presidents of the XXI Century

On the date supposed to be of Marcos's inauguration, 25 February 1986, took place the sworn in of Corazón Aquino as the first female president of the Philippines. Corazon Aquino had wide popular support but no political organization and her vice president, Salvador H. Laurel, had an organization but almost no popular support. The military, namely generals Enrile and Ramos, also had large stakes in a coalition government. The coalition government fell apart very soon and there were unsuccessful military coups, to oust Aquino. She survived them and was succeeded in 1992 by general Ramos who worked on coalition building and he was able to convince right-wing soldiers, communist insurgents, and Muslim rebels to cease their activities against the government.

Joseph Estrada, who was Ramos's vice president and enjoyed great popularity was elected president in 1998. Within a year, Estrada's popularity declined amid allegations of corruption and failure to remedy poverty. In 2000 Senate investigators accused Estrada of accepting bribes from illegal businesses. Following street protests and the withdrawal of the support by the armed forces, on 20 January 2001, Estrada was forced out of office.

Gloria Macapagal-Arroyo (Vice president and the daughter of President Diosdado Macapagal) was sworn in as Estrada's successor on the day of his departure. Macapagal-Arroyo's initial term in office characterized by fractious coalition politics and by a military mutiny in Manila in July 2003. She declared a nationwide state of rebellion and charges filed against more than 1,000 people. Macapagal-Arroyo was re-elected and sworn in for her own six-year term as president on June 30, 2004. With this new mandate that ended on June 30, 2010, she was able to move on her political and economic reform agenda.

Benigno Simeon Cojuangco Aquino III was the 15th president of the Philippines from 2010 to June 30, 2016. He is the son of politician Benigno "Ninoy" Aquino Jr. and President Corazon Aquino. He is a fourth-generation politician as part of the Aquino family. He was sworn into office as the 15th president of the Philippines on 30 June 2010, succeeding Gloria Macapagal Arroyo. Under his presidency, the Philippines nation's economy grew at the highest rates in decades. Characterized for his confrontational foreign policy; his administration filed an arbitration case, *Philippines v. China*, before the Permanent Court of Arbitration or PCA (a non-UN intergovernmental organization located in The Hague, Netherlands) in an attempt to invalidate China's claims in the South China Sea and assert the Philippines' claims in the area; the court ruled in favor of the Philippines. This arbitration case launched by the Philippines against China stands as the most significant, and most closely watched, development for specialists and observers of the maritime disputes in the South China Sea. To help observers navigate through this foggy proceeding see the article of Ramón Paterno. This article tries to supply a focused overview of the arbitration case and developments in the bilateral dispute between the two parties, Paterno (2016).

Vicente Duterte was born in Maasin, Southern Leyte, and studied political science at the Lyceum of the Philippines University, graduating in 1968, before obtaining a law degree from San Beda College of Law in 1972. He was a lawyer and a prosecutor for Davao City. He became mayor of the city in the wake of the 1986 People Power Revolution. Duterte served as mayor of Davao for over 22 years, during which he transformed Davao in a peaceful and friendly city. During his presidency Duterte focused on combating the illegal drug trade by initiating the war on drugs, fighting crime and corruption, and intensified efforts against terrorism and communist insurgency. He launched a massive infrastructure plan, initiated economic reforms, and proposed a shift to a federal system of government which was unsuccessful. He also oversaw the government's response to the COVID-19 pandemic. Duterte pursue an independent foreign policy and strengthened relations with China and Russia. He initially announced his candidacy for vice president in the 2022 election, but in October 2021, he retired from politics.

Ferdinand "Bongbong" Romualdez Marcos Jr., commonly referred to by the initials BBM or PBBM, was born September 13, 1957 and is the 17th and current president of the Philippines, World Atlas (2022). President Marcos Jr. Previously, served as a senator from 2010 to 2016. He is the second child and only son of former President Ferdinand Marcos Sr. And former first lady Imelda Romualdez Marcos. He became Governor of Ilocos Norte in 1983, holding that office until his family was ousted from power by the People Power Revolution and fled into exile in Hawaii in February 1986. After the death of his father in 1989, President Corazon Aquino eventually allowed his family to return to the Philippines to face various charges. Marcos and his mother, Imelda, are currently facing arrest in the United States for defying a court order to pay U.S.$353 million in restitution to human rights abuse victims during his father's dictatorship. In 2021, Marcos announced that he would run for President of the Philippines in the 2022 election, under the Partido Federal (PFP). He received 59% of the votes. He assumed office on June 30, 2022.

6 The U.S.-Philippines Alliance

Secretary of State Antony J. Blinken traveled the 6th of August 2022 to Manila, where he met President Ferdinand Romualdez Marcos Jr. and Secretary of Foreign Affairs Enrique Manalo to reaffirm the U.S.-Philippines Alliance and the U.S. commitment to the Indo-Pacific region. The U.S. Department of State released a statement on the U.S.-Philippines relations. These strong relations are based on historical and cultural linkages and shared values and interests.

Economic and security and defense cooperation between the Philippines and the United States supply the opportunity to engage on a range of global, bilateral, and regional issues. The Philippines' participation in the Summit for Democracy Year of Action supplies an avenue for continued engagement and collaboration on democracy, human rights, and rule of law. The U.S. and the Philippines enjoy strong people-to-people connections. At least four million Filipino-Americans live in the U.S. and almost 300,000 U.S. citizens reside in the Philippines. Almost 21,000 Filipinos have taken part in U.S. Government sponsored people-to-people exchange programs between the U.S. and the Philippines. The Statement on U.S.-Philippines relationship published the 5 of August 2022 is highly informative and explains the deep and the lasting relations of the two countries supporting the development of the Philippines:

> The Philippines is one of the top three trading partners of the U.S. and the United States is one of the largest foreign investors in the Philippines. For the past 60 years, the United States Agency for International Development (USAID) has worked with the Philippine government and local authorities and organizations to share development goals, investing since 1961 more than $5 billion to support the Philippines. Current development priorities include adapting to climate change, promoting renewable energy, favoring economic recovery, fighting corruption, and defending human rights. The United States has also been the Philippines' strongest partner in countering the COVID-19 pandemic, providing over $39 million in pandemic-related aid and as of July 2022 donating more than thirty-three million vaccine doses.

The cooperation of the U.S. and the Philippines on clean energy and the contribution of USAID is also well explain in the document. But the more innovative collaboration is on nuclear civilian cooperation and on cybersecurity:

> The United States and the Philippines collaborate closely with one another on clean energy. USAID's $34 million Energy Secure Philippines (ESP) supports a more competitive, secure, and resilient Philippine energy sector by working to improve the performance and efficiency of energy utilities, deploy renewable energy systems, enhance competition in the power sector, and bolster energy sector cybersecurity. ESP will help mobilize more than $750 million in private sector investment into the sector and develop at least five hundred megawatts of added clean energy

generation capacity. The United States and the Philippines also collaborate closely with one another on nuclear energy. In March, the United States and the Philippines signed a Memorandum of Understanding Concerning Strategic Civil Nuclear Cooperation (NCMOU), which supplies a framework for cooperation and a mutually aligned approach to nonproliferation on civil nuclear issues. The United States also helps the Philippines through our Foundational Infrastructure for Responsible Use of Small Modular Reactor Technology (FIRST) program which deepens our strategic ties, supports energy innovation, and advances our technical collaboration with the Philippines on secure, safe nuclear energy infrastructure

On 22 September 2022 President Joseph R. Biden, jr. and President Marcos met in New York and the made the following remarks:

President Joseph R. Biden, Jr. Met today with President Ferdinand Marcos Jr. of the Philippines in New York. The leaders reflected on the importance of the U.S.-Philippines alliance. President Biden reaffirmed the United States' ironclad commitment to the defense of the Philippines. The leaders discussed the situation in the South China Sea and underscored their support for freedom of navigation and overflight and the peaceful resolution of disputes.

The leaders discussed opportunities to expand bilateral cooperation on a wide range of issues, including energy security, climate action, and infrastructure. The leaders also discussed Russia's war against Ukraine and its implications for energy prices and food security, as well as ASEAN matters, the crisis in Myanmar, and the importance of respect for human rights.

7 Security Cooperation U.S.-Philippines

The mentioned Statement on the U.S.-The Philippines relationship published 5 August 2022 reflects the importance of U.S.-Philippines relations and specially on security cooperation, U.S. Department of State (2022). The statement makes clear that bilateral defense agreements continue to supply the foundation for the defense relationship. They enable critical U.S. military support, presence, and interoperability. The 1951 U.S.-Philippines Mutual Defense Treaty (MDT) supplies a solid foundation for our robust post-World War II security partnership. The 1999 Visiting Forces Agreement (VFA) and the 2014 Enhanced Defense Cooperation Agreement (EDCA) are supposed to supplement the MDT and reaffirm mutual security cooperation between the United States and the Philippines. These agreements build ability for U.S. forces and the Armed Forces of the Philippines by enabling greater interoperability, capability development, and modernization. Furthermore, the mentioned agreements expand opportunities for bilateral training, augment the U.S. ability to aid in the Philippines in cases of natural disasters, and support efforts to uphold the rules-based order in the South China Sea. That order protects the rights, freedoms, and lawful uses of the sea to all nations. The General Security of Military Information Agreement between the Philippines and the U.S. complements information-sharing and equipment modernization. The U.S. supports the Philippines' counterterrorism efforts against ISIS and other terrorist groups. U.S. counterterrorism aid improves the Philippines' ability to respond to terrorist attacks and enhance law enforcement ability to effectively investigate and prosecute cases of terrorism.

U.S. Secretary of State Anthony Blinken arrived in Manila the night of August 5, 2022, after attending the ASEAN meetings in Phnom Penh, Cambodia, where he joined his counterparts including Chinese and Russian ministers. ASEAN foreign ministers called for "maximum restraint" as China mounted war drills around Taiwan and moved against the U.S., fearing the situation "could destabilize the region and eventually could lead to miscalculation, serious confrontation, open conflicts, and unpredictable consequences among major powers. Antony Blinken met President Ferdinand "Bongbong" Marcos Jr. n August 6, 2022, at the Malacañang Palace in Manila. Marcos Jr. Praised the vital relationship between Manila and Washington, which are treaty allies, and U.S. aid to the Philippines over the years. Blinken reiterated Washington's commitment to the 1951 Mutual Defense Treaty with the Philippines and "to collaborating with you on shared challenges." He also discussed with Marcos Jr. Strengthening democracy and U.S. commitment to work with the Philippines to defend the rule of law, protect human rights, freedom of expression and safeguard civil society groups. Addressing the press after the meeting, Blinken described the Philippines as "an irreplaceable friend," and he also reiterated to the president that an armed attack on Filipino forces, public vessels, or planes in the South China Sea "will invoke U.S. mutual defense commitments."

Meetings in Manila were for discussions on U.S.-China tensions over the Taiwan visit of U.S. House of Representatives Speaker Nancy Pelosi, However, Blinken said a 70-year-old defense pact with the Philippines was "ironclad." This comment of the Secretary made it clear that the U.S.-Philippines Mutual Defense Treaty (MDT) and other security cooperation agreements were particularly important for the peace and stability in the South of China Sea region.

The visit of Blinken was truly relevant for Philippines policies in the JSCS/WPS and for the future of the presidency of Marcos Jr. In fact, when U.S. Secretary of State Antony Blinken assured the Philippines on the 6 August 2022 that the United States would come to its defense if attacked in the South China Sea, the role of the Philippines in the region was strengthen. Furthermore, Philippine's politicians will be able to better use the UN arbitral court ruling invalidating China's claim and making possible for them to gain global support. In any case, President Duterte's overtures towards China and his anti-U.S. rhetoric damaged United States-Philippines ties. In the coming years, the Philippines' role in the South China Sea region and around the world will strengthen.

8 The West Philippine Sea

The disputes concerning the West Philippine Sea in the South China Sea, put the United Nations Convention on the Law of the Sea or the Law of the Sea Convention (LOSC) as an essential international instrument affecting the maritime entitlements of the Philippines. The Philippine state, a maritime nation, needs to understand the Law of the Sea and the LOSC, which is its primary reference material in dealing with its public maritime concerns, see Yano (2007).

In the South China Sea context, the posture of the Philippines is central to counter China's aggressive claim to the South China Sea/West Philippine Sea (SCS/WPS) through on bilateral discussions, and by an ASEAN collective approach, Shead (2017). West Philippine Sea abbreviated as WPS is the official designation by the government of the Philippines to the parts of the South China Sea that included in the country's exclusive economic zone. The term is incorrect to refer to the entire South China Sea. As mentioned before, to strengthen its position using the UN, the Philippines tried to use the arbitral court ruling invalidating China's claim and to gain global support. Its position improved obtaining secured clarification from the U.S. that the Mutual Defense Treaty (MDT) covers the South China Sea. However, President Duterte administration undermined these advantages negotiating chips in the hope of securing economic benefits. President Duterte announced the Philippines was discarding its traditional alliance with the U.S. and announced the termination of the Visiting Forces Agreement (VFA). He even called the UN arbitral ruling as little more than a piece of paper. Banking on his personal friendship with China's Xi Jinping, Duterte preferred bilateral talks. President Duterte ended his term and the promised benefits have not materialized. Meanwhile, China, has increased its aggressive actions to control this waterway with its rich fishing grounds and rich potential deposits of hydrocarbons.

Within ASEAN, negotiations on a Code of Conduct on the South China Sea are having little progress. In fact, being the South China Sea issue considered by ASEAN members as a dispute between China and the United States. With economic realities in favor of China, there has been little enthusiasm among ASEAN countries to choose sides. Indonesia and Vietnam have stood up to assert their sovereign rights in the face of Chinese incursions, but collectively, ASEAN has been so far ineffective in any regional effort to moderate China's aggressive behavior.

Other developments in terms of regional alliance could prove to be practical options for the Philippines position moving forward. In 2007 came into being the Quadrilateral Security Dialogue, Romulo (2021), referred as Quad, formed of Australia, India, Japan, and the United States. From the very beginning, Quad members viewed the Security Dialogue as a response to China's rise as a world power. It was for that reason that Australia, under Kevin Rudd as prime minister, after withdrew from the dialogue, but rejoined following his departure. The Quad was formally reconvened in 2017 and has since then started to become a more formal body following the increase of bilateral disputes between China on the one side and India, Australia, and Japan on the other. President Biden's desire to revitalize relations with allies may hasten this process. Later, it took place a meeting of the Quad-Plus dialogue which included Vietnam, South Korea, and New Zealand. At the same time, the term "Indo-Pacific" has come to be a widely recognized regional concept used to define America's current security strategy in East Asia. The United States, Australia, Japan, India, France, the United Kingdom, Indonesia, and ASEAN adopted "Indo-Pacific" as a policy symbol. "The Spirit of the Quad," a joint statement published in 2021 by the Quad members, described a common vision of a free and open Indo-Pacific, see Quad Leaders' Joint statement (2021).

9 Conclusions

The situation of the Philippines in the South China Sea is a geopolitical factor that is now more important than ever for the country influencing its international policy. The

Republic of the Philippines has 7,641 islands, of these islands (only 2,000 are with habitants) and has been and still is an ardent supporter of the development of the concept of archipelagic states in the Law of the Sea.

Early inhabitants arrived from Indonesia and other places 30.000 years ago, followed for people arriving from China and other places. The Filipino population has quickly assimilated various migrations throughout its history. The arrival of the first Spanish explorers in 1516 began a period of 333 years of common history with Spain. The separation ended in 1898 after a turbulent period in which the support of the United States was instrumental in the separation of the metropolis. The period of guardianship of the United States lasted 48 years and ended on July 4, 1946. Manuel Roxas y Acuña was the first president of the Philippines and although the Americans continued with more than twenty bases and facilities in the territory, the independence of the country combined in the following years despite periods of crisis. The Philippines has close historical ties with the United States and with Spain. The relationship with the United States has had difficulties during the twentieth century but has strengthened in the twenty-first century. The U.S.-Philippines Mutual Defense Treaty (MDT) signed on 1951, supplied a solid foundation for our robust post-World War II security partnership. Last year the Statement on U.S.-Philippines relationship published the 5 of August 2022 is highly informative and explains the deep and the lasting relations of the two countries supporting the development of the Philippines.

President Joseph R. Biden, jr. and President Marcos met in New York on 22 September 2022, and they made remarks on which the two leaders reflected on the importance of the U.S.-Philippines alliance. President Biden reaffirmed the United States' ironclad commitment to the defense of the Philippines. The leaders discussed the situation in the South China Sea and underscored their support for freedom of navigation and overflight and the peaceful resolution of disputes.

These remarks are particularly important for the Philippines. In fact, Spratly Islands are considered geographically part of the Philippine archipelago and is just one hundred kilometers away from Palawan Island. It means that they are much closer to the Philippines than any other countries. According to 1982 United Nations Convention on the Law of the Sea (UNCLOS), the Spratly Islands lie within the Philippines' 200-mile Exclusive Economic Zone. On January 22, 2013, the Philippines instituted an arbitral proceeding against the People's Republic of China (PRC) over the disputed islands to UNCLOS. However, China rejected and returned the notification. The final ruling occurred on July 12, 2016, when the PCA published the tribunal's arbitration award. The tribunal ruled on most points in favor of the Philippines and against China. The Philippines tried also to get support on ASEAN but the negotiations on a Code of Conduct on the South China Sea are having little progress.

Spratly Islands could be the source of billion tons of oil reserves and natural gas and are one of the most productive fishing in the area. It is also the busiest areas of commercial shipping traffic. Thus, it is important for economic development of the Philippines. Also disputed with China are the Scarborough Shoal and other traditional fishing grounds inside the Philippines' exclusive economic zone.

The Philippines is a unique country in Asia and has its cultural roots in Europe and America without renouncing its Asiatic origins. Its close ties with the United States make its defense linked under various treaties with the defense of its American ally. The democratic advance and economic progress will make the Philippines an essential pillar for stability in Southeast Asia.

References

Bautista Maximiano, J.M.: Remembering the Philippines' 1986 People Power Revolution (2022). https://www.preda.org/2022/remembering-the-philippines-1986-people-power

Blanco Pitlo, L.: The Philippines and the West Philippine Sea (2013). https://www.ThePhilippinesandtheWestPhilippineSea-TheDiplomat

Cartwright, M.: Manila Galleon. Galleon - World History Encyclopedia (2021). https://www.Manila

Churchill, R., Lowe, V., Sander, A.: The Law of Sea: Fourth edition (2022). https://books.google.es/books/about/The_Law_of_the_Sea.html?id=SL

Gojo Romelino, R.: The Hukbalahap movement (1984). https://www.globalsecurity.org/military/library/report/1984/GRR.htm

Márquez Montero, C.: Real Academia de la Historia. Fernando de Magallanes (2021). https://dbe.rah.es/biografias/12661/Fernando-de-magallanes

Montecalvo, R.: The royal company of the Philippines (2014). https://prezi.com/2xrgy7t98vz6/the-royal-company-of-the-philippines/

One World-Nations online. History of the Philippines (2011). https://www.HistoryofPhilippines(nationsonline.org)

Ordaz Gargallo, J.: José Rizal, poeta y político de la independencia de Filipinas (1947). https://www.cervantesvirtual.com/obra-visor/jose-rizal-poeta-y-politico

Paterno, R.: The maritime review. Philippines vs China (2016). https://maritimereview.ph/author/rpaterno/

Philippines: Official Gazette of the Republic of the Philippines 2022 (2022). https://www.officialgazette.gov.ph.about.Philippines

Puig-Samper Mulero, M.A.: Alexander von Humboldt. Real Academia de la Historia (2019). https://dbe.rah.es/biografias/16469/alexander-von-humboldt

Quad Leaders' Joint statement: The Spirit of the Quad (2021). https://in.usembassy.gov/quad-leaders-joint-statement-the-spirit-of-the-quad/

Rizal, J.: Epistolario Rizalino. Tomo Tercero (1930). https://books.google.es/books/about/Epistolario_Rizalino.html?id=1FseAAAAMAAJ&redir_esc

Romulo, R.: Indo-Pacific Quad: Relevance to Philippines (2021). Quad: Relevance to Philippines | Philstar.com https://www.Indo-Pacific

Shead, B.: The Philippines's relationship with ASEAN (2017). https://www.aseanbriefing.com/news/Philippines-relationship-ASEAN

Severino, R.: Where in the World is the Philippines? https://www.bing.com/search?q=WHERE+IN+THE+WORLD+IS+THE+PHILIPPINES%3F&form

Salvador, E.: The Revolution of 1898: The Main Facts (2002). file:///G:/Liberalism%20in%20the%20Philippines.mhtml

U.S. Department of State: Statement on U.S.-The Philippines relationship, 5 August 2022. https://www.STL.News/TheUnitedStates-PhilippinesRelationship

U.S.-Philippines Mutual Defense Treaty MDT (1951). https://www.officialgazette.gov.ph/1951/08/30/mutual-defense-treaty

World Atlas: List of The Presidents of The Philippines (2020). https://www.worldatlas.com/articles/presidents-of-the-philippines

World Atlas: ASEAN countries (2021). https://www.worldatlas.com/geography/asean-countries.html
Yano, J.: The Problematic "West Philippine Sea" (2007). https://maritimereview.ph/the-problematic-west-philippine-sea/

Artificial Islands in the South China Sea. Territorial Disputes in the Area. United Nations Conference of the Law of the Sea Proposals

Jordi Regí Rodríguez(✉)

Nebrija–Santander Chair on Analysis and Resolution of Conflicts, Antonio de Nebrija University, Madrid, Spain
jregi@nebrija.es

Abstract. Artificial Islands construction is a rising phenomenon. The ones constructed by the People's Republic of China in the South China Sea are a set of gains for the country, but they do not respect international law and specifically the United Nations Convention of the Law of the Sea (UNCLOS). China's actions regarding the construction of these islands have succeeded in raising the tension in the region.

The consequences of China's actions could have repercussions on international competitiveness with strong economic and political tensions also due to disputes over the limits of the jurisdiction of each of the States around the South Sea. China prefers the South China Sea issue to be resolved among the stakeholders of the region and with no external interference but in a globalized world, this situation should not be accepted. It is not only a question of economic exclusive zones (EEZ) but the control of essential maritime routes and oil and gas reserves in the area.

Keywords: Artificial islands · Territorial disputes · United Nations conference of the Law of the Sea · South China Sea

1 Introduction

The people's Republic of China, as a coastal country, has a huge dependence on maritime transport, as well as on the exploitation of its natural resources and its foreign trade -through which it exports an enormous number of products manufactured–. For this reason, the race for the right exploitation of subsoil natural resources has become one of the priorities over which focuses its geopolitical strategy on Asia-Pacific.

The Asian Power is increasingly undeniable. China advances in its economic growth and its commercial and financial development. This process affects also its direct area of influence; at the same time, puts China in a position ever more relevant in international scenarios, whether they be economic, political, financial, or military.

The great opportunities that exploitable resources on the seabed would provide make the region one of the sea basins with the greatest tensions between states, especially accentuating since the end of 2016 when China began to move away from discreet

J. Cayón Peña and J. M. Ramírez (Eds.): *Threats to Peace and International Security: Asia versus West*, ASTSA, pp. 111–131, 2023.
https://doi.org/10.1007/978-3-031-28336-9_7

politics. The exploitation of these resources is one of the cornerstones around which conflicts emanate and given the geographical vastness of the South China Sea, the existence of millions of islands and reefs of emerged land and the coexistence of numerous coastal states, make the region a difficult area to control, favoring threats and the illegal exploitation of resources, as well as territorial disputes (Fig. 1).

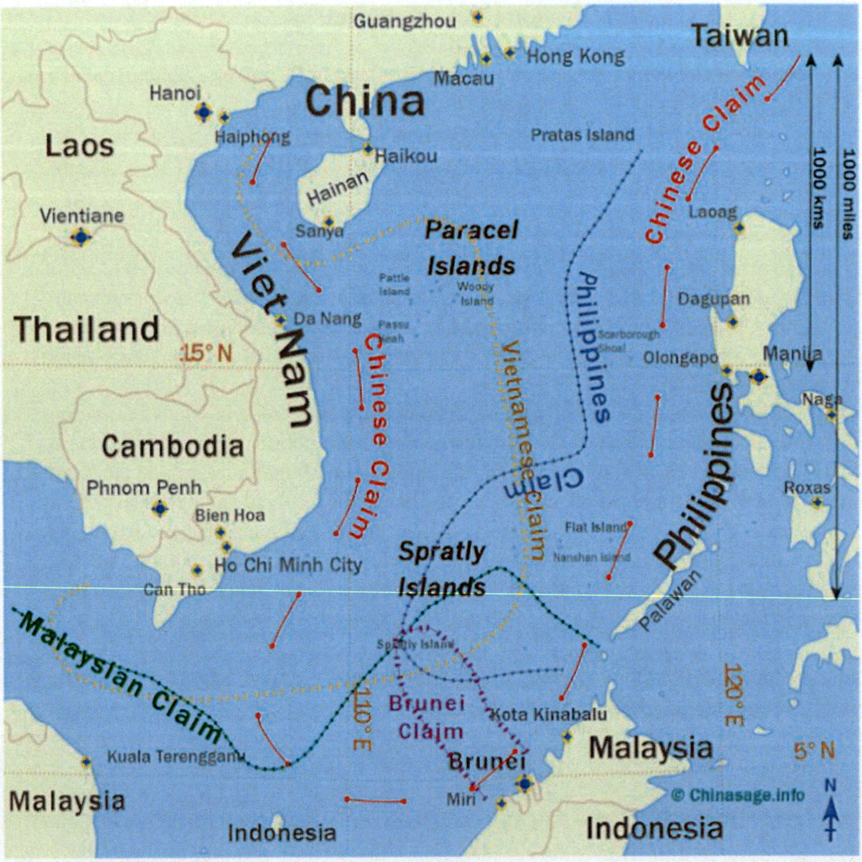

Fig. 1. South China sea map. Link: www.chinasage.info/south-china-sea.htm.

The South China Sea is surrounded by China, Brunei, Indonesia, Malaysia, the Philippines Islands, Vietnam, and Taiwan, and all of them have several disputes and claims motivated by the strategic interests of the islands.

The South China Sea is incredibly rich in natural resources with 11 billion barrels of oil, 190 trillion cubic feet of natural gas, and 10% of the world's fisheries. Most importantly though, 30% of the world's shipping trade flows through here to the booming population centers and economic markets of Southeast Asia where 5.3 trillion dollars of commerce goes over that water each year. It's an extremely important body of water. With oil reserves of several billion barrels, an estimated nine hundred trillion cubic feet of natural gas (Afrin, 2017).

We may clearly distinguish between three different dimensions (Sreekumar and Hassan, 2020), economic, strategic and geopolitical, and maritime dimensions. One of the principal dimensions of an artificial island is an economic dimension which primarily corresponds to commercial and industrial purposes. Mostly, artificial islands are constructed for exploring and extracting resources such as oil, coal, petroleum, minerals, and even fishery products. For instance, the Upper Zakum Islands of Abu Dhabi were constructed to extract oil and petroleum from the seabed. Strategic and Geopolitical, in many cases, they are constructed to keep watch on the neighboring countries and as a site for building military and defense infrastructure. These artificially constructed islands can be used to attack enemy countries using warships and missiles and maritime dimension, Maritime security is a word that is gaining popularity and importance in international relations. There is no exact definition or consensus on maritime security definition yet.

The United Nations Conference on the Law of the Sea (United Nations, 1982 is clear about that:

> "Article 121. Regime of the Islands, 1. An island is a naturally formed area of land, surrounded by water, which is above water at high tide. 2. Except as provided for in paragraph 3, the territorial sea, the contiguous zone, the exclusive economic zone and the continental shelf of an island are determined in accordance with the provisions of this Convention applicable to other land territory, 3. Rocks which cannot sustain human habitation or economic life of their own shall have no exclusive economic zone or continental shelf." (United Nations, 1982)

UNCLOS was established on April 30, 1982, to establish the limits of the zones maritime areas over which States have sovereignty. The areas established in the Convention and that will be of great relevance throughout this text are the internal waters, the territorial sea, the contiguous zone, the exclusive economic zone, the continental shelf, and the high seas.

These artificial islands cannot be considered as islands and obviously nor the ones constructed by the PRC with dredge ships, and it can neither give more territorial sea based on that illegal fact. In many cases, they are constructed to keep watch on the neighboring countries and as a site for building military and defense infrastructure. These artificially constructed islands can be used to attack enemy countries using warships and missiles. Also, maritime security is a word that is gaining popularity and importance in international relations and clearly shows a threat to the rest of the countries.

For instance, the Fiery Cross Reef as we can see in the next image, was a natural reef and in 2016 there is a harbor, military infrastructure, and a small airport (Fig. 2).

In this article, we will analyze the historical situation regarding the territorial dispute in the South China Sea. The violations and proposals for a solution according to the United Nations Convention of the Law of the Sea (United Nations, 1982).

However, the very fact that PRC represents a great influence political, economic, commercial, and military, questions the effectiveness of the cooperation from other states and the abundance of international pressure.

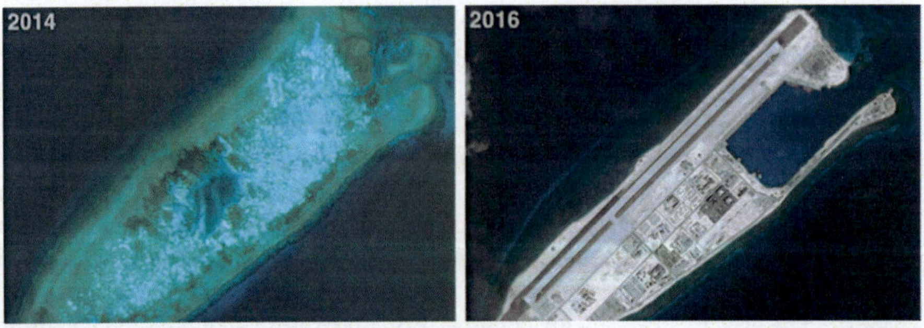

Fig. 2. Fiery Cross Reef slider. Link: https://storymaps.arcgis.com/stories/6d8a684e762f4f4ca90c1a19121fcf8c/print.

Also, the environment is an important element because the construction of these islands is directly causing great damage to the seabed and coral reefs in the SCS (McManus, 2017).

2 Territorial Disputes in the South China Sea

Territorial disputes in the South China Sea are based on the claim of islets and archipelagos by the People's Republic of China (or mainland China), the Republic of China (or Taiwan), Vietnam, the Philippines, Malaysia, and Brunei, from the southern area of the China Sea, also called in other ways depending on the point of view that is considered (Fig. 3).

These islets and archipelagos are not inhabited, despite the presence of military bases which, on the other hand, along with trade, are the central axis of the conflict in question.

China claims the line called "Nine dash-line" which the old Chinese nationalist government marked out in the 1940s and that all neighboring countries reject. Within this line are the Paracelsus Islands, but above all the Spratly Islands, most of them rock islets that today are in the hands of several countries with military confrontations. The importance of this claim is that if accepted internationally it would make the South China Sea Chinese territorial waters, and not international ones as they are now. And this would allow China to control the navigation of ships. This would imply having control over half of the total tons that are moved in the world. This line encompasses 90% of the waters of the South China Sea.

In this sense, it is worth highlighting the historical context in which the claims over the territories are written. Before Japan's defeat in World War II, the South China Sea was under the influence of the Japanese empire and, therefore, the islands in the area were under its sphere of power and effective control. With the defeat of Japan and the signing of the San Francisco Peace Treaty in September in 1951, this country renounces its former overseas domains. Specifically, in article two of said treaty, Japan renounces all rights, titles, and claims to the Spratly Islands and the Paracel Islands (United Nations Treaty of peace with Japan, 1951). However, the treaty did not contemplate awarding the administration of these territories to any State. In this gap conflicts arose over the control of the islands in the South China Sea, the consequences of which have transcended

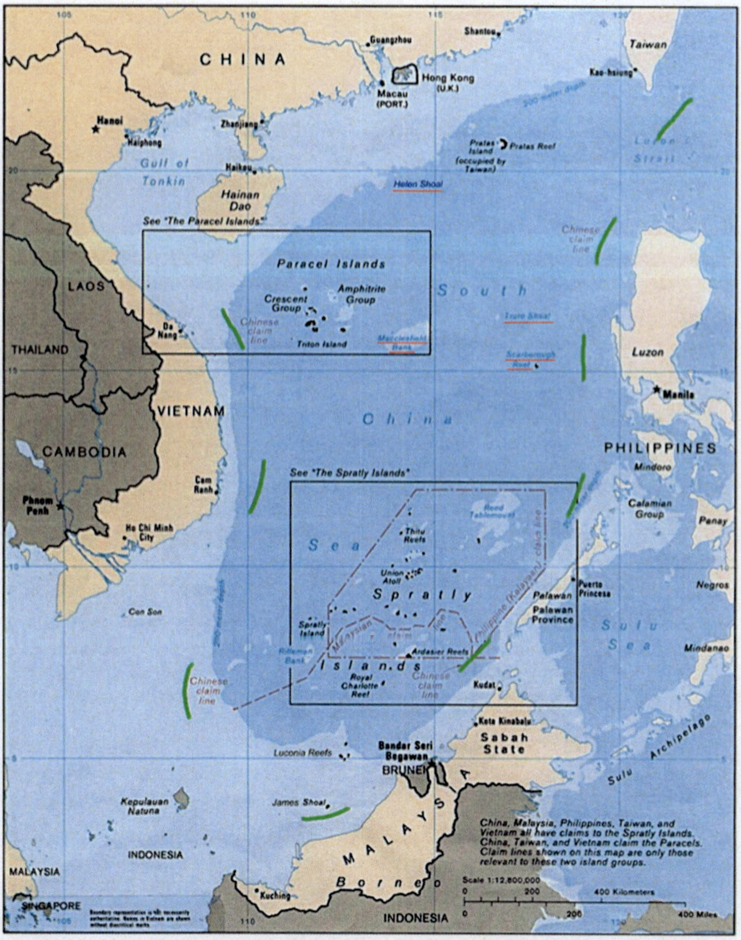

Fig. 3. Nine dash-line in green. Source: U.S. Central Intelligence Agency

to the present day. As Seokwoo Lee maintains "the lack of precision in key diplomatic documents, especially the San Francisco Peace Treaty of 1951, allowed certain territorial disputes to arise". (Lee, 2002).

The Chinese government did not accept any claims of the rest of the states in the South China Sea and several armed conflicts happened during the last 20 years of the last century (Chang, 1991), mainly based on showing the neighboring countries his determination about not accepting any kind of negotiation about its sovereignty.

The construction of artificial islands has since been protested by neighboring countries, especially by the Philippines and Vietnam governments who highlight the breach of the status quo by these unilateral construction activities (PHILIPPINES UN, 2014).

This construction started with the occupation of rocks and reefs in the SCS, like the one shown in the following image (Figs. 4 and 5).

Fig. 4. Chinese soldiers in an islet in SCS. Source: Reuters

But as it is clearly shown in the next image, PRC, dredging vessels are building islands in the Mischief Reef in the disputed Spratly Islands in the South China Sea.

Fig. 5. Dredging vessels in a reef in the SCS. Source: Reuters. P-8A Poseidon surveillance aircraft provided by the U.S. Navy, May 21, 2015

The people's Republic of China has focused its maritime strategy on the fight for hegemony and control of the sea, leading to disputes with all the coastal nations of the

South China Sea. The conflict for control of these waters began after the end of the 2nd World War as it has been said and, in the absence of an international agreement in which is known to establishes a division of the archipelagos, every nation has taken a stand unilaterally based on historical justifications, and principles of sovereignty or control territorial to defend the claim of its waters.

> "China has undertaken drastic efforts to dredge and reclaim thousands of square feet in the South China Sea. It has deployed anti-ship and anti-aircraft missile systems on the Spratly Islands, according to the U.S. Department of Defense, and constructed military infrastructure on several artificial islands, such as such as runways, support buildings, loading piers, and communications facilities. China's land development has profound security implications. The potential to deploy aircraft, missiles, and missile defense systems to any of its constructed islands vastly boosts China's ability to project power, extending its operational range south and east by as much as 1,000 kilometers." (Council of Foreign Relations, 2019).

In the following map, we can see the area of projection gained by the artificial islands at Subi Reef in the SCS (Fig. 6).

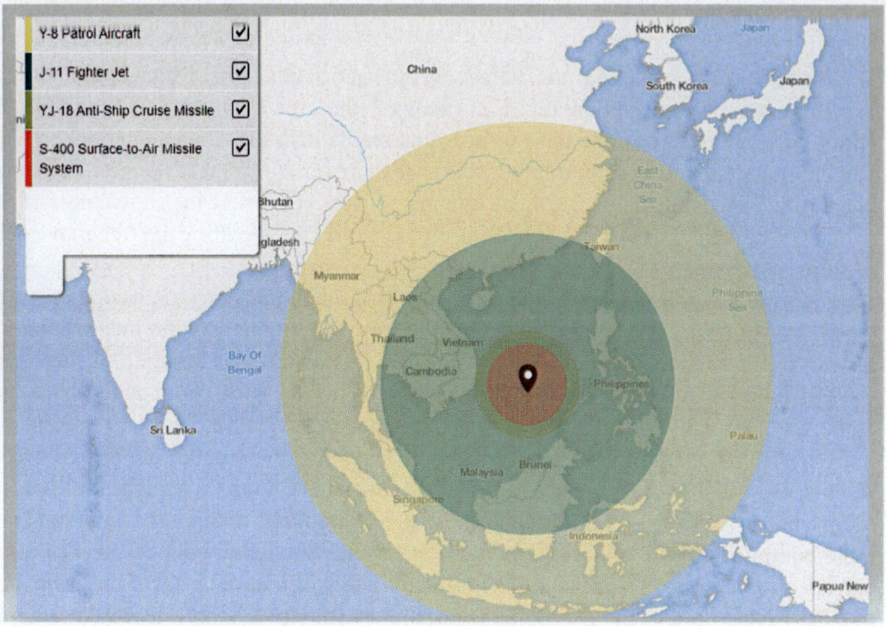

Fig. 6. Range of the Chinese weapons in the SCS. Source: Global GIS Data, Globalsecurity.org

But Beijing's primary strategy in the South China Sea is to use civilian and paramilitary pressure to coerce its Southeast Asian neighbors into abandoning their rights. (Poling, 2020).

> "China has constructed 72 fighter jet hangars at its three airbases in the Spratlys — Fiery Cross, Mischief, and Subi Reefs — along with another 16 on Woody Island in the Paracels. It has so far held off on deploying combat aircraft to the Spratlys but rotates J-11 fighters frequently through Woody. Assuming it was the first mover in a conflict, it would be able to deploy combat aircraft rapidly to the airfields in the Spratlys, instantly establishing air dominance in the theater. Unless the Chinese happened to pick a fight when U.S. forces were engaged in a major exercise like Balikatan in the Philippines, the closest U.S. ground-based combat aircraft would be in Okinawa and Guam, approximately 1,300 and 1,500 nautical miles away, respectively. The only U.S. military planes in the region would be patrol aircraft in the Philippines and potentially Malaysia.
>
> China has, meanwhile, deployed YJ-12B and YJ-62 anti-ship cruise missiles to its outposts in the Spratlys and Paracels, backed by longer-range missile capabilities from the mainland. And it has invested heavily in radar and signals intelligence capabilities on all the islands, making it a safe bet that it sees just about anything moving on or above the South China Sea. A U.S. Navy vessel sailing in those waters would be well within the range of Chinese fire when hostilities broke out. Lacking supporting ground-based fire or air cover, the only rational option would be to pull back to the Sulu and Celebes Seas, and probably beyond, as quickly as possible." (Poling, 2020)

The other states in the area are completely opposed to this claim, which until February 17, 2016, was strictly diplomatic. For example, the area claimed by China collides with Singapore in its commercial spirit. China maintains sixty-one open conflicts with neighboring states. It is important to note that there are a few with the United States, due to some islets that they have there, and this fact can determine the seriousness of the conflict. The Americans have given themselves the role of defending the free movement of ships in the area.

Half of the world's commercial traffic passes through this corridor, as does most of the oil consumed by Asian countries. If China were to turn this sea into internal waters, instead of international waters as they are now, its power over the trade of the entire world would be immense. The Paracelsus Islands, to the north, is disputed by a few countries, especially Vietnam and the two Chinas, but the Chinese military presence is indisputable. The same does not happen in the Spratlys, with the enormous difficulty that this means, where several countries —Vietnam, mainland China, Taiwan, the Philippines, Malaysia, and Brunei— control the islands, islets, and reefs, making the situation even more complicated and volatile in military terms and without any doubt, the 11 billion barrels of untapped oil and the 190 trillion cubic feet of natural gas that are estimated to exist in that area, (Asia Maritime Transparency Initiative, 2020), represent another decisive factor in the territorial dispute.

While the PRC, Taiwan, and Vietnam claim all the archipelagos, the rest of the countries defend a division partial and equidistant.

The numerous complaints in which the PRC is immersed reflect the importance of the blue economy, given that its geo-economic interests focus on trade maritime as the main and fundamental means for the export of your products, and due to the existence of raw materials most necessary to sustain power with an energy demand that is increasing greater time.

Although PRC ratified UNCLOS on June 1996 (United Nations, 1996), China filed a reservation statement in 2006 which excludes all forms of dispute settlement in Sect. 2 of part XV of UNCLOS (United Nations, 2006) declaring its clear position on the problem.

In 2016, according to press reports, the Permanent Court of Arbitration in The Hague ruled that there was "no legal basis" for China's claim in the dispute over control of the area over which China believes to be entitled (in the South China Sea), after a claim filed in 2013 by the Philippines over the Scarborough Reef dispute, which China places within its maritime space. The sentence agreed with the Philippines and, according to the Ara newspaper, "warns that China is interfering with Manila's fishing rights in the Scarborough reef, generating serious risks of collision with its neighbor's ships." (Permanent Court of Arbitration, 2016).

However, the Chinese government responded by rejecting the ruling, saying it did not recognize the court's legitimacy because it does not consider historical elements.

In August 2017, Chinese Defense Minister Chang Wanquan emphasized the importance of maritime safety and loomed a possible "people's war at sea" to safeguard Chinese sovereignty, after the failure of the Court of the Hague before the claim's history of China in the region.

PRC will require foreign ships to report in what they consider to be their territorial waters (Krishnan, 2021). A decision that will affect many countries, including India, which estimates that 55% of their trade would be affected by it, by using the South China Sea routes and the Strait of Malacca. China's newly passed coast guard legislation authorizes its maritime law-enforcement fleets to use lethal force on foreign ships operating in China's waters, including the disputed waters claimed by China. (China Government, 2021).

> For over a decade, China has implicitly indicated that it does not need to wage war to achieve its goals. Beijing has opted for a slow-intensity conflict approach or low-intensity coercion by which China uses incremental steps to expand its de facto control over disputed territories. Beijing has used the South China Sea as a ground to test and refine its coercive policy toward smaller claimants. These policies can be duplicated and enacted by China elsewhere, including its disputes in the East China Sea. (Trung, 2021)

This political style of PRC leaders is now starting to change with the aforementioned China Coast Guard law that is in clear contradiction with international law and specifically with the UNCLOS. (Okada, 2021).

Article 21 of the CCG Law stipulates that if a foreign warship or government vessel violates China's domestic law in waters where China claims jurisdiction, the CCG will take enforcing measures, up to and including forced eviction and towing. Article 22 permits the CCG to use weapons against foreign organizations and individuals that infringe on China's sovereign rights and jurisdiction at sea. However, UNCLOS Articles 32, 95, and 96 stipulate that warships and government ships are completely immune from the jurisdiction of any country other than the flag state. Therefore, if the CCG implements the actions defined in Articles 21 and 22 of the CCG Law, it would violate international law. Taking illegal coercive measures against other countries' warships and government ships causes an increased risk of armed conflict. (Okada, 2021).

This new situation is not given a good perspective to solve the conflict but is a great source of problems. According to Suxian Luo:

> Internally, China should establish transparent processes to curb disproportionate use or abuse of force by local personnel and further bring its maritime law enforcement operations in line with international practice. Unauthorized, impulsive behavior resulting from the "excessive zeal or incompetence" of local commanders, according to Sean Lynn-Jones, an international security scholar at Harvard University's Belfer Center, bears the primary responsibility for the occurrence of incidents at sea.
>
> There are several internal mechanisms that China can consider installing to discourage such acts: 1) documenting and reporting incidents involving the use of force, 2) investigating and evaluating the appropriateness of using force, 3) making appropriate revisions to the procedures, and 4) taking necessary disciplinary actions on personnel found inappropriately using force.
>
> China's intention to clarify and standardize operations of its coast guard should be welcomed. But Beijing needs to understand why its coast guard law has aggravated concerns in the region and reassure its neighbors by expanding engagement and transparency. (Luo, 2021)

The SCS problem and all of the problems in the area seem only to raise a new step into the militarization of the sea and looks as if these artificial islands tend to find their sense. We would, however, be very wrong if we thought that this crisis is only of an economic or legal nature. This situation has a substratum even broader and deeper within the strategic vision you want to adopt in China. In this change, it shifts its continental vocation towards the sea, aware that its future as a superpower depends on the control of the oceans.

3 Artificial Islands Status According to the United Nations Conference on the Law of the Sea (UNCLOS)

The conflict is based on the "Nine-dash line", defined in the maps published by China in 1947 to delimit territorial waters in the South Sea from China. Additionally, Beijing has built military infrastructure on artificial islands located within the disputed territory.

It is necessary to understand this problem and how it is applied in the UNCLOS. For the particularity of this case, there is no regulation within the Convention, however its importance lies in the establishment of maritime zones that due to artificial islands it has extended the Chinese territory and its jurisdiction in the sea.

These islands are found above the surface of the sea, which means that they do not count as part of the continental territory and this results in extending the baseline from which the nautical miles begin to be counted, making China the owners of 2.25 million km2 in the Southern Sea, which in total has 4.25 million km2 and with the right to exploit its resources.

According to what Singh and Yamamoto declare, these artificial islands are against both the Declaration on the Conduct of the Parties in the South China Sea and UNCLOS:

> These sustained constructions in SCS have repeatedly raised concerns about a breach of the 2012 Declaration on the Conduct of the Parties in the South China Sea (ASEAN, 2002). This Declaration underlines respect for freedom of navigation in and overflight above the South China Sea, as provided by the UN Convention on the Law of the Sea (UNCLOS) but recent past has witnessed contested interpretations and narratives on their provisions which need to be addressed and examined. (Singh and Yamamoto, 2016)

Satellite images have shown unprecedented activity by China at Subi and Fiery Cross reefs in the Spratlys, including the possible construction of heliports, landing strips, docks, and radar and surveillance structures. Also from China, the Spratlys are claimed by Malaysia, the Philippines, Vietnam, and Taiwan. The construction of artificial islands and infrastructure by China is increasing its potential power projection capacity in the region. We can monitor the construction of these islands by visiting the website https://amti.csis.org/island-tracker/china/, where there are satellite images of the area from the origin of the activity until now. (Asia Maritime Transparency Initiative, 2021).

Various high-resolution photos taken by the Asia Maritime Transparency Initiative, beginning in 2013, show the efforts of Chinese vessels creating or reclaiming land atop submerged reefs in several areas of the Spratly Island chain, including the Fiery Cross Reef, the Johnson South Reef, the Gaven Reef, the Subi Reef, the Hughes Reef, and the Mischief Reef. (Asia Maritime Transparency Initiative, 2021).

In the following image with a year of difference, we can see the original reef and in the photo on the left the dredge ship is destroying the natural reef and creating the beginning of an artificial island in the SCS (Figs. 7 and 8).

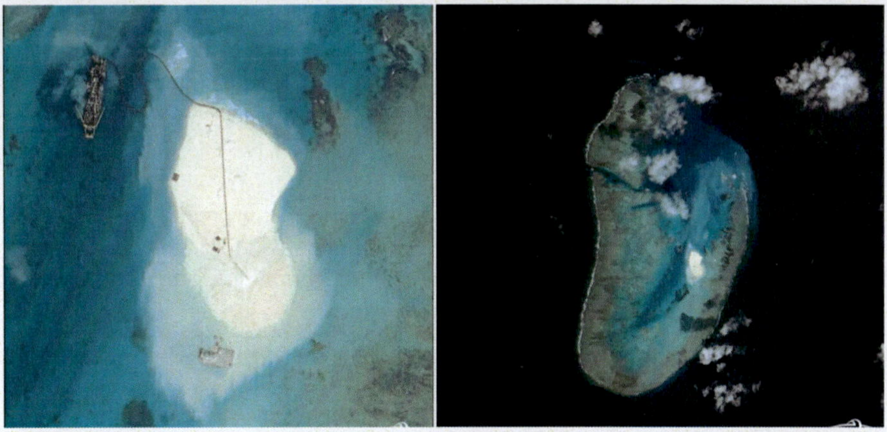

Fig. 7. North reef. Link: https://amti.csis.org/island-tracker/china/ (Asia Maritime Transparency Initiative, 2020)

The environmental issue is also very important because of the non-respecting methods of creating these islands with dredge ships. Van is quite precise about that:

Fig. 8. Mabini reef in SCS evolution. Source: Official Website of the Philippine Department of Foreign Affairs. (2014)

The environment is being disrupted due to the disturbances that we are doing to the area. From the construction of the artificial islands to the fisheries over harvesting and damaging the ecosystems in the area, the environment is one thing that countries around the Spratly Islands should have mutual terms for. Preserving the ecosystem is important to focus on especially since an extreme amount of damage was already done to the reef and marine life. All parties have an economic interest in maintaining sustainable fishing in these waters. By implementing these suggestions of different fishing methods, coast regulators, replanting reefs, creating large marine protected areas (MPA's), and an expansion of land over seafloors instead of expanding on top of reefs, it will give more opportunity for the environment and marine life to recover and thrive.

However, this extension implies overlapping with those of the contiguous States, so this becomes an internment conflict not regulated by UNCLOS. This is where the Responsibility of the States plays a very important role since this jurisdiction is applied to everything that has international regulation, which means that the State, being the major international actor must be subject to international law and respond to them as stipulated. (Van, 2020)

But the definition of UNCLOS doesn't accept as an island an artificial one, and the consequence of not being considered an island is that it will not generate territorial sea and cannot be used as the base point for measuring the territorial sea even when these are located within territorial waters (Singh and Yamamoto, 2016, 13).

If we try to analyze this situation, we may find what Gottman said in 1952:

> Accessibility is the determining factor: areas to which men have no access do not have any political standing or problems. The sovereignty of the moon has no importance whatsoever today, because men cannot reach it nor obtain anything from it. The Antarctic had no political standing before navigators began going there, but since it was made accessible by its discoverers, the icy continent has been divided into portions like an apple pie… (Gottman, 1952)

Is fundamental that a change in UNCLOS is probably a must, Papadakis said in 1977 that artificial islands were *de lege ferenda* and would be best dealt with by a new international convention to determine their status in international law (Papadakis, 1977). But in the negotiations of UNCLOS, maybe because they were trying to find a major consensus, nothing was considered as we all know.

The only legal reference in UNCLOS about artificial islands is clear about them and they are only authorized in the economic exclusive zone, but without accepting the possibility of making them a part of the territorial sea.

"Artificial islands, installations, and structures in the exclusive economic zone

1. In the exclusive economic zone, the coastal State shall have the exclusive right to construct and to authorize and regulate the construction, operation and use of:

    (a) artificial islands.
    (b) installations and structures for the purposes provided for in article 56 and other economic purposes;
    (c) installations and structures which may interfere with the exercise of the rights of the coastal State in the zone.

2. The coastal State shall have exclusive jurisdiction over such artificial islands, installations and structures, including jurisdiction with regard to customs, fiscal, health, safety and immigration laws and regulations.
3. Due notice must be given of the construction of such artificial islands, installations or structures, and permanent means for giving warning of their presence must be maintained. Any installations or structures which are abandoned or disused shall be removed to ensure safety of navigation, taking into account any generally accepted international standards established in this regard by the competent international organization. Such removal shall also have due regard to fishing, the protection of the marine environment and the rights and duties of other States. Appropriate publicity shall be given to the depth, position and dimensions of any installations or structures not entirely removed.

4. The coastal State may, where necessary, establish reasonable safety zones around such artificial islands, installations, and structures in which it may take appropriate measures to ensure the safety both of navigation and of the artificial islands, installations, and structures.
5. The breadth of the safety zones shall be determined by the coastal State, taking into account applicable international standards. Such zones shall be designed to ensure that they are reasonably related to the nature and function of the artificial islands, installations, or structures, and shall not exceed a distance of 500 m around them, measured from each point of their outer edge, except as authorized by generally accepted international standards or as recommended by the competent international organization. Due notice shall be given of the extent of safety zones.
6. All ships must respect these safety zones and shall comply with generally accepted international standards regarding navigation in the vicinity of artificial islands, installations, structures and safety zones.
7. Artificial islands, installations and structures and the safety zones around them may not be established where interference may be caused to the use of recognized sea lanes essential to international navigation.
8. Artificial islands, installations and structures do not possess the status of islands. They have no territorial sea of their own, and their presence does not affect the delimitation of the territorial sea, the exclusive economic zone or the continental shelf." (United Nations, 1982)

UNCLOS is extremely clear about the regime of the artificial islands: They have no territorial sea of their own, and their presence does not affect the delimitation of the territorial sea, the exclusive economic zone or the continental shelf, so the Convention is not silent but clear about the status of this islands.

But the preamble also gives us an answer when says that: "Affirming that matters not regulated by this Convention continue to be governed by the rules and principles of general international law" (UNCLOS, 1982).

The geographical characteristics of the Paracel and Spratly Islands are the ones that cause the most problems according to their nature from the point of view of their different natural formations and origins. The Highest index of island development activity by China takes place in the Paracel and Spratly Island chains. Beijing has claimed since the end of 2015, more land than all other claimants combined in the last 40 years.

The SCS arbitration (Permanent Court of Arbitration, 2016), accepted that the Chinese-built artificial islands in the area were in fact islands according to article 60 of UNCLOS.

> China's activities at Mischief Reef have since evolved into the creation of an artificial island. China has elevated what was originally a reef platform that submerged at high tide into an island that is permanently exposed. Such an island is undoubtedly 'artificial' for the purposes of Article 60 (Permanent Court of Arbitration, 2016).

But the Permanent Court of Arbitration determination, in that case, may have legally resolved that territorial dispute, but it does not provide clear guidance for determining the legitimacy of a state constructing an artificial island in international waters, not within its own Economic Exclusive Zone or an EEZ belonging to another state. This open question is important because several of China's artificial islands in the South China Sea fall into that category.

But following Saunders there:

> It is not merely a consequence of the State's sovereignty over the sea, but rather the act of making the land itself that gives the State further rights in international law – more rights than the untransformed sea could ever have given it. Properly understood then, it is the very process of creation that makes the new land territory and awards the rights that flow from this territory.
>
> This illustrates why judging the territorial status of an artificial island on its pre-reclaimed nature is a fallacy. The reclaimed land was once sea – but its status in international law is judged on its post-reclamation reality, otherwise, baselines could never be affected. (Saunders, 2018).

And of course:

> The argument so far is that if artificial islands fulfill certain criteria, then they can be considered territory at international law. Proximity does not determine whether an artificial island is territory but does determine how title to territory is demonstrated (or if it can be). It must be acknowledged that this argument leads to certain repercussions, some of them negative. 200 In particular it could be argued that treating artificial islands as territory will legitimize the actions of China in the South China Sea – actions that have been found illegal by an Arbitral Tribunal.
>
> How does this serve the coherence of international law? Further and more generally, it could be argued that it may lead to a grab and ransack type mentality, where States build artificial islands recklessly to increase their territorial holdings: the very thing that commentators have warned against for decades. However, these problems are addressed when artificial island building is viewed through the lens of legality. (Saunders, 2018).

In Trigg´s words "Changes in territory through accretion, erosion and avulsion are not accurately described as roots of title. Rather, states acquire any new territory formed through such natural processes by effective occupation and acquiescence" (Triggs, 2010). And also, he is clear about what happens in the case of protests:

> "It is quite another step...to argue that protests can prevent a state from acquiring territory that is terra nullius. On this reasoning, it is unlikely that protests can be a permanent bar to acquisition of territory by effective occupation. If, by contrast, the disputed territories communis, persistent objections from a majority of the international community could prevent consolidation of the title" (Triggs, 2010)

We must finish considering that artificial islands are built illegally, the building state cannot acquire title to the territory unless the occupation is permitted or legitimized by the international community. (Saunders, 2018).

4 United Nations Conference of the Law of the Sea and the Conflict and Other Actors in the Area

China has produced a challenge to stability, regional security, and prosperity. Given the importance of the region in the economic world, the instability in the South Sea of China may have global serious consequences.

The effects of an armed conflict could have a devastating impact on the region and the world, given the geostrategic importance of the disputed area and that the two largest world economies would be involved.

Despite the widespread regional condemnation, China has continued to pursue an aggressive policy and expansionist in the region. His actions in the South China Sea have been their resistance to accept adopted positions by other countries in the region. This has been seen as aggravated by their reluctance to comply with the provisions of UNCLOS.

ASEAN has become an important regional actor and contributes greatly to international cooperation, so its role as a mediator of the problem to ease tensions would be beneficial.

International dialogue is one of the most used tools within the international community, so this would be the first step towards a rapprochement between States to propose a solution and dissolve tensions and questions regarding security threats.

On the other hand, respect for International Law must be one of the main objectives when proposing a solution to the conflict. The legal loopholes found in UNCLOS make the process difficult, as well as implementing the responsibility of the States while respecting their sovereignty.

A solution to the international dispute would bring the case before the International Court of Justice (ICJ), which is in charge of settling disputes concerning International Law. Through the court, the case could be presented and guidelines to be followed following the regulation of international standards could be established. According to this same idea, resorting to the ICJ would take a weight off the States since an external body would be the one to make the decisions.

But according to Kohl´s opinion the leading actor of UNCLOS is not clear about that as it has been shown in this paper:

> Despite UNCLOS having contemplated states constructing artificial islands, the Convention leaves much to be desired in terms of how the law determines the legitimacy and entitlements of artificial islands.
>
> UNCLOS operates ineffectively when a state constructs an artificial island outside its own EEZ or that of another state (Khohl, 2018).

As we know, the international system is constantly evolving through the interactions between all its actors, which is why International Law must find a way to keep abreast of advances, especially technological ones, to regulate it.

After 38 years of establishment, UNCLOS must adapt its international regulations, so the Convention must make new regulations regarding the issue of artificial islands, which can be done through the ICJ.

The solutions cover all the surroundings of the conflict, trade routes, international security, and international interests. The important thing is to achieve progress in the regulations regarding this issue to have a clearer idea of the consequences or effects that they could bring to the States. Similarly, safeguarding the well-being of the affected States should be involved in the decisions that the ICJ could make once the situation is presented to it.

Under State Responsibility, this case would enter into an objective liability, where the acts performed are not unlawful since they do not exist a norm that prohibits it but that brings international repercussions.

A 'possible solution for this case may be the Convention for the Protection of the Environment since the construction of the islands affects the oceans, despite that this convention is important, it is not relevant to the main problem, but it is good to consider it. Lawful actions carried out by the State can cause consequences in international law, whether concerning the Convention for the Protection of the Environment, what is permitted and established in the Convention of the Sea or threaten international security. Due to the complexity involved the application of international jurisdiction concerning the problem is necessary to formulate new proposals for solutions, whether they are practical for resolving the latent conflict of international tensions or the correct application of international standards.

For conflict resolutions to take place, it is important strong international pressure on other countries, even more so in the case that China has an even greater influence within the international context.

The support of the other States will lead to the ICJ not only holding responsible China for the consequences but that there is an advance within the regulation of UNCLOS that manages to avoid future problems according to the advanced technologies that can be used by different countries.

This is a complicated conflict to solve, and Singh and Yamamoto are clear about that:

> However, the solution to overlapping and contested sovereign claims in SCS seems still far from being achievable in the short or even long term. States continue to prefer to ignore the jurisdiction of international courts as also conventions and declarations they have signed and ratified. Instead of rule of law, security considerations of geopolitics seem to determine national policies.
>
> International law no doubt provides the most agreeable framework as also a promise of a certain degree of legitimacy to official parleys, yet it seems evolving contours of geopolitics rather than rule of law are increasingly determining equations amongst all these major stakeholders and claimants. The Chinese government does not seem to worry too much about the fact that artificial islands do not generate EEZ or that no continental shelves can be drawn from them as they simply do not consider any country's claims over SCS. Access, control, and denial seem to be China's approach which has been working so far (Singh and Yamamoto, 2016).

Also, Afrin is clear about that:

> China has created a climate where it will be very hard for China to exist in this state of fraternal relations with its neighbors. In Chinese parlance, they say, 'core interest' means there is no room for compromise. There would be serious political costs for such an action, not least international opprobrium.
>
> There is nothing in the UN Convention on the law of the Sea to resolve sovereignty disputes over land and no chance that the claimants will submit their claims to the International Court of Justice or another arbitration body. Therefore, the UNCLOS does not provide any specific mechanisms to solve competing claims of sovereignty over such maritime features.
>
> The jurisdiction over artificial islands finds no ad hoc origin in the UNCLOS. In view of this fact, the determination of the relevant jurisdiction over artificial islands is established depending on the different maritime zones found in the UNCLOS. Artificial islands are not given any further distinct rights other than those determined by their placement in the maritime zones.
>
> UNCLOS fail to declare who owns what in the South China Sea. The new islands allow China to harness a portion of the sea for its own use that had previously been relatively out of reach. Although there are significant fisheries and possible large oil and gas reserves in the South China Sea, China's efforts serve more to fortify its territorial claims than to help it extract natural resources. (Afrin, 2017).

Maybe the failure of UNCLOS in that problem is proven but also it is important to understand that the convention signed in 1982 in Montego Bay, could not be the philosopher's stone to find a solution to a conflict that exists many years before the existence of UNCLOS.

As it has been said Environmental Conventions may be a key to solving this conflict and probably in an ever time more polluted world a good solution.

5 Conclusions

The concluding statements focus on the fundamental arguments demonstrated in the preceding text:

I. In conclusion, In International Law there are several challenges that countries face, despite this, there must be a starting point and limits to the behavior of the States, because without limits it's impossible to build a new international order.

II. Interactions within the international system are subject to a series of norms and obligations, but the breach of these affects in a generalized way to the whole system of balance among the states of the world and specifically between the actors of this conflict that mainly wants to solve this problem in terms of a more domestic solution among them

III. Regardless of the result of this conflict. It is important to recognize the importance of all the elements and their relationship with International Law to fully understand the scenario which is based on a long conflict.

IV. It is important to find a solution to the conflict and International Law should be more focused on the regulation of international jurisdiction and the evolution of the global picture. Environmental issues or reform proposals of the international conventions should be a good solution to this problem.

V. The problem in general entails the direct involvement of International Law by paving the way for its evolution and adaptation to the new tendencies that are established by the States that tried to be more independent and less cooperative.

VI. Every time greater and better regulations must arise within the international context to be able to harmonize international relations under the same legal framework since compliance with international standards is of great importance to safeguarding international peace and security in the area and with other actors.

VII. However, the very fact that China represents a great influence in political, economic, commercial, and military questions the effectiveness of the cooperation from other states and the abundance of international pressure that may be able to help. In general, Southeast Asia presents great complications when establishing territorial limits, however, the United Nations Convention on the Law of the Sea does not establish the resolution of these controversies easily and some countries are not accepting their jurisdiction.

VIII. Not only is regulation necessary under technological advances, but existing maritime zone regulations also need to be strengthened and shared with other states. UNCLOS should be adapted to a new era in terms of international relations. This represents a challenge to International Law and to the will of the States of taking responsibility for their actions when there is no international jurisdiction clear about the consequences. Maybe new Conventions talking about important aspects as Global Commons should be more universal with a more open-minded vision.

IX. For this problem, the most important challenge on which much of the resolution of the conflict depends is the application of the responsibility of the State and the adequate fulfillment of the sanctions or the international regulations, without new standards and regulations that fulfill new situations, we are not going to be able to build a better and more global world.

X. State sovereignty is one of the most important elements within the international system, however, it is also a challenge when it comes to accounting for compliance with international standards. Environmental regulations in the XXI century could not accept the attack of the People's Republic of China against the biodiversity of the South China Sea using dredge ships.

XI. Finally, this problem may not be solved only with the intervention of the actors in the area. A global solution is completely necessary.

References

Afrin, S.: The construction of China's Artificial Island in the South China Sea. The failure of UNCLOS. J. Conflict Integrat. **1**(2), 66–97 (2017). http://www.dbpia.co.kr/Article/NODE07296391

Asia Maritime Transparency Initiative. South China Sea Energy Exploration and Development (2020). https://amti.csis.org/south-china-sea-energy-exploration-and-development/

Asia Maritime Transparency Initiative. China Island Tracker (2021). https://amti.csis.org/

Association of Southeast Asian Nations. Declaration on the Conduct of the Parties in the South China Sea (2002). https://asean.org/declaration-on-the-conduct-of-parties-in-the-south-china-sea-2/

Chang, T.K.: China's claim of sovereignty over spratly and paracel islands: A historical and legal perspective, case western reserve. J. Int. Law **23**, 399–420 (1991)

China Government. Coast Guard Law (2021). http://www.xinhuanet.com/politics/2021-01/23/c_1127015293.htm

Council of Foreign Relations. China's Maritime Disputes (2019). https://www.cfr.org/chinas-maritime-disputes/#!/chinas-maritime-disputes?cid=otr-marketing_use-china_sea_InfoGuide#overview

Gottman, J.: The political partitioning of our world: An attempt at analysis. World Politics **4**(4), 512–519 (1952)

Khohl, A.: China's artificial island building campaign in the South China Sea: Implications for the reform of the United Nations convention on the law of the sea. Dickinson Law Rev. **122**, 937 (2018)

Krishnan, A.: China to require foreign vessels to report in territorial waters. The Hindu (2021). https://www.thehindu.com/news/international/china-to-require-foreign-vessels-to-report-in-territorial-waters/article36170508.ece

Lee, S.: The 1951 San Francisco peace treaty with Japan and the territorial disputes in East Asia Pacific. Rim Law Policy J. Assoc. **11**(1), 62–143 (2002)

Luo, S.: China's Coast Guard Law: Destabilizing or Reassuring? The Diplomat (2021, Jan. 29). https://thediplomat.com/2021/01/chinas-coast-guard-law-destabilizing-or-reassuring/

McManus, J.W.: Offshore coral reef damage, overfishing, and paths to peace in the South China sea. Remote Sens. Ecol. Conserv. (2017). https://doi.org/10.1163/15718085-12341433

Okada, W.: China's Coast Guard Law challenges rule based order. The Diplomat (2021). https://thediplomat.com/2021/04/chinas-coast-guard-law-challenges-rule-based-order/

Papadakis, N.: The International Regime of International Islands. Sijthoff Publications on Ocean Development (1977)

Permanent Court of Arbitration. The South China Sea Arbitration (The Republic of Philippines v. The People's Republic of China) (2016). https://pcacases.com/web/sendAttach/2086

Philippines Government. Mission to the United Nations, "Statement by Secretary Albert del Rosario". In: 69th Session of the United Nations General Assembly, High Level General Debate (2014). https://www.un.org/en/ga/69/meetings/gadebate/pdf/PH_en.pdf

Philippines Government, Department of Foreign Affairs (2014). https://dfa.gov.ph/

Poling, G.: The Conventional Wisdom on China's Island Bases is Dangerously Wrong. War on the Rocks (2020). https://warontherocks.com/2020/01/the-conventional-wisdom-on-chinas-island-bases-is-dangerously-wrong/

Saunders, I.: Artificial Islands in International Law. Vanderbilt J. Trans. Law **52** (2018). https://papers.ssrn.com/sol3/papers.cfm?abstract_id=3273152

Singh, S., Yamamoto, L.: China's Artificial Islands in the South China Sea: Geopolitics versus Rule of Law. Rev. Direito Econ. Socioamb. Curitiba **8**(1), 4–23 (2016). https://dialnet.unirioja.es/descarga/articulo/6172750.pdf

Sreekumar, K., Hassan, G.: A study of artificial island. Centre for Public Policy Research (2020). https://www.cppr.in/policy-briefs/a-study-of-artificial-islands

Triggs, G.: International Law: Contemporary Principles and Practices. LexisNexis (2010)

Trung, N.T.: How's China Coast Guard Law has changed the regional security structure. Asia Maritime Transparency Initiative (2021). https://amti.csis.org/how-chinas-coast-guard-law-has-changed-the-regional-security-structure/

United Nations. United Nations Treaty of Peace with Japan (1951). https://treaties.un.org/doc/publication/unts/volume%20136/volume-136-i-1832-english.pdf

United Nations. United Nations Convention of the Law of the Sea, UNCLOS (1982). https://www.un.org/depts/los/convention_agreements/texts/unclos/unclos_e.pdf

United Nations. People Republic of China ratification of the Treaty (1996). https://treaties.un.org/doc/Publication/CN/1996/CN.197.1996-Eng.pdf

United Nations. China Reservation Statement (2006). http://www.un.org/Depts/los/convention_agreements/convention_declarations.htm#China%20Upon%20ratification

Van, A.: Artificial islands in South China Sea (2020). https://storymaps.arcgis.com/stories/6d8a684e762f4f4ca90c1a19121fcf8c/print

Thus, the dispute over the South China Sea, is poisoning the relations of the Southeast Asian countries, with a difficult solution considering the relevant role of one of the claimants, China, both in political and economic terms in the region and the dependence of the other claimants and neighbours of China for their development.

On the other hand, in reaction to China's policy, the United States of America (US) and its allies are proceeding with shows of force in the area to prevent Chinese territorial claims from gaining traction. In particular, they are resorting to so-called freedom of navigation operations (FONOPs) -in some places around the world since the US Freedom of Navigation Program was formally established in 1979, but also in the waters of the South China Sea years ago-, to ensure freedom of navigation for ships and prevent Chinese expansionism in the area (United States of America, 2018). Those activities, together with the China countermeasures are escalating the situation and putting in danger the international peace and security.

In this context of a multifaceted dispute in the South China Sea, one of the claimants, the Philippines, had recourse to one of the jurisdictional means of peaceful settlement of disputes set up in the United Nations Convention on the Law of the Sea (UNCLOS). Indeed, by notification and Statement of Claim dated 22 January 2013, the Philippines initiated arbitration proceedings against China pursuant to Articles 286 and 287 of the UNCLOS and in accordance with Article 1 of Annex VII of the same Convention. On 21 June 2013, the Arbitral Tribunal was constituted and on 12 July 2013, the Tribunal issued Administrative Directive No. 1, pursuant to which the Tribunal formalised the appointment of the Permanent Court of Arbitration (PCA) as Registry for the Arbitral Tribunal (*The Philippines vs. China*, 2015, parrs. 31–34, pp. 16–17). According to the Arbitral Tribunal, the notification of the Philippines aimed at "[…] resolving a dispute over the Parties' respective "maritime entitlements" and the lawfulness of Chinese activities in the South China Sea" (*The Philippines vs. China*, 2015, parr. 2, p. 1).

China, as the defendant in the case, since the unilateral initiation of the arbitration proceedings, had made it clear that it would neither accept nor participate in the arbitration unilaterally initiated by the Philippines. Therefore, notwithstanding the position of China, the Arbitral Tribunal convened a hearing on jurisdiction and admissibility in July 2015 and issued an award on jurisdiction and admissibility on 29 October 2015, deciding some jurisdictional issues and deferring others for further consideration. The Arbitral Tribunal then convened a hearing on the merits from 24 to 30 November 2015 and, on 12 July 2016 the Arbitral Tribunal rendered an award addressing the issues of jurisdiction not decided in the Award on Jurisdiction and Admissibility and the merits of the Philippines' claims over which the Tribunal had jurisdiction.

It is my understanding that the unilateral recourse to arbitration to settle such a geographically, economically, environmentally and historically important dispute involving no less than one of the permanent members of the Security Council is of very significant importance for testing the scope of the means of dispute settlement under Part XV of UNCLOS. But in addition to the technical legal scope for international law of the South China Sea arbitration, we believe that the case is of particular interest in the context of both regional and global geopolitics, as the interests of the major superpowers are at stake, and that it fits perfectly into the context of one the issues highlighted by the organisers of the 62nd CICA International Conferences on Security, which is: Geopolitics: the situation in Southern Asia, including sovereignty in the South China Sea, and of course, the overall theme of the conference, "Threats for Peace and Security: Asia vs. the West".

To achieve these objectives, we will divide our paper into three sections, in addition to the introduction. In the second, we will analyse the scope of the South China Sea arbitration within the framework of the means of peaceful settlement of disputes under Part XV of the Convention. In the third, we will question the scope of the arbitral decision to resolve the actual dispute between the two parties to the case, but also to resolve the general dispute in the area over sovereignty, jurisdictional and navigational rights in the waters and geographical features of the South China Sea. Finally, we will present our conclusions.

2 Relevance of the South China Sea Case in the Context of the Settlement of Disputes Under Part XV of UNCLOS

By the mid-1960s the state of the law of the sea, mainly embodied in the four 1958 Geneva Conventions on the Law of the Sea, satisfied few, and for many reasons it became clear that a new conference was needed to calm the waters of the deep conflicts of interest that were causing great instability and legal uncertainty. To this end, the General Assembly of the United Nations convened a third Conference on the Law of the Sea for 1973 by Resolution 2750 C (XXV) of 1970. The General Assembly also instructed the Committee on the Peaceful Uses of the Sea-bed and the Ocean Floor beyond the Limits of National Jurisdiction to act as preparatory body for the conference (UN, General Assembly, 1970).

The third Conference on the Law of the Sea, in which 160 States participated, held eleven sessions between 1973 and 1982, as the interests at stake in the regulation were very varied and all of them had to be brought together since the underdeveloped States imposed the idea that the Conference should aim at establishing the complete legal regime of the Law of the Sea and not limit itself to a few aspects. In addition, the work took so long, as the method of adopting the Convention was set to be consensus, which was in keeping with the need to reach a global solution to all the problems. However, it is well known that this method, while it has the enormous advantage of the ease with which a consensus text is accepted, has the disadvantage of the slowness it imposes in having to accommodate all the tendencies. In fact, although the consensus method was followed throughout the Conference, the Convention was finally adopted by vote, as the Government of the United States of America had changed in the meantime and the new administration did not agree with what had already been decided. In the end, UNCLOS was provisionally adopted on 30 April 1982 in Jamaica by 130 votes in favour, 4 against and 17 abstentions and finally adopted on 17 December 1982, containing 320 articles and 9 annexes. The Convention entered into force on 16 November 1994, one year after the 60th instrument of ratification was collected, as set forth in article 308. All the States involved in the South China Sea dispute are parties to the Convention, since all of them have ratified it.

As we know, the peaceful settlement of disputes arising out of the application and interpretation of UNCLOS is regulated in Part XV. After offering in Sect. 1 the possibility for the parties to settle their dispute by means of Conciliation regulated in Article

284 UNCLOS, Sect. 2 regulates the compulsory procedures leading to binding decisions, although it provides for their subsidiary nature in relation to any other means that the parties may have chosen. It is noteworthy that Article 286, which heads Sect. 2, establishes that when it has not been resolved by the means agreed by the parties, it shall be submitted, at the request of any of the parties to the dispute, to the court or tribunal that has jurisdiction in accordance with the provisions of the same Sect. 2. A flexible system is established, allowing States Parties to choose, by a written declaration deposited with the Secretary-General of the United Nations, between one or more of the jurisdictions referred to in Article 287, the International Tribunal for the Law of the Sea (ITLOS) established by UNCLOS itself, the International Court of Justice (ICJ), an Arbitral Tribunal constituted by Annex VII of the Convention, or a Special Arbitral Tribunal constituted in accordance with Annex VIII of UNCLOS.

It should also be noted, however, that the Convention establishes in Article 287.5 the subsidiary nature of arbitration governed by Annex VII of the Convention, since, according to the text of this paragraph: "If the parties to a dispute have not accepted the same procedure for the settlement of the dispute, it may be submitted only to arbitration in accordance with Annex VII, unless the parties otherwise agree". This provision had its origin in the current of thought that emerged during the sessions of the Third United Nations Conference on the Law of the Sea, which was constituted by the opinions of that group of States that considered that a future International Tribunal for the Law of the Sea, or in general any pre-established tribunal, would be too rigid, since the parties would not be able to choose as judges experts in the matters involved in the dispute, and in addition a pre-established procedure, already slow and costly, would have to be accepted. This group of States proposed, on the contrary, to favour arbitration characterised by a flexible and agile procedure, in which the choice of arbitrators and the speedy delivery of decisions are made possible.

On top of that, Article 298. 1 allows States and entities to declare that they exclude the application of the compulsory binding procedures for the settlement of disputes under UNCLOS with respect to certain specified categories of disputes.

Furthermore, it must be pointed out that UNCLOS provides for the residual jurisdiction of the ITLOS in the case of the urgent need to order, modify or revoke provisional measures in the absence of the constitution of the arbitral tribunal to which the dispute was submitted, by virtue of the provisions of Article 290.5 UNCLOS. In addition, Article 287.2 of UNCLOS also provides, as a special case, for the exclusive jurisdiction of the Seabed Disputes Chamber of the ITLOS provided for in Part XI of UNCLOS, to hear all disputes relating to the seabed and ocean floor and subsoil thereof beyond the limits of the jurisdiction of States.

The reality following the adoption of the Convention has proved unfounded the fears of the aforementioned group of opinion regarding States' reluctance to have recourse to international courts and tribunals.

Indeed, on the one hand, regarding Article 287 declarations, it is worth mentioning that, up to March 2022, 44 States have chosen ITLOS as their preference among the jurisdictions referred to in Article 287. None of them is any of the seven States involved in the South China Sea dispute. Another group of 22 States have chosen the ICJ as the first choice among those jurisdictional means of pacific settlement of disputes. None of them is any of the seven States involved in the South China Sea dispute neither. Only 8 States have decided to give preference to Arbitral Tribunals set up in accordance with Annex VII of ITLOS, but none of them is any of the seven States involved in the South China Sea dispute. For their part, 7 States have chosen the Special Arbitral Tribunals constituted in accordance with Annex VIII of the Convention, but none of them is any of the seven States involved in the South China Sea dispute[1].

On the other hand, when it comes to the specific jurisdiction that States have chosen in the nearly three decades since the entry into force of the Montego Bay Convention, it should be noted at the outset that not many cases have been submitted to arbitration. Indeed, up to June 2022, 15 arbitrations were conducted pursuant to Annex VII of the Convention[2].

However, it is necessary to qualify this fact by pointing out that, although States were initially reluctant to submit their disputes to the arbitration provided for in Annex VII, since 1998 there has been a growing trend in the opposite direction. Another undeniable fact of appreciable relevance is the propensity to use the services of the Permanent Court of Arbitration (PCA) to act as the Secretariat of the established arbitral tribunals, a circumstance that has also allowed this century-old institution to experience a kind of second youth. Indeed, since the 1982 Convention came into force in 1994, the PCA has served as registry for 14 arbitrations under Annex VII of UNCLOS. Next to the one that we are studying in this chapter, among the States involved in the South China Sea dispute, Malaysia and Singapore submitted the *Land Reclamation by Singapore in and around the Straits of Johor (Malaysia v. Singapore)* to the PCA also[3].

It has to be pointed out also that some cases initiated under Annex VII were subsequently transferred by agreement to the ITLOS, probably, as underlined by Robin Churchill, to reduce the cost of litigation (Churchill, 2016). On the contrary, little success has got the Arbitration in accordance with Annex VIII of the Convention, as no case has been submitted to it since its entry into force (Churchill, 2016).

When it comes to weight the recourse to the Law of the Sea Tribunal, it should be pointed out that the ITLOS has gradually taken increasingly solid steps, exercising its preferential jurisdiction in matters of provisional measures and prompt release of vessels and their crews, but also gaining ground in the office of hearing cases on the merits. The requests for an advisory opinion and for maritime delimitation, respectively, have helped the Tribunal to consolidate and move towards stability and maturity.

[1] United Nations Treaty Collection, Chapter XXI, Law of the Sea, 6. United Nations Convention on the Law of the Sea, Declarations and Reservations, https://treaties.un.org/Pages/ViewDetailsIII.aspx?src=TREATY&mtdsg_no=XXI-6&chapter=21&Temp=mtdsg3&clang=_en. United Nations, Division for Ocean Affairs and the Law of the Sea, 1. Settlement of disputes mechanism under the Convention: Choice of procedure under article 287 and optional exceptions to applicability of Part XV, Sect. 2, of the Convention under article 298 of the Convention, https://www.un.org/depts/los/settlement_of_disputes/choice_procedure.htm.

[2] Permanent Court of Arbitration,"Contribution of the Permanent Court of Arbitration to the Report of the United Nations Secretary-General on Oceans and the Law of the Sea, as at 17 June 2022, https://docs.pca-cpa.org/2020/06/7977fb42-contribution-of-the-permanent-court-of-arbitration-to-the-report-of-the-....pdf.

[3] https://pca-cpa.org/en/cases/108/

As far as recourse to the ICJ is concerned, it is fair to point out that States have continued to rely on the Court for their disputes on the law of the sea since the entry into force of UNCLOS, as they did from the very beginning of the Court, and even at the time of the Permanent Court of International Justice, although it should be noted that many of the cases submitted to the Court, in addition to law of the sea aspects, often involve other legal aspects (Sepulveda Amor, 2012, p. 6).

We should add that of the seven states involved in the South China Sea dispute, only China, Malaysia and Singapore have made declarations under Article 298 of UNCLOS.

Turning now on the context of the case before the PCA, as we already know, China had from the beginning let clear that it did not want that the Arbitral Tribunal should solve the dispute. In such situation, as any international tribunal should do, the Arbitral Tribunal had to look for if it had jurisdiction in the case, even in the presence of the actual opposition of the respondent State after the presentation of the claim.

Thus, the Tribunal had first to decide whether both States were parties to the UNCLOS. It made the verification and added that, accordingly, they were "[...] both bound by the dispute settlement procedures provided for in Part XV of the Convention in respect of any dispute between them concerning the interpretation or application of the Convention" (*The Philippines vs. China*, 2015, parr. 106, p. 37). Then, the Tribunal recalled that Part XV of UNCLOS, on the settlement of disputes, is structured in three Sections. Section 1 sets out general provisions, including those aimed at reaching agreement through negotiations and other peaceful means. Section 2 provides for mandatory procedures involving binding decisions, which apply where agreement has not been reached using Sect. 1, but are subject to the provisions of Sect. 3, which sets out a number of specific limitations and exceptions to jurisdiction (*The Philippines vs. China*, 2015, parr. 108, p. 38). Therefore, the Tribunal pointed out that Article 287 of the Convention accords parties a choice of procedures for the settlement of their disputes and that neither the Philippines nor China had made a written declaration choosing one of the particular means of dispute settlement set out in Article 287.1. For the Tribunal, in that case, according to the provisions of Article 287.3, both Parties were deemed to have accepted arbitration in accordance with Annex VII to the Convention (*The Philippines vs. China*, 2015, parr. 109).

Moving forward, the Tribunal added that its jurisdiction depended on the finding that the Parties actually had a dispute and that the dispute concerned the interpretation or application of the Convention. Further, the Tribunal also stated that, as required by Article 286, it had to be convinced that no settlement had been reached by recourse to other peaceful means of dispute settlement as contemplated in Sect. 1 of Part XV, and that none of the specific limitations and exceptions set out in Sect. 3 of Part XV of the Convention apply to the case (*The Philippines vs. China*, 2015, parr. 110).

On top of that, the Tribunal held that China's decision not to participate in the proceedings did not imply the Tribunal's lack of jurisdiction and that the Philippines' decision to initiate arbitration unilaterally did not constitute an abuse of the Convention's dispute settlement procedures (*The Philippines vs. China*, 2015, parrs. 112–129, pp. 39–44).

After considering the claims submitted by the Philippines, the Tribunal rejected the argument presented in China's Position Paper of 7 December 2014 that the dispute between the Parties actually concerned territorial sovereignty over the islands in the South China Sea and therefore did not fall within the jurisdiction of the Tribunal, according to the Declaration filed by China in 2006 with regard to article 298 of UNCLOS, where China excluded the disputes over sovereignty related to maritime features (*The Philippines vs. China*, 2015, parr. 153, pp. 59–60).

The Tribunal also rejected the argument set out in China's Position Paper that the dispute between the Parties was really about the delimitation of the maritime boundary between the two countries and therefore did not fall within the jurisdiction of the Tribunal by virtue of the declaration submitted by China in 2006. On the contrary, the Tribunal considered that each of the Philippines' submissions discloses disputes between the two States concerning the interpretation or application of the Convention (*The Philippines vs. China*, 2015, parrs. 155–157, pp. 60–61).

The Tribunal also holds that no other State is indispensable to the proceedings. For the Tribunal the fact that it was not ruling on sovereignty, the rights of Viet Nam and other States that have claims to the islands of the South China Sea did not need to be determined before the Tribunal could proceed (*The Philippines vs. China*, 2015, parrs. 179–188, pp. 71–74).

With respect to the preconditions for the Tribunal's jurisdiction set out in Sect. 1 of Part XV of the Convention, the Tribunal rejected the argument set forth in China's Position Paper according to which the 2002 Declaration between China and ASEAN on the Conduct of Parties in the South China Sea constituted an agreement to resolve disputes relating to the South China Sea solely by negotiation. On the contrary, the Court held that the China-ASEAN Declaration was a political agreement that did not purport to be legally binding and was therefore irrelevant to the provisions of the Convention that give priority to dispute settlement by any means chosen by the parties. Similarly, the Tribunal considered that certain other agreements and joint declarations by China and the Philippines did not preclude the Philippines from resorting to the Convention to resolve its dispute with China. Furthermore, the Tribunal considered that the Philippines had complied with its obligation under the Convention to exchange views on the settlement of its dispute and had sought to negotiate with China to the extent required by the Convention and general international law (*The Philippines vs. China*, 2015, parrs. 189–353, pp. 75–123).

The Tribunal then referred to the limitations and exceptions set out in Sect. 3 of Part XV of the Convention, which excludes disputes on certain matters from compulsory settlement. The Tribunal considered that the question of whether these limitations and exceptions applied to the Philippine claim was, in some cases, related to the merits of the claim. For example, the question of whether the Tribunal had jurisdiction over historic rights in the South China Sea might depend on the Tribunal's analysis of the nature of the rights claimed by China. Similarly, the question of whether the Tribunal had jurisdiction to deal with China's activities in the South China Sea might depend on the Tribunal's decision as to whether the maritime features claimed by China were islands capable of generating overlapping maritime zones with those of the Philippines. The Tribunal also noted that the location of certain activities and the exception included in the Convention regarding military activities might affect its jurisdiction over certain Philippine claims (*The Philippines vs. China*, 2015, parrs. 354–396, pp. 125–140).

In light of the above, the Tribunal considers that it was then in a position to determine that it had jurisdiction to deal with the issues raised in seven submissions by the Philippines. The Tribunal concluded, however, that its jurisdiction over seven other submissions by the Philippines would have to be considered in conjunction with the merits (*The Philippines vs. China*, 2015, parrs. 397–412, pp. 140–147).

Therefore, in its Award of 12 July 2016, the Tribunal, under the basis that, on 25 August 2006, China had issued a declaration pursuant to Article 298 of the Convention, activating all of the optional exceptions to jurisdiction foreseen in that clause, had to considered mainly whether the other Philippines' Submissions were affected by any of those exceptions from jurisdiction that it had not dealt with in its previous award on jurisdiction and admissibility. Thus, first, the Tribunal had to decide whether the claim concerning Chinese historic rights and the 'nine-dash line' were affected by the exception from jurisdiction for disputes concerning "historic title" in Article 298 of the Convention (*The Philippines vs. China*, 2016, parrs. 215–229, pp. 96–97).

The Tribunal concluded that the exception to jurisdiction in Article 298 is limited to disputes involving historic titles and, due to the fact that China did not claim historic title to the waters of South China Sea, but rather a constellation of historic rights short of title, therefore, it held that it had jurisdiction to consider the Philippines' Submissions in question (*The Philippines vs. China*, 2016, Parr. 229, p. 97).

Second, the Tribunal should get into the question whether the Philippines' claims could be considered as included in the exception from jurisdiction set forth in Article 298 for disputes concerning sea boundary delimitation. However, the Tribunal indicated that there was no possible basis for the application of the exception to jurisdiction because it did not exist any legal basis for any entitlement by China to maritime zones in the area contemplated and therefore, no delimitation was required (*The Philippines vs. China*, 2016, parr. 633, p. 256). Third, the Tribunal was obliged to decide whether the claimant Submissions were affected by the exception from jurisdiction in that article regarding law enforcement activities in the Exclusive Economic Zone (EEZ) (*The Philippines vs. China*, 2016, parrs. 690–695 and 733–734, pp. 277–279 and 291).

But the Tribunal, having determined that the maritime features in question were low-tide elevations, which, as such, generate no entitlement to maritime zones of their own, and that no high-tide feature in the area in question could generate an entitlement to an EEZ, the Tribunal concludes that it has jurisdiction with respect to the Philippines' Submission (*The Philippines vs. China*, 2016, Parrs. 693–694 and 733–734, pp. 278 and 291). And finally, the Arbitral Tribunal studied whether the Philippines' submissions could be in any way affected by the exception from jurisdiction embodied in Article 298 for disputes concerning military activities (*The Philippines vs. China*, 2016, parrs. 932–938; 1024–1028; 1150–1165, pp. 371–373; 411–413; 452–457). On that point, the Tribunal pointed out that the essential facts in exam in one of the areas concerned were the deployment of armed forces and warships from both parties and therefore that it lacked jurisdiction to consider the Philippines' Submissions No. 14(a) to (c) 38, but it held its jurisdiction to consider Submission 14 (d) on the basis that China itself did not consider the activities in the other area concerned to be military (*The Philippines vs. China*, 2016, Parr. 1164, p. 457).

Having rejected most of the exceptions to its jurisdiction, the Tribunal examined the merits of the claims submitted by the Philippines. Thus, first, in relation to historical rights and the 'nine-dash line', concluded that, as between the parties in the dispute before it, China's claims to historic rights, or other sovereign rights or jurisdiction, with respect to the maritime areas of the South China Sea encompassed by the relevant part of the 'nine-dash line' were contrary to UNCLOS and without lawful effect to the extent that they exceed the geographic and substantive limits of China's maritime entitlements under the Convention (*The Philippines vs. China*, 2016, par. 278, p. 117).

Second, the Tribunal went on to consider the status of certain elements claimed by China and its consequent entitlement to surrounding extensions of water. The Tribunal, based on its previous analysis, noted that none of the features claimed by China could generate an EEZ or a continental shelf. Therefore, the Tribunal considered that it could declare that certain maritime areas were within the Philippines' EEZ without delimiting a boundary –something excluded from the dispute before the Tribunal-, because those zones do not overlap with any possible rights of China (*The Philippines vs. China*, 2016, pars. 643–648, pp. 259–260).

Third, the Tribunal examined the question of the legality of China's actions in the South China Sea. In this regard, the Tribunal found that China had violated the Philippines' sovereign rights in its EEZ by interfering with Philippine fishing and oil exploration, by constructing artificial islands and by failing to prevent Chinese fishermen from fishing in the area. The Tribunal also found that China had caused a serious collision and danger to Philippine vessels and personnel by its activities in the vicinity of certain areas (*The Philippines vs. China*, 2016, parrs. 696–716, pp. 279–286).

Fourth, about the allegation of Philippines according to which since the commencement of the arbitration in January 2013, China had unlawfully aggravated and extended the dispute between the parties, the Tribunal found that the claimant was right, because China had, in the course of the proceedings, aggravated and extended the disputes between the Parties through its dredging, artificial island-building, and construction activities (*The Philippines vs. China*, 2016, Par. 1181, p. 464).

Finally, when it comes to the submission of the Philippines about the future conduct of China regarding its obligations under UNCLOS, in general and particularly in respect to the Philippines, the Tribunal ended up its decision by stating that it considered it beyond dispute that both Parties were obliged to comply with the Convention, including its provisions regarding the resolution of disputes, and to respect the rights and freedoms of other States under the Convention. And the Tribunal added that, since neither the Philippines nor China had contested that, it was not necessary or appropriate for it to make any further declaration over the matter (*The Philippines vs. China*, 2016, Par. 1201, p. 469).

To sum up, regarding the relevance of the awards of the Arbitral Tribunal of the South China Sea dispute in the context of the interpretation and implementation of UNCLOS, it has been underlined that they were like a "legal game changer" (Anh, 2016, 369). More precisely, with regard to the settlement of disputes under part XV of UNCLOS, it's clear that they prove a preoccupation to highlight both the unity of the whole Convention and the relevance of the resolution of disputes system embodied in Part XV to avoid unilateralism by the part of States (Tanaka, 2019, pp. 226–228). In that line, for example, for professor Oxman: "Among the effects over the long term may be the […] avoidance of dangerous law enforcement tactics at sea, and increased appreciation of the contributions of the Law of the Sea Convention and its compulsory dispute settlement system to the rule of law in international affairs (Oxman, 2016, 281)". In the latter respect, the contribution of these decisions in reminding States Parties of their obligation to submit any dispute concerning the interpretation or application of the Convention to a jurisdictional body leading to a binding decision, where no settlement has been reached about any other peaceful means of their own choosing, cannot be overstated. Even more if we consider that it was rendered against the will of a permanent member of the Security Council of the United Nations and one of the hegemonic States in the international society of this time.

3 Acceptance of the Parties of the Awards and Implication for the Solution of the Dispute in the Area

It would not surprise anybody that China has not accepted the arbitral award after it was rendered in 2016, in the view of its position since the submission of the case unilaterally by the Philippines. Among the various manifestations of refusal, it is relevant to highlight the fact that, some days before the rendering of the Arbitral Award in July 2016, the Ministry of Foreign Affairs of the People's Republic of China already announced that China adhered "[…] to the solemn position of non-acceptance of and non-participation in the arbitration, and will stay committed to settling the relevant disputes with the Philippines in the South China Sea through bilateral negotiation" (Ministry of Foreign Affairs of China, 2016).

On the other hand, in August 2016 China's Supreme People's Court issued a regulation stating that China has a clear legal basis to safeguard maritime order in the disputed region (China Daily.com, 2016; Leddy, 2021, p. 788).

Next to that, the Chinese doctrine also adheres to the official position. Thus, in the introduction to the 500 pages long "Critical Study" that the Chinese Journal of International Law consecrated to the Awards on jurisdiction and the merits in the South China Sea Arbitration between the Philippines and China, it was stated that:

"These awards are not conducive to solving the dispute between China and the Philippines in the South China Sea; instead, they have complicated the related issues. They have impaired the integrity and authority of the Convention, threaten to undermine the international maritime legal order, run counter to the basic requirements of the international rule of law, and also imperilled the interests of the whole international community" (Chinese Society of International Law, 2018, 218).

Not surprisingly, several authors have strongly disapproved the "Critical Study". For example, as it was stated by Professor Douglas Guilfoyle; "[…] it is certainly intriguing that a major scholarly society would chose to very obviously re-litigate a case and produce its output in English for international consumption. I am unaware of any parallel effort by a national scholarly society of a permanent member of the Security Council in relation to a major international legal decisión" (Guilfoyle, 2018).

On the other hand, according to the official manifestations of position of third States, there are not unanimity about the necessity for China to abide by the Arbitral Award. Indeed, according to a tracker of official public stances on the arbitration set up by the Asia Maritime Transparency Initiative of the Center for Strategic and International Studies (CSIS), 8 States have publicly called for the ruling to be respected, while 35 that have issued generally positive statements noting the verdict, but have stopped short of calling for the parties to abide by it, and 8 that have publicly rejected it (*Center for Strategic and International Studies*, Arbitration Support Tracker). No strong consensus can therefore be discerned in favor of the need for China to comply with the 2016 arbitral tribunal decision.

In light of the above, it is obvious that the Arbitral Tribunal's award has not resolved the dispute on the ground. As for China's position, it cannot be denied that this State has intensified its actions in defence of its territorial claims in the area (Zhao, 2020, p. 491). A good demonstration of this has been provided by the recent military manoeuvres around Taiwan on the occasion of the visit of the Speaker of the American House of Representatives, Nancy Pelosi in August 2022, and the accompanying argumentation, such as the assertion that the Taiwan Strait is not an international waterway (United States of America, 2022).

In my opinion, nothing could better represent China's attitude in the region, although it is of course a particularly hot spot because of the question of Chinese unity, than the words of the Chinese representative, Zhang Jun, at the UN Security Council at the beginning of his rotating presidency in August 2022. Indeed, the one who should be the main defender of the principles and purposes of the United Nations Charter, as President of the UN Security Council, warned, when asked for his opinion on Nancy Pelosi's visit to Taiwan that: "if such a visit were to occur, it would undermine the "One China" principle, China's sovereignty and territorial integrity, and stability and peace in the Taiwan Strait". He went on saying that the above-mentioned visit would also undermine relations between China and the United States. Finally, he ended up noting that "[...]Taiwan's tendency towards independence is further developing with the support of external forces" and that "if we do not take appropriate, forceful action to stop this, the situation might be out of control" (United Nations, Security Council, 2022).

On the other hand, it's true that Members of the Association of Southeast Asian Nations (ASEAN) and China have been discussing the possibility of a code of conduct to manage maritime and territorial disputes in the South China Sea (CoC) for more than two decades (*Center for Strategic and International Studies*, Blueprint; Institute for Peace and Conflict Studies, 2021). The Code aims to manage tensions that may arise from disputes between claimants in the region, including Brunei, China, Malaysia, the Philippines, Taiwan, Vietnam and Indonesia. Without binding engagements, nevertheless the idea progressed, and after several years of inconclusive negotiations, China and ASEAN settled for a nonbinding "Declaration on the Conduct of Parties". Regarding the principles that should govern the relations between the States in the area, the point three of that declaration underline that: "The Parties reaffirm their respect for and commitment to the freedom of navigation in and overflight above the South China Sea as provided for by the universally recognized principles of international law, including the 1982 UN

Convention on the Law of the Sea (Governments of the Member States of ASEAN and China, 2012).

Since then, some advances can be tracked, but in the summer of 2022 is difficult to predict whether the process will end up successfully, notwithstanding the statement of the Asean Foreign Minister's meeting of 3 August 2022 underscoring "the importance of the full and effective implementation of the 2002 Declaration on the Conduct of Parties in the South China Sea (DOC) in its entirety" (ASEAN, 2022). Indeed, it cannot be ruled out that, as some experts have pointed out, that China "has been using the ongoing CoC negotiations as a pretext to gain time for fortifying its claims in the South China Sea" and "it has also been modernizing its military capabilities to ensure a strengthened bargaining position while negotiating the CoC, offsetting the U.S. military presence in the region" (Institute for Security & Developpment Studies, 2020).

4 Conclusions

We have seen how, despite China's refusal to allow the Arbitral Tribunal appointed under Annex VII of UNCLOS to hear the case and its absence from the proceedings, the Tribunal issued decisions on jurisdiction and admissibility of the claim in 2015 and on the merits in 2016, respectively.

For us, the relevance of these awards lies on its contribution to underline the unity of the whole Convention and the importance of the resolution of disputes system embodied in Part XV.

There is absolutely no doubt that the resolution of the award in absentia is not the best situation to resolve the dispute and of course an explicit acceptance by China to submit the dispute to the arbitral tribunal would have been more desirable. However, no one can deny that the respondent State had already given its consent to submit future disputes by accepting the provisions of the Convention providing for the submission of such disputes to jurisdictional instances.

As for the scope of the arbitration decision in pacifying the dispute between the States affected by the South China Sea, it should be noted that China has refused to implement it and that there has not been a great consensus among the third States as to the need to abide by it. There is no doubt that the fear of taking a stance against this great giant has conditioned the attitude of the States in the region on this issue. Indeed, China has continued its policy of increasing its show of force and sovereignty in the area to reinforce its claimed legal titles.

On the contrary, the situation has become increasingly complicated in recent months. For example, in November 2021 the Spokesperson for Foreign Affairs and Security Policy of the European External Action Service brought forward that coastguard vessels of the People's Republic of China had blocked two Philippine supply boats on their way to Second Thomas Shoal, 105 nautical miles west of the province of Palawan (Philippines) in the South China Sea and used water cannons against them. Furthermore, in that press release the Spokesperson added that the incident was not an isolated one, because that episode followed other unilateral actions by vessels of the People's Republic of China in the South China Sea over the previous months (EEAS, 2021). In that line, we recall as well China's large-scale military operations in the vicinity of Taiwan in reaction to the Speaker of the United States House of Representatives visit in the summer of 2022 and the real risk of an invasion of the island that hangs in the air.

Some hopes were raised by the emergence and evolution of the so-called Code of conduct to manage maritime and territorial disputes in the South China Sea, an instrument of a doubtful juridical nature that has been discussed over by ASEAN members and China in the last two decades in order to avoid disputes in the area. Nevertheless, one should be reasonably cautious about its actual adoption in the recent future.

In short, can we say that the non-respect of the arbitral decision on the South China Sea is another sign of the contempt of some of the great powers, in particular the autocratic ones, for international law in recent times?

References

Anh, N.T.L.: The South China Sea Award: Legal implications for Vietnam. Contemp. Southeast Asia: J. Int. Strateg. Affairs **38**(3), 369–374 (2016). https://www.muse.jhu.edu/article/647374

ASEAN. Joint Communiqué of the 55th Asean Foreign Ministers' Meeting (2022, Aug 3). https://asean.org/wp-content/uploads/2022/08/Joint_Communique-of-the-55th-AMM-FINAL.pdf

China Daily.com. News. China's supreme court clarifies maritime jurisdiction (2016, Aug 2). https://www.chinadaily.com.cn/china/2016-08/02/content_26311388.htm

Chinese Society of International Law: The South China Sea Arbitration Awards: A critical study. Chin. J. Int. Law **17**, 207–748 (2018)

Churchill, R.: Compulsory' Dispute Settlement under the United Nations Convention on the Law of the Sea – How has it operated?, PluriCourtsBlogs. Centre for the Study of the Legitimate Roles of the Judiciary in the Global Order (2016, June 9). https://www.jus.uio.no/pluricourts/english/blog/guests/2016-06-09-churchill-unclos-pt-2.html

EEAS. South China Sea: Statement by the Spokesperson on recent incidents(2021, Nov. 11). https://eeas.europa.eu/headquarters/headquarters-homepage/107619/south-china-sea-statement-spokesperson-recent-incidents_en

Ehle, J.: Keynote Adress at the 12th South China Sea International Conference (2020, Nov. 11). https://eeas.europa.eu/headquarters/headquarters-homepage/88945/keynote-address-rear-admiral-j%C3%BCrgen-ehle-senior-military-advisor-eeas-12th-south-china-sea_en

Guilfoyle, D.: A new twist in the South China Sea Arbitration: The Chinese Society of International Law's Critical Study. EJIL: Talk! Blog Eur. J. Int. Law (2018). https://www.ejiltalk.org/a-new-twist-in-the-south-china-sea-arbitration-the-chinese-society-of-international-laws-critical-study/

Governments of the Member States of ASEAN and the Government of the People's Republic of China. Declaration on the Conduct of Parties in the South China Sea (2012, May 14). https://asean.org/declaration-on-the-conduct-of-parties-in-the-south-china-sea-2/

Institute for Peace and Conflict Studies. Bhadri, V.: ASEAN, China, and a Code of Conduct for the South China Sea (2021, April-21). http://www.ipcs.org/comm_select.php?articleNo=5762

Institute for Security & Developpment Studies. Panda, J.P.: Code of Conduct needed for South China Sea (2020). https://isdp.eu/publication/code-of-conduct-needed-for-south-china-sea/

Jia, B.B., Talmon, S.: Introduction. In: Talmon, S., Jia, B.B. (Eds.). The South China Sea Arbitration: A Chinese Perspective (pp. 1–14). Hart Publishing Ltd., London (2014). https://doi.org/10.5040/9781474201933.ch-001. Accessed 11 Aug 2022

Leddy, K.: Competing claims: The developing roles of international law and unilateral challenges to maritime claims in the South China Sea. Vanderbilt J. Trans. Law **54**(3), 785–830 (2021)

Oxman, B.H.: The South China Sea Arbitration Award. Univ. Miami Int. Comparat. Law Rev. **24**, 235–284 (2016). https://doi.org/10.2139/ssrn.2835534

PCA Case Nº 2013–2019. Arbitration before an Arbitral Tribunal constituted under annex VII to the 1982 United Nations Convention on the Law of the Sea, The Philippines vs. The People's Republic of China, Award on Jurisdiction and Admissibility 29 Oct. 2015. https://pcacases.com/web/sendAttach/2579

PCA Case Nº 2013–2019. Arbitration before an Arbitral Tribunal constituted under annex VII to the 1982 United Nations Convention on the Law of the Sea, The Philippines vs. The People's Republic of China, Award of Award of 12 July 2016. https://pcacases.com/web/sendAttach/2086

Ministry of Foreign Affairs of the People's Republic of China, Statement on Settling Disputes Between China and the Philippines in the South China Sea Through Bilateral Negotiation (2016, June 8). https://www.fmprc.gov.cn/mfa_eng/wjdt_665385/2649_665393/201606/t20160608_679464.html

Sepulveda Amor, B.: The International Court of Justice and the Law of the Sea. Anuario Mexicano de Derecho Internacional, Décimo Aniversario, pp. 3–26 (2012)

Tanaka, Y.: The South China Sea Arbitration: Toward an International Legal Order in the Oceans. Hart Publishing, Oxford (2019)

United Nations, General Assembly, A/RES/2750(XXV) C. Reservation exclusively for peaceful purposes of the sea-bed and the ocean floor, and the subsoil thereof, underlying the high seas beyond the limits of present national jurisdiction and use of their resources in the interests of mankind, and convening of a conference on the law of the sea (1970, Dec. 17)

United Nations, Security Council. Press Conference by Security Council President on Programme of Work for August (2022, Aug. 1). https://press.un.org/en/2022/220801_SC.doc.htm

United States of America. Under Secretary of Defense for Policy. U.S. Department of Defense. DoD Annual Freedom of Navigation (FON) Reports. Annual Freedom of Navigation Report, Fiscal Year 2017 (2018). https://policy.defense.gov/Portals/11/FY17%20DOD%20FON%20Report.pdf?ver=2018-01-19-163418-053

United States of America. Press Briefing by Press Secretary Karine Jean-Pierre and National Security Council Coordinator for Strategic Communications John Kirby (2022, Aug. 1). https://www.whitehouse.gov/briefing-room/press-briefings/2022/08/01/press-briefing-by-press-secretary-karine-jean-pierre-and-national-security-council-coordinator-for-strategic-communications-john-kirby-2/

Zhao, S.: East Asian Disorder. China and the South China Sea Disputes. Asian Surv. **60**(3), 490–509 (2020)

Global Perspective

Jihad in Europe: Towards a Predictive Model for the Neutralization of Terrorist Threats

Oliver Pérez López(✉)

Guardia Civil, Madrid, Spain
operezlopez@guardiacivil.es

Nowadays, most people can remember where they were when the Twin Towers attack happened, and something similar happens to the Spaniards at a national level, when the attacks on the Madrid trains took place on March the 11th 2004, and more recently in August 2017 with the attacks that occurred successively on Las Ramblas in Barcelona and on the promenade of the town of Cambrils in Tarragona.

The terrorist barbarity and the impact caused by the attacks, which take hundreds or even thousands of lives happen near our homes and shake the very foundations of our security will always live on our memory. Everything that came after, and which is so important in the media, from the life stories of the victims to the profile of the author or authors, will be analyzed in depth for a long time.

It will also arouse all kind of feelings and reflections: from the grief for the lives lost to the incomprehension of the reasons that, for example, pushed some young residents in a town in Tarragona to carry out an attack that shocked the Spanish society as a whole in that summer of 2017.

In my case, I remember perfectly well that on August the 17th 2017 I was in the office, it was just after 4:30 p.m., and I received a call from the Head of the Intelligence Section that our police force has in Catalonia. He told me that there had been a multiple hit-and-run at Las Ramblas and that, based on the first information received, it made the semblance of a terrorist attack.

This last shade was key as in recent times there had been several run overs, albeit of lesser severity, which after the relevant investigations had turned out to be unintentional accidents, but until they were ruled out as a terrorist attack, they had to be treated as a priority.

In this case, the first data from Barcelona allowed the investigators, in a matter of minutes, and by using their usual analysis techniques as well as the information available in the different databases, to draw up from scratch a composition of the acting cell that turned out to correspond completely with the acting terrorists and their possible collaborators.

Among the information available, it stood out the fact that most of the people who were subsequently investigated lacked specific records for terrorism, which from the standpoint of investigators specialized in this matter meant that there were no initial theoretical motivations to suspect about them. Only the one who was identified as the leader of the terrorist cell, a male who was far older in age than the rest of members of the terrorist structure, had been involved or related in the past with radical individuals with criminal records.

J. Cayón Peña and J. M. Ramírez (Eds.): *Threats to Peace and International Security: Asia versus West*, ASTSA, pp. 149–167, 2023.
https://doi.org/10.1007/978-3-031-28336-9_9

All these set of facts obtained in the subsequent investigation have sparked important reflections in the investigators' mind. On the one hand, because even after having the police reconstructed the terrorist plot, from its beginning with the radicalization processes, through the preparatory acts to the final chain of events ending with a great explosion prior to the final improvised attacks, none of the security forces with CT competence managed to notice the structure and activity of this large cell. On the other hand, from the first information that appeared on the authors until the day of the trial, there was a strong focus on the profile of the attackers, their youth, their apparent integration and the unexpectedness of everything that happened as the prototype of the attack expected was of another typology.

Therefore, it should be assessed that, although the reality of the difficulty of anticipating the action of certain types of terrorist attackers is widely accepted, the feeling that this important specific case arouses is that all services failed to a greater or lesser extent, and they could not prevent the death of a high number of innocent people. Questions such as *what went wrong?* Or *what would it take to be able to act with guarantees next time?* must be answered in order to improve the possible future response to this type of tragic situations.

1 Objectives and Methodology

This investigation aims to provide a broad vision about the variety of terrorist profiles and the specific aspects that characterize the Jihadist threat at a European and Spanish level, and the importance that this fact has on the response of the security forces in the fight against terrorism.

Thanks to this knowledge based on the different data and reflections that will be provided throughout this document, a final list of indicators will be provided, which taken into account in a timely manner, would allow improving CT action by directing it towards a predictive model that - adapted and applied to each specific situation at the time - would enhance preventive capabilities by establishing the degree of security risk that a potential terrorist attack could pose.

The description of a real terrorist attack situation such as the one that took place in Barcelona in 2017, and the approaches and questions that could be asked about it, will be followed by several reflections about the importance to identify and set a group of possible indicators that help to recognize a terrorist profile.

Subsequently, two differentiated inductive methods will be used to achieve the widest possible range. On the one hand, on a sample of terrorist attacks that took place in Europe and, on the other hand, on the arrests of Jihadist terrorists carried out in Spain. In both studies, the working period would be from 2018 to the current date of completion of this article.

To this end, secondary sources specializing in terrorism will be combined with studies conducted by the author and derived from his more than fifteen years of experience devoted to fight terrorism as a Head of a specialized police unit.

2 Context of the Study/State of Play

There are many specialized studies on terrorist profiles in Spain. To the existing studies from years ago focused on the Basque Nationalist Liberation Movement where the new ETA terrorists were recruited and from which lasting conclusions were drawn over time about the requirements that new candidates had to meet, there have been researches into the profiles of Jihadist terrorists that have yielded far less specific results.

In the Spanish case, and to introduce some recent data of interest, in the period between 2013 and 2016, the detainees related to Daesh were radicalized both, in physical and virtual environments, and the prisons were already beginning to appear as places to take into consideration (Reinares and García-Calvo 2016). However, this period seems too far away from the current aspects of the phenomenon because, as it was mentioned above, this terrorism has a huge capacity for mutation. Among other issues to be taken into account, the following ones should be noted: the attacker's profile has changed since the returned FTFs have not acted on Western ground since 2016 (Pérez López 2021) and the use of social networks and messaging applications have been gaining prominence both in radicalization processes and in other daily uses by the main terrorist organizations (Municio 2017).

At an international level, it is worth highlighting the report by the Memorial Center for the Victims of Terrorism of February 2018 that studies the impact of Jihadist terrorism in the countries of the European Union between 1994 and 2017. Precisely, the alleged study will aim to give temporary continuity to the content of this publication and to update the data in the following years in order to extract common elements and characteristics that, properly elaborated and combined in the future, allow to support the development of preventive systems. Nowadays, a variety of security services and international private companies are directing some of their capabilities to this end.

3 Terrorist Profiles

3.1 Changing Threat, Changing Profiles

Within the framework of the fight against security threats, as a general rule, which is not fully effective, investigators are usually up-to-date on procedures and their application, so they have a realistic assessment of each situation as well as the current trends.

This circumstance has reached a degree of excellence precisely in recent years at the same time as Daesh was born. This has happened when both terrorist and counter-terrorist actions have skyrocketed exponentially in terms of statistics. This has allowed the law enforcement to acquire much more experience and, as a consequence, and although Jihadism is a tremendously dynamic and changing threat, the analyst and the investigator, far beyond what the existing analysis techniques allow, are able to issue preliminary assessments that would be difficult to achieve otherwise.

As well, as the Internet has become the "cornerstone" that has expanded the capabilities of this type of terrorism, the intelligence analysts will know how to adapt police procedures to this situation and how to take advantage of it in order to direct police action to neutralize the threat. Given that, within the framework of the European space, the lone attacker is being considered as the one having a profile with the greatest probability of acting in a potential next attack. A large part of the available resources is redirected, as far as possible, to the investigated targets that meet these requirements. However, far from suffering the expected action of a "lone wolf attacker", the type of attack committed in 2017 in Barcelona came from a group that was both incredibly large and unexpected, in which its members did not use the Internet, which has been detected to date in the highest percentage of those individuals who were investigated and arrested in previous years.

Did the terrorist make no mistakes or leave no clues to follow that alerted of their plans? Were they really so integrated into their social environment that, at no time, did they show that they were immersed in a radicalization process?

3.2 Indicators in the Attacks in Catalonia in 2017

Taking up again what was stated at the beginning of this paper about the terrorist cell that carried out the attacks in Barcelona and Cambrils (Tarragona), and as an example of the terrorist profiles who plan and execute an attack, it is worth mentioning that several members of the cell underwent a radicalization process that manifested itself as a change in their physical appearance and some behaviors, as reflected in different parts of the Summary Proceeding 5/2018, a case that was prosecuted in Spain.

Physically, they started to abandon aspects related to Western culture, and they let their beards grow. In some cases, they even strictly shaved their mustaches, and began wearing religious orthodox clothing, changing their usual way of dressing.

In terms of behavior, it was noticed that some of them increase their visit to the mosque, also there are evidence of several incidents with Muslim community people, because the latters were not coming to pray. All members of the cell adopted this rigorous practice of religion over time, in some cases reaching a high degree of aggressiveness when talking about religion, causing fear to part of their social environment.

Several of these terrorists stopped their daily activities that they had hitherto been doing normally, such as playing sports, partying, listening to commercial music, etc. In general, they changed their behavior towards women to the point of not looking at or talking to them (Teixidor 2020), and they tried to convince some of their relatives to do the same. Likewise, those who were still studying began to miss classes.

In dates closer and closer to the attacks and in private conversations with people outside the group of the terrorists, they expressed statements against Jews and Spaniards, and they even started to show their radical views on some issues related to religion in other conversations publicly and in well-known social networks.

The issues referred to in the preceding paragraphs were objective facts that, after the terrorist attacks, acquired a different perspective from the moment in which they occurred. All this information could have been enough as a a wake-up call to react but, nevertheless, there are many other issues that must also be considered.

On the one hand, several of these facts, which could well be measured as indicators of radicalism, are in fact closely linked to the free and legal practice of the religion. In this sense, any preliminary observation, not to mention the police use of any of those aspects, could generate a victimization of Islam and the Muslims.

On the other hand, even if the people, who were able to observe this radical evolution in the appearances and/or behaviors of these individuals, had informed the security forces, what could investigators have done about it?

It is indeed a good opportunity, and in many cases, it would even be the only one, to focus on these people as potential targets to be investigated. The reality, on the contrary, is that, at the same time as the possibility of a new investigation arises, the investigators – no matter what security force they are in -, as stated in several parts of this paper, face constantly new and endless challenges, in which precisely the volume of information and the opening of lines of investigation is constant. Therefore, it is quite difficult to be able to delve into all of them, which may have been necessary.

Based on this section, if law enforcement would have criminal records, or even this type of behavior information, it might have been possible to detect subsequent weird activities, such as the purchase of precursors or the sale of gold. However, it will never be known with absolute certainty. Even if, after the events and having plenty of time to conduct a good academic research, elements of interest would have been obtained that could have substantiated an investigation, the reality is that, in real time and at that moment, there would always be many different unknown and out of control factors and variables. Anyhow, it would be indeed a hopeful start and, duly systematized as far as the treatment of indicators is concerned, could provide an indisputable opportunity to be able to solve similar situations in the future.

In this way, even when the results must be deemed negative for all purposes, it is possible to justify and defend the actions of those responsible for the security when facing these difficulties. These last frenetic years in the fight against terrorism have revealed the dynamism, variety, diversity and the huge mutation capacity shown by this threat. This can be considered as a determining factor for police action and intelligence services that are constantly surprised by new situations, different terrorist profiles - who are able to move at international level -, and the fact that when something happens thousands of kilometers away from the European soil, it also has a decisive influence on the internal security. These and other elements shake the existing security policies to the point that it is necessary to introduce constant adaptations in many different regulatory areas.

Furthermore, this broad threat constantly generates new security challenges to deal with that rarely support a single or systematic response over time. Therefore, when the enemy itself is changing, and its profile is ill-defined, everything becomes more difficult from one minute to the next, and it is practically impossible to anticipate the move to action in real time, even when the target is being actively investigated.

In fact, these statements are not something new. The conclusion was already reached in studies made two decades ago: it is not possible to establish a single profile of a member of the Jihadist networks that were operating at the beginning of the year 2000 since, based on the reasonable variables used at the time of the study, a very different image of its members was obtained (Jordan et al. 2016).

Given the above, it would be reasonable to think that it is not feasible to establish a single terrorist model (Municio 2017), but it would be more feasible to identify indicators based on which to work the profiles of those investigated people in order to catalog and classify their behavior, dangerousness, or being able to assess information that is obtained about certain people at specific times. At a time like the present, where there is great experience in the fight against terrorism, both nationally and in terms of Jihadism, and given that there is a well-established criterion on the reality and the existing needs to improve, it is deemed that the study of those profiles is truly important because if we want to defeat the enemy, we need to know it first (Municio 2017).

3.3 Early-Stage Indicators Detection: Law Enforcement Responsibility Under a Great Difficulty

Unfortunately, a current debate is still focused on the effectiveness of law enforcement counterterrorism. Investigators are constantly under the scrutiny at every level: judges and prosecutors as well as rulers and the public opinion. There is no margin for error when it comes to neutralizing an attack before it is executed. For this reason, their situation is frankly complicated. Despite the above, this section is worth reading given that it provides an understanding of the work carried out by the professionals in this field because the quality of their work goes unnoticed unless something transcends the public opinion. However, the day an attack occurs, the police action will be the target of all the questions.

There have been several cases where, after an attack, it has been initiated a cleaning process of the responsibilities of those in charge at a police level in the CT fight. A very graphic and well-known example of this, although not the only one, was the case of the attacks in Toulouse (France) by Mohamed MERAH (Jordan 2012). His terrorist activities and the subsequent investigation showed that there was room for improvement on the part of the security services and it ended up with the dismissal of the main people responsible of the DGSI (General Directorate of Internal Security).

What should the French investigators have done in this case? It is difficult to deal with a terrorist or a group of terrorists who are precisely taking measures not to be neutralized and who take advantage of all the possibilities offered by our State of Law to act with great freedom.

It is at this moment when all the limitations, which investigations on terrorism matters have - both in the field of pure intelligence and of law enforcement - gain more value: a scenario where uncertainty usually predominates and where it is accentuated the fact that the authors of the current jihadist terrorism are very different from the terrorists with whom investigators have been used to deal with years ago.

In Spain, the terrorist organization ETA operated for many years and put the Government ant the society on the ropes on several occasions. In that time, investigators faced a terrorist profile that is very close to the traditional values and customs of the native culture. Ideological distance was not an important or determining factor when it came to investigating this threat since there was a common cultural factor between investigators and the investigated individuals. This meant that the former could develop lines of investigation more effectively because they could understand and comprehend this type of terrorist, and in many cases their action could even be anticipated.

Everything changed with the jihadist terrorist phenomenon in European societies in general, and in Spain in particular. The profile of this type of terrorist, who act in the name of religion, moves within unfamiliar parameters compared to those that existed until very recently. This is translated in an added problem for investigators, who do not find clarity or ease in their work, where their instinct and previous experience are not as useful as would be desirable. Moreover, indicators that previously betrayed the ETA terrorists and that were totally controlled by the investigators are now invalid. An eminently operational commitment doesn't facilitate finding convincing evidence that would lead to broad judicial sentences anymore. Now, a huge number of analysts needs a lot of time and work to be able to draft pieces of writing that end up in a prison sentence or in the expelling of the terrorist profile.

The indicators that previously served as a warning to show that a person could be collaborating or integrated in ETA are not at all applicable to the current wave of terrorism. The analyst and the investigator will have to open their minds to new ways and techniques that allow paying attention to issues that have gone unnoticed and that could have helped to make better assessments in general. Perhaps, the key precisely lies in working more specifically and systematically on studies of indicators that are not as intuitive as before and that allow establishing early detection mechanisms.

3.4 Terrorist Profiles

In addition to the above, please find below a summary of some of the terrorist roles that will necessarily be taken into consideration in this study and that will undoubtedly affect the obtained results.

First of all, we will list the profiles that could pose a direct threat:

- Lone actors: those who, as a rule, do not have direct contact with any terrorist organization but are inspired by them.
- Lone directed actors: those who, although acting autonomously and not needing operational support from any group or organization, have had, at some point, contact with their members and have received instructions.
- Returned *foreign terrorist fighters*: those who travelled and physically joined terrorist structures operating in conflict zones and returned subsequently to other countries, with the intention of continuing to operate in favor of the terrorist cause.

With regard to them, it is important to note that there has been an evolution towards a trend of attacks perpetrated mostly by lone actors who rarely had a direct relationship with terrorist organizations. They did not have, therefore, prior training and generally underwent a mostly autonomous radicalization process in their country of residence.

Other roles of major concern in the fight against this type of terrorism are those played by collaborators involved in key logistical facets, among which stand out the participation in actions linked to the shipment of material to conflict zones and the facilitation of activities for European territory-based terrorist elements.

Also, the work of recruiters and the networks for sending material have played an important role in recent years, facilitating the exodus of fighters to the conflict zone.

Furthermore, it is apparent that another key activity of growing importance, in light of the evolution of new trends such as cryptocurrencies, is being carried out in the field of financing and by the terrorists engaged in it.

Another example of this variety would be the instrumentalization of the internet, turning it into the real axis around which the jihadist threat currently revolves. Its transversality has allowed maintaining the terrorist pressure over time, regardless of the fact that the terrorist organizations did not control territories of their own. Therefore, those who consume terrorist propaganda, and especially those who spread it, are priority permanent targets of the security forces.

Finally yet importantly, there are the individuals in prison, either because of terrorism or for any other criminal typology, who are radicalized or are potential candidates for undergoing a process of this nature.

3.5 Study of the Actors: Attacks in Europe and Arrests in Spain

Existing studies and publications on perpetrators of major attacks in Europe and on detainees in Spain, assess not only rather general aspects such as the attacker's gender, age or nationality or the method or means used, but also more profound facets such as their primary socialization environment, educational level, way of life, link with other terrorist typologies, time in prison, degree of mental derangement or use of internet platforms.

This set of factors, which shows how wide-ranging the jihadist terrorist profile is, will also serve as a first step towards a proposal for the establishment of the set of indicators that in the law enforcement agencies' experience of recent years would be identified as representative and preventive, in order to detect potential terrorists.

In this study, unlike in many others conducted before and which reflect the actual state of research, the specific characteristics of the place where attacks were committed are not going to be explored, except in relation to the fact that they were actually carried out on European soil. At Spanish national level, the data offered also ignore the place where the arrests took place, as it is not of interest in the present investigation.

3.5.1 Attacks in Europe

Now, a perspective will be introduced of the attacks occurred on European soil from 2018 to present day. Data will be provided in order to both draw some conclusions but also shed some light on what could be the determining and common features of the profile of potential terrorists who may pose a security risk.

Regarding the objective of the attacks, the most relevant data is that the attacks target civilian population or uniformed security forces. The most affected countries are France, the most significant example where lone actors have executed between three and six attacks each year, United Kingdom and the Russian Federation.

The latter, however, will be excluded from this study in order to focus strictly on European countries since, although the attacks they have suffered are obviously and effectively jihadist, most of them have been committed within the framework of the particular conflict between that country and Chechen groups. Terrorists from that origin have quite a different and even lesser impact in Europe than they do there.

Likewise, it will not be necessary to mention that practically all the attackers are men, with a slight presence of female terrorists, in conjunction with the role of women and the uses and customs advocated by the radical jihadist groups.

Moreover, in the context of a temporal overview, it should be noted that, in recent years, the number of attacks in Europe has been progressively declining, except for a rebound in 2020, in the time of COVID and the restrictions derived from the measures that were adopted.

The generic data offered below in the following paragraphs comes from a summary table that has been prepared in real time as the attacks occurred using information from different specialized media outlets and secondary sources. The specific details about the perpetrators, which, on the other hand, are decisive to be able to identify possible indicators, have been extracted by the author and will be talked in depth in the following section that talks about key indicators.

In this way, regarding the attacks that took place on European soil throughout 2018, it is worth noting that up to 15 attacks were recorded. From those, 6 occurred on French soil and 3 on British soil, oscillating the age range of the attackers between 19 years the youngest and 52 years the oldest.

Despite the difficulty of having exact data, the typology of terrorists responds in most cases to individual attackers who acted alone or in a targeted manner. This last piece of information is not always easy to confirm because, in subsequent investigations, it is sometimes not possible to prove the previous link with other terrorists and, in many cases, it is necessary to resort to possible subsequent claims of the attack.

Even though it has been verified that there is variety of origins of the attackers, it predominates the little elaboration in the planning, having resorted, as a general rule, to the use of knives. In fact, in most of the attacks where a firearm was used, it was because the perpetrator got the weapon from the security force agents who were precisely the targets (Igualada Tolosa 2018).

Another aspect to take into consideration is that there is a significant number of cases in which the attacks occurs shortly after the terrorist had been released from prison.

These previous aspects also predominate with respect to the attacks suffered in Europe in 2019 where 9 attacks were recorded: 4 of them in France and 2 in the United Kingdom, which were carried out individually by perpetrators between 20 and 45 years of age.

Something statistically different happens in 2020, the year of the pandemic, when the data practically doubles, accounting for 18 terrorist attacks: 10 in France, 3 in United Kingdom and 2 in Germany.

This year's data also highlights the fact that ten of the perpetrators had previously served time and many of them were known by the security services for their alleged radicalism. In both cases, the average increases considerably with respect to previous years in what could be an important trend to take into account for the following years and for the design and adoption of any preventive measures.

Likewise, and directly related to the previous data, from 2018 to this year, a significant number of attacks, practically half, have been carried out inside prisons.

In 2021, the evolution of the attacks on European soil returns to the trend before 2020 with 10 attacks: 4 of them in France, 2 in the United Kingdom and another two in Germany. So, while the number of attacks has been going down with respect to the immediately preceding years, from 2014 and 2017, when the pseudo-caliphate Daesh was at its peak, there was a progressive increase in the role of lone actors to the detriment of those carried out by organized groups or returnees. Likewise, directly related to the previous data, the majority of attacks were carried out using knives followed far behind by any other procedure, be it through running over, firearms or the use of explosives.

From this study of attacks, it has been identified some other common features that appear in quite a high number of attackers and that could constitute a key element to define indicators of interest.

On the one hand, although the age ranges, as seen in the previous data, are very wide between the oldest and the youngest, the average age of the vast majority was between 20 and 35 years. This average age has been approximately constant for more years in samples corresponding to the years 2016 and 2017.

On the other hand, it has been detected that, in a high coincidence index, the terrorist attacker would have been previously involved in other criminal activities linked to common crimes. Possibly, this aspect is also associated with the fact that many of these attackers have also served time, before taking action, for reasons other than terrorism.

This circumstance would not be accidental since the situation in prisons is of increasing concern in the European environment, since, to the apparent difficulty of reintegration of those convicted of terrorism, we must add the high rate of radicalization that exists among common inmates.

Through the little reliable information that is sometimes available regarding some attacks, it can be assessed that many of the attackers lavished face-to-face in physical environments associated with Muslim culture, that is, mosques or Islamic communities. This issue is becoming more and more common and takes place as the same time as the paradigm of lone actors who spend a lot of time connected to the internet inside their homes developing an introverted profile, interacting and accessing terrorist propaganda content through different social networks and messaging applications.

In a representative number of cases, it was detected the existence of possible mental disorders diagnosed in the attackers. On this aspect, it is difficult to have reliable statistics given the high possibility that the terrorist has not followed any medical parameters or has been previously diagnosed. However, police experience specializing in terrorism indicates that the impact of this medical issue could be much more important than that attributed to date in the different studies.

3.5.2 Arrests in Spain

In a similar format to the previous section, it will be presented a study based on the available data of the individuals who have been arrested in Spain for their alleged actions in favor of jihadist terrorism between the years 2018 and 2022. According to the statistics of the Spanish Internal Affairs Ministry corresponding to this period of time count with quite a high number of detainees. Therefore, it is difficult to talk about specific details so there will be a tendency to extract common denominators that support the investigation.

It is worth noting that the highest number of detainees and exploited operations in Spain occurred between 2015 and 2017, lowering the annual figures by half in 2018. This trend would continue in the following years, possibly with the justification that the reform of the Spanish Criminal Code of 2015 collected new criminal forms related to behaviors linked to jihadist terrorism and this implied an upturn both in lines of investigation initiated at a judicial level and in those that could be resolved at that time. As of 2017, at the same time as the judicial resolutions of these investigations were issued and their non-adaptation to initial expectations took place, it had a negative impact on the continuity of its application as of 2018.

It is also necessary to consider that, in an adequate alignment with the objectives of the general study to identify valid indicators applicable to a preventive system, it will not be decisive to contemplate the nationality of detainees since it is a type of data that must be subject to the its importance in terms of the origins of the attackers in Europe.

That being said, and beginning with the analysis of the arrests carried out in 2018, it is worth noting that 287 operations were carried out compared to the 52 and 74 people arrested previously. The ages of the detainees were between 19 and 52 years old, although the majority of cases were between 26 and 38 years old (Igualada Tolosa 2018).

This year, without a doubt, was marked by the Operation Escribano, in which twenty people under investigation were questioned for their links with the so-called "prison front". With this action, the directed and systematized evolution of the phenomenon of radicalization in prisons in Spain was made clear. A trend that is also wide spreading in the rest of Europe and that precisely reinforces the need to focus specific attention on prevention in the future.

Later on, in 2019, we had 33 operations with the arrest of 60 people, whose ages were mostly between 26 and 31 years of age.

One of the most interesting reflections that can be extracted from the age ranges is that the range that goes up to 38 years of age is associated with individuals who have been arrested for instrumentalizing the use of new technologies to support terrorism while those whose age exceeded 40 years were more circumscribed to logistics and financing activities.

In 2020, 38 arrests were made belonging to 24 operations and, although there is a wide range of ages, the largest number of detainees were between 32 and 38 years old, with no data on their profile that could be significantly different from those detained years before them.

During the following year, in 2021, 24 operations were completed with the result of 40 people arrested. 100% of the individuals arrested that year were male, which consolidated the already known downward trend about the participation of women in this particular terrorist role. Most of the detainees were not older than 25 years (27%), and when talking about nationality, the majority of these detainees were Moroccan (42%), Spaniards and Algerians.

Finally, from January to September 2022, 35 people have been arrested in Spain for their links to terrorism, with 48% of those arrested being between the ages of 30 and 39. Likewise, 37% of the detainees have police records from various criminal areas other than terrorism.

In all the cases of the previous samples, both the attacker in Europe and those arrested in Spain, and of course once there has been an investigation into them that allows knowing in depth certain characteristics of their lives, there is the possibility of identifying different aspects, which properly focused, could become relatively quantifiable indicators based on which to make classifications.

4 Key Indicators Identification

When studying the profile of a person, it is possible give an assessment from the most basic and personal aspects such as the nationality, sex or age of the individual to aspects related to the ideology, medical issues or police records. Precisely, it will be in the deepening of these personal particularities where the best arguments will be found to extract generalities that can be extrapolated into a model, which could be applied to new individuals so that they are assessed.

In this way, both in closed questions and in others that are more open to interpretation, it is proposed a list of characteristics that are present, to a greater or lesser extent, in the individuals that made up the two samples, whose treatment and measurement based on the appropriated factors could be key to carry out assessments on individuals about their dangerousness.

- Age: this is an important aspect that is directly assessable due to the data previously offered with the age ranges of the people who carried out attacks.

  In the case of attacks in Europe between 2018 and 2022, the average age was between 20 and 25 years.
- Gender: as it was mentioned above, the impact of the role of the female gender in the parameters of this threat is relegated to a very secondary level with very little prominence in both attacks and arrests.

  In the sample of both cases, attackers in Europe and detainees in Spain, the total predominance is that of males with the exception of very specific cases corresponding to women, which hardly reach 10% of the annual arrests in Spain.
- Origin: the origin of the attackers is very diverse, although there are several predominate nationalities. The same has been discovered in the case of places of birth of those detained by the Spanish security forces. Likewise, it is worth noting the increase in importance of the role of the native of the European countries, whether from second or third generation immigrants and the case of converts.

  This indicator, regardless of the results of attacks in Europe, should be adapted by each country and its analysts to the idiosyncrasy of the social reality of its territory since it will probably directly affect the results that can be collected locally.
- Profession: despite the wide professional casuistry detected in the two samples, where people with jobs of relative importance have been combined with others who did not have a known occupation, repeated correspondences to certain specific sectors have been observed. Specifically, the services sector and unskilled labor have been the most frequent sectors with a high number of unemployed people who had received subsidies at different times.
- Conflictive primary socialization environments: as in any other aspect of study unrelated to terrorism, the development of childhood or youth in broken families or with problems can decisively condition personal evolution in the future.
- Studies/Technical qualification/Courses: this is quite a decisive aspect in importance since a person without academic training could be more easily manipulated than others. Likewise, the fact that the person under investigation has a specific qualification in certain specific sectors could mean access to components for explosives or the ease of making certain devices. Regarding the sample, the technical qualification or the

training received in most cases corresponding to the profile of the attackers was framed in levels of basic studies or oriented to technical professional development.

- Management of social networks: this skill, which is basic in developed societies, can become a key indicator because the jihadist terrorist circuit extended its use to conduct propaganda tasks. In fact, this aspect has been present in different categorizations in many individuals from both samples.
- Behavior patterns: these aspects are quite important both in individuals with a visible initial level of socialization, which at any given time suffer a considerable change, as well as in subjects who develop a way of life without assessable social features and who spend much of their time at their homes. In quite a high number of attacks in Europe, both in the case of the investigated individuals and the detainees in Spain, it was possible to appreciate a change in their behaviors. This has also been backed up by the explanations given about the individuals who made up the cell that attacked in Barcelona back in 2017.
- Acquisition of skills/specific practice of sports: in a significant number of cases in real investigations, it has been possible to verify that the individual under observation had developed a fondness for physical activities related to contact sports or military simulation.
- Military training: the knowledge and experience in the use of weapons and explosives is a factor that could reasonably pose a high level of danger.
- Externalization of ideology: this would be a very valuable indicator to reliably identify a person who is immersed in a radicalization process or who has a highly significant degree of radicalization. By itself, and even if it is public and notorious, it does not have to imply the commission of any crime as it can be limited to freedom of speech. However, taken together with other elements, it has enough of an importance for the security forces to develop information needs on this person. It has been verified how, in a high number of studied cases, the terrorist had verbalized in several of his social circle's rejection of Western lifestyles and societies.
- Lack of integration: this is an additional aspect together with verbal comments that can become evident through visible actions of rejection of the uses and customs of the social environment in which they live.

  In many of the investigated cases, this fact has been corroborated at some point.
- Feeling of victimization: the way in which an individual personally perceives being the victim of an injustice or a grievance due to the treatment they received in relation to certain religious, political or ideological issues.

  This aspect has been very frequent in many of the cases of recent perpetrators under the modality of "lone actors".
- Terrorist links: in the jihadist terrorist casuistry of recent years, there has been a wide facility of communication between terrorist operatives and serious candidates. Some of the driving elements behind this trend are social networks, the high number of fighters who traveled from a large number of countries to join terrorist structures and the situation in prisons.

  This issue is faithfully reflected in both samples since many of the perpetrators and detainees in Spain had previous links with other people related to the jihadist circuit.

- Diminished mental faculties: unlike other terrorist typologies, within the jihadist terrorist organizations, the instrumentalization of people with mental disorders has been promoted mainly to be used as suicide bombers in conflict zones and to act as lone actors on Western soil.

  Although it would be a difficult indicator to measure without the existence of a medical verdict, in many of the cases that appear in the two samples, investigators have considered that possibility in quite a high number of cases.

  All those disorders, both psychotic and/or schizophrenic disorders and those associated with the use of substances, which could be instrumentalized in favor of the terrorist cause, should be contemplated within this indicator.
- Feeling in tune with terrorist organizations: this indicator is highly related to activities on the internet or the verbal externalization of the ideology but it ends up being exclusively referred to expressing sympathy towards a terrorist organization or to advertise its propaganda products.

  Regarding the individuals arrested in Spain, this characteristic has provided, in recent years, and in the absence of other elements, the judicial framework to be able to urge several measures against potential terrorists.
- Prison time: currently, there is a serious problem with the phenomenon of radicalization in European prisons as well as with the prompt release of inmates sentenced for terrorism after serving very short prison sentences.

  This is visibly objective and it has happened once and again in a very high number of the studied cases. The perpetrator has served a prison sentence and it is during the time in prison when the individual ends up radicalized. It also highlighted that a high number of attacks perpetrated in recent years had been committed inside prisons.
- Existence of prior intelligence: in almost all the cases of attacks in the sample, the individuals were known by the security forces for their alignment with the jihadist terrorist cause. However, they did not have the necessary set of indicators or the appropriate evidence to issue a specific measure against them.
- Consumption of jihadist propaganda: the fundamental role of the internet in the jihadist threat has led to both social networks and commercial messaging applications becoming places of access to terrorist propaganda. The great impact that this has on self-indoctrination processes has already been demonstrated.

  In more than 90% of the studied cases, both perpetrators and detainees have stored different kinds of propaganda material (video, audio and image) on their digital devices.
- Links with criminality: in many cases, the attackers as well as those detained for terrorism in Spain had been previously involved or even have been actively involved in the commission of other types of crimes of a nature other than terrorism.
- Suspicious international movements: the proclamation of the pseudo-caliphate Daesh and the territorial control that this terrorist organization had in Syria and Iraq generated a calling effect on radical Muslims from over the world, who moved to these countries to join the ranks of the terrorist organizations that were operating there. This issue had as an added consequence the fact that the displaced ended up receiving instructions and gaining experience in the handling of weapons and explosives, which increased their level of dangerousness in the event of a return to their places of origin or even to other places. The above-mentioned international movements would not only be

limited to this casuistry, but also would have to be extended to other cross border movements, whose purpose was to maintain contact with operational members of terrorist organizations.

- Pledge of allegiance to a terrorist organization: although it is a difficult aspect to corroborate at any stage of the investigation, it should be seen as key evidence of radicalism and final determination to be a strong candidate for taking action. In fact, back in 2015, there was a pledge of allegiance in 64% of known attacks cases and, in 2016, in 38% of the cases (Vidino and Marone 2022).

As it will be explained in the final conclusions of this document, it would be possible to create a risk assessment system to assess the danger that an individual could pose by listing all the above indicators and breaking them down into possible sub-indicators and categorize them at different levels. By doing so, it would be possible to propose a preventive and predictive system that could anticipate when a known individual or a target who is being investigated could have a greater probability of taking action.

5 Limitations to the Investigation

In order to take advantage of what it has been written down in this study, it is necessary to have a set of data that will only be known in the case of people who are being thoroughly investigated. Wouldn't have been then valid to use it to anticipate a response in the case of the Barcelona attacks back in 2017? Sadly enough, with the investigation procedures that are currently in place, the answer would be no. Therefore, new reflections should be raised within the framework of some procedures such as in the fight against radicalization, where there is still much room for improvement in western societies, so that attention could be directed towards the few "warnings" that investigators receive before it is too late to neutralize the threat.

As a matter of fact, in recent years, security forces have been overwhelmed by the amount of work they have to face, which is quite difficult to handle given the dimensions of the agencies. The huge volume of information received in these investigation units has become quite a challenge in itself at the time of treating the information accordingly. All of this without even taking into consideration the quality behind that information, which at first is not something easy to appreciate or even asses. That being said, both the information directly linked to a credible attack and the information linked to an action that is less possible to verify needs to be equally dealt with. This is the feature that most defines what it means to work on a threat in which any data received can be a key element in avoiding a disaster tomorrow or even in five years. The above-mentioned volume of information limits the response capacity and this forces us to have broad structures of different diversified work teams given the high number of existing areas of expertise in the jihadist phenomenon that must be specifically addressed.

Given the latest contributions, it can be assumed that the Barcelona attacks, based on all the variables that surrounded this plot, could have hardly been avoided except for a matter of instinct or pure luck that unfortunately did not occur.

When we talk about jihadist terrorism with a retrospective vision of the recent years, it is even easier to understand the difficulties that security forces have to face. Along the way, there have been coined different terms to specifically explain that this type of terrorism has many faces and a polymorphism of many aspects to which devote resources in a diversified manner. On the one hand, there are all those profiles that could be a threat such as returned foreign terrorist fighters (FTF), lone actors, both directed actors or organized groups. On the other hand, there are those whose action is individually circumscribed to the collaborative field or even those people who facilitate the action for the terrorists in any imaginable way: documentation, logistics, weapons, etc.… or many others who, during these last years, at the dawn of the new technologies, have consumed, edited and/or disseminated propaganda material in favor of the terrorist cause.

Moreover, it should not be forgotten any and all elements that could support the terrorist action and that should also be faced by security forces to try to diminish the backbone capabilities of these organizations instead of just tackle the problem by arresting the individuals who appear as a threat. Things such as propaganda, financing or radicalization must be addressed by making use of specific and comprehensive strategies and procedures, sometimes assumed by the same investigators who are devoted to neutralize operatives who intend to act.

Due to these previous factors and many others that, to a greater or lesser extent, and depending on the moment or the scenario, will also have an influence to take into account, we must be aware that any improvement in the fight against terrorism will always constitute a progress but that the implementation of these progresses will need a long period of adaptation until it can be effective.

Anyhow, this effectiveness is constantly under risk of end up being affected by the constant change that exists in the jihadist universe. Changes that, to a greater or lesser extent, can see the entry and exit of trends in different aspects that further affect the level of importance of the different terrorist roles at each moment, the origin of the terrorists, the procedures used and so on. In short, they can affect the importance of the indicators that are intended to be highlighted in this investigation. As some other studies mentioned (Calle Prado and López Melero 2022), we need to resort to the geographical and cultural place of origin of the terrorist since there will be some differentiating factors which encourage crime in order to draw a profile.

On the other hand, the data used in this investigation on the attacks carried out in Europe and the arrests conducted in Spain has been extracted from various specialized publications as well as the investigator's own data due to his profession. The different figures contrasted through the different sources do not fully correspond as there are certain margins of interpretation when doing the appropriate accounting.

The figures set out in this document have been based preferably on the available data collected during the period of time corresponding to the years covered in the study that contemplate the most extensive version of both police operations, including those with no arrests, and the attacks whose alleged terrorist inspiration can be questioned in some way.

Obviously, it must also be duly taken into account that the profile of the perpetrators of terrorist actions may not be the same as that of those who have simply been arrested for other types of activities or of those in whom the final element of willingness to take action or the predetermination to plan an attack is not present. However, the difference in profiles can precisely allow a greater enrichment with regard to the identification of indicators and the importance that can be assigned to each one of them.

6 Conclusions

In recent years, it has been demonstrated, and therefore written down in this study, that a factor to take into account is the attackers self-radicalization process, which prevents security forces from being able to anticipate their action.

Even in cases in which it has been possible to arrest the perpetrators, it turns out that they carry out the terrorist action inside prisons or after serving time. Therefore, a prompt detection can't really guarantee an effective neutralization.

Besides this, it would be important to note that security forces are facing a high number of challenges on a daily basis, which never cease to need greater dimensioning to guarantee the minimum security to our fellow citizens at all times.

For these reasons and given all the above, it is necessary to conclude with the need to have the greatest number of means and resources possible while making the most out of any past and/or recent experience from which to extract lessons learnt that can be applied in the future.

In this sense, and given that the activities conducted by security forces are quite focused on reacting to incidents, it is key to work more in the field of prevention, where precisely the assessment of risks on individuals would allow establishing priorities and an order of potential terrorists based on the degree of dangerousness they pose if they would conduct a terrorist action, generating the possibility of a needed proactivity.

The categorization of some of these indicators would be based on objective data. However, the categorization of other ones would be conducted by applying subjective assessments that, in any case, should be carried out by experienced analysts in the fight against terrorism with a great knowledge of the matter.

The key to being able to establish a predictive system lies in the combined application of past experience and current information. On the one hand, it is essential to take advantage of the experience from the fight against terrorism in general, and of what has been learnt in depth about the profile of the attackers in particular. On the other hand, there would be the information available at each present moment about the individuals who are being investigated or who, in any way, are deemed to be assessed. The adequate interrelation of these two areas could allow obtaining graphic and numerical results based on which to make certain types of decisions.

The way to do this would depend on the temporal and physical context in which is to be applied as well as on the perspective of the analysts who are in charge of this task. This means that the parameters of this work model would not be the same in Europe than in North America or Africa. Terrorist problems and their conditioning factors are different in each one of the regions and each indicator and its categories would have a different impact and importance, which would have to be regulated and adapted to the local casuistry.

Obviously, the final result behind the integration of every single aspect would not harbor an indicative value or evidence that could be taken into account before a competent court in terrorist cases beyond the possible attention that each of the factors could awaken individually in the corresponding prosecutors or judges for being considered as an objective or additional element that is present in a specific type of crime.

The possibility of establishing a decision-making model linked to the specific priorities developed thanks to multiple integration criteria would be a tool of great value in the field of action for the security forces because it would allow resources to be directed towards those elements deemed of interest due to the danger they could pose to the detriment of other objectives that reasonably come to occupy another less critical position in the scale of priorities.

However, the benefits and advantages that the adoption of a prioritized work system based on the explained criteria could entail should not be understood as the definite tool that will put an end to terrorism since the reality is that its application could only become effective in the case of known individuals and about whom there is a lot of information. A different issue is that of relative to the radicals who are outside the radar of the security forces and who could lead the next attack tomorrow.

In this case, the attack disruption necessarily goes through the involvement of all the sectors that could help in the fight against this endless scourge in the same way that was orchestrated against terrorist organizations of the past, which were defeated. Much of this leading role will reside in the citizens and in the power they have at the time of reporting on quite a large part of the above-mentioned indicators and that will be unknown by those responsible for the security until, unfortunately, an attack has to be reconstructed through an investigation.

The society, duly made aware and with adequate knowledge of the threat, would be the means through which to name and face possible individuals of interest on whom to work in terms of security to be able to apply this new approach to preventive methodology. With the normalization of this aspect, perhaps potential terrorist actors such as those that made up the cell that attacked Barcelona in 2017 would have been discovered and neutralized in time.

References

Terrorismo Internacional. El paradigma en la mutación del modus operandi terrorista; Biblioteca fundamental de criminología; Delta Publicaciones (2022)

De La Corte Ibañez, L.: La yihad de Europa. Desarrollo e impacto del terrorismo yihadista en los países de la Unión Europea (1994–2017); Report nº4 del Centro Memorial de las Víctimas del Terrorismo (2018)

García-Calvo, C., Reinares, F.: Atentados en Barcelona y Cambrils: (I) formación de la célula de Ripoll, radicalización de sus miembros y preparación de unos actos de terrorismo a gran escala; Real Instituto ELCANO. Retrieved Agost 3, 2022 (2022). https://www.realinstitutoelcano.org/documento-de-trabajo/atentados-en-barcelona-y-cambrils-parte1-formacion-de-la-celula-de-ripoll-radicalizacion-de-sus-miembros-y-preparacion-de-unos-actos-de-terrorismo-a-gran-escala/

Igualada Tolosa, C.: Atentados y actividad yihadista global en 2018; Observatorio Internacional de Estudios sobre Terrorismo (OIET); Colectivo de Víctimas del Terrorismo (COVITE) (2018)

Igualada Tolosa, C.: Operaciones policiales contra el yihadismo en España en 2018; Observatorio Internacional de Estudios sobre Terrorismo (OIET); Colectivo de Víctimas del Terrorismo (COVITE) (2018)

Jordan, J., Mañas,F.M., Trujillo, H.: Perfil sociocomportamental y estructura organizativa de la militancia yihadista en España. Análisis de las redes de Abu Dahdah y del 11-M; Jihadmonitor.Org. (2016). Accessed 2016. https://www.academia.edu/2324653/Perfil_sociocomportamental_y_estructura_organizativa_de_la_militancia_yihadista_en_Espa%C3%B1a_An%C3%A1lisis_de_las_redes_de_Abu_Dahdah_y_del_11_M

Jordan, J.: El caso de Mohamed Merah en el contexto actual de la amenaza terrorista; Grupo de Estudios en Seguridad Internacional (GESI); University of Granada (2012). Accessed 24 Mar 2012. https://www.ugr.es/~gesi/analisis/3-2012.pdf#:~:text=Por%20tanto%2C%20la%20campa%C3%B1a%20terrorista%20de%20Mohamed%20Merah,los%20Juegos%20Ol%C3%ADmpicos%20de%20Londres%20el%20pr%C3%B3ximo%20verano

Municio Mújica, N.: Evolución del perfil del yihadista en Europa; Instituto Español de Estudios Estratégicos (2017)

Pérez López, O.: Retornado Yihadista: ¿La mayor amenaza contra occidente?; End-of-Master's Project in Analysis of Intelligence and Cyber intelligence; University of Nebrija (2021)

Proceeding 5/2018. Spanish National High Court, Judicial Chamber for Criminal Cases, Section 3, Ruling 15/2021

Reinares, F., García-Calvo, C.: Estado Islámico en España; Real Instituto Elcano (2016)

Teixidor, A.: Los silencios del 17-A; Diéresis (2020)

Vidino, L., Marone, F.: Jihadist attacks in the west: 2014 – 2022; Program on extremism at George Washington University (2022)

However, there is a long path towards achieving an ultimate success, which truly demands more capacity- and trust-building initiatives between and among the regional countries.

In this paper, the readers shall have an opportunity to get familiar with a first-hand personal review of the past lessons and anticipation of the future perspective of the new policy.

1 Introduction

The following is the personal analysis of the author and is not the position of the VIIMES.

In this paper, general information on particularities of Iran and its neighbours, by referring to the views of some international analysts, is followed by some personal comments. In order to factually reflect the foreign policy of the new government and its implementation since President Raisi took office, I have prepared a compilation of official statements, mostly with quotation, as documentary.

Which Developments Require the New Iranian Government to Give a Higher Priority to Its Neighbouring Countries?

- President Raisi took office amid high internal expectations and external challenges, perhaps the most difficult since the 1979 Revolution.
- The new government was elected by its constituencies after the previous policy with specific priority to the West had failed.
- The degree of frustration vis-à-vis Western countries by supporters of the previous government, especially those with a so-called western mindset orientation, as a result of the hostile US policy in the Trump era and the weakness of the EU, despite the narrative that the previous government did put almost all eggs in the Western basket, was a unique phenomenon in Iran since the triumph of the Islamic Revolution.
- Given such environment with a negative attitude towards the West, the proposal of Dr. Raisi to materialize the great potential of the region, specifically neighbouring countries at least as an alternative and worthy to try, sounded attractive and was welcomed by the majority of the constituencies.
- New Iranian Government, in contrast to the preceding one, which linked the revival of Iran's economy with solving the nuclear issue with the West and integrating it into international economy, has envisaged a policy with more emphasis on the East, based on strengthening economic ties with Iran's neighbours and key non-Western powers as the long-term strategy that serves Iran's geoeconomics and geopolitical interests.
- President Raisi defends Iran's involvement in the region, which he sees as relevant power factor, saying: *Iran's regional power is more important than the country's defence and missile capabilities.* America and Israel know that Iran has great operational capability and supremacy. No balance is possible in the region without the consent of the Islamic Republic of Iran.
- Raisi government reiterated that it is also pursuing friendly relation with other countries, beyond its immediate orbit, the strategy of balancing foreign relations.
- Regional countries, particularly the Persian Gulf states, hope that the new president will start a fresh chapter of regional relations based on cooperation and build bridges of trust to guarantee the stability and security.

External powers have always planned to interfere in this region.

It is recalled that, less than a year of the triumph of Islamic Revolution by Iran, the US president Jimmy Carter, in his State of the Union address of January 23, 1980, announced that "An attempt by any outside force to gain control of the Persian Gulf region will be regarded as an assault on the vital interests of the United States of America. And such an assault will be repelled by any means necessary, including military force."

The imposed war by Saddam against Iran which started on 22 September 1980, shortly after that statement, with fully fledged support of US, especially after the strategic meeting of Rumsfeld with Saddam on 20 December 1983, are concrete indications of the US intervention policy in the region. The security threat in the Persian Gulf did not come from the Communist bloc as the US always portrayed.[1]

The end of the imposed war and the collapse of the Soviet Union did remove the excuse of the American involvement. However, the Iraqi invasion of Kuwait and the subsequent Desert Storm war paved the way for the next preplanned military invasion of Iraq.

American officials do not miss a beat in their warnings to the GCC that Iran is the real long-term threat to the region (fn.1).

As long as the GCC states insist on the presence of foreign military forces, specifically the US in the Persian Gulf, tension between Iran and these states will remain and prevent a drastic change in the regional cooperation.

While some analysts (fn.1) are of the view that the model of Islamic democracy in Iran with dynamic reforms coping with international developments, worry the Arabs neighbours, but the Islamic Republic of Iran has always reiterated its full respect for the people's choice and sovereignty of all countries.

Following the end of the Saddam War and the Iranian position opposing the Iraqi occupation of Kuwait helped Iran's standing among the GCC states and improved Arab Iranian relations.

Apparently, the trade is still the *raison d'être* of Persian Gulf security (fn.1). External actors are still concerned about access to and control of the supply of a valued commodity, today defined as oil, and they seek access to regional markets. The flow of oil to end consumer is regarded as a key element of international security, and thus protection of lines of communication is as vital as ever.

2.2 Caspian Sea

The Caspian region is a resource-rich area with a unique locality that connects Europe and Asia in more than just geography. Caspian basin's classification and resources have made this region strategically important for all those states that reside on its shores and even beyond it. From Caspian's own littoral states Russia, Iran, Azerbaijan, Kazakhstan, and Turkmenistan to external actors like Turkey, European Union, China, United States, and India are all involved in the geopolitics of the Caspian.

Despite ranking among the world's leading oil producers and the second largest producer of natural gas, Iran's share of the Caspian oil and gas reserves is therefore

[1] Security in Persian Gulf: Origin, obstacles the search for consensus Edited by Lawrence G. Potter and Gary G. Sick, Palgrave, ISBN: 0–312-23950–5.

Opportunities

- The failure of past policy vis-à-vis West, with non-compliance specifically on JCPOA, demand of people for an immediate foreign policy shift,
- The crystal-clear signals by neighbouring countries on their frustrations with reliance on the West, specially US, and their willingness and determination for a change and for promotion of the bilateral relation with Iran,
- The coherence and close collaboration between the three branches, legislation, judiciary, and executive,
- More convergence and cooperation between officials in charge of diplomacy and regional security front,
- The people and various stakeholders ready to focus on resilient economy and relinquish reliance on sanction relief as the result of negotiation for revival of the JCPOA.

4 Part-III: Promotion of Bilateral Relations with Neighbouring Countries

In the following documentary, the performance of the new government with the orientation on neighbourhood policy is reviewed. Evidently, there is a still long way to go towards the realization of the long list of objectives which Dr. Raisi echoed during the election campaign and committed himself to.

Promotion of Iran-Iraq Relation

A-Iraqi PM Mustafa Al-Kadhemi Becomes First Foreign Leader to Meet President Raisi on September 12, 2021, After His Election

In a joint news conference[3] President Raisi said:

- I hope despite the aims of the enemies of the two countries, we will witness expansion of good relations between Iran and Iraq,
- Iraq had agreed to waive visas for Iranian pilgrims to Shi'ite holy sites in Iraq on the occasion of Arbaeen, marking the end of the 40-day mourning period for Imam Hussein, Prophet Mohammed's grandson.

B-President Raisi made the following remarks in a phone call with his Iraqi counterpart Barham Salih on 3 April 2022:[4]

- Any country in the region that neglects the hegemonic goals of the United States, and the Zionist Regime will both disregard the interests of its nation and will spur Muslim nations' anger.
- The Islamic Republic of Iran supports the unity, independence, security, and the promotion of regional and international position of Iraq.
- We consider the slightest insecurity in Iraq to be to the detriment of the whole region, so we welcome the realization of the interests of the Iraqi people and the establishment of a strong government in this country.
- Good steps have been taken to develop and deepen relations between the two countries and we are determined to promote the level of relations and cooperation between the two countries in all fields to the full capacity and the development of bilateral and regional relations between Tehran and Baghdad, and lead to closer relations at the international level.
- The passage of time has proved the legitimacy of the Supreme Leader's statement that the United States is not sympathetic to the Muslim nations in the region, especially Iraq, and today, it has become clear to everyone that outsiders are only pursuing their own interests and domination.

Iraqi President Barham Salih stressed:

- The need for cooperation between the two countries to overcome regional challenges,
- Establishing stability and security in the region is very important and, in this regard, we hope for the active role of the Islamic Republic of Iran.
- Tehran and Baghdad have many common goals and objectives at the regional and international levels, and by strengthening the level of cooperation and coordination, we can take useful and effective steps to ensure the interests of our nations and the nations of the region.
- The solution to the crises in the region is merely with the will of the countries themselves, and intra-regional solutions without the interference of outsiders.
- The economic capacities of the two countries can serve the interests of the two nations.

C-2nd Visit of Iraqi Foreign Minister Fuad Hussein, on April 14, 2022, After Iran's New Government[5]

President Raisi emphasized on:

[3] https://en.mfa.ir/portal/newsview/651456/Ayatollah-Raisi-in-A-joint-press-conference-with-the-Iraqi-Prime-Minister-Despite-enemies%E2%80%99-will-Iran-Iraq-ties-to-develop-in-all-fields.

[4] https://www.president.ir/en/135514.

[5] https://english.almanar.com.lb/1582715.

- The security and interests of Tehran and Baghdad are intertwined, and the enemies can never undermine their ties.
- The support of the territorial integrity of Iraq and the unity among all ethnic and religious groups in Iraq.
- Tehran seriously expects its neighbouring countries, especially Iraq, to not allow any presence that poses a threat to Iran's security, either in areas controlled by the federal government or in areas controlled by the Kurdistan Regional Government in the country.
- Neighbouring countries need to be vigilant against the conspiracies of the enemies.
- The Islamic Republic of Iran is closely monitoring the movements by the Zionist regime, and cooperation with this child-killing regime cannot be concealed, and we will not allow them to endanger the security of the region in any country, including Iraq.

Iraqi Foreign Minister emphasized on:

- Iraq's commitment to strengthening the level of cooperation with Iran in various bilateral, regional, and international levels.
- Iraq considers itself not only a neighbour but also an ally and friend of the Islamic Republic of Iran.
- Iraq is ready to cooperate with Iran extensively, including in the field of security, to prevent any threat to the interests of the Islamic Republic of Iran.

Note: Iraq's National Security Adviser Qasim al-Araji and Head of the Iraqi Interior Ministry's intelligence service, Ahmed Abu Ragheef, have accompanied Iraqi FM.

Improving Iran-Saudi Relation

- New governments are opting for melting the ice, welcome initiatives to reduce tension and open a new chapter.
- Iran has welcomed the Iraqi initiative for Iran-Saudi talks in Baghdad.
- 5 meetings have been held so far. The last one in March 2022 was however suspended after the mass execution of 81 men, among them 41 Shia Muslims, in Saudi Arabia.
- MFA of Iraq announced: 5th round of meeting was held. Next round will be at diplomatic level.
- Though some western analysts are of the view that Iran's recent interest in de-escalating tensions with Saudi Arabia comes as Riyadh, coming under increasing pressure from Yemeni Houthi and ultimately has no choice but to come to terms with the Islamic Republic, but the author is of the belief that Raisi's regional policy is genuine with political will.

Promotion of Iran-UAE Relation

A process of rapprochement between Iran and the United Arab Emirates (UAE) began. In fact, the regional dialogue is already picking up speed. UAE Vice President and Prime Minister Sheikh Mohammed bin Rashid Al Maktoum was among the first senior figures in the region to congratulate Raisi on his election victory.

On 1 September 2021, the Foreign Minister of Iran gave following comments on his meeting with the Prime Minister of the United Arab Emirates on the side-lines of a regional summit in Baghdad:[6]

- I had positive and cordial talks with Prime Minister of the United Arab Emirates Sheikh Mohammed bin Rashid Al Maktoum on the side-lines of the Baghdad Conference for Cooperation and Partnership.
- In line with mutual cooperation, Iran and the UAE can make great strides and achieve neighbourly diplomacy.
- In this conversation, we talked about the positive intentions and determination of the leaders of the two countries to bolster ties and stressed the importance of brotherly relations between the two countries. In order to enhance bilateral ties and the realization of regional cooperation, we will consult our neighbours, and cooperate and empathize with them. The 13th Iranian administration prioritizes working with neighbouring countries.

The UAE prime minister also commented on the meeting:

- I wish him success in his new duties through the development of positive relations with neighbouring countries and consolidating relations based on the principles of wisdom and the interests of nations.
- As always, our greetings to the Iranian nation, a neighbour, and a friend.

Promotion of Iran-Oman Relation

[6] Iran FM hails talks with UAE PM - Tehran Times.

A-Iranian Foreign Minister Hossein Amir-Abdollahian welcomed his Omani counterpart, Sayyid Badr Albusaidi, upon his arrival on 23 February 2022, with the visit scheduled to focus on bilateral and international affairs, as nuclear talks between Iran and world powers continue in Vienna.[7]

B-In a phone call[8] on 19 March 2022 with Iranian Foreign Minister Hossein Amir-Abdollahian, Omani Foreign Minister Sayyid Badr Albusaidi expressed hope that Iran and the P4 + 1 group of countries would take final steps to reach an agreement on the revival of the landmark 2015 agreement in the Austrian capital of Vienna as soon as possible.

Amir-Abdollahian said Tehran and Muscat enjoy close relations and hoped the two sides would further improve ties. He commended Oman's "constructive" role in resolving some issues pertaining to the release of two British prisoners.

Promotion of Iran-Turkey Relation

A-Turkey and Iran signed an agreement to comprehensively improve relations in a meeting at the 15th Economic Cooperation Organization (ECO) summit held in Turkmenistan's capital Ashgabat on 29 November 2022.[9]

According to the tweeter by Iran's foreign minister the meeting of the head of states including the talks behind closed doors was historic. He further said, "It was agreed

[7] The New Arab Staff & Agencies.

[8] https://www.presstv.ir/Detail/2022/03/19/678851/Iran-Oman-Amir-Abdollahian-Sayyid-Badr-Albusaidi-ties-Vienna-talks-JCPOA-prisoners-

[9] https://www.dailysabah.com/politics/diplomacy/turkey-iran-agree-to-up-ties-as-erdogan-raisi-meet-at-eco-summit.

to talk about the comprehensive improvement of relations and the removal of some obstacles." A high commission is planning the visit of the PM of Turkey to Iran in the near future.

B-It is recalled that in October 2021, the interior ministers of Turkey and Iran signed a memorandum of understanding designed to prevent terrorism and illegal activities the countries face, particularly along their borders.[10]

The two countries are part of the Astana Process, which was initiated by Turkey, Iran and Russia to bring the warring sides in Syria together to find a permanent solution to the decadelong war.

Meanwhile, Iran's Ambassador to Ankara Muhammad Farazmand recently said that Iran supports Erdoğan's initiative to establish a 3 + 3 peace mechanism in the Caucasus region.[11]

Promotion of Iran-Afghanistan Relation

A-Iran's Expectation of Taliban[12]

On 13 Oct. 2021, the Chairman of Iran's Strategic Council on Foreign Relations, former FM Kamal Kharrazi urged Taliban, the new ruler of Afghanistan:

- Try to eliminate terrorists in the country Afghanistan as their first and foremost duty.
- The current Afghanistan rulers are duty-bound to fight against terrorism and prevent the terrorist group of Daesh (ISIS) from carrying out massacres and killing innocent people in schools and Shia mosques
- Main duty of any government is to fulfil people's rights one of which is security.
- While eliminating terrorism, the current Afghanistan rulers should pay attention to the fact that the oppressed Shia people in Afghanistan have a natural right to defend themselves.
- Whether the current Taliban - after taking power over Afghanistan - is different from the past, is yet to be judged based on their treatment of ethnic groups and different Afghan religions.
- They should also take due measures to establish [good] relations with neighbours and serve the neighbouring countries' legitimate interests,
- So, the Islamic Republic of Iran carefully and closely observes Taliban's policies and behaviour in Kabul and other parts of Afghanistan.
- To serve their interests, Taliban should change their behaviour in order to bring about peace to Afghanistan and establish good ties with neighbours.
- The Islamic Republic of Iran is not after interfering in Afghanistan's internal affairs.
- To observe Iran's legitimate interests include border security, prevention of terrorist activities and terrorists' entry to the Islamic Republic's soil, prevention of transit of illicit drugs to Iran; respect for rights of Shia and other Afghan groups, preservation

[10] https://www.hurriyetdailynews.com/iranian-turkish-interior-ministers-meet-in-tehran-168786.

[11] https://www.dailysabah.com/politics/diplomacy/iran-supports-turkeys-33-mechanism-for-south-caucasus-envoy.

[12] https://en.irna.ir/news/84503138/Elimination-of-terrorism-duty-of-current-Afghanistan-rulers.

and expansion of Persian Language as part of Afghans' heritage; development of trade cooperation between Iran and Afghanistan, and preparing the ground for return of Afghan refugees residing in Iran to their homes.

- Afghanistan's political independence should be preserved; and this is not just a national interest but a necessity to regional peace and stability.
- The presence of foreign forces which lasted for several decades in Afghanistan caused many tragedies for the nation which should be used as lessons by the current rulers in a bid to prevent their land from becoming a scene for international and regional powers.
- The Islamic Republic of Iran will be ready for any kind of cooperation with the Afghan nation and government if the policy in the neighbouring country moves towards formation of an inclusive government, preservation of rights and security of all groups, fight against terrorism and adoption of policy on good neighbourliness.

B-Iran-Afghanistan Joint Committees of Cooperation Kick off[13]

On 17 November 2021, Iran-Afghanistan joint committees of cooperation were held in Kabul with the participation of the Iranian delegation, and the caretakers of the ministries of Agriculture, Immigrants Affairs, Information and Culture, Economy, Trade and Industry of the Taliban.

[13] Iran-Afghanistan joint committees of cooperation kick off - IRNA English.

The President's Special Envoy on Afghanistan, Mr. Kazemi Qomi, heading Iran's delegation highlighted:

- Iran and Afghanistan's interests are intertwined,
- Due to the presence of foreigners, many problems have arisen for the people of this country,
- A roadmap for joint cooperation and a 5-year to 10-year perspective should be drawn.

The Special Envoy met with Taliban Acting Foreign Minister Amir Khan Muttaqi and discussed various issues including political, economic, and refugee affairs, bilateral relations, and regional and international cooperation.

4.1 C-Promotion of Industrial Cooperation

Iranian Minister of Industry, Mine and Trade, following talks with his counterpart, said on 17 March 2022:[14]

- Iran and Afghanistan will cooperate to mine iron ore.
- Afghanistan is rich in mineral reserves. A huge deposit of an Iranian iron ore mine named Sangan which is situated in Khaf, lies in Afghanistan. With its high-tech know-how, Iran can help exploit the iron ore in Afghanistan. This will be mutually beneficial.
- Afghanistan is one of the poorest nations in the world, he said, noting that the country lies at the crossroads of Central and South Asia and is sitting on mineral deposits worth nearly $1 trillion, including critical industrial metals such as lithium.
- Iran is Afghanistan's largest trading partner, accounting for nearly a third of its total trade volume. However, transactions are about to fall short of the $2.7 billion target set for this year, he added.
- A diverse range of issues including Tehran's plans to launch joint venture projects with neighbouring countries are under discussion.
- We have already held talks with several regional countries including Oman, Qatar, Syria, Uzbekistan, Pakistan, and Armenia. By doing so, we can distance from exporting raw materials and boost sustainable exports. Joint ventures are mutually beneficial and offer a guaranteed marketplace by serving the common interests of nations.
- Iran is embarking on using transit capacities of neighbouring countries too.
- Regional countries can also invest in Iran and benefit from its trade capacities. Iran is open to foreign investments.

Promotion of Iran-Turkmenistan Relation

Referring to his visit to Turkmenistan, President Raisi highlighted the following points during a phone call with President Berdymukhamedov on 15 March 2022:[15]

[14] https://en.irna.ir/news/84689049/Iran-Afghanistan-to-mine-iron-ore.

[15] https://en.irna.ir/news/84685853/Pres-Raisi-stresses-need-for-activating-North-South-Corridor.

- The importance of North-South Corridor and hope that the two countries will witness evermore usage of their economic capacities,
- Iran's will to broaden relations with Central Asian countries, especially with Turkmenistan.

Promotion of Iran-Azerbaijan Relation

In a message to his Azeri counterpart Ilham Aliyev on the 30th anniversary of the establishment of diplomatic relations between Tehran and Baku, President Raisi underlined the following points on 14 March 2022:[16]

- The need for further expansion of economic and trade relations between Iran and Azerbaijan which he said would benefit the interests of both nations.
- The two countries have experienced warm relations coupled with mutual respect over the past 30 years of bilateral relations.
- Regional and international situations double the need for strong and regular relations between neighbouring countries, particularly those with cultural, historical, and civilizational common grounds.

16 https://www.tehrantimes.com/news/471054/Raisi-felicitates-30th-year-of-Tehran-Baku-diplomatic-ties.

Promotion of Iran-Tajikistan Relation

In a message to Iran's President Ebrahim Raisi on 11 February 2022, President Emomali Rahmon of Tajikistan felicitated Iran on the 43rd anniversary of the Islamic Revolution victory, calling for development of all-out cooperation between Dushanbe and Tehran.[17]

Expressing satisfaction from remarkable achievement following vast cooperation between the two countries, the Tajiki president highlighted that:

- Expansion of mutual ties in different areas to protect both nations' interests,
- Iran and Tajikistan enjoy mutual understanding and confidence-building; so, continuation of efforts in this regard, including constant consultations at high-ranking level, is of utmost significance.
- He is sure the existing capacities for development of Iran-Tajikistan relationship in all fields will be utilized properly because of joint determination and constructive efforts.

Note: As the first country to establish an embassy in Dushanbe, Iran was one of the first states to extend diplomatic recognition of the newly independent Tajikistan in 1991. The

[17] https://en.irna.ir/news/84647209/Tajikistan-calls-for-expansion-of-all-out-ties-with-Iran.

Islamic Republic also provided diplomatic assistance and constructed new mosques in Tajikistan.

Promotion of Iran-Russia Relation

President Putin and President Raisi discussed the development of bilateral economic relations and international cooperation in Moscow on 19 January 2022.[18]

The Russia–Iran geopolitical convergence in the Caucasus–Caspian region and Central Asia is based on their shared opposition to the NATO expansion, popular unrest against region's autocratic leaders as Western-backed 'colour revolutions' and their shared belief that regional powers should shape the security architecture in Eurasia. Moscow considers Iran's participation as necessary in settling regional crises in Syria, Iraq and Afghanistan.

Bilateral trade doubled in the last two years from being US$ 2 billion in 2019 to US$ 4 billion in 2021, with the value of Iran's exports to Russia passing US$ 1 billion for the first time. Iran and Russia had a trade turnover of US$1.595 billion in 2019, of which Russia exported US$1.198 billion to Iran, and imported goods to the value of US$392 million from Iran. Most of this trade is within the energy sector, but there are avenues to develop trade in the agricultural and electronics industries.[19]

---

[18] Article by Dr Deepika Saraswat, published by Manohar Parrikar, IDSA (Institute for Defense Studies and Analyses).

[19] Russia-Iran Trade Ties Set To Boom As Raisi Visits Moscow - Russia Briefing News (russia-briefing.com).

The impressive growth comes after Iran and the Eurasian Economic Union (EAEU) implemented in October 2019 a three-year preferential trade agreement which stipulated that during this period the two parties must accept the conditions for achieving a full free trade plan for tariff-free essential commodities. One has to note that since 2019, more than 50 per cent of the total bilateral trade is being conducted through national currencies as both countries seek to break the dollar dominance in trade and finance. Even though the Iranian financial institutions have been cut-off from Brussels-based Swift since November 2018, Iran's trade ties with Russia and the member states of EAEU have remained unimpeded as Russia's alternative financial messaging system called SPFS or the System for Transfer of Financial Messages was introduced to the banks of the EAEU in October 2019.

Iran has also joined the Shanghai Cooperation Organisation (SCO) which will sure have a positive impact on bilateral relations even beyond the economic domain.

Iran with her long border with Afghanistan, is a key partner in the SCO plans to stabilize and reconstruct this country after decades of occupation and destruction of its infrastructure.

With regard to international cooperation, Russia and Iran are able to assist the Syrian government, as that country also recovers from civil war. Note that Syria recently joined China's Belt and Road Initiative, while Iran has signed off a 25 year cooperation agreement with Beijing and opting for a 20 year agreement with Moscow.

During this historical visit, further developing bilateral economic, trade, cultural, political, and military relations with Russia, President Raisi said:[20]

- In the current, very exceptional conditions, where there is opposition to the unilateral actions of the West, including the United States, we can create synergy in our interaction.
- Iran would continue to develop despite Western sanctions and threats and would work on establishing mechanisms for the gradual lifting of all sanctions and restrictions.
- Common understanding of the two countries on regional and international issues is the basis of cooperation.
- We have a very good experience of cooperation with the Russian Federation in the fight against terrorism in the region… Such a very good experience can create the preconditions for us to apply this experience in many other areas.
- Iran-Russia ties are on the path to become strategic relations.

Following the meeting with President Putin, President Raisi spoke in Duma, the lower house of Russia's parliament:

[20] https://iranprimer.usip.org/blog/2022/jan/21/raisi-russia.

President Raisi highlighted the following main points:

- The United States has not fulfilled its obligations under the nuclear deal.
- Iran is serious about reaching an agreement if the other parties are serious about lifting the sanctions effectively and operationally.
- The strategy of domination has now failed, and the United States is in its weakest position, and the power of independent nations is experiencing historic growth.
- US weaken independent governments from within through "economic sanctions, destabilization, promotion of insecurity, and false narratives of events."
- The Islamic Republic of Iran has the necessary will and readiness to develop and expand relations with the Russian Federation.
- Today, fortunately, there are very clear horizons for cooperation between the two countries at the bilateral, regional, and international levels.
- Strengthening Iran-Russia relations in bilateral and multilateral forms will boost the economies of the two nations and strengthen regional and international security. The abundant, yet complementary economic and trade capacities of the two countries, along with the power and influence of each of our two countries in their geographical areas, can strengthen the convergence between the regions.
- The experience of an international system based on domination shows that its output was nothing but war, violence, insecurity, and division among nations. The failure of the policy of military occupation and forcing the United States to flee Iraq and Afghanistan stems from one concept: resistance of nations. The idea of resistance serves the independence of countries. In modern times, the concept of resistance plays a central role in deterrence equations. The successful model of cooperation between Iran and Russia in Syria has also ensured the independence of the countries and the consolidation of regional security in the continuation of the resistance of the Syrian

people and government. In this regard, we have enjoyed the cooperation of the Russian Federation with the intelligent leadership of Mr. Putin, which is commendable and can be considered an effective model for the development of cooperation in various fields.

- However, the war on terrorism has been part of the war on hegemony because terrorism is one of the by-products of hegemony. The strategy of domination has now failed, and the United States is in its weakest position, and the power of independent nations is experiencing its historic growth. The important thing in this age, which requires vigilance, is that the desires for domination have not disappeared and new forms of domination are on the agenda. The most important goal of this agenda is to weaken independent governments from within, which is pursued through economic sanctions, destabilization, the promotion of insecurity, and false narratives of events in such a way that they try to change the place of the oppressor and the oppressed in public opinion.
- The 'evil alliance' of the United States with terrorists is clear to the world, especially to the nations of West Asia, from Syria to Afghanistan. There are now complex plans to send takfiri terrorists on new missions from the Caucasus to Central Asia. Experience has shown that it is pure Islamic thought that can prevent the formation of extremism and takfiri terrorism.
- NATO, on the other hand, seeks to infiltrate various geographical areas with new coverings that threaten the common interests of independent states. Promoting pro-Western governments and confronting independent democracies based on national identities and traditions is part of NATO's cultural projects that reflect the hypocrisy of this diminishing pattern of behaviour.
- Sanctioning nations is a common form of new domination, and countering it requires the cooperation of independent states and a collective response. Otherwise, sanctions will affect all countries, even US allies, under various pretexts. The United States claims that the sanctions are due to the Islamic Republic of Iran's nuclear activities. Everyone knows that these activities are legal and under the constant supervision of the International Atomic Energy Agency. But the reality is that in different historical periods of Iran's development, whenever our nation has raised the banner of nationalism, independence, or scientific development, it has faced sanctions and pressures of the Iranian nation's enemies.
- The policy of the Islamic Republic of Iran, according to the fatwa of the Supreme Leader of the Islamic Revolution, is that we are not looking for a nuclear weapon, and such weapons have no place in our defence strategy. America seeks to oppose the rights of our nation. Our philosophy is also clear: 'We do not relinquish the rights of our nation.' Those chanting 'America is back' have not yet fulfilled their obligations under the nuclear deal. We are not satisfied with anything less than our rights. The Islamic Republic of Iran is serious about reaching an agreement if the other parties are serious about lifting the sanctions effectively and operationally.
- The policy of maximum interaction of the Islamic Republic of Iran with independent governments is original and will continue regardless of the developments in the international environment. The Islamic Republic of Iran is the winner of two battlefields against terrorism and the campaign of maximum economic pressure. At the same time, the Islamic Republic of Iran has extensive economic potential, especially in the fields

of energy, trade, agriculture, industry, and technology, which pave the way for beneficial cooperation for any bilateral or multilateral interaction with different countries. In this regard, basic agreements were reached between the Islamic Republic of Iran and the Russian Federation, which will cause a significant leap in bilateral economic relations for the benefit of the two nations, and effective regional cooperation for the benefit of peace and stability of nations in different regions

- The privileged geographical location of Iran, especially the north-south corridor, can make trade from India to Russia and Europe less expensive and more prosperous. Stabilizing and benefiting the relations between the two countries requires the expansion of cooperation in the fields of science, society, culture, and media, and we are ready for the maximum development of stable and long-term relations. To this end, we believe that the relations between the two countries should be designed in such a way that, while providing mutual benefits, they are also safe from the interference of third parties.

Promotion of Iran-Pakistan Relation

A-In his message to his counterpart in Pakistan on 23 March 2022, the Iranian chief executive expressed satisfaction with the amicable ties between the two neighbouring countries, expressing hope that the mutual exchanges will expand and consolidate more than ever.

Raisi also addressed the Pakistani prime minister saying that the brotherly and friendly relationship between the Islamic Republic of Iran and the Islamic Republic of Pakistan can expand increasingly as a result of empathy and cooperation among authorities of both states in various fields and in line with ensuring interests of both nations.[21]

B-Pakistani President Proposes Using Local Currency to Boost Trade with Iran

According to Daily Business Recorder, on 16 Feb 2022, President Arif Alvi who held an important meeting in Gwadar last month with the aim of strengthening border cooperation with neighbours has directed State Bank of Pakistan (SBP) and Federal Board of Revenue (FBR) to make all necessary arrangements in this regard.

In November 2021, the President of Pakistan, during a meeting with his Iranian counterpart Dr. Raisi on the side-lines of the ECO Summit in Turkmen capital, emphasized utilization of barter trade mechanism with Tehran.

The president, who wants clear timelines for implementation on the decision taken in the meeting, directed all stakeholders particularly Government of Baluchistan, chairman of FBR, Advisor on Commerce and Investment, to expedite the process of establishing border markets as well as facilitation of people on all crossing points at Afghan and Iran border.

[21] https://en.irna.ir/news/84693689/President-Raisi-felicitates-Pakistan-Day.

With regard to provision of electricity to Gwadar from Iran, it was decided that the demand of 120 MW already made to Iran will materialize on an urgent basis with continuous supply for the entire year.

Regarding trade in local currency, the President directed Governor State Bank of Pakistan, and Federal Board of Revenue to make all necessary arrangements for trade in local currency with Iran and Afghanistan. The president also directed that all private banks should open branches on all crossing points.[22]

The Prime Minister of Pakistan Imran Khan during a meeting with the Minister of Interior of the Islamic Republic of Iran in Islamabad on Monday expressed satisfaction with the progress and positive measures in developing brotherly relations between the two countries and stressed the importance of close cooperation to strengthen joint trade.

Trade of Iran and Pakistan complement each other, and many problems can be eliminated by expanding cooperation in freight transport, tariff reduction, and the creation of border markets.

C-Gas Pipeline from Iran to Pakistan[23]

Pakistan's Finance Minister, Shaukat Tarin, in his interview with the Financial Times, expressed hope on 12 March 2022, that if the JCPOA is revived the gas pipeline project would also be revived since it is suspended due to US imposed sanctions.

He also spoke about a Russian-built gas pipeline that will transport liquefied natural gas from southern Pakistan to its north.

He said that Pakistan "will go ahead with this deal", as it is "the best alternative as of now", despite the West's pressure on Russia over its military operation in Ukraine.

"This was obviously done before Ukraine," the Pakistani minister added.

Note: Iran proposed in early 2000 the "Iran-Pakistan-India Peace Pipeline", a project which could contribute to sustainable development and reduce security tension between the two nations neighbouring Iran. The project was stopped by the US pressure on India. However, the Iran-Pakistan pipeline project is going on, though not as efficiently as expected by the Pakistani side.

D-Pakistan and Iran FMs Discuss Ways to Expand Bilateral Ties

Foreign ministers of Iran and Pakistan, during a phone conversation on 15 March 2022, discussed ways to further strengthen bilateral relations.[24]

According to the joint statement:

- Both sides agreed to intensify efforts to further expand bilateral cooperation in all areas of mutual interest,
- Pakistan and Iran enjoy close fraternal relations, rooted in shared history, common culture, and people-to-people linkages, the statement said, adding that the two countries share perspectives on a range of regional and global issues of mutual interest.

---

22 https://en.irna.ir/news/84652909/Pakistani-President-proposes-using-local.

23 https://en.irna.ir/news/84688576/Minister-JCPOA-revival-enables-Pakistan-to-revive-gas-plan-with.

24 https://en.irna.ir/news/84684346/Pakistan-Iran-FMs-discuss-ways-to-expand.

E-Darakht-E-Dosti, Epitomizing Pak-Iran Relationship, Roundtable & Exhibition[25]

The Centre for Afghanistan, Middle East & Africa (CAMEA) at the Institute of Strategic Studies Islamabad (ISSI) held a Roundtable and Exhibition on 22 Feb 2022, in collaboration with the Embassy of the Islamic Republic of Iran and the Iran-Pakistan Institute of Persian Studies titled Darakht-e-Dosti, Epitomizing Pak-Iran Relationship: Celebrating Linguistic Linkages. Islamabad, Pakistan.

5 Part-IV: Promotion of Cooperation with Regional and Interregional Organizations

1. Realization of Membership of the Islamic Republic of Iran at the Shanghai Cooperation Organisation (SCO)
2. New momentum in Economic Cooperation Organization (ECO)
3. Participation at Summit of Gas Exporting Countries Forum (GECF)

1-Realization of Membership of the Islamic Republic of Iran at the Shanghai Cooperation Organisation (SCO)

At the 21st Summit of the SCO, held in Tajikistan on 17 September 2021, upon unanimous decision, the Islamic Republic of Iran became a new member of the SCO. This is considered as a turning point.

In his statement[26] at the Summit, President Raisi addressed pivotal points:

- Cultural development is the first agenda of cooperation between civilised countries. Most of the world's cultural and spiritual treasury is located in Asia. Asia is the cradle of human civilisation, and its beating heart has been in China, India, Tajikistan and Iran. Asian culture and civilisation have always been associated with harmony, patience, politeness, mutual respect and benevolence, and in a nutshell, wisdom and justice. The greatest Abrahamic religions have arisen in Asia.
- Spirituality is the eternal need of humanity and what today's man has lost. The crisis of spirituality is the foundation of all crises in the world.
- Monopolies, violence, and human rights abuses are manifestations of the consequences of staying away from spirituality; Iran can play an important role in the development of cultural regionalism.
- My foreign policy orientation is focusing on "economic multilateralism" and strengthening "neighbourhood policy" in its broadest sense and strengthening its presence in regional organisations.
- The combination of the Eurasia and One Road-One Belt initiatives can be an objective realisation of this approach, and the vast potential of the Islamic Republic of Iran in terms of geopolitics, population, energy, transportation, human resources, and most importantly spirituality, culture and civilisation can cause a significant stimulus to this outlook.

---

[25] https://en.irna.ir/photo/84658841/Darakht-E-Dosti-Epitomizing-Pak-Iran-Re.

[26] https://president.ir/en/131307.

- This region has had a great cohesion throughout history, and the restoration of this cohesion is one of the features of the Shanghai Pact and emphasised by the Islamic Republic of Iran.
- Asia is a land rich in civilisations and values.
- Asia's role in the international stage requires maintaining harmony between its nations and civilisations. Iran strengthens the harmony among Asian nations and civilisations.
- The world has entered a new era. Hegemony and unilateralism are declining.
- The international system is changing towards the polarisation and redistribution of power in favour of independent states.
- At present, world peace and security are threatened by hegemony and challenges such as terrorism, extremism, and separatism; threats targeting a wide range of countries around the world, especially members and partners of the Shanghai Cooperation Organisation.
- As in the not-so-distant past, Asia is at the centre of global change.
- Maintaining and strengthening peace in this vast area is not a choice but a necessity. The Shanghai Cooperation Organisation and its "governing spirit" - mutual trust, common interests, equality, mutual consultation, respect for cultural diversity and common development - are key tools for maintaining peace in the 21st century.
- Peace and development are achieved through the cooperation and coordination of key countries in the region. In this direction, the formation and strengthening of infrastructure bonds between different countries is important and necessary.
- The One Belt-One Road Initiative, the Eurasian Economic Union and the North-South Corridor, as key projects in the field of infrastructural links, can play a role in strengthening the common interests of developing countries and strengthening peace in the region. These projects are not competitors but complement each other. Iran is the link between the above three infrastructure projects. Iran could be the connecting link between South and North Eurasia through the North-South Corridor, connecting Central Asia and Russia to India. The north-south corridor can strengthen the convergence infrastructure in the form of the "Great Eurasia". Iran is on the route of One Belt-One Road Initiative corridors, the China-Central Asia-West Asia Corridor, and could connect East and West Eurasia. Also, Iran's large port of Chabahar has the capacity to become an exchange centre for several member and neighbouring countries in a special way, which with the efforts of members can be a symbol of cooperation of all members of the Shanghai Organisation.
- The foreign policy of the Islamic Republic of Iran has always been based on active participation in international organisations, multilateralism and opposition to unilateralism based on justice, cooperation, mutual respect, and the need to play a constructive role in facing international and regional challenges.
- Today, the international system faces many challenges and problems that cannot be solved by one government alone. The first challenge is the corona pandemic, which not only targets the health of the nations of the world but also has significant social, economic, political and security consequences. We appreciate the efforts of the members of the Shanghai Cooperation Organisation, especially China, Russia, and India, for assisting in the global vaccination, and we appreciate it in contributing to the spirit of international cooperation.

- Any disruption to the process of helping human health through global vaccination under the pretext of sanctions is against human rights and is in fact crimes against humanity. Solving this problem strongly requires international cooperation, and the members of the Shanghai Pact have great potential in this field, and the Islamic Republic of Iran is ready to actively cooperate in this field.
- Sanctions or economic terrorism is another challenge that has become the most important tool of the hegemons to impose their will on others. Sanctions or economic terrorism are key obstacles to promoting regional harmony.
- The SCO needs to design structures and mechanisms for a collective response to sanctions. Unilateral sanctions are not limited to one country but, as it has become clear in recent years, include more independent countries, especially members of the Organisation. It is important and necessary to design mechanisms for collective confrontation with unilateral sanctions in the framework of this organisation.
- Insecurity hinders development and terrorism hinders sustainable economic growth. With a history of more than 40 years of relentless confrontation and fight against terrorism and extremism, the Islamic Republic of Iran has rendered worthy services for the realisation of peace and justice in the West Asian region. We have been allies of Iraq and Syria in fighting ISIL and other terrorist movements. The strategic partnership between Iran and Russia in the fight against terrorism and extremism in Syria is a valuable experience and a successful model for future cooperation with other regional and supra-regional partners.
- I extend my hand of cooperation to all countries participating in this Summit for the realisation of peace and alliance in the fight against terrorism and extremism.
- We need collective action to ensure security and justice as key infrastructures for development and progress.
- Unfortunately, more than two decades of US show-fighting terrorism in Afghanistan and Iraq have resulted in the loss of many opportunities for the two countries to provide security and prosperity for their people. The United States has been exporting this unsuccessful model to Syria for several years. The centres for US' military presence in Syria are the most insecure and unstable parts in the country.
- The Islamic Republic of Iran believes in common security and does not consider security to be segregated.
- The way to ensure common security is an indigenous way, which is possible only with the participation of regional powers and without foreign intervention.
- The responsibility for the situation in Afghanistan lies entirely with the United States and its allies during this period. But we, the countries of the region, must create the conditions for the people of Afghanistan to overcome their problems and chart a path to a secure future.
- The Islamic Republic believes that this will be achieved only through the assistance of the countries of the region to the effective participation of all ethnic groups in the future governance of Afghanistan. Naturally, the countries of the region have only a facilitating role. Foreign intervention in Afghanistan adds to the problems and, ultimately, leads to instability in that country.
- The Islamic Republic of Iran is ready to devote all its efforts to the establishment of an inclusive, comprehensive, and independent government in Afghanistan, and rush to their aid like all these difficult years that we have been with our Afghan brothers and

sisters. However, I would like to emphasise that the realisation of such a goal cannot be achieved by any country alone and requires joint and organised work in the form of regional mechanisms.

- Ensuring the rights of the Iranian people in the area of a peaceful nuclear programme is a guarantee of the common interests of developing countries. Nothing can stop Iranian's peaceful nuclear activities, which are carried out within the framework of international regulations. Diplomacy is one of the means of securing the national interests of countries, but diplomacy is effective when all parties adhere to it in practice. Threats and pressure weaken diplomacy and tie its hands. Unfortunately, some parties think that they can use diplomacy as a tool to threaten and pressure diplomacy in their own favour, while with this trick, they practically remove diplomacy from the table and make it ineffective.
- The Islamic Republic of Iran, while respecting the independent actions of the SCO member states and the non-recognition of US' unilateral sanctions and non-compliance with its illegal sanctions policies, considers strengthening bilateral cooperation, especially in the economic field, as an important factor in promoting the SCO strategic role in the global economy.
- The need to cooperate on environmental issues, technology development, post-corona cooperation, cyber security, public diplomacy, and strong communication with the people and dealing with organised crime, drugs and terrorism.
- I believe that the members of the Shanghai Organisation, relying on their deep-rooted history of civilisation, can establish existing methods for achieving and promoting peace and security based on diplomacy and comprehensive interaction based on justice and spirituality.

2-New momentum in Economic Cooperation Organization (ECO)

November 2021 in Ashgabat, Turkmenistan.

President Raisi while referring to the need for identification and removal of barriers hindering fulfilment of ECO objectives underlined the importance of the role which could be played by the Secretariat in this regard through initiation and development of the comprehensive plans.[27]

President Raisi also highlighted:

- Each one of the ECO member countries has huge economic capacities which can be used to give a boost to the economic prosperity of the region.
- Iran attaches special significance to the expansion of regional cooperation within the framework of the Organization.

3- Gas Exporting Countries Forum (GECF)

Upon an official invitation to participate in the 6th Summit of the Gas Exporting Countries Forum (GECF), Iran president visits Qatar on 21 February 2022.[28]

In a press conference President Raisi said,

[27] https://www.eco.int/news/88768-ECO-Secretary-General-calls-on-the-President-of-the-Islamic-Republic-of-Iran.html?t=News.

[28] https://president.ir/en/131307.

- This visit is taking place at the invitation of Sheikh Tamim bin Hamad, the Honourable Emir of Qatar, with the two goals of our bilateral relations with the friendly, brotherly, and neighbourly country of Qatar, and participating in the forum of countries producing and exporting gas.
- We hope that this visit will be a step towards improving political, economic and trade relations between the countries of the region and the countries of the Persian Gulf.
- Iran has proven its loyalty to all regional countries at difficult times.

On the sideline of the GECF, 14 agreements and memoranda of understanding were signed between the officials of the two countries.

It has to be recalled that prior to the GECF Summit, the foreign minister of Qatar met President Raisi on 27 January 2022.[29]

During the meeting President Raisi emphasized on:

- The expansion and deepening of ties and cooperation with the countries of the region and neighbouring countries as a priority of the foreign policy of the Islamic Republic of Iran in the new period,
- Tehran welcomes regional cooperation in the interests of peace, security, and the progress of the nations of the region,
- We are ready to activate all areas for the expansion of bilateral and regional cooperation in the interests of both nations,
- The presence of foreign powers in West Asia increases insecurity and concern,
- Foreign countries do not respect the identities and personalities of the nations and states of the region and think that they are the world rulers, while they destroy the spirit of the abandon arrogance and recognize the identity and culture of nations.

6 Part-V: National, Regional, and International Security and Their Interrelations/Interactions

A-Joint Ministerial Statement of the Second Meeting of Foreign Ministers of Afghanistan's Neighbouring Countries[30]

The Foreign Ministers of the Neighbouring Countries of Afghanistan, including China, Iran, Pakistan, Tajikistan, Turkmenistan and Uzbekistan and Russia, held a meeting in Tehran on 27 October 2021.

The meeting was inaugurated by the Vice-president of the Islamic Republic of Iran, and a video message by the Secretary General of the United Nations.

The Ministerial Joint Statement highlighted:

- Noting that situation in Afghanistan has changed fundamentally and stressing support for the national sovereignty, political independence, unity and territorial integrity of Afghanistan, and non-interference in its internal affairs,

[29] https://www.qatar-tribune.com/latestnews-article/mid/506/articleid/8455/iranian-president-meets-with-qatar-S-foreign-minister.

[30] https://www.fmprc.gov.cn/mfa_eng/wjb_663304/wjbz_663308/activities_663312/202110/t20211030_10404009.html.

- Recalling the universally accepted principles of international law in particular the Afghan people's right to decide on their own future independently, and respecting the aspiration of the Afghan people for realizing durable peace, hope to see an Afghanistan enjoying stability, development, prosperity, and harmonious relations with its neighbouring countries,
- Expressing deep concern over complicated security, governance, socio-economic, humanitarian situation in Afghanistan,
- Agreeing that countries primarily responsible for the difficulties in Afghanistan should earnestly deliver on their commitment, and provide Afghanistan with urgently needed economic, livelihood and humanitarian assistance to help realize a stable transition of the situation in Afghanistan,
- Noting that an inclusive and broad-based political structure with the participation of all ethno-political groups is the only solution to Afghanistan issues,
- Expressing the strong support of neighbouring countries of Afghanistan to achieve peace, stability and national reconciliation in the country and encouraging all parties, including Taliban to continue political dialogue and consultations for the solution of the outstanding issues, and future development of the nation,
- Emphasizing that international and regional organizations in particular the United Nations agencies and relevant members of the UN Security Council should abide by their responsibility for political settlement of Afghanistan issues, rendering support to Afghans to develop the socio-economic infrastructure and providing economic and humanitarian assistance,
- Taking with great concern into consideration the deteriorating economic situation in Afghanistan and urging the international community to provide humanitarian assistance on urgent basis,
- Condemning with strongest term the terrorist attacks in all shapes and forms including those against ethnic and religious groups particularly the recent terrorist attacks on mosques.

Declare the following:

1. Support a durable and realistic settlement of differences through dialogue and negotiation among relevant parties for achieving national reconciliation, lasting political solution, and formation of an inclusive government.
2. Call on the relevant Afghan parties to implement modest and prudent internal and external policies, return to the normal order of the society as soon as possible, realize the effective operation of government agencies, provide basic public services to people, take actions to improve people's livelihood and protect the fundamental rights of ethnic groups, women and children in Afghanistan.
3. Take note the assurances and commitments of relevant responsible Afghan parties to the international community that the territory of Afghanistan will not pose any threats to the neighbouring countries and will not be used by criminal, terrorist and separatist groups, and cut ties with all kinds of terrorist groups, strike and eliminate them in a decisive manner.
4. Call on the Afghan relevant parties to abide by their all-undeniable responsibilities, take friendly approach toward neighbouring countries and respect recognized

universally accepted principles of international law and fundamental human rights and protect the safety and legitimate rights of foreign nationals and institutions in Afghanistan.

5. Encourage the relevant Afghan parties to confront various threats and challenges including terrorism, drug smuggling and human trafficking, crack down on organized crime and other criminal acts originating from Afghanistan and taking into consideration the terrorism threats and counter-terrorism effectiveness in Afghanistan, discuss through bilateral or multilateral channels the possibility of restarting counter-terrorism cooperation with Afghanistan in due course.
6. Call on the relevant parties of Afghanistan and the international community to address the root causes of refugees and forced displacement in Afghanistan to avoid any destabilizing activity that would deteriorate the situation and cooperate to bring a permanent solution for the protracted situation of Afghan refugees;
7. Call on the international community and donor countries to provide continued, adequate and proportionate financial support to the host countries of Afghan refugees, especially the Islamic Republic of Iran, the Islamic Republic of Pakistan and other neighbouring countries of Afghanistan.
8. Call on the international community to further provide Afghanistan with more urgent humanitarian assistance including food, medicines, winter utilities etc., to prevent humanitarian crisis and refugee wave in Afghanistan, and prevent new shock to neighbouring countries and the international community.
9. Call on the international community to take concrete actions to provide Afghanistan with help against COVID-19, and curb the spreading of the virus;
10. Start the function of the mechanism of regular meetings of Special Envoys (representatives) for Afghanistan affairs as well as regular meetings of the representatives of Embassies in Kabul at an early date (as mentioned in the first round of foreign minister's meeting joint statement) to jointly promote and hold consultations on details of relevant cooperation regularly for more concrete achievements.
11. Reiterate call on international community to remain positively engaged with Afghanistan and develop long term roadmap to advance the agenda of political engagement, economic integration, and regional connectivity.

7 B-Iran's Regional Security Policy and Concerns

The following latest position was announced by President Raisi on the occasion of the Army Day on 18 April 2022:[31]

[31] https://www.president.ir/en/135815.

- The Army of the Islamic Republic of Iran today has shown the face of an experienced, well-equipped, and ready armed force.
- Because of its brilliant record, the Army is trusted by the people, and the people see this force as a support.
- The Army of the Islamic Republic of Iran has also left famous figures among the martyrs who are a source of pride for all of us and what remains of the army in our minds has become a lasting model for ages and generations and will never be forgotten.
- Empathy and unity of the Army of the Islamic Republic of Iran and our Islamic Revolutionary Guard Corps, as two powerful arms of the Commander-in-Chief, and cooperation of these two and other forces are a model in various fields in the country.
- The most central capability of the Armed Forces of our country is having sincere, believing, and spiritual-oriented personnel in the field of confrontation with the enemy.
- Our armed forces are experienced, skilled, disciplined, and revolutionary and have a valuable spirit of defending the holy system of the Islamic Republic and obeying the orders of the Supreme Command of the Armed Forces,
- Our proud army used the opportunity of sanctions in the best way to be self-sufficient and empowered, and today our country's military industry, including the army, is in the best condition.
- During the Corona pandemic, the Army of the Islamic Republic of Iran used all its health and medical capacities to serve the people and has always been at the service of the people when natural disasters or other problems occur.
- Iran will never start a war but will face any aggression with a remorseful and decisive response, with the high readiness of the country's military forces and the high intelligence elite of these forces in the face of regional and international developments.

- The slightest movement of the enemy will not be hidden from the sharp eyes of our armed forces.
- The Zionist Regime that is seeking to normalise relations with some regional countries must know that the slightest move it makes will not be hidden from the sharp eyes and intelligence of the Armed Forces and intelligent forces of the Islamic Republic of Iran.
- Any movement of the Zionist Regime against our country will lead to a decisive response from the Armed Forces of the Islamic Republic of Iran. Beware (to the leaders of the region) that the great and formidable power of the Armed Forces of the Islamic Republic of Iran will not leave you as you are for a second.
- Those who long to confront the Islamic Republic of Iran should learn from the fate of Saddam Hussein's forces and, on the other hand, see the confession of the White House leaders who explicitly admit that they have suffered a disgraceful defeat against the Islamic Republic of Iran.
- Today, the army is in the hearts of the people and is ready to carry out assigned missions under the command of the Supreme Commander of the Armed Forces, and this preparation is a great success for the Islamic Republic of Iran.

Other Dimensions of Regional Security

Lots could be said, but in a nutshell, it seems the security networking among neighbours is the best possible solution. Inclusive approach to all states, participating based on the purposes and principles of the UN Charter, including sovereign equality of states, refrainment from threat or use of force, peaceful resolution of conflicts, respect for territorial integrity, non-intervention in domestic affairs and respect for self-determination of states by their own people, with exclusion of any foreign interference, is the reliable sustainable security option.

The following is a short review of the impacts of specific developments which has undeniable impact of regional security and has hindered the promotion of relations with neighbouring countries.

Impact of Arab Spring & It's Possible Remnant on Iran-Arab Relation

… according to research made by the Geneva Centre for Security Policy[32]:

From the late 2010, peaceful mass protests have spread from Tunisia to most other Arab countries and prompted considerable political change referred to as the 'Arab Spring.' In spite of various differences, the protests expressed long standing popular grievances such as growing socio-economic inequalities. Closely related to policies of selective economic liberalization they were exacerbated since 2008 by the increase in world food prices and the (nonetheless mitigated) effects of the global financial crisis.

Popular contestation, responses by the ruling regimes and ensuing political dynamics in the Middle East and North Africa have a number of security implications. Contested as it is, the concept of security focuses on the protection of individual or collective actors from physical harm and from threats do other attributes of their existence ranging from accustomed ways of life to prosperity and self-determination.

[32] Series n° 10, January 2013, the Security Implications of the Arab Spring, Eberhard Kienle.

In need of continuous US military support the Gulf monarchies content themselves with occasional statements and attempts to revive the Saudi inspired Arab peace plan of 2002 (in which the Arab states declared their readiness to recognize Israel in exchange for the creation of a Palestinian state). To an extent, many in the Gulf see Israel as an undeclared strategic ally against Iran, albeit an uncontrollable one whose action, especially military, may also seriously backfire.

Balanced and sustainable socio-economic development is no less important to address key concerns of political actors and forces whose influence has increased after the departure of the old autocrats. Such balanced development may challenge some 'Western' interests but is an essential plank of attempts to ultimately overcome the vision of an unbalanced global order dominated by the 'West' that is shared by Arab nationalists, representatives of the left and most Islamists.

In the same context, Martin Chulov's recent article in The Guardian on 3 April 2022, somehow concludes that the regional countries are reconsidering their past policy vis-à-vis the West, in particular the United States:[33]

As Joe Biden moved to open US strategic oil reserves, his two biggest oil-producing allies have kept their tanks firmly shut. The UAE and Saudi Arabia continue to rebuff the US president as he attempts to counter soaring oil prices prompted by Russia's invasion of Ukraine. And both countries have been unusually frank about their refusal to step in.

The five week old war is bringing tensions to a head in several parts of the world, but perhaps nowhere is a regional order more under strain than the Middle East, where two of America's biggest allies are now seriously questioning the foundations of their relationship.

The Saudi and Emirati refusal to bail Biden out – or even to take his calls – has pushed relations between the Gulf states and Washington to an unprecedented low. The extraordinary flow of Russian wealth to Dubai, just as the US and Europe try to strangle Putin's economy, has inflamed things further. Usually opaque and often inscrutable, officials in Abu Dhabi and Riyadh have in recent weeks been uncharacteristically blunt to visiting diplomats about the nature of their grievances, and how far they are prepared to take them. One western diplomat told the Guardian that a Saudi counterpart had said: "This is the end of the road for us and Biden, but maybe the US also."

Al-Yahya contrasted Washington's demands with Beijing's no-strings diplomacy, saying: "While American policy is beset by baffling contradictions, Chinese policy is simple and straightforward. Beijing is offering Riyadh a simple deal: sell us your oil and choose whatever military equipment you want from our catalogue; in return, help us to stabilise global energy markets.

Professor Abdulkhaleq Abdulla, a noted scholar in political science, described the crisis with washington as the worst in "50 Years".

"What made matters worse was the Biden administration's objection to sovereign Emirati decisions, such as receiving Bashar al-Assad … and putting pressure on Abu Dhabi to increase its oil production outside the context of the Opec agreement.

"All this comes at a time when America is no longer the only superpower in the world, which prompted the UAE and other countries to diversify partners."

---

33 https://www.theguardian.com/us-news/2022/apr/03/us-relations-saudi-arabia-uae-oil-crisis.

Considering the above analysis, the region, specifically Arab neighbours are facing a dilemma of what option to choose, Iran or the West, mainly the US. The developments since the Arab Spring, including the fate of Arab rulers, show that they have to change the hostile policy vis-à-vis Iran to a cordial/respectful relation if not to a close and even strategic one.

Terrorism as well as the menace of the Mafia of Narcotic Drugs, are serious threats to the national security of all states in this region. Records show that both have been triggered and manipulated by outside powers.

8 A-Iran Vis-À-Vis Terrorism, Extremism, and Violation

Since triumph of the Islamic Revolution in Iran, Iranians have faced with extremists, the so-called MEK, supported by the US and its regional allies, then harboured in EU and US, as safe heaven, after they escaped following the massacre of over 17000 innocent people, including children. From the top, the supreme leader, to the individual citizens in the street.

Iranian people are the main victim of terrorism in the region and also the most active in combating the ugly phenomenon of extremism and terrorism, specifically in the name of religion, such the ISIS, known as Daesh.

In order to promote a global fight against violence and extremism, Iran proposed to the United Nations General Assembly a resolution called "World Against Violence and Extremism". It was adopted by consensus on 18 December 2013.[34]

As a matter of fact, no tangible measures were witnessed as the result of the UN calls. The ISIS occupied vast area in Iraq and Syria and claimed Caliphate, to rule the Muslim world. As documents showed on many occasions the ISIS received sophisticated arms and money from US and couple of regional countries.

As for the root cause of such terrorism in the Middle East, I just refer to official statement of the United States:

Reuters reported on 11 August 2016: *Republican Donald Trump called President Barack Obama and Democratic rival Hillary Clinton the "co-founders" of Islamic State, ratcheting up his assertion that they are responsible for the rise of the militant group.*[35]

Mr. Trump confessed that 7 billion dollars was spent in the Middle East, under the motto "The *Global War on Terror" (GWOT).* No result other than bloodshed leaving millions of innocent victims and refugees, augmentation of terrorism, and breeding hate leading to further terrorism.

Ms. Clinton too confessed in one of her books and also orally[36], that the US created Al-Qaida to combat the Soviet Union:

"Let's remember here... the people we are fighting today we funded them twenty years ago.

"They [the Soviets] *invaded Afghanistan... and we did not want to see them control Central Asia and we went to work...* ***And it was President Reagan in partnership with***

34 A world against violence and violent extremism, A/68/L.31, UNGA, 10 December 2013.

35 https://www.reuters.com/article/us-usa-election-trump-idUSKCN10M146.

36 Hillary Clinton: "we have helped to create the problem we are now fighting" - YouTube.

the Congress, led by Democrats, who said you know what it sounds like a pretty good idea… let's deal with the ISI and the Pakistani military and let's go recruit these mujahideen.

"And great, let them come from saudi arabia and other places, importing their wahabi brand of islam so that we can go beat the Soviet Union.

"So, there is a very strong argument which is… it wasn't a bad investment to end the soviet union but let's be careful with what we sow… because we will harvest".

These two terrorist groups massacred hundreds of thousand innocent Muslims, Christians, Yazidis in the region specially in Afghanistan, Iraq, and Syria, as well as Iranians.

The only option was to physically fight with the ISIS in Iraq and Syria, stop its advancement, and free the occupied lands. General Ghassem Soleimani, the commander of Quds Branch of the IRGC, started the historic battle with ISIS. He was supported by hundreds of volunteers from the region including Iraq, Afghanistan, Lebanon. Upon request and in full coordination with the governments of Iraq and Syria, he freed strategic provinces such as Mussel in Iraq, and rescued thousands of women and children, especially Yazidis, from blood thirsty members of the ISIS.

The successful fight put an end to the most horrified chapter of our contemporary age. The crystal-clear message to Iran's neighbours is that they could count on Iran to defend them in case of any terrorist threat, by non state actors or state terrorists.

The anti-terrorist global hero was however assassinated by the US in Baghdad airport, while on his official visit to Iraq to resolve the disputes between Saudi Arabia and Iran. The determination of Iranian people to fight terrorists has augmented after this horrific assassination.[37]

9 B-Triangle Initiative on Drugs

According to the reports of the UNODC, Iran is the war front of drug smuggling with about 80% of confiscation, sacrificing over 4000 law enforcement martyrs, preventing transition of drugs to Europe. Apart from short diplomatic words, Europe has refrained from real shared responsibility and appreciation.

In 2008, the author proposed on behalf of the Islamic Republic of Iran, the "Triangle Initiative", a plan for close collaboration between Iran-Afghanistan-Pakistan, to combat drug trafficking under the auspices of the UNODC. Noteworthy, that the author was then directly involved from the submission of the initiative to the UNODC and the establishment of the operation headquarters in Tehran. Since then, a number of joint operations have been successfully conducted. In fact, this initiative has changed the security threat to an opportunity for convergence and cooperation.

10 C-Iran's Security Initiatives for the Persian Gulf Region

There are various obstacles that have hindered the establishment of stable and sustainable security in the Persian Gulf region. The demand by some Persian Gulf States for

[37] Paper by A.A.Soltanieh on International Cooperation Against Terrorism. TRT World Forum on "Envisioning Peace and Security in a Fragmented World", Istanbul, Turkey; 3–4 October 2018.

dominance over the region, political and ideological differences, and the competitive procurement of weapons have all caused friction among states, thereby preventing them from cooperating with one another in creating security in the region. The first step is to accept differences and emphasis on inclusivity rather than to ignore conflicts of interests.

The initiative called "Regional Dialogue Forum" proposed by Iran in 2017. I recall that the UNSC resolution 598 of July 1978[38], ending the imposed war by Saddam against Iran, has called for such security dialogue and arrangement, but the region has so far not responded to Iran's readiness in this regard. Later, on 25 September 2019, Iran proposed the Hormuz Peace Initiative, Hormuz Peace Endeavor, so-called "HOPE"[39], at the UN General Assembly.

Though such constructive initiatives were proposed with good intention and based on the realities on the ground, it was not realized due to lack of political will and feeling urgency by states on the other side of the Persian Gulf then.

I expect a change in attitude and conduct of countries in the Persian Gulf vis-à-vis Iran from now on, given the fact that the new government has already extended hands.

11 Message of the New Government to the United Nations

President Raisi highlighted the following points at the 76th UNGA on 21 September 2022:[40]

- Iran is the land of culture and civilisation. The land of knowledge and spirituality. The land of perseverance and independence. The Iranian people are monotheist and patriotic. They have their unique identity and love to explore the world.
- For hundreds of years, our nation has safeguarded their right to self-determination and freedom against the hegemons and have made their country the most progressive in the election-based political system in the west of Asia.
- The Islamic Revolution was indeed a great leap for the fulfilment of national and Islamic ideals of Iranians including freedom, independence, and religious democracy.
- I, as the elected President of the great people of Iran, am honoured to be their representative to convey to the world at large the message of rationality, justice and freedom which are the three most fundamental principles of the life of the contemporary man Freedom and justice as two sacred and innocent words that are too broad to define, are indeed very tough and intricate when it comes to practicing. Freedom means the right to think, decide and act for all the human beings. Peace and lasting security are tied to the administration of justice and, basically, the divine prophets emerged so that people would demand justice and exercise their rights. Justice and freedom may be achieved only when the rights of all nations are fulfilled. As a matter of fact, any violation of the rights of nations will, more than anything, endanger global peace and security. However, those three principles that all the Abrahamic religions have in common will not be able to attain their purpose without spirituality,

[38] UNSC Resolution 598, 20 July 1987, https://digitallibrary.un.org/record/137345.

[39] UNGA, Hormuz Peace Endeavour, 25 September 2019.

[40] https://www.president.ir/en/131476.

- This year, two scenes made history: one was on January the 6th when the US congress was attacked by the people and, two, when the people of Afghanistan were dropped down from the US planes in August. From the Capitol to Kabul, one clear message was sent to the world: the US' hegemonic system has no credibility,
- Over the past decade, the US has been making the mistake of modifying its "way of war" with the world instead of changing its "way of life",
- Today, the world doesn't care about "America First" or "America is Back". If rationality prevails in the minds of the decision-makers, they have to realise that nations' perseverance is stronger than the power of the superpowers,
- The US' organised crime against humanity must be recorded as a symbol and reality of the so-called American human rights,
- Sanctions are the US' new way of war with the nations of the world. Sanctions against the Iranian nation started not with my country's nuclear program; they even predate the Islamic Revolution and go back to the year 1951 when oil nationalisation went underway in Iran, which in turn led to a military coup backed by the Americans and the Britons against the then government of Iran that was elected by the people. Sanctions, especially sanctions on medicine at the time of the COVID-19 pandemic, are crimes against humanity,
- It is the strategic policy of the Islamic Republic of Iran to consider the production and stockpiling of atomic weapons as forbidden based on the religious decree by His Eminence, the Supreme Leader, and Nukes have no place in our defence doctrine and deterrence policy,
- The Coronavirus is a wake-up call for the whole world, reminding us once again that the security of all human beings is interdependent,
- The fact that modern lives have become devoid of meaning and spirituality as well as the spread of poverty, discrimination and oppression have helped the rise of terrorism. The increasing growth of indigenous terrorism in the West bears witness to this bitter truth. Even more bitter is the use of terrorism as an instrument for foreign policy because you cannot fight terrorism with double standard. An arbitrary attitude is not the way to solve terrorism and you cannot fight terrorism with double standards,
- The military presence of the US in Syria and Iraq is the biggest hindrance to the establishment of democracy and will of nations
- The solution to the Yemeni issue is the speedy and unconditional stop to the Yemeni aggression and facilitation of constructive talks between Yemeni groups,
- While decisively defending all is rights and the interests of its people, Iran is keen to have large-scale political and economic cooperation and convergence with the rest of the world. I seek effective interaction with all the countries of the world especially with our neighbours and shake their hands warmly.

12 Immediate Economic Achievements of the New Neighbouring Focused Policy

In Line with the New Policy Indicators Show a 43% Increase in Trade with Neighbouring Countries[41]

[41] https://en.irna.ir/news/84713581/Iran-S-trade-with-neighbors-up-by-43.

Alireza Moghadasi, the head of the Islamic Republic of Iran Customs Administration (IRICA) announced: The value of Iran's non-oil trade with its neighbours from March 2021 until March 2022, 100 million and 131 thousand tons of goods worth $51.875 billion were exchanged between Iran and 15 neighbouring countries. 75.445 million tons valued at $26.29 billion, with a 29% rise in value and a 12% growth in weight.

Major export destinations of the Iranian non-oil goods were Iraq with $8.9 billion, Turkey with $6.1 billion, the United Arab Emirates (UAE) with $4.9 billion, Afghanistan with $1.8 billion, and Pakistan with $1.3 billion in imports from the Islamic Republic, followed by Oman, Russia, Azerbaijan, Turkmenistan, Armenia, Kazakhstan, Kuwait, Qatar, Bahrain, and Saudi Arabia. Iraq's main purchases from Iran are agricultural products, engineering services, construction materials, and energy, such as electricity and natural gas. Baghdad has received waivers from Washington allowing it to buy Iranian electricity and natural gas.

A short comparison shows that Iran had exported $11 billion worth of food and agricultural products to Iraq in five years. However, the export has drastically increased during last year, around $9 billion of Iran's $12.5 billion in exports. Iraq also exported to Iran on a larger scale over the year. Iraq exported $1.2 billion worth of goods to Iran, marking a 790 percent increase.

One has to note also that according to the head of Iran's customs, Iran currently exports non-oil commodities to 40 European countries, 21 Asian countries, 28 African countries, and 12 American countries, while importing from 41 European countries, 31 Asian countries, 12 American countries, and 11 countries in Africa.

Analysis of Crisis Management Systems in the Context of the Global Economic Crisis and Military-Political Changes

Lucia Kurilovska[1](✉) and Jana Mullerova[2]

[1] Faculty of Law, Department of Criminal Law, Criminology and Criminalistics, Comenius University in Bratislava, P.O. BOX 440, Šafárikovo Námestie 6, 81499 Bratislava, Slovakia
lucia.kurilovska@flaw.uniba.sk

[2] Department of Public Administration and Crisis Management, Academy of the Police Force in Bratislava, Sklabinská 1, 83517 Bratislava, Slovakia
jana.mullerova@akademiapz.sk

Abstract. Crisis management is experiencing turbulent times at all levels of governance globally on all continents. Governments have to respond to growing economic problems, military challenges, civilian emergency planning issues, as well as foreign policy changes that negatively affect the stability of many previously very stable sectors. The text examines the crisis management tools used by Western and Eastern countries, their different positions and strategies, and their approaches to dealing with current problems. The common approach for both East and West remains the same in the case of emergencies of a natural or technical nature as well as integrated rescue systems. There are many common features of the most advanced models of crisis management in the East and in the West. The text analyses the crisis management model in the USA, Russian Federation, China and in selected European countries.

Keywords: Emergency management system · Civil emergency planning · System analysis · Comparison

1 Introduction

In general, Crisis Management and Civil Protection Systems concentrate on threats of a non-military nature. However, a significant part is the protection of the civilian population from the consequences of military attacks involving CBRN weapons. The original focus of civil defence during the Cold War changed to civilian protection after the collapse of the Eastern bloc. A particular issue is preparedness and response to terrorist attacks, which has become more serious after 11 September 2001, as well as after the Islamist attacks in Paris, Berlin, Barcelona and, most recently, Vienna.

The strategy of the European countries to date has quite logically concentrated on natural hazards, i.e. floods, fires, storms, snow calamities, earthquakes, volcanic eruptions, tidal waves and catastrophic droughts, in line with their frequent occurrence, massive

J. Cayón Peña and J. M. Ramírez (Eds.): *Threats to Peace and International Security: Asia versus West*, ASTSA, pp. 205–228, 2023.
https://doi.org/10.1007/978-3-031-28336-9_11

scale and enormous damage. The structure of crisis management, the legislative environment, the staffing, as well as the material and technical equipment, prevention and response measures, fully reflect the predominance of the above-mentioned types of risks. The integrated rescue system was never intended for military purposes. On the other hand, it is applicable in dealing with the consequences of military attacks, including bombing and other military actions. Crisis management is valid for fire fighting, decontamination of chemical contamination, deactivation of radiation contamination, fire fighting, debris removal, extrication of persons, provision of pre-medical and medical assistance, evacuation of threatened areas.

Although a military conflict was not included in the top 10 risks in terms of likelihood, nor in the top 10 risks in terms of impact in the World Economic Forums recently published risk ranking published in Garcia-Segura (2020)[1]. Nevertheless, we foresee a potentially enormous impact of the ongoing military operation of the Russian Federation in Ukraine, as well as a negative economic impact on the security of the countries of the European Union, the USA, China and Russia itself in terms of the guarantee of crisis management functions.

The aim of the analysis of national crisis management systems is to define the structural characteristics, to reveal potential weaknesses in the light of the ongoing economic crisis and war conflicts.

2 Crisis and Emergency Management System in USA

The system of protection and security in the US has been built since the end of World War II. Therefore, it belongs to the most sophisticated and effective systems in the world. In the USA, information support for crisis management is used. This includes Ready.gov a public online Infobook system, which is used by FEMA (Federal Emergency Management Agency).

US National Emergency Shelter Information System (NSS) is a comprehensive web-based database created to support federal, state, and local government agencies and voluntary organizations responsible for mass care and emergency relief. The term "shelter" can be thought of as the deployment and provision of emergency shelter and basic needs to residents who are victims of an emergency. Authorities at this level also organise a variety of humanitarian aid and include voluntary organisations that help each other in their local communities. We can compare this, for example, with our Volunteer Fire Brigades Associations or the various voluntary organisations, for example, during the floods.

The NSS is a planning system that provides federal, state, or local agencies and emergency managers a tool for sharing information pertaining to emergency housing of residents or, for example, food options, provision of potable water, basic services in the event of emergency (tornado, hurricane, widespread flooding, etc.)

[1] The list of the top ten most likely security risks did not foresee the possibility of a hot military conflict within Europe. However, the list of the top ten risks with the greatest impact placed weapons of mass destruction at the top.

The system also provides the user with an extensive mapping program that allows the creation of user maps that mark on a map which facilities could be affected by the event. Kailes (2020) divides the user interface into:

1. Natural emergencies,
2. Evacuation routes,
3. Critical infrastructure.

The system helps emergency managers specify the capabilities and capacities of each facility; provides detailed information regarding more than 170 data points on the map. The FEMA organization, in partnership with IBMs Division of Global Services, provides technology support for the NSS system in two ways, providing automatic exchange of NSS data between the American Red Cross and the organization FEMA. Any U.S. resident can obtain regular information on the status of individual emergency locations accommodations, including but not limited to those available for iPhone mobile phones.

U.S. Department of Homeland Security (2017) states the Fire and Rescue Service is made up of 163,300 professionals, volunteers and temporary staff and 151,000 civilian employees. With 71% of all registered fire departments fully staffed by volunteers and 56% of all firefighters are volunteers.

The Federal Emergency Management Agency (FEMA, 2022) employs more than 20,000 people nationwide. Headquartered in Washington, D.C., with 10 regional offices located across the country. FEMA is able to leverage a tremendous capacity to coordinate within the federal government to make sure US is equipped to prepare for and respond to disasters. FEMA is comprised of Program Offices and Regional Offices located throughout the United States. The workforce can swell to over 50,000 active members during major disasters.

FEMA collects vast amounts of data on multiple aspects of emergency management—Disaster Information, Individual Assistance, Public Assistance, Hazard Mitigation, National Flood Insurance Program (NFIP), and Grants. Data sets are available for download, along with an application programming interface (API) that provides data in an easily digestible, machine readable format.

By making FEMAs data publicly available, OpenFEMA promotes government transparency and accountability, as well as enables collaboration with community partners—such as banks, financial companies, insurance companies, mortgage and real estate companies, private sector companies, universities/academia, journalists, non-profits, federal/state/local government agencies, and citizens/individuals—to improve outcomes in support of disaster survivors.

FEMA declares following goals.

1. Release high value data sets to the public in machine-readable formats and via an application programming interface (API) in accordance with Federal Open Data directives, executive orders, and legislation.
2. Institutionalize the OpenFEMA data release process throughout FEMA.
3. Engage with internal and external partners to leverage FEMAs data to improve outcomes in support of disaster survivors.

FEMA operates the Integrated Public Alert & Warning System (IPAWS), the national system for local alerting that provides authenticated emergency and life-saving information to the public through mobile phones using Wireless Emergency Alerts, to radio and television via the Emergency Alert System, and on the National Oceanic and Atmospheric Administrations Weather.

2.1 US emergency Key Agencies and Systems

Ready.gov
Ready.gov is an official website of the U.S. Department of Homeland Security. Ready is a National public service campaign designed to educate and empower the American people to prepare for, respond to and mitigate emergencies, including natural and man-made disasters. The goal of the campaign is to promote preparedness through public involvement.

Ready.gov is the preeminent portal for emergency system communications with the public. There are three main features of this attractive portal. It is a venue for communicating the prevention of a wide range of emergencies to any individual who can learn about damage minimization measures in an attractive way. The second function is the recruitment of volunteers. The third function is the appeal for financial support for rescue units.

IPAWS is the name for a system through which emergency management authorities can inform the U.S. population about emergencies through various channels. FEMA is the operator of this system. IPAWS is a modernized integrated system for the national warning infrastructure. This system can be used at the federal, state, and local levels to warn the public. IPAWS allows the system to link individual local information warning systems that use the CAP protocol on which IPAWS operates. IPAWS provides an effective way for emergency management personnel to alert and warn the public of a serious emergency situation through the use of individual early warning systems, such as the Central Alert System (EAS), the Wireless Alert Alert System (WEA), the radio service operated by NOAA, and other public warning systems.

U.S. Oceanic and Atmospheric Administrations Oceanic and Atmospheric Administration Information Service
This is an information service of the National Oceanic and Atmospheric Agency (NOAA), or the U.S. Office of Oceanic and Atmospheric Administration, which operates under the U.S. Department of Commerce. One of the tasks of this office is to inform US residents about current and potential changing climatic conditions and the changing environment where they live. The office operates an information service on the web website at www.noaa.gov, where one can obtain a variety of information on weather

forecasts, warnings storm warnings, and keep track of weather events. These forecasts are displayed via map applications on various geo-information platforms.

National Terrorism Advisory System
Cyber-terrorist attacks could disrupt the public information network, the Internet, and thus the functionality of computer information systems. This form of terrorism could not only prevent communication between emergency management agencies during an ongoing emergency, but also, for example, limit the availability of information resources to the public. Therefore, constant effort is necessary to secure these communication infrastructures precisely because of the potential misuse by modern-day terrorists who aim to deliberately damage a functioning system and cause chaos, with negative consequences for all citizens.

That is why the Department of Homeland Security (DHS) has established a special terrorism threat information system (National Terrorism Advisory System) to provide always up-to-date information about a potential terrorist attack to the public, foreigners, government agencies, emergency services, public sector organizations, transportation companies, airports, etc.

The emergency system has a horizontal structure with a high degree of autonomy and therefore a number of regional and local differences. Federal FEMA units are deployed in emergencies that exceed the capabilities of the affected state or states. The US emergency management system is likely to be highly sensitive to economic stability. It can be anticipated, that the current economic crisis will reduce the amount of raised funds to operate the system. At the same time, it is high likely expected, that the number of volunteers on whom the system is vitally dependent will be reduced consequently.

3 Wide Range Emergency Management in Russian Federation

The Ministry of Russian Federation for Civil Defence, Emergencies and Elimination of Consequences of Natural Disasters (EMERCOM of Russia - also called the Ministry for Extraordinary Situations or MCHS) was established on January 10, 1994, according to the President of Russias Ordnance. EMERCOM grew out of the Russian Rescue Corps, which was established in December 1990 with the purpose to provide swift and effective response in the event of emergencies. The Rescue Corps were transformed into the Emergency and Civil Defence State Committee in 1991, and General of the Army Sergey Shoigu was appointed head of the committee.[2]

When the Soviet Union broke apart, the complete Civil Defence apparatus was transferred to EMERCOM except for the underground bunker system of command and

[2] Sergei Shoigu, currently Minister of Defence. It proofs the tide connection among the emergency management structures and military structures of Russian Federation. EMERCOM organisational structure involves armed forces.

control, which the Ministry of Defence kept for its own use. EMERCOMs missions correspond closely to the missions of the U.S. Federal Emergency Management Agency (FEMA) and many of the disaster relief/assistance missions of the US National Guard.

EMERCOM is the worlds largest rescue professional organisation. It has 288,500 employees (2018). The structure is vertical, from the national to the provincial and regional level. EMERCOM has 6 regional centres, which include The Volga-Ural Regional Centre, the Siberian Regional Centre, the Central Regional Centre, the North-western Regional Centre, the Southern Regional Centre, and the Far Eastern Regional Centre. EMERCOM is subdivided into several departments. These include the Department for Protection of the Population and Territories; the Department for Disaster Prevention; the Department of Forces; the Department for International Cooperation; the Department for the Elimination of Consequences of Radiological and other Disasters; the Department for Science and Technology; and the Management Department.

EMERCOM's Crisis Management Centre (CMC) is the main body for the day-to-day management of the Unified Emergency Prevention and Response State System (UEPRSS). It is therefore tasked with the provision of firm and continuous management of the forces and assets allocated for emergency prevention and response, provision of necessary information for the system as a whole, and for the coordination of all UEPRSS activities. CMC principal services are on stand-by duty round the clock. Apart of communications and hardware experts, duty service comprises chief duty officer and duty shift officers. Chief duty officer is to organize an immediate initial response on an emergency situation until eventual deployment of the emergency response temporary HQs.

Forces and facilities are divided into:

- National Crisis management Centre,
- Fire department,
- Search and Rescue Service,
- Aviation,
- Paramilitary rescue units,
- Paramilitary mine rescue units,
- State small vessel inspectorate.

Very important is the role of Scientific organizations (EMERCOM, 2022):

- All-Russian Centre for Monitoring and Forecasting of Emergencies of the EMERCOM of Russia (Centre "Antistikhiya")
- All-Russian Research Institute for Civil Defence of the EMERCOM of Russia (the Federal Science and High Technology Centre)
- The Federal State Budgetary Institution "The Research Institute of Fire Protection of All-Russian Order "Badge of Honor" of the EMERCOM of Russia"
- Centre for Civil Defence Strategic Research of Russian Emergencies Ministry
- Federal State Institution "Noginsk Rescue Centre of the EMERCOM of Russia"
- Federal State Institution "Leader Centre for High Risk Rescue Operations"
- Federal State Institution "Don Centre of the Russian Emergencies Ministry"
- Paramilitary Rescue Units

- Federal State Public Institution “Ruza Logistics Centre for Control Units of the Russian Emergencies Ministry”
- Nikiforovs All-Russian Centre for Emergency and Radiation Medicine
- Information Centre OKSION
- Central Hospital No. 72 of the EMERCOM of Russia
- Federal State Institution “Centre for Emergency Psychological Aid of the Russian Emergencies Ministry (CEPA)”
- Federal State Institution “Financial Centre of the EMERCOM of Russia”;
- Federal State Public Institution “State Central Airmobile Rescue Team of the Russian Emergencies Ministry” («Centrospas»)
- Spasatel Recreation Centre of the Russian Emergencies Ministry
- National Airmobile Rescue and Academic Centre for Training of Mine Rescuers and Miners
- Agency for Support and Coordination of Russian Participation in International Humanitarian Operations.

EMERCOM represents a typical system with a vertical structure with an emphasis on centralised management. The Ministry is the absolute dominant provider of emergency services. It employs professional staff trained in a wide range of specialized institutions. Considerable emphasis is placed on education among the population so that each citizen becomes as competent as possible in various aspects. The existing role of voluntary non-government organizations is not determinant for the functioning of the rescue system. The financing of the system is directly dependent on the state budget. Problems or significant cuts in the funding of rescue services are not expected to occur, even in the light of the current economic sanctions by Western countries. The possibility of using rescue personnel for the purposes of a military operation also remains open.

4 Chinese High-Potential Crisis Management System

The centralisation of the Chinas crisis management system (inspired by Russian model) started just a few years ago. Ministry of the Emergency Management of the Peoples Republic of China was created by merging the crisis management departments of several ministries in 2018. According the Ministry (2022), it took over the functions of the former paramilitary Firefighting Corps of the Peoples Armed Police, which is today the State Firefighting Service of the Ministry of Emergency Management. China Earthquake Administration and State Administration of Coal Mine Safety is affiliated to the new ministry, while the State Administration of Work Safety was dismantled. The aim of establishing a centralised Ministry of Emergency Situations is to make it easier and therefore more efficient for emergency services to respond to a wide range of emergencies.

It organises the preparation of the overall national emergency response plan and planning, guide the work of all regions and departments in responding to emergencies, and promote the construction of emergency response plan systems and plan exercises. Establishing disaster reporting system and releasing disaster information in a unified manner, coordinating the construction of emergency forces and material reserves and unifying their dispatch in disaster relief, organising the construction of disaster relief system, guiding emergency relief for safety production and natural disasters, and undertaking the work of the National Command for Special Major Disasters. Guiding the prevention and control of fire, flood and drought disasters, geological disasters, etc. Responsible for the comprehensive supervision and management of production safety and supervision of production safety in industrial, mining and trade industries, etc.

The Ministry (2022) states the aim after the conversion of public security fire forces and armed police forestry forces, together with the health safety and other emergency rescue teams is the implementation of special management methods and policy to improve the sense of professional honour, to maintain a living force and combat power. The Ministry of Emergency Management should handle the relationship between disaster prevention and relief, clarify the division of responsibilities with relevant departments and localities and establish a coordination and cooperation mechanism.

The Chinese crisis management system with a central ministry and a vertical structure of centralised management resembles the Russian system headed by the EMERCOM ministry. As this system is undergoing dramatic development, there are still many missing auxiliary structures. On the other hand, it has the advantage of the versatility of the firefighting units that form the basis of the system, as well as the possibility of using the army, which carried out civil protection tasks during the quarantine measures of the Covid-19 period. The Chinese army has forces and means capable of dealing with emergencies over large areas.

5 Variable Models of EU Countries

There is a long-standing debate between two groups of opinion at the level of the European Union. On the one hand, there are the advocates of maintaining the coexistence of models and, on the other hand, the advocates of structural convergence. At the same time, the roles of the main private actors, the place of citizens in the crisis management system, the consideration of the human factor in organisations, the important role of crisis communication and the emergence of global security management standards must all be taken into account. This European overview demonstrates the need for a transversal approach in order to develop a culture of crisis, safety and risk management.

Beyond the concept of crisis management, which is quickly addressed, the focus on seven Member Countries, the subject of the study (Spain, France, Germany, Italy, Sweden, the United Kingdom and the Czech Republic), raises the question of the preservation of specific national cultures and the possibility of convergence towards a single European model.

The countries studied from a crisis management perspective can be divided into two traditional groups. The first is characterised by horizontal subsidiarity, which preserves the autonomy of local actors (Germany, Spain, Italy, UK), and the second by vertical subsidiarity, which favours collective reactivity by adapting the level of response to the scale of the crisis (France, Sweden, Czech Republic, Slovakia), often in a deconcentrated or even decentralised framework. The numerous structural or major crises that we have studied in these countries have modified this initial division of the Member Countries. An examination of the developments, similarities and differences between models reveals the existence of a veritable mosaic of systems.

In Germany, civil protection in peacetime is traditionally the responsibility of the Lands according to the Basic Law of 1949.The federal government is only responsible for civil protection in a state of defence. Due to a lack of resources during the Elbe flood in 2002, the German model was amended in 2009 as part of a political consensus in the event of nationwide disasters by providing the State with a federal office, an information system for emergency prevention, a joint operational monitoring centre between the Federation, the Lands and the organisations involved.

Following the Madrid bombings in 2004 and the violent forest fires in 2005, Spain, aware of the insufficient management of the crisis, took note of the inadequacies of the organisation of crisis management and rescue resources. In 2005, it created a military emergency unit attached to the Ministry of the Interior, following the example of the French civil security training and intervention units. Spain, one of the most decentralised countries in Europe, is strengthening civil-military cooperation by recognising a major role for the State in the event of a serious crisis to compensate for the fragmented nature of its system and the fragility of the response of certain autonomous communities.

In the last ten years or so, marked by natural disasters and a major migratory by natural disasters and a major migratory crisis, Italy has evolved the implementation of civil protection. Organised around four levels (communal, provincial regional, national), the Italian model is similar to the French system for the management of major crises by strengthening the prerogatives of the President of the Council while relying on the resources of the autonomous regions, the mobilisation of fire brigades and volunteer units.

Based on an entirely decentralised logic, the UKs crisis management organisation is management organisation was severely destabilised after the London bombings in July 2005. However, the British government had already redesigned its organisation in 2004, which specified the central governments role as coordinator, the distribution of missions between the territorial levels and the definition of three levels of intensity. While the local system reflects the decentralising tradition of the decentralising tradition of British administration, this complex models the organisation of the real-time response.

Some Member Countries belonging to the horizontal model (Spain, United Kingdom), faced with dysfunctions in the organisation of the response, have been able to improve their response. They led to strengthen coordination at the central level because of the acceleration of major crisis situations. The difficult application of the subsidiarity principle in the event of serious crisis has necessitated internal legislative adaptations.

An overview of the different crisis management systems distinguishes between countries with a vertical and a horizontal crisis management system (Table 1). For example, Austria, England, Spain, Germany or the United States have a typical horizontal structure. A vertical crisis management structure exists in France, Belgium, the Czechia, Slovakia, Russia and China. In the following lines, we will analyse the systems in several EU countries in order to better understanding their diversity, specificities and trends in structural and organisational change.

Table 1. Models of government crisis organisation

Country	Ministry responsible	Local responsibility	Subsidiarity model
Austria	Interior	Mayor/Governor of Land	Horizontal
Belgium	Interior	Mayor	Vertical
China	Ministry of the Emergency Management	Territorial/Regional	Vertical
Czech Republic	Interior	Mayor	Vertical
England	Prime Minister	Mayor/Police	Horizontal
France	Interior	Mayor/Prefect	Vertical
Germany	Home Affairs	Mayor/Governor of Land	Horizontal
Italy	Prime Minister	Mayor/Prefect	Horizontal
Russian Federation	Minister of Civil Defence	EMERCOM Republic/ Territorial/Regional	Vertical
Slovak Republic	Interior	Mayor	Vertical
Spain	Interior/Defence	Mayor/Head of autonomous region	Horizontal
Sweden	Prime Minister	Mayor/County Governor	Vertical
Switzerland	Defence, Civil Protection and Sport	President of Canton/ Mayor	Horizontal/Vertical
United States	Department of Homeland Security	Local/County/State	Horizontal

5.1 Germany

A 100-year Elbe and subsequent inundation caused by more than a week of heavy rainfall devastated Europe, causing billions of euros of damage in the Czech Republic, Austria, Germany, Slovakia, Poland, Hungary, Romania and Croatia. The heavy rainfall in the eastern Alps led to flooding in northern Italy. The Elbe reached more than 9 m, the city of Dresden was largely destroyed.

National Crisis Management Organisation During the Event
Germany is organised - administratively and politically - according to a federal structure, inherited both from the history of its formation as a nation state and from the constitutional foundations that have governed it since the end of the WWII. As a result, each of its regions (Land) has a high degree of autonomy, particularly in the organisation of police and civil security services and in municipal law. Each Land is itself subdivided into districts, districts and municipalities - and each of these levels has extensive, heterogeneous, powers in the field of civil protection.

In addition, Germany has a large support force of volunteers (500,000 volunteers), the volunteer fire brigade (1,200,000 people) and the Federal Agency for Technical Relief (THW −40,000 people). However, this is tending to erode, due to both demographic and sociological factors.

Prior to 2002, Germany had adopted a largely decentralised crisis management system, in which the principle of subsidiarity was the rule among the various layers of the administrative structure of the territory - both constitutionally and operationally.

According to the Basic Law (Constitution) of 1949, the federal state was only responsible to ensure civil security only in a state of defence, while civil protection in peacetime was devolved to the Lands. In addition, the armed forces were significantly less involved in civilian operations due to the historical background of the country.

Highlights on Crisis Management and Feedback

This model was significantly amended, following the Elbe floods in August 2002, which highlighted a problem of reactivity and resources. Indeed, from that date onwards, the Federation and the Lands agreed, by political consensus, on the new strategy for the protection in Germany, which emphasises the joint responsibility of the federal and state governments in the event of exceptional disasters nationwide.

The federal government subsequently established:

- Federal Office for Civil Protection and Disaster Relief (BBK), which acts as the a Federal Office for Civil Protection and Disaster Relief (BBK), which acts as a technical authority;
- a joint operational monitoring centre for the Federation and the Länder (GMLZ) to coordinate information between the Federation, the Länder and the organisations involved,
- an information system for the prevention of emergency situations,
- an inter-Länder exercise protocol (LÜKEX),
- an academy for crisis management, emergency planning and civil protection (AKNZ) for the theoretical and practical training of civil protection officers.

On 9 April 2009, the Civil Defence and Disaster Assistance Act the reform process by providing a new legal basis for the protection of the population.

It is important not to see these actions as centralising tendencies, as the country is both attached to its decentralised functioning and legitimately proud of the efficiency of its relief and assistance services, but as a of the efficiency of its emergency and assistance services, but as a complement to existing structures for the existing structures for large-scale threats.

5.2 Spain

On 11 March 2004, several bomb explosions by Moroccan terrorists occurred on trains in the Madrid suburbs. It was the deadliest attack since Lockerbie in 1988. Thirteen devices were detonated, killing 191 people. The attack takes place three days before the legislative elections, which the government will lose because of the disastrous management of crisis communication. Indeed, the government blamed the attacks on the ETA (Euscadie Ta Askatasuna - Basque Country and Freedom), while the Islamist track will become more and more obvious as time goes by.

National Crisis Management Organisation during the Event

The 1978 Constitution marked a break with the old Francos model of territorial organisation in Spain. Model of centralised territorial organisation. As a fundamental norm for the political organization of the nation, it led to the creation of a national crisis management organization. In just 20 years it led to a major transfer of competences from the general administration of the State to the Autonomous Communities, making Spain one of the most decentralised countries in Europe. Thus, Spain, parliamentary hereditary monarchy, built a horizontal model of crisis management during the 1980 s and 1990 s. A horizontal model of crisis management.

While the municipal level was the reference element, the Autonomous Communities had strong competences in this field, allowing the principle of subsidiarity to be applied in accordance with the law of 21 January 1985, the fundamental on which the entire civil protection system was based. However, the States competence in this area provided for the possibility of regulating by law the duties of citizens in the event of the occurrence of a major risk. In Spain, civil protection was defined as "the physical protection of the population and property in the event of a serious risk, public calamity or extraordinary disaster in which the life and physical integrity of people is in danger" The action of the public authorities combined with citizen action was to minimise, avoid or repair damage to people, property and the environment. This was a comprehensive concept of civil protection.

Nevertheless, this horizontal subsidiarity organisation created a competition of competences between the State and the Autonomous Communities. If the prerogatives of the civil governor, the States representative in the provinces 1998, the latter remained in principle the guarantor of the proper functioning of the institutions. However, the local level of crisis management was favoured because it was the most legitimate and promoted resilience. But the principle of the Autonomous Communities and ministries was applied more or less well unless local authorities were overwhelmed by the scale or technicality of the event to be managed. However, this architecture, virtuous on a theoretical level, had demonstrated its limits in the face of the complexity and gravity of natural or human disasters. The search for greater collaboration between the various administrations was a key element in the development of the The search for increased collaboration between the various administrations could not compensate for the systems structural weaknesses. Indeed, the citizens contribution remained very limited and centred on prevention and safeguard measures, despite the existence of more than measures, despite the existence of over 1,300 local volunteer associations. Moreover, although regulatory obligations were imposed on economic actors, they were also without any real economic actors, they were also without real constraint. The main principles of prevention were more like objectives around which self-protection obligations were based.

Despite the introduction of an emergency planning system in 1992, the development and implementation of territorial or special plans required coordination, which was lacking in some cases due to the diversity of their effectiveness.

Highlights on Crisis Management and Feedback

The principle of state competence has been progressively reaffirmed. It is based on the "damage likely to be done to the national interest when the emergency is supra-territorial in scope in that it affects several autonomous communities or when the scale of the crisis requires national leadership national direction" requiring the coordination of the different administrations to be organised.

The civil protection intervention forces led by the Ministry of the Interior until 2005 relied on units that were difficult to project in a highly degraded environment. In the aftermath of the terrorist attacks of 11 March 2004 in Madrid, and the violent forest fires of 2005, Spain recognised the inadequacies of its crisis management and rescue resources by creating a Military Emergency Unit in 2005, similar to the training and intervention units and of the French civil security system (UIISC). Attached to the Ministry of Defence, this unit is placed under the authority of the Ministry of the Interior during rescue missions. Today, the governance is shared at national level between the Ministries of the Interior (Directorate General for Civil Protection and (Directorate General for Civil Protection and Rescue) Defence under the direction of a crisis cabinet under the authority of the Prime Minister.

Thus, the Spanish model of crisis management has gradually evolved by recognising a major role for the State, in particular by strengthening civil-military cooperation. Aware of the limits of the fragmented nature of its crisis management system, in 2014 Spain introduced a National Security Strategy (NSS) and a national civil protection system in 2014.

The principles of this comprehensive strategy are based on unity of action, anticipation and prevention, efficiency and sustainability of means and resilience or capacity for resistance and recovery. This new framework is seen as an essential instrument to ensure the coordination, cohesion and efficiency of public policies in the field of civil protection, notably through the new European mechanisms and international cooperation.

5.3 Czech Republic

The Example of the 2013 Floods

In May and June 2013, large parts of Central Europe were affected by catastrophic floods, which damaged homes and disrupted infrastructure and disrupted services.

The toll of the floods in the Czech Republic, meanwhile, was very high: 14 dead, 220,000 people evacuated due to flooding that affected 700 municipalities. Thousands of homes were left without electricity, water and gas.[3]

National Crisis Management Organisation During the Event

Following the floods in August 1997, which highlighted the difficulties of organising

[3] Brazova,V.K. Matczak, P. & Takacs, V. (2015) Evolution of civil security systems: the case of three Central European countries. p.800.

Czech civil protection, the national services reorganised themselves along the lines of the French civil protection model. These floods are thus the catalyst event for strengthening Czech-French cooperation and assistance in the field of civil protection, prevention and emergency management.

The floods forced the Czech Republic authorities to open locks in the south of the country, in order to reduce the pressure of water on the dykes. In return for this action, huge masses of water rushed towards Prague, drowning a large part of the city. Although the floods were more severe and extensive in 2013, the overall amount of damage was less than in the previous year in the Czech Republic. This is partly due to the relative effectiveness of protection and risk control measures put in place since 2002, but it is felt that much more efforts needs to be done for the future.

In addition, the EU assistance mechanism has been called upon, with the Czech Republic submitted a request for financial assistance on 8 August 2013. The total direct damage. The total direct damage was estimated at EUR 637 million.[4] Crisis management in the Czech Republic has been designed in a pyramidal manner, with the head of government at the top of the pyramid. It is based on the act of 28 June 2000 on the integrated emergency system. This involves the fire & rescue system, first aid, the police, the armed forces, the voluntary associations and voluntary citizens. It also determines the competence of the governmental and territorial authorities, the rights and obligations of all actors in the preparation of emergency-in preparedness and reaction, but also in the protection of the population at all stages of a crisis.

Civil protection, which was formerly the responsibility of the Ministry of Defence now belongs to the Ministry of the Interior. Shortly afterwards, in 2001 the fire brigade (organised into a general directorate and 14 regional directorates) and and 14 regional directorates) and the civil protection services were merged to create an Integrated rescue system. At the national level, the State Security Council aims to plan the preparedness of the emergency services units to face future crisis events.

It is responsible for crisis management in coordination with the central crisis staff. It is placed under the presidency of the Prime Minister and the Minister of the Interior. It should be noted that the action is under the responsibility of the elected official of the region.

Among the strong points of the Czech crisis management system can be recognized: The definition of the organisation of crisis management structures by legislative texts as well as the definition of the rights and obligations of crisis management actors by legislative texts. Current system has proved its worth in several recent crises situations.

5.4 Slovak Republic

The national security system, including the crisis management system, is very similar to that of the Czech Republic. This is logical given the common development within Czechoslovakia. The transformation of the crisis management system started at the time of the Czechoslovak Federation (1990–1992) and continued in the same direction after the establishment of the independent republics. The transformation of civil defence into civil protection as well as the establishment of the integrated rescue system took place in

[4] Ibidem.

both republics in an almost identical way. The main difference lies in the position of the Police within the Integrated Rescue System. In the Czech Republic, the Police is one of the basic components, in Slovakia it is one of the other components. However, despite the above, in both countries the police have practically identical competences and tasks in dealing with crisis situations.

Similarly, to the Czech Republic, Slovakia has a strong centralised management headed by the President of the Fire and Rescue Corps and the President of the Police Corps within the Ministry of the Interior.

The entire crisis management structure is vertically oriented with clear demarcation of competences and rules of cooperation between the individual professional rescue services as well as voluntary rescue associations and the police. The commander or head of the intervention is always clearly defined.

Slovak emergency services also contribute to the EU civil protection system. Slovakia has several functional modules ready to respond to large-scale fires, floods or refugee crises, which have been deployed abroad in large-scale emergencies. Now, for the first time in its modern history, Slovakia has become a recipient of rescue modules. The reason for this is to cope with the migration wave from Ukraine as a result of the armed conflict. Specifically, these are medical modules aimed at managing infectious diseases, modules providing electricity as well as modules for emergency accommodation (Fig. 2).

The crisis management system has demonstrated a relatively high level of flexibility and preparedness to respond to the refugee surge and related challenges.

6 Switzerland

Switzerland, as a traditionally neutral country, has built a comprehensive crisis management system that combines the advantages of both vertical and horizontal structures. Switzerland is also known for its high level of technology and facilities for emergency services.

The National Emergency Operations Centre is the federal authority responsible for dealing with emergency incidents. It also serves as national reporting and situation centre and as the staff unit of the Federal Civil Protection Crisis Management Board. The NEOC is a division of the Federal Office for Civil Protection FOCP within the Federal Department of Defence, Civil Protection and Sport DDPS.

One of the NEOCs responsibilities is to constantly monitor and assess the general situation. If natural, technical and society-related disasters occur (e.g. events resulting in increased radioactivity, biological or chemical disasters, a satellite crash or a breakdown in infrastructure), the NEOC informs its partner organisations, presents the overall situation and acts as the coordinating authority. In the case of emergencies leading to increased radioactivity, the NEOC can take measures to protect the population. In certain emergencies, e.g. major chemical incidents or a potential satellite crash, the NEOC carries out further situation-specific tasks, and may at any time be assigned additional tasks by the Federal Council.

The NEOC is designed so that it can be operationally ready at all times and poised with a minimum of staff to make a preliminary assessment and link up with partner organisations. In the event of an emergency, the NEOC can expand its capacities rapidly according to the situation. In addition to its permanent staff of around 30 employees, the NEOC can bring various other units into play in order to have sufficient manpower and ensure sustainability.

The NEOC is available to its partner organisations round the clock 365 days a year. Every year, some 400 cases call for a situation assessment by persons on standby and, if needed, the involvement of specialists from NEOC or its partners. In its work, the NEOC relies on high-performance, crisis-resistant and redundant links to partners such as the cantonal police forces operations centres.[5]

Around 40 people work for the NEOC. Native speakers of all of Switzerlands national languages are well represented. Having a workforce with good language skills is important for a national specialist service like the NEOC. The majority of NEOC employees come from a scientific or technical background, specialising in fields like geophysics, physics, chemistry, meteorology, engineering and telecommunications. NEOC is divided into six sectors and one staff unit.

Planning and Management Staff Unit oversees internal coordination and administrative processes. It is also responsible for managing the development of NEOCs concepts and network of domestic, foreign and international partner organisations.

Staff Unit Strategy and Coordination

This unit provides internal coordination and administration. It is in control of the development of partner network in Switzerland, our network with foreign partner organisations and international organisations.

Reporting and Situation Centre identifies and assesses Bevölkerungsschutzrelevante Lageareas of relevance to civil protection efforts (BREL) and ensures that NEOC partner organisations receive key information. Partner organisations can also access BREL information on the Electronic Situation Display (ESD NEOC). When an incident occurs, BREL information is supplemented with situational and customised communication products. It identifies and assesses the radiological situation, manages the federal sampling and measurement system and produces radioactivity-specific documentation.

Rescue Operations are managed by the NEOC Warning Centre, operational documentation and operational training for NEOC staff. It also oversees the processes of the NEOC Warning Centre and the NEOC standby service, as well as the NEOCs key operational processes, and carries out regular reviews of the NEOCs operational readiness.

Operational Systems operate a highly-available IT infrastructure. It also is responsible for maintaining and developing operational applications. It takes the lead on operation-specific IT projects for all Civil Protection partners, in areas such as the coordinated incident monitoring system, the exchange of data and alert channels.

Federal Civil Protection Crisis Management Board runs the Federal Civil Protection Crisis Management Board (BSTB). It also develops and attends to the processes of the different parts of the BSTB during preparatory phases (Directors Conference, planning element) and ensures coherence and links between the work of the BSTB and that of the federal and cantonal agencies and infrastructure operators. During operations, it acts as the staff unit of the Federal Civil Protection Crisis Management Board.

[5] About the NEOC https://www.naz.ch/en/naz.

If an incident with national implications is imminent or has occurred, the Federal Civil Protection Crisis Management Board, under Article 4 paragraph 2 of the Ordinance on the Federal Civil Protection Crisis Management Board, is responsible for:[6]

- ensuring both the flow of information and the coordination with other federal and cantonal staffs and offices, the operators of critical infrastructures and the responsible authorities abroad
- assessing the overall situation, in particular where it comprises a combination of different situations
- providing the information that the Federal Council and the responsible federal department or office need to make their decisions
- coordinating expert knowledge at federal level
- coordinating the deployment of national and international resources.

The National Emergency Operations Centre NEOC acts as the operations and support unit for the Federal Civil Protection Crisis Management Board.

The Federal Civil Protection Crisis Management Board comprises the directors conference, a planning unit made up of experts from the authorities involved, and the operations and support units.

The National Emergency Operations Centre, as the Federal Management Boards operations and support unit, is responsible for convening the Federal Management Board rapidly in the event of an emergency and providing it with information and continuing updates on developments in both the overall situation and the situations in the various sectors. Reports on these individual situations are compiled by the authorities and specialist bodies concerned and made available via National Emergency Operations Centre.[7] Figure 1 shows the organisation of communication with the media and the public during a crisis situation of national scale.

The Swiss model is a successful hybrid of vertical and horizontal crisis management systems. The backbone consists of state structures, downstream cantonal authorities up to the district level, while relying on more than a million civil protection volunteers who are ready to intervene in a wide range of emergencies, including military threats.

7 The Tools of the European Civil Protection Mechanism

The Emergency Response Coordination Centre (ERCC) is operational 24/7 since 1 October 2013. It is the result of the merger of the (ECHO) and the Monitoring and Information Centre (MIC) in the European Union: Monitoring and Information Centre (MIC) in the field of civil protection. It is part of the European Commission (DG ECHO).

States have access to a platform of civil protection assets available in all participating states. Any state, inside or outside the EU, can request assistance through the centre. The centre acts as a hub between the participating States, the affected State and the

[6] About the NEOC https://www.naz.ch/en/naz.

[7] The Federal Civil Protection Crisis Management Board's operations and support unit https://www.naz.ch/en/naz/eo.

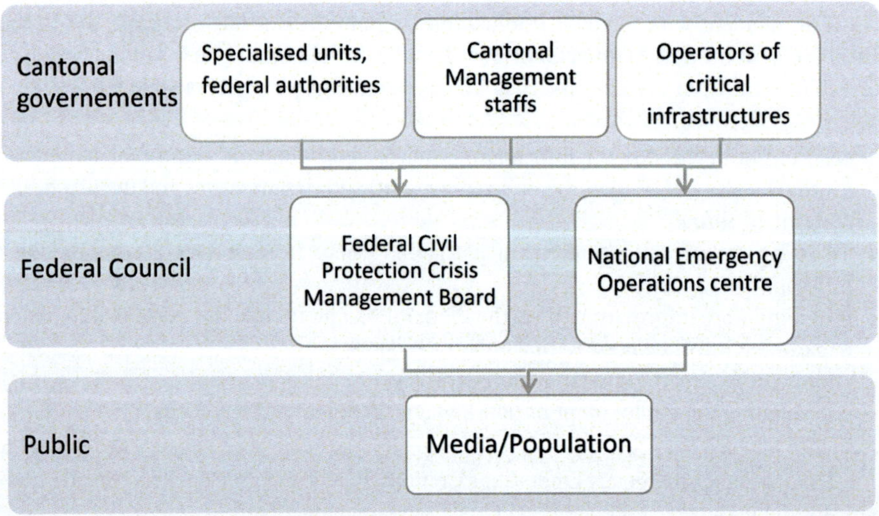

Fig. 1. Swiss task force organisation in the event of national emergencies related to civil protection. *Source* The Federal Civil Protection Crisis Management Boards operations and support unit https://www.naz.ch/en/naz/eo

experts sent to the field. The centre also plays a coordinating role by matching offers of assistance from participating States with the needs of the disaster-stricken State. In addition, it provides regular information on ongoing emergency relief activities.[8]

7.1 The Common Emergency Communication and Information System (CECIS)

The mechanism provides for emergency communication and monitoring instruments managed by the ERCC through the Common Emergency Communication and Information System (CECIS) managed by the ERCC. This is a web-based notification and alerting application, which aims to facilitate emergency communication between participating states.

The European Emergency Response Capability: EERC The creation of a European Emergency Response Capacity (EERC) is the main advance reform of the Mechanism in 2013, which was further developed in 2014. The EERC takes the form of a pool of capacities allocated in advance on a voluntary basis by the Member Countries. These capabilities may include civil protection modules, other response capabilities and the provision of experts.

The Commission is responsible for defining the quantity and quality of the capability to meet the needs of the European Emergency Response Capability (EERC). It sets up a system for the certification and registration of the response capabilities that it and

[8] European Civil Protection and Humanitarian Aid Operations. European Civil Protection Pool. https://civil-protection-humanitarian-aid.ec.europa.eu/what/civil-protection/european-civil-protection-pool_en

registration of the response capacities that Member Countries make available to the EERC.[9]

These response capacities made available to the EERC are available for operations under the Union Mechanism when a request for assistance has been made through the Emergency Response Coordination Centre (ERCC). The final decision to deploy them is taken by the countries that have registered response capabilities concerned. In the event of a national emergency, major disaster or, in exceptional cases, for serious reasons, a Member Country is not in a position to make its response capacities available in the event of a disaster, that country shall inform the Commission as soon as possible. In case of deployment, the response capacities of the States remain under their command and control, while the direction of the relief effort is the responsibility of the requesting State.[10]

When the ERCC receives a request for assistance, it forwards it to the contact points of the other Member Countries, collects validated information on the situation. The Commission may make recommendations, in consultation with the requesting Country, for the provision of assistance through the Union mechanism, based on the needs identified on the ground and any relevant pre-established plans in the requesting Country. It may invite Member Countries to deploy specific means and facilitate the coordination of the assistance requested.

Any Member Country to which a request for assistance is addressed through the mechanism, shall promptly determine whether it is in a position to provide the assistance and shall inform the requesting Member Country of its decision via the CECIS, specifying the scope, modalities and, where appropriate, the cost of the assistance it could provide. The ERCC informs the other Member Countries.

The EU member countries + Norway have certified rescue modules that are available for emergency response purposes at the request of the affected country. An overall up-to-date overview of the certified modules is shown in the figure below. In addition to the modules shown, which represent the highest category, each country has a multiplication of modules that are seeking certification and are also available on request. The modules shown on the map (Fig. 2) are available immediately without the need to approach the official country locations, reducing the response and departure time of the module to the affected location. Modules move and then operate completely autonomously for 7–10 days with their own food, fuel, accommodation supplies without the need for resupply from local authorities.

The system of civil protection modules serves not only for non-military threats. As it has been shown, some modules can also serve in military conflicts. Currently, the only certified civil protection module of the Slovak Republic is focused on emergency accommodation. The Samaritan Unit deployed this module near the Slovak-Ukrainian border to meet the needs of refugees after the outbreak of the hot conflict in Donbas.

The European Commission upgraded the EU Civil Protection Mechanism and created rescEU to protect citizens from disasters and manage emerging risks in 2019. It is

[9] Emergency Response Coordination Centre (ERCC). https://civil-protection-knowledge-network.europa.eu/emergency-response-coordination-centre.

[10] Emergency Response Coordination Centre (ERCC). https://civil-protection-knowledge-network.europa.eu/emergency-response-coordination-centre.

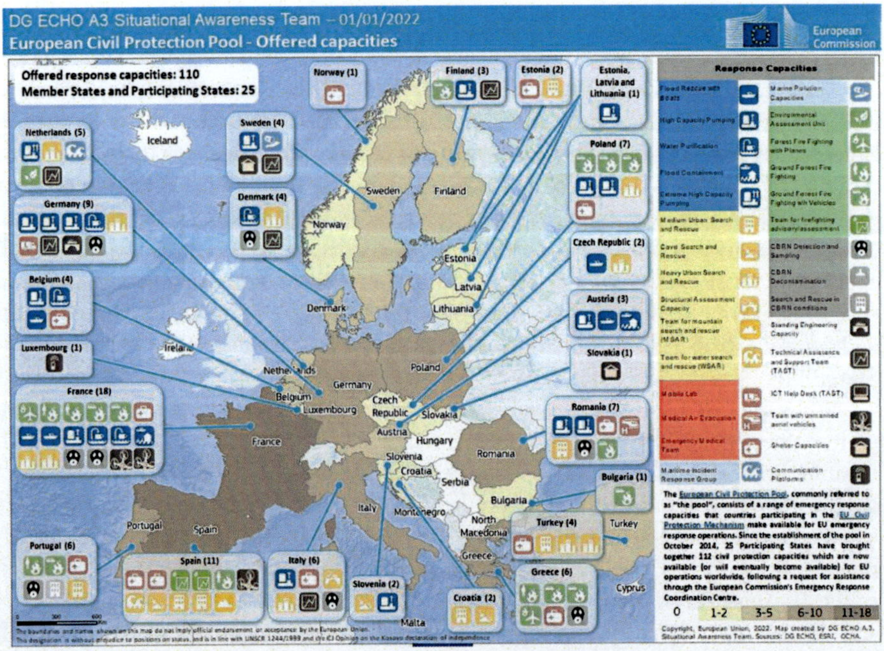

Fig. 2. European Civil Protection Pool – Offered Capacities 01/01/2022. *Source* Emergency Response Coordination Centre. October 10, 2022. https://erccportal.jrc.ec.europa.eu/DesktopModules/Response Capacity/Documents/20220101_CivilProtectionPool_offered.jpeg

fully financed by the EU. RescEU has established a new European reserve of resources including a fleet of firefighting planes and helicopters, medical evacuation planes, and a stockpile of medical items and field hospitals that can respond to health emergencies, mobile shelters for those displaced. Furthermore, the EU is also developing a reserve to respond to CBRN incidents.

7.2 European Civil Protection Reaction on Ukraine Crisis

EUs Civil Protection and Humanitarian Aid Operations have been operating in Ukraine since February 2014. Since then, the EU and Member Countries have provided around €1.3 billion in humanitarian aid including €425 million financial value of in-kind assistance and emergency operations and €348 million humanitarian aid from EU member countries in 2022.[11]

The map below shows the current status of humanitarian assistance provided and received for war-affected Ukraine. The wide range of assistance includes emergency shelter modules, mobile hospitals, medical supplies, fire-fighting modules, power generators, fuel, CBRN protective equipment and other miscellaneous equipment (Fig. 3).

[11] European Civil Protection and Humanitarian Aid Operations - EU humanitarian aid in Ukraine 26/08/2022 https://civil-protection-humanitarian-aid.ec.europa.eu/where/europe/ukraine_en#facts--figures-as-of-2608.

France is the largest provider of humanitarian aid. In addition to Ukraine itself, modules are provided to neighbouring countries, i.e. Moldova, Poland, Slovakia as well as the Czech Republic, which receives a significant number of migrants from Ukraine, in order to cope with the refugee wave. In total 31 European countries provide effective assistance related to immigrant wave from Ukraine and civil security inside the country. The map below clearly shows the type of assistance provided by the specially oriented civil protection modules from individual EU Member Countries, as well as an overview of the recipient countries that use this assistance on their own territory. For example, Slovakia not only provides its own assistance to refugees, but rescue modules from other countries operate on its territory and focus on assisting persons arriving across the Ukraine-Slovakia border (Fig. 3).

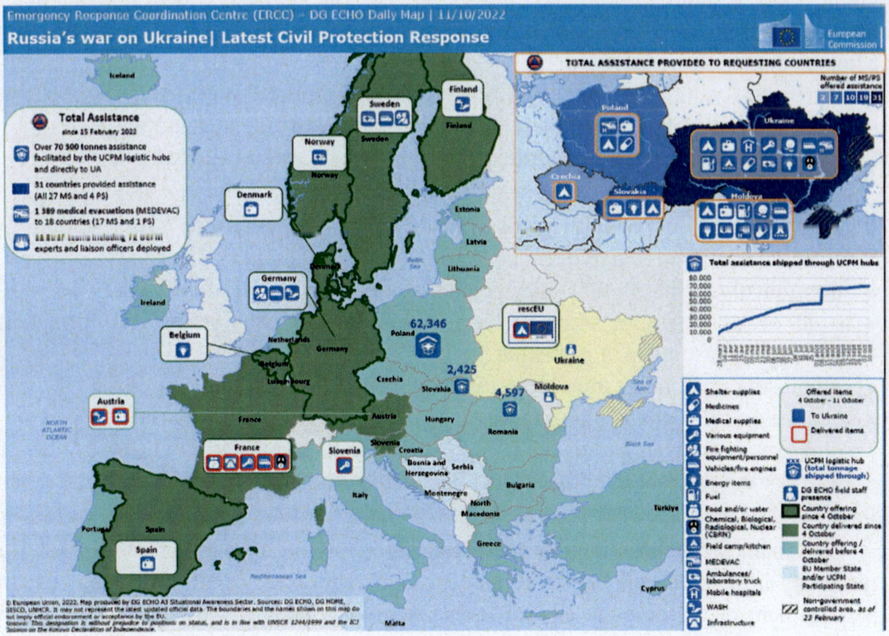

Fig. 3. Russias war on Ukraine – Latest civil protection response. *Source* Emergency Response Coordination Centre Daily Map 11/10/2022. Emergency Response Coordination Centre. October 11, 2022. https://erccportal.jrc.ec.europa.eu/ECHO-Products/Maps[12]

Resume

The adaptability of national crisis management or civil protection systems depends on their structure, functions, competences as well as funding, staffing and material support.

The crisis management system in the USA differs from those in Russia and China primarily because of its decentralised horizontal structure. The system is heavily dependent

[12] Emergency Response Coordination Centre 11/10/2022 https://erccportal.jrc.ec.europa.eu/ECHO-Products/Maps

on volunteers, who make up the majority of emergency personnel, especially firefighters. The decentralised funding system, heavily dependent on private financial or material donations, can be directly threatened in times of economic crisis.

The Russian system is a vertically structured crisis management system complemented by a number of supporting state-run institutions of an educational and scientific research nature. Its functioning is fully dependent on the state budget, as is the case in EU countries. Volunteers are only a complement to civil protection civil servants. The system also includes response to military threats.

The Russian system is a vertically structured crisis management system complemented by a number of supporting state-run institutions of an educational and scientific research nature. Its functioning is fully dependent on the state budget, as is the case in EU countries. Volunteers are only a complement to civil protection civil servants. The system also includes response to military threats. The Chinese system is dynamically developing along the Russian model. Like Russias Emercom, it is managed by a single Ministry for Crisis Situations.

European countries can be divided according to their governance system into horizontally and vertically structured, both approaches having their limits.

The comparison of vertical model countries reveals several similarities:

- Distribution of responsibility for crisis management and response resources on territorial level with a real deconcentration on the conduct of operations;
- strong involvement of crisis management at the central level of the State;
- based on a system of piggybacking on the implementation of civil protection intervention resources in particular;
- call on supranational resources (equipment, command structure, expertise, etc.);
- to make up for national shortcomings, capacity to manage the crisis by relying on a solid administrative system which, in the event of insufficiency, will be able to benefit from assistance from the higher level (sending experts, material aid, etc.).

The main differences include the presence or missing of national civil protection resources in reserve capable of supporting and reinforcing territorial resources; the management of the crisis at central level does not necessarily rely on an interministerial centre that takes charge of the entire crisis; the amount of autonomy granted to the local level varies from country to country. For example, very autonomous in USA and very centralised in Russia under the direction of the prefectural chain; the ability to pass on the direction of crisis management with fluidity from one level to the other.

The question of the preparedness of countries crisis systems for the risks arising from military and economic threats remains an open one, and only the reality of the situation can fully illuminate the functioning of the system. However, it can be concluded that countries with a well-developed vertical state-led structure complemented by elements of horizontal governance are better prepared than countries with a typically horizontal structure. There are several main reasons for this. The protection of life, health, property and the environment is the main priority of the state, not only during crisis situations, and in times of economic crisis the emergency services will remain primarily financed from the state budget, while voluntary associations can also be used. Conversely, funding based largely on voluntary donor contributions may be insufficient at a critical time and may lead to the breakdown of crisis management structures.

The EU has developed a wide range of tools that enable the Union to play a role in a joint response to a variety of crises. The combined resources of 27 member states and the distinct competence the EU has developed over the years have made the EU a unique actor in the international crisis arena.

References

ANVIL: Civil Security and the European Union : a survey of European civil security systems and the role of the EU in building shared crisis management capacities (2015). Retrieved August 18 2022. https://anvil-project.net/

Brazova, V.K., Matczak, P., Takacs, V.: Evolution of civil security systems: the case of three central European countries. J. Risk Res. **18**(6), 789–806 (2015)

Boin, R.A., Ekengren, M., Rhinard, M.: The European Union as Crisis Manager. Cambridge University Press, Patterns and Prospects (2013). https://doi.org/10.1017/CBO9781139565400

Bossong, R., Hegemann, H.: Cooperation under Diversity? Exploring Cultural and Institutional Diversity in European Civil Security Governance. In: Bossong, R., Hegemann, H. (eds.) European Civil Security Governance. NSCS, pp. 27–49. Palgrave Macmillan UK, London (2015). https://doi.org/10.1057/9781137481115_2

Di Camillo, F., Marrone, A., Silvestri, S.,Tessari, P., Ungarno, A.R.: The Italian Civil Security System. Edizioni Nuova Cultura (2014)

EMERCOM - Ministry of the Russian Federation for Civil Defense, Emergencies and Elimination of Consequences of Natural Disasters (2022). Retrieved August 21 2022 https://www.mchs.gov.ru/deyatelnost/bezopasnost-grazhdan/antiterror_1

European Civil Protection and Humanitarian Aid Operations.: European Civil Protection Pool. Retrieved August 26 2022. https://civil-protection-humanitarian-aid.ec.europa.eu/what/civil-protection/european-civil-protection-pool_en

European Civil Protection and Humanitarian Aid Operation.: EU humanitarian aid in Ukraine. Retrieved August 26 2022. https://civil-protection-humanitarian-aid.ec.europa.eu/where/europe/ukraine_en#facts--figures-as-of-2608

Federal Office for Civil Protection. National Emergency Operational Centre : About the NEOC Retrieved September 13 2022. https://www.naz.ch/en/naz

Federal Office for Civil Protection FOCP National Emergency Operations Centre. (2022) The Federal Civil Protection Crisis Management Boards operations and support unit. Retrieved September 13, 2022 https://www.naz.ch/en/naz/eo

FEMA. Reports & Data. (2022) Open FEMA. Retrieved September 11, 2022 https://www.fema.gov/about/reports-and-data/openfema

Garcia-Segura, L.A.: The necessary link between security culture and data protection in the European Union. In: Ramirez, J.M., Biziewski, J. (eds.) A Shift in the security paradigm - Global challenges: Is Europe ready to meet them?, pp. 235–250. Springer (2020)

Kailes, J.: The National Shelter System and Physical Accessibility – Time to Look Under the Hood. The partnership for inclusive disaster strategies (2020). Retrieved August 20, from https://disasterstrategies.org/blog-post/the-national-shelter-system-and-physical-accessibility-time-to-look-under-the-hood/

Kirchner, E., Fanoulis, E., Dorussen, H.: Civil security in the EU: National persistence versus EU ambitions? Eur. Secur. **24**(2), 287–303 (2014). https://doi.org/10.1080/09662839.2014.968133

Ministry of the Emergency Management of the Peoples Republic of China. (2022). Main Responsibilities. Retrieved September 15, 2022 https://www.mem.gov.cn/jg/

U.S. Department of Homeland Security. (November, 2017) Emergency Services Sector Profile. Retrieved August 29, 2022 https://www.cisa.gov/emergency-services-sector

Pedagogy of Peace: The Key to Understanding Between East and West

Valentín Martínez-Otero(✉)

Universidad Complutense de Madrid, Madrid, Spain
valenmop@edu.ucm.es

Abstract. Peace is a very broad concept both from a theoretical and practical point of view, but it is indisputable that its educational promotion is called to play a fundamental role in today's seriously threatened globalized world. The school, lato sensu, cannot ignore its responsibility for security and coexistence, particularly if we consider that conflicts and international insecurity have increased. among the efforts that western countries dedicate to a new international order based on security and human rights, the pedagogical strategy enriched with multidisciplinary research around notions such as global citizenship, the construction of just societies, understanding between the east and the west, and the expansion of peace culture. Education for planetary coexistence would be located within this framework, in accordance with the objectives for sustainable development (unesco, 2017), a consensual way at a global level to face challenges and prevent threats.

Keywords: Pedagogy of peace · Coexistence · Threats · Understanding between the East and the West · Globalization

1 Introduction: Peace on the Dynamic Global Stage

The notion of peace has a long history, largely because of the concern generated by war. Jiménez & Jiménez (2004) recall the relevance of the concept of peace in Greco-Roman culture, a rational peace that could be understood as the absence of war or a break between conflicts. Peace (Greek: *Ειρήνη*) was also synonymous with harmony, a state of tranquility in the villages and in the city-state. In this Hellenic context, and taking the person as the center, it was also related to tranquility. In the case of Rome, the absence of wars or rebellions was guaranteed by a powerful military machine. The *Pax Romana* constituted a system of order, control, and legal relationship, but it did not guarantee justice.

The interest in peace will be seen later in other areas. Let us think, for example, of Christianity, in whose essence the message of peace and fraternity is clearly discovered, although some interpretations throughout history have endeavored to pervert it.

The idea of peace, now with a socio-political or anthropological character rather than a theological or religious one, exalts us and springs from the aspiration that human life be presided over by harmonious coexistence. Although some circumstances endanger

J. Cayón Peña and J. M. Ramírez (Eds.): *Threats to Peace and International Security: Asia versus West*, ASTSA, pp. 229–241, 2023.
https://doi.org/10.1007/978-3-031-28336-9_12

this coexistence, our vocation is not, as we wish, war, although it is true that it has accompanied us for as long as we can remember. Nor do we want to refer to the "peace of the cemetery" or to a precarious peace, but to a peace, which as advocated by Kant (1999), is fertile and mature, fruit of moral and cultural development. Although the philosopher of Königsberg founded perpetual peace on law, considering that a project of harmony among human beings must be inscribed in a legal framework, it is evident that for this program of harmony not to be a chimera, it must be accompanied by a true ethical effort. The fragility of peace, wherever threatened, demands a permanent vigil over it.

Peace, in fact, calls for a plenary conjunction of efforts that must be promoted in all areas. But beware, since without justice, peace becomes unattainable. Peace is an expression of equity, progress and humanity that is learned and strengthened through exercise. Its development is equivalent to advancing firmly along the path of harmony, reciprocity, and rapport. While it is true that it is sometimes said that peace is nothing more than a beautiful idealism, an anticipation of a still distant future, it cannot be denied that it is a necessary illusion, a torch of hope that illuminates, guides, and comforts.

This is how Don Quixote must have understood it because he put all his effort into promoting peace in his own way, often aggressively. Although it is shocking, the explanation is given by himself when referring to weapons in one of his famous speeches: "… Which have as their object and end peace, which is the greatest good that man can desire in this life." (I, 37). With these words, the self-knighted gentleman expresses a yearning for peace, a peace that is intimately linked to war. In all its harshness, war endangers stability and coexistence, threatens chaos and suffering. That is why weapons must be put to the service of protection, security, order and the common good, even more so at a time when Russia has brought war to the European continent.

At the time of writing, the summit of the North Atlantic Treaty Organization (NATO) corresponding to the year 2022 is being held in Madrid (Spain). Its main theme is that of the Russian invasion of Ukraine, although other related issues are also addressed, such as Sweden and Finland's membership, or the challenge made by China. From the Western perspective, Russia and China represent authoritarian threats to world peace and NATO makes its goal of ensuring the freedom and security of its members through political and military means explicit. Politically, because it promotes democratic values and allows its members to consult and cooperate on issues related to defense and security to solve problems, build trust and prevent conflicts. Militarily, because it is committed to the peaceful resolution of conflicts, although if diplomatic efforts fail, it claims the ability to take military action.[1]

In the document entitled NATO *Strategic Concept 2022*, NATO states that the global geopolitical scenario is increasingly dangerous and competitive, to the point that the Euro-Atlantic zone is not at peace and the security of allied countries is threatened. He blames Russia for violating the rules by invading Ukraine and establishing a strategic partnership with China that champions the authoritarian undermining of the rules-based international order. NATO points to these and other challenges and threats to its interests, security, and values: terrorism, climate change, the emergence of disruptive technologies, the weakening of arms control, disarmament and the non-proliferation architecture.

[1] https://www.nato.int/nato-welcome/index.html Accessed on 29 June 2022.

In these circumstances, NATO, from an integrated and coherent approach aimed at promoting national and alliance-wide resilience, strengthens its strategic engagement with its members in three main areas– deterrence and defense, crisis prevention and management, and cooperative security.

Based on the global and interconnected risks previously mentioned, NATO does not rule out the use of weapons to defend allied territory and preserve the sovereignty and integrity of all its members against any aggression. In parallel, the alliance reaffirms its "Open Door" policy to all European democracies by virtue of shared fundamental values and its strategic interest in Euro-Atlantic peace and stability.

NATO's new strategic concept is exposed in broad strokes. Threats from Russia and China have strengthened the role of the alliance and favored a collective redefinition of the identity of the Euro-Atlantic area.

For some authors, however, the current critical situation generated by the invasion of Ukraine is the result of the progressive exclusion of Russia from the economic and security architecture of the West after the Cold War, and the consequent emergence of internal Russian nationalism at the same time as pro-Western sentiments in the post-Soviet space increased. Especially in Ukraine and Georgia (Cafruny et al., 2022). Here we find a heterodox line of argument, because instead of explaining the invasion of Ukraine from the "proven Russian aggressive tendencies" and the "well-known ambition of Putin", as is usually done from the Western orbit, the United States is held responsible for its unbridled global expansion through NATO and other ideological and political-military means. From this perspective, the triumphalism that the end of the Cold War could awaken led Russia to gradually adopt a defensive and confrontational strategy against the "Western threat".

In the face of escalating war, this paper analyzes and focuses on the role that peace education can play. The search for peace in a changing and threatened geopolitical environment is a priority objective incorporated into the policies of Western countries. An overview of the pedagogy of peace as a way of understanding between East and West, and, consequently, of expansion of security and defense, stability, democratization, and world development, is presented.

2 The Search for Peace: Pedagogical Dimension

The differences noted when explaining the current crisis generated by the invasion of Ukraine do not reduce the concern about it and coincide in highlighting the danger that hangs over the world. In a scenario characterized by dynamism, complexity and multiple risks, the demands of the era in which we live lead us to strengthen the commitment to peace and to ask ourselves about the role that pedagogy can play in achieving this goal. It should not be overlooked, however, that to achieve peace we must work for it, something that seems to be increasingly distant if one thinks of the proliferation of hostile decisions on the part of Russia: calling for pseudo-referendums in the occupied territories of Ukraine, calling up 300,000 reservists and nuclear threat. The rise of these measures in an extremely critical situation should not prevent us from appreciating, on the contrary, the value of peace, unconditionally desirable and enabling understanding, justice, freedom, and coexistence.

The cultivation of peace does not aim at the suppression of all kinds of combative inclination, which, below the romantic cloak, would be profoundly absurd. In the current conjuncture, the pedagogy of peace can be understood as a scientific field of education, at once rational and experiential, normative and orientative, committed to coexistence, prevention and resolution of conflicts, democratic participation, intercultural understanding, and justice.

The pedagogy advocated here, in line with the consensual tripartition of education - formal, non-formal and informal - extends to the different age groups and to the various areas of human life, not only to the family and school. This decisive notional advance of the educational universe and of the pedagogy itself as a science opens endless possibilities for reflection and action to promote individual and collective development in scenarios of peace, in aspects as diversified as the reduction of interpersonal violence or the prevention of war at the international level. From this perspective, the words of Harris (2004) when he stated that the approaches to peace education— international education, rights education, development education, environmental education, and conflict resolution education— are not exclusive, but rather complementary, acquire full meaning.

One of the most important contributions of pedagogical science to the cause of peace lies in becoming aware of the diversified sources of violence, which may be distributed in five interrelated areas, these being personal, family, relational, organizational, social/environmental. The promotion of peace inside and outside of the classroom involves identifying the origin of the various forms of violence and traveling alternative paths, characterized by rationality and ethics.

The pedagogy of peace, in its dual condition of scientific and humanistic project, provides keys for the prevention of rivalry and discord, for the elimination of barriers and for the cultivation of understanding at different levels and in various scenarios. A pedagogy sensitive to fraternity, grounded in hope, realistic and, at the same time, ready to promote the improvement of a world that in many ways turns against itself.

3 Education for Peace, Beyond School

Whatever area we focus on, we must know the conditions for the possibility of peace through in-depth analysis. Peace education may lose its orientation and become a vague aspiration if the fundamentals of the intended action in a particular scenario are ignored. An anchorage is needed to develop the pedagogical scaffolding and its complex strategy. Therefore, it is necessary, as indicated by Gross (2017), that initiatives in education for peace, conflict prevention and resolution, peacebuilding and promotion of social cohesion know their socio-historical roots, while remaining linked to visions of the future.

To transform reality, extremely varied, you must first know it. We can contemplate in its full configuration different areas, each with its specific problems, but interconnected, as well described by the systemic model, which would require a macroanalysis (planet), although the gaze may also be directed mainly towards a closer scenario (family, school, work environment). The proposals of the educational process for peace, whatever the context of intervention, must not collide with those that may be made for other areas. A harmonious vision at the global level may be utopian, but it constitutes a necessary frame of reference for the pedagogy of peace. Such a horizon, achievable, encourages deepening the relationships between socio-political, economic, cultural, religious aspects, etc., as well as in the interdependence of scenarios. Violence is a global problem and the search for peace requires every effort, however modest they may seem and despite the pitfalls that may exist.

The family and the school, directly educational institutions, are appropriate environments for learning peace. Parents and other family members play a particularly important role in this education. From a pedagogical perspective, it must be recognized that the family is the first and main educational institution, a natural and cultural environment supposedly distinguished by love, in which its members, especially during the infant stage, should find protection, attention, welcome, affection and warmth, as befits a true home (in Spanish, hogar, from the word *focus,* 'fire'). However, although it is paradoxical, the family is often a violent institution in which aggressions usually remain invisible and silenced from the outside because it is a private environment of behaviors in which force is used to harm a member of the family group, may it be on the physical, psychological/emotional, sexual, economic, or other level. The non-accidental damage generated, sometimes even of a "negative" nature, that is, by omission, as happens in negligence, may lead to death. No one is exempt from suffering domestic violence since it occurs in the home. However, it is usually carried out by those who are older, or have greater power, strength, or economic dominance over the most vulnerable members, usually children, women, the elderly and people with functional diversity (Martínez-Otero, 2020).

The school institution, on the other hand, should also be an environment of coexistence, although peace is often broken in educational centers to the point of making learning impossible. With this atmosphere of conflict, of manifest violence, educational work becomes impossible. As Zurita (2018) has pointed out, the serious consequences of school violence, not only on the people and institutions directly involved, but also on democratic life and the exercise of human rights, make prevention a pressing task.

The accumulated experience in the prevention and resolution of school violence allows us to point out some general considerations, which are synthesized in the enrichment of interpersonal communication and in the real inclusion of students in the activities of the educational community. We must advance in the construction of humanized schools, built on rationality, the social dimension, affectivity, and ethics, in which the participation of families play a fundamental role.

The family and the school are the pillars in this education for peace, but in addition to these great institutions, we must remember the influence of other environments, such as work, which constitutes a fundamental aspect of human life that demands commitment in the face of violence, among other conditions that degrade it. That commitment is embodied through rights, but also through values, knowledge, skills, and permeates relationships. Therefore, it is essential to promote in work environments a culture of peace based on cordiality (*cor, cordis* = heart), mutual respect and dignity of the human being (Martínez-Otero, 2022).

The pedagogy of peace is not limited to these environments (family, school, and work), but also extends its concern to external scenarios of a political, social, economic, and cultural nature, particularly if they are distinguished by their negative influence on coexistence. In general, the approach of an "ethos of peace" is presented as a necessary alternative to the "*ethos* of violence" that proteatically characterizes many forms of relationship. A democratizing socio-cultural change is required at the global level, albeit differentially, to free it from the many damages caused by negative conflicts.

As defended by Caireta (2013), from the closest to the most global levels, a pedagogy for peace that provides tools that help people relate healthily to each other, with their immediate environment and with the world, based on values and human rights, a type of education aimed at preventing and overcoming violence by enhancing the capacity to critically analyze problems, to act and participate responsibly, as well as to promote the positive dimension of conflicts and foster harmonious and cooperative relations is necessary.

We share the reflection of Morin (2011) when he states that globalization has provided the infrastructure of a world-society, with numerous permanent intercommunications, although required by a regulated and ethically oriented globalized economy, which does not lose sight of the awareness of community of destiny of the entire planet. Unfortunately, Morin complains that globalization has provoked a planetary crisis of multiple faces and, although the United States maintains techno-economic and military hegemony, a multipolar world dominated by blocs with both cooperative and conflicting interests is developing, where numerous problems increase the need for collaboration, but also the risks of conflict.

The concern is heightened if we think of the real danger of the outbreak of the Third World War. Faced with the clear risk that peace in the world will break down again in this twenty-first century, particularly after the Russian invasion of Ukraine, pedagogical strategy must play an important role in the search for harmonious solutions to problems. That invasion constitutes the greatest threat to peace and security in Europe since the end of the cold war.

4 The Complex Construction of Peace

From the international perspective, since 1945 UNESCO has been promoting the right to quality education and scientific advances applied to the development of the knowledge and skills required to achieve economic and social progress as well as peace and sustainable development. This United Nations organization leads and coordinates the Education 2030 Agenda, a program that is part of a global movement to eradicate poverty by achieving 17 Sustainable Development Goals (SDGs) by 2030. Goal number 16, on "Peace, justice and strong institutions" is: "Promote peaceful and inclusive societies for sustainable development, provide access to justice for all and build effective, accountable and inclusive institutions at all levels." (UNESCO, 2017, 42). The learning of peace that it establishes is not limited to the cognitive aspect, while recognizing its importance, for example, in what refers to the concepts of justice, inclusion and peace, but extends to the socio-emotional dimensions (empathy and solidarity with those who suffer injustices, etc.) and behavioral (critically evaluate, demand, and publicly support the development of peace policies, resolve conflicts, etc.). Although, as indicated in the document itself, educators may use these SDGs, specifically SDG 16, to design exercises, textbooks, courses, and exhibitions in formal education institutions, while they may also serve as a reference for trainers in vocational training programs, NGO staff in the design of non-formal education offerings and education policy makers.

The educational concern for peace is not limited to schools; it also extends to the whole community, since peace is expressed at the personal, social, and planetary levels. It is based on the premise that education for peace, governed by rationality and ethics, enables international understanding, the expansion of human rights, security, and harmonious coexistence. A brief reflection on what we have said allows us to notice that we are facing very general and diversified approaches. Despite this variability and the fact that peacebuilding is complex, the effectiveness of experiences for its educational promotion must be recognized (Cremin and Bevington, 2017; Van Dijk, Haan and Winter, 2020; Jordan et al., 2021; Roque-Hernandez, 2022; Hietamäki and Tucci, 2022) in different scenarios, since the pedagogical path for the promotion of a culture of peace is distributed in several interrelated areas: family, school, media/information, labor, community/social, legal and civic-political. It is undoubtedly an arduous task ahead. Peace is a universal aspiration whose achievement requires coordination of efforts, *mutatis mutandis*, at all levels and sectors, in all age groups and in all people. Although peace education covers all stages of life, it has a greater impact on infants. This influence is based on the greater plasticity of childhood. Inspired by Rojas (1996), it can be said that the seeds of peace are sown in the early years, they are cultivated and unfolded during childhood, and they begin to bear their beautiful and benign fruits in adolescence, until they become an inseparable part of the adult personality.

Human violence is due more to sociocultural characteristics than to genetics. As Alonso Fernández (1994) states when describing contemporary *Homo brutalis*, whose essence harbors potentially high danger and cruelty, the increase in malignant aggressiveness of the human being is due more to learning than to the influence of heredity. According to our argumentation we could contrast this human type, whose destructive power has skyrocketed during the current technological era and with the arms race escalation, to *Homo pacificus*, in whose profile traits such as empathy, openness, respect and the tendency to resolve conflicts through dialogue stand out, that is, a set of qualities capable of being promoted educationally from early childhood.

Efforts are increasing to investigate what personality type influences attitudes of peace. There is recent empirical evidence that awareness/responsibility, openness to experience, emotional stability, and affability are associated with attitudes of peace (Cavarra *et al.*). The pedagogical perspective allows us to add, with inherent healthy optimism, that these dimensions of personality can be worked on educationally in the subjects and in the environments themselves. The possibilities of introducing modifications are easier in the family and at school, but significant steps are also being taken in work environments and even in social environments, provided there is political will and sufficient collaboration from the media and citizens. It should be remembered that subjects and psychosocial climates influence each other. Just as open, respectful dialogue and responsible people encourage the construction of environments of coexistence, so environments and societies characterized by true civility leave their mark on subjects in the form of tolerance, self-criticism and understanding.

The pedagogy of peace is born from encounter and dialogue. It is realistic and does not ignore the fact that conflict is consubstantial to human nature, but it does not renounce harmony and, therefore, opts for the path of respect, interaction, and the strengthening of mutual understanding. It is a pedagogy that combats everything that blocks or slows down mutual understanding, such as prejudices and injustices. Among its purposes is the promotion of positive changes in the socio-educational and relational sphere, which requires greater participation, exchange, and appreciation of what is considered different. Moreover, the pedagogy of peace becomes difficult without profound transformations in political, school, media, administrative and socio-economic structures, which should be based more on being than on having. Without the presence of an environment of coexistence, wherever it happens, personalization is considerably complicated, which, far from being interpreted as meaningless such a pedagogy in contexts impregnated with violence, makes it more pressing in environments of conflict, injustice, and exclusion, as Bajaj (2015) has emphasized.

5 An International Pact for Coexistence

The already bleak panorama of violence on the planet is currently increasing with the risk of world war after the Russian invasion of Ukraine, which has caused devastating destruction, thousands of deaths, and millions of displaced persons. Russia represents a major challenge for the West, even more so with its association with overpopulated and powerful China. The gross domestic product (GDP) of the Asian giant could surpass that of the United States in the early 2030's and its currency could compete with the established financial power and liquidity of the US Dollar (Ajami and Karimi, 2021). NATO's concern is growing about the alliance of the world's two most powerful authoritarian states.

As conflict and violence become more complex, policymakers and peacekeepers are looking for novel strategies to address new challenges (Voukelatou et al., 2022). To face the challenges (armed conflicts, terrorism, socio-economic crises, energy shortages, misinformation, food insecurity, environmental damage, etc.) that transcend national borders and the demands of peace that the world has, it's necessary everyone makes the effort. Organizing a plan of coexistence at the international level requires will, coordination and an unequivocal orientation towards the *pactum,* a Latin term sharing its root with the word 'peace'. Although the anthropological pessimism of Hobbes (1998, 10) led him to say that "pacts that do not rest on the sword are nothing more than words, without strength to protect man, in any way", what the peace agreement requires is compliance with international law. Rousseau (2017), with an optimistic vision of the human being and one of the precursors of the policy of the pact or social contract, had already indicated the need to support the State by its foreign relations through the law of nations, that is, the predecessor legal rules of current international law.

For Kant (1999), it is the public right of humanity to favor a continuous approach to perpetual peace, a peace that is not a vain fantasy, but a problem that must be solved progressively.

There is nothing more opposed to arbitrariness or authoritarianism than a pact founded on rationality and ethics. Therefore, the priority objective is to encourage States to initiate truthful negotiations, based on free consent and good faith (United Nations, 2005), to prevent or end conflicts within the framework of international law. Once the treaty is established, it is binding under the *principle pacta sunt servanda*, "covenants are to be fulfilled", enshrined in the 1969 Vienna Convention.

The establishment of an agreement or convention involves answering the question of what peace is desired for the global order. The answer cannot be given exclusively from education, since it is an issue of enormous complexity that must be addressed from all possible fronts with the appropriate political leadership. Progress in the projected pact or, what is equal, in the construction of peace is the subject of intense debate on the chessboard of international relations and must be made based on the principles of a policy of humanity. Such a framework, sociohistorically contextualized, encourages pedagogy to systematize its transformative action, and vice versa, since, in one way or another, educational advances serve as a spur to politics.

The *phenomenology of peace*, to the extent that it may be spoken in these terms, allows us to notice, in the first place, a process of consciousness distinguished by peace and tranquility. Along with this inner dimension or intrapersonal peace, we find all its external projections,—interpersonal, social, international, and universal—, longed-for expressions of psychic peace, concretions of difficult demarcation in relational life, whose effective materialization requires knowledge and effort.

The richness and complexity of peace is reflected in the vast conceptual field, which may complicate the establishment of specific actions. The distinction made by the Norwegian irenologist Galtung (1969) between "negative peace" or absence of direct violence and "positive peace" or overcoming violence -direct, cultural, or structural- which is accompanied by social justice, allowing one to guide the formal construction of peace, through harmonious coexistence based on values such as freedom, equality, solidarity, justice and even fraternity. In the public arena, peace is made possible by laws and regulations. The peace sought, whatever the level at which we find ourselves, requires a consensual, ethically grounded regulation. The conquest and the exercise of coexistence in peace are expressed in a legitimate legal system. As a counterpoint, peace by force imposed by authoritarian powers is itself violence.

After the conceptual bifurcation of peace into negative and positive, other notions have emerged such as "imperfect peace" (Muñoz, 2004) or "neutral peace" (Jiménez, 2021), although the difficulty of putting into practice the desire for peaceful coexistence persists.

Peace, perhaps better without adjectives, must penetrate and circulate through our lives, orienting it harmoniously. It is a hopeful horizon for which humanistic and scientific studies are needed. High politics, nourished by disciplines and diverse approaches, cannot remain in abstraction, but must lead to a planning, managing, and promoting activity of coexistence.

Although the concrete conditions of peace vary according to many circumstances – among them, the areas in which it is to be safeguarded or promoted and the willingness of the parties to reach a *consensus* – the art of politics, as Morin (2011) argues, forces us to navigate between *realpolitik* and *idealpolitik*, which requires, without ignoring an ideal of peace, a commitment to reality to modify it. From the field of political science, the balance between both conceptions, apparently irreconcilable, while still having our feet on the ground, elevates us to a higher level in which, given the situation in the world, only understanding is possible. A political science that sought to reduce the problem of international relations to one of two approaches would be seriously and regrettably simplified. Therefore, the efforts of irenology (science of peace), which provides valuable assistance to political science and politics itself, are not aimed at solving the antinomy by the expeditious procedure of eliminating one of its terms, but at its harmonious and synergistic encounter, a task that, of course, is not easy.

The two orientations just mentioned are also located in the educational field and, in general, in social sciences as a whole. One could even speak of *realpedagogik* and *idealpedagogik,* which would represent respectively pedagogical realism, more practical, technical, and empirically based, and pedagogical, even critical, idealism of a more speculative nature. Both trends are complementary and together offer richer solutions to education, in general, and specifically to peace education.

6 Peace and a New World Order

It has been said that the center of world power corresponds to the United States, as a hegemonic superpower, in a situation of the international political system described as "unipolar" (Zahirinejad, 2022) and although it may have seemed until recently that other powers were incapable of altering this *status quo,* at least Russia and China are challenging US primacy.

The serious invasion of Ukraine and the disturbing Russian - Chinese alliance have set off alarms. From the Western perspective, Russian expansionist pretensions destabilize the world order and threaten American power. It is not surprising that East-West relations are viewed with trepidation and that attempts are being made to avoid direct military confrontation and nuclear war.

On the contrary, from the Russian and Chinese perspectives, the United States represents the main threat to world peace, by far from any other country. That is why a new balance is sought in international relations, in pursuit of a multilateral order, far from Western hegemonism and the power politics of the Cold War.

Russia aspires to maintain and expand its informational, cultural, linguistic, and socio-economic presence in the post-Soviet space. From a historical and geopolitical point of view, it refuses to lose influence and does not seem, at least until now, that it really wants peace.

China, for its part, presents itself as neutral, a "neutrality" that will have to be seen how it materializes. Biba (2022) speaks of China's "pro-Russian neutrality" in relation to the war in Ukraine and adds that this positioning has gone against the great hopes, particularly European, that the Asian country would improve its tarnished international reputation. For this researcher, the Kremlin is China's most important partner in its global strategic rivalry with the United States, although he does not rule out the fact that China may push Russia to end the war, especially if it obtains concrete benefits, which requires a more pragmatic policy on China, incorporating tangible incentives in aspects such as trade and investment, health, climate change and nuclear non-proliferation. The need to take visible steps in this Western policy toward China could be a basic principle in the pursuit of peace.

The construction of peace is the object of permanent vindication, but unfortunately, despite the indisputable efforts, the threat of war is increasing throughout the world. If, as Öjendal *et al.* argue (2021), peacebuilding as a general project is fragmented, without sufficiently shared lexicon and without solid institutional support, it seems necessary, first of all, to establish a clarifying dialogue between the different actors around goals, difficulties, terms and concepts, values and interests, studies and initiatives, agencies, practices and experiences, without ignoring geostrategic relations at the international level, territorial integrity, legality, economic interdependence, human rights, social justice and arms conflicts. It is an arduous negotiating task, but it is necessary, especially if we start from the premise that the path toward peace is not straight. The idea that peace is a dynamic, winding, and complex process that requires creative, innovative, malleable, and durable approaches based on local, national, regional, and international rights (Paffenholz, 2021) is making its way (Paffenholz, 2021).

The process of joint peacebuilding cannot be closed to non-Western perspectives. The project of world peace must be a constant stimulus for its multilateral construction. Peace is the path and goal, a permanent project that, more now that we are immersed in a deep world crisis, must maintain open, ethical, and rational communication, realism in analysis and idealism in aspiration. The peace of the world is a daily, collaborative, multilevel task, which must consider the present and move towards a desirable future.

School, family, and social pedagogy must assume its commitment to collaborate in the prevention of conflicts and in the promotion of coexistence at all levels, attuned to Sustainable Development Goal 16 (SDG) (UNESCO, 2017), aimed at promoting just, peaceful, and inclusive societies. Education for peacebuilding is necessary at the intrapersonal, interpersonal, intergroup, national, and international levels. From this broad perspective, it is easier for the efforts made by different scenarios and agents in the fight against violence, in any of its variants, and in the safeguarding of peace, which is now seriously threatened, to converge synergistically.

References

Ajami, R.A., Karimi, H.A.: The emerging global order: China's outreach within a managed and competitive framework for the quads and others. J. Asia-Pacific Bus. **22**(2), 105–108 (2021). https://doi.org/10.1080/10599231.2021.1905491

Alonso Fernández, F.: Psicología del terrorismo. Masson-Salvat (1994)

Bajaj, M.: Pedagogies of resistance and critical peace education praxis. J. Peace Educ. **12**(2), 154–166 (2015). https://doi.org/10.1080/17400201.2014.991914

Biba, S.: How to make China help bring the war in Ukraine to an end (GIGA Focus Asien, 3). German Institute for Global and Area Studies; Leibniz-Institut für Globale und Regionale Studien, Institut für Asien-Studien (2022). https://doi.org/10.57671/gfas-22032

Cafruny, A., Fouskas, V.K., Mallinson, W.D.E., Voynitsky, A.: Ukraine, multipolarity and the crisis of grand strategies. J. Balkan Near Eastern Studie*s*. Advance online publication (2022). https://doi.org/10.1080/19448953.2022.2084881

Caireta Sempere, M.: Peace and coexistence education in school settings: A teacher training perspective. Escola de Cultura de Pau; Evens Foundation (2013). https://escolapau.uab.cat/img/programas/educacion/informe.pdf

Cavarra, M., Canegallo, V., Santoddì, E., Broccoli, E., Fabio, R.A.: Peace and personality: tThe relationship between the five-factor model's personality traits and the Peace Attitude Scale.

Peace and Conflict: J. Peace Psychol. **27**(3), 508–511 (2021). https://doi.org/10.1037/pac0000484

Cervantes Saavedra, M. de.: Don Quijote de la Mancha. RBA Editores (1994)

Cremin, H., Bevington, T.: Positive peace in schools: tackling conflict and creating a culture of peace in the classroom. Routledge (2017). https://doi.org/10.4324/9781315304236

Galtung, J.: Violence, peace and peace research. J. Peace Res. **6**(3), 167–191 (1969)

Gross, Z.: Revisiting peace education: Bridging theory and practice-international and comparative perspectives-introduction. Res. Comp. Int. Educ. **12**(1), 3–8 (2017). https://doi.org/10.1177/1745499917698290

Harris, I.M.: Peace education theory. J. Peace Educ. **1**(1), 5–20 (2004). https://doi.org/10.1080/1740020032000178276

Hietamäki, S., and Tucci, I.: Behind screens: Challenges and opportunities of participatory online peace education in Finland. J. Peace Educ. Adv. online publication (2022). https://doi.org/10.1080/17400201.2022.2087610

Hobbes, T. (1998). El Estado. Fondo de Cultura Económica

Jiménez Bautista, F.: Paz positiva versus paz imperfecta: El poder de la verdad. Revista de Cultura de Paz **5**, 7–33 (2021)

Jiménez Bautista, F., & Jiménez Aguilar, F. (2014). Una historia de la investigación para la paz. *Historia Actual Online*, *34*, 149–162. https://doi.org/10.36132/hao.v0i34.940

Jordan, R., et al.: Peace engineering in practice: A case study at the University of New Mexico. Technol. Forecast. Social Change, **173**, Artículo 121113 (2021). https://doi.org/10.1016/j.techfore.2021.121113

Kant, I.: Hacia la paz perpetua. Biblioteca Nueva (1999).

Martínez-Otero, V.: Orientaciones educativas para la prevención de la violencia familiar. In: Ramírez, J.M., Martínez-Otero, V. (Dirs.) La violencia en la familia, pp. 27–41. Dykinson (2020)

Martínez-Otero, V.: La inteligencia afectiva en el mundo del trabajo: Prevención de la violencia y fomento de la convivencia. In: Ramírez, J.M., Martínez-Otero, V. (Dirs.) Violencia y trabajo, pp. 35–55. Dykinson (2022)

Morin, E.: La vía: Para el futuro de la humanidad. Paidós (2011)

Muñoz, F.A.: La paz imperfecta. En F.A. Muñoz (Ed.), La paz imperfecta (pp. XX-XX). Eirene (2001)

North Atlantic Treaty Organization. (2022). NATO 2022 strategic concept: Adopted by Heads of State and Government at the NATO Summit in Madrid, 29 June 2022. https://www.nato.int/nato_static_fl2014/assets/pdf/2022/6/pdf/290622-strategic-concept.pdf

Öjendal, J., Bachmann, J., Stern, M., Leonardsson, H.: Introduction: peacebuilding amidst violence. J. Intervention Statebuilding **15**(3), 269–288 (2021). https://doi.org/10.1080/17502977.2021.1913006

Organización de las Naciones Unidas para la Educación, la Ciencia y la Cultura. (2017). Educación para los Objetivos de Desarrollo Sostenible: Objetivos de aprendizaje. https://unesdoc.unesco.org/ark:/48223/pf0000252423

Paffenholz, T.: Perpetual peacebuilding: a new paradigm to move beyond the linearity of liberal peacebuilding. J. Interven. Statebuilding **15**(3), 367–385 (2021). https://doi.org/10.1080/17502977.2021.1925423

Rojas, L.: Las semillas de la violencia. Espasa-Calpe (1996)

Roque-Hernández, R.V.: Building a culture of peace in everyday life with inter- and transdisciplinary perspectives. Front. Educ. **7**, Artículo 847968 (2022). https://doi.org/10.3389/feduc.2022.847968

Rousseau, J.J.: El contrato social. PRD (2017)

van Dijk, A., de Haan, M., de Winter, M.: Voicing versus silencing: education for peace in contexts of violence. Int. J. Educ. Res. **102**, Artículo 101581 (2020). https://doi.org/10.1016/j.ijer.2020.101581

Vienna Convention on the Law of Treaties, 1969. United Nations, Treaty Series, vol. 1155, p. 331. https://legal.un.org/ilc/texts/instruments/english/conventions/1_1_1969.pdf

Voukelatou, V., Miliou, I., Giannotti, F., Pappalardo, L.: Understanding peace through the world news. EPJ Data Sci. **11**(1), 1–30 (2022). https://doi.org/10.1140/epjds/s13688-022-00315-z

Zahirinejad, M.: Conflict and integration in the Middle East and North Africa. Peace Studies J. **15**(1), 43–56 (2022)

Zurita, Ú.: Violencia escolar. Eunomía: Revista en Cultura de la Legalidad, **14**, 299–309 (2018). https://doi.org/10.20318/eunomia.2018.4171

Author Index

J. Cayón Peña and J. M. Ramírez (Eds.): *Threats to Peace and International Security: Asia versus West*, ASTSA, p. 243, 2023.
https://doi.org/10.1007/978-3-031-28336-9